THE REAL HISTORY OF WORLD WAR II

A NEW LOOK AT THE PAST

Alan Axelrod

STERLING

New York / London
www.sterlingpublishing.com

Library of Congress Cataloging-in-Publication Data Available

10 9 8 7 6 5 4 3 2 1

Published by Sterling Publishing Co., Inc.
387 Park Avenue South, New York, NY 10016

Distributed in Canada by Sterling Publishing
c/o Canadian Manda Group, 165 Dufferin Street
Toronto, Ontario, Canada M6K 3H6
Distributed in the United Kingdom by GMC Distribution Services
Castle Place, 166 High Street, Lewes, East Sussex, England BN7 1XU
Distributed in Australia by Capricorn Link (Australia) Pty. Ltd.
P.O. Box 704, Windsor, NSW 2756, Australia

Book design and layout: Oxygen Design/Sherry Williams, Tilman Reitzle

Printed in China

Sterling ISBN: 978-1-4027-4090-9 (hardcover)
Sterling ISBN: 978-1-4027-7999-2 (paperback)

For information about custom editions, special sales, premium and corporate purchases, please contact Sterling Special Sales Department at 800-805-5489 or specialsales@sterlingpublishing.com.

For Anita and Ian

To some generations much is given.
Of other generations much is expected.
This generation . . . has a rendezvous
with destiny.

—PRESIDENT FRANKLIN D. ROOSEVELT,
SPEECH TO THE 1936 DEMOCRATIC
NATIONAL CONVENTION,
JUNE 27, 1936

CONTENTS

The Real History of World War II

PART ONE

Prelude and Outbreak

PART TWO

Britain Alone

PART THREE

Infamy

PART FOUR

Underbelly

PART FIVE

The Pacific War

PART SIX

Crusade in Europe

PART SEVEN

Devastation and Recovery

DRAMATIS PERSONAE

Alexander, Harold (1891–1969) British general who became Allied commander in charge of the Mediterranean Theater late in 1943.

Arnim, Hans-Jürgen von (1889–1971) Key German panzer (tank) commander in Operation Barbarossa (June 21, 1941–December 1941) and, later, in North Africa under Rommel.

Arnold, Henry "Hap" (1886–1950) From March 1942, commanding general of U.S. Army Air Forces.

Badoglio, Pietro (1871–1956): After becoming Italy's head of state following the removal of Mussolini in 1943, concluded an armistice with the Allies.

Bormann, Martin (1900–45?) Hitler's private secretary and one of the most powerful men in the Nazi Party.

Bradley, Omar Nelson (1893–1981) American commander of the 12th Army Group in Europe, popularly known as the "G.I. General."

Braun, Wernher von (1912–77) Scientist who created Germany's V-2 rocket weapon.

Brooke, Alan, 1st Viscount Alanbrooke (1883–1963) Chief of the British Imperial Staff, Britain's most senior officer during the war.

Canaris, Wilhelm (1887–1945) Leading figure of German espionage, who was also a covert agent of the anti-Nazi underground.

Carlson, Evans (1896–1947) U.S. Marine leader of Carlson's Raiders, a Pacific theater special operations unit.

Chamberlain, Neville (1869–1940) British prime minister who disastrously attempted the "appeasement" of Adolf Hitler, co-signing the Munich Pact in 1938 with French premier Édouard Daladier.

Chennault, Claire (1890–1958) Creator and commander of the American Volunteer Group, the famed "Flying Tigers" of Burma and China.

Chiang Kai-shek (1887–1975) Leader of Nationalist China during World War II and an important but troublesome ally in the war against Japan.

Churchill, Winston (1874–1965) Prime minister of Britain and, with Franklin Roosevelt, the Allies' greatest war leader.

Clark, Mark (1896–1985) Commander of the Fifth U.S. Army in the costly and protracted Italian campaign.

Cunningham, Andrew (1883–1963) As Britain's First Sea Lord, a principal naval planner of Operation Overlord (the D-Day landings at Normandy, June 6, 1944).

Daladier, Édouard (1884–1970) French premier who reluctantly signed, with Britain's Prime Minister Chamberlain, the Munich Pact in 1939 to appease Hitler.

Darlan, Jean-François (1881–1942) Commander of Vichy French forces in North Africa, who concluded an armistice with the Allies following Operation Torch (November 8, 1942).

Dönitz, Karl (1891–1980) Commander in chief of the German navy, who served as head of state after Hitler's suicide on April 30, 1945, and authorized Germany's surrender.

Donovan, William "Wild Bill" (1883–1959) Chief of the U.S. Office of Strategic Services (OSS), predecessor of the CIA.

Doolittle, James "Jimmy" (1896–1993) U.S. Army Air Forces officer who led the Doolittle Raid (April 18, 1942) on Japan and later commanded the U.S. Eighth Air Force.

Dowding, Hugh (1882–1970) Commander in charge of British Fighter Command during the Battle of Britain (July 10, 1940–October 31, 1940).

Dulles, Allan (1893–1969) Spymaster chief of the U.S. Office of Strategic Services (OSS) in Europe.

Eichelberger, Robert (1886–1961) U.S. field commander under Douglas MacArthur in the Pacific theater.

Eichmann, Adolf (1906–62) Nazi SS officer instrumental in carrying out the "Final Solution," the Holocaust.

Einstein, Albert (1879–1955) America's most famous expatriate German physicist, whose letter to President Roosevelt prompted the Manhattan Project to create an atomic bomb.

Eisenhower, Dwight D. (1890–1969) U.S. general who served as Supreme Allied Commander, Europe, commanding all Allied forces.

Fletcher, Frank (1885–1973) U.S. admiral who participated in every major action in the Pacific theater.

Gaulle, Charles de (1890–1970) Principal leader of the Free French during the Nazi occupation of France, and president of the provisional French government from June 1944–January 1946.

Geiger, Roy (1885–1947) U.S. Marine Corps general whose command in the Pacific culminated with victory in the Okinawa campaign (April 1, 1945–June 21, 1945).

Goebbels, Josef (1897–1945) Minister of propaganda for the Third Reich.

Göring, Hermann (1893–1946) Third Reich Reichsmarschall (Imperial Marshal) and head of the Luftwaffe (German air force).

Groves, Leslie (1896–1970) U.S. Army Corps of Engineers general who headed the Manhattan Project to produce an atomic bomb.

Guderian, Heinz (1888–1953) German panzer general who was one of the architects of blitzkrieg ("lightning war").

Halsey, William "Bull" (1882–1959) U.S. admiral in the Pacific theater famed for his aggressive audacity.

Harris, Arthur "Bomber" (1892–1984) British air marshal who was one of the prime architects of strategic bombing.

Hess, Rudolf W. (1894–1987) Deputy Nazi Party leader who made a quixotic overture of alliance to Britain in May 1941.

Heydrich, Reinhard (1904–42) SS leader who was a key perpetrator of the Holocaust.

Himmler, Heinrich (1900–45) Adolf Hitler's top lieutenant in the administration of the Nazi Party and the Third Reich.

Hirohito (1901–89) Emperor of Japan during World War II and after.

Hitler, Adolf (1889–1945) Founder of Nazi Party, absolute dictator of Germany, and the man who began World War II.

Ho Chi Minh (1890–1969) Communist nationalist leader of Vietnamese anti-Japanese guerrilla resistance in World War II.

Hodges, Courtney (1887–1966) General who commanded the First U.S. Army in Europe.

Hopkins, Harry (1890–1946) Franklin Delano Roosevelt's powerful personal emissary and adviser.

Hull, Cordell (1871–1955) U.S. Secretary of State during most of World II.

Jodl, Alfred (1890–1946) Chief of the operations staff of the German High Command (OKW) during all of World War II and close military adviser to Adolf Hitler.

Keitel, Wilhelm (1882–1946) German field marshal who was Hitler's top military adviser and liaison to the army.

Kesselring, Albert (1885–1960) Able German general who fought in the Western Front blitzkrieg, North Africa, and the Italian Campaign.

Kimmel, Husband E. (1882–1968) As commander in charge of the Pacific at the outbreak of World War II, Admiral Kimmel, with army counterpart, General Walter Short, absorbed principal blame for defeat at Pearl Harbor, December 7, 1941.

Kimura, Hyotaro (1888–1948) Japanese general who led the defense of Burma at the end of World War II.

King, Ernest (1878–1956) U.S. chief of naval operations (December 1941–March 1942), commander in chief of the U.S. Fleet (from March 1942), and a principal architect of Allied naval strategy.

Kinkaid, Thomas (1888–1972) U.S. admiral in the Pacific theater.

Kleist, Paul Ludwig von (1881–1954) Commander of German Army Group A during the invasion of the Soviet Union.

Kluge, Günther von (1882–1944) German commander defeated at the Battle of Kursk in the Soviet Union (July 4, 1943–July 20, 1943).

Krueger, Walter (1881–1967) German-born U.S. general instrumental in the liberation of the Philippines.

Kurita, Takeo (1889–1977) Imperial Japanese Navy admiral defeated at the Battle of Midway and the Battle of Leyte Gulf (October 23–26, 1944).

Leahy, William (1875–1959) U.S. Navy admiral who was a close military adviser to Franklin Delano Roosevelt.

Leclerc, Philippe (1902–47) Leading field commander of the Free French Army.

Leigh-Mallory, Trafford (1892–1944) British air officer who was commander in charge of the Allied Expeditionary Air Force during the Normandy Landings (D-Day, June 6, 1944).

LeMay, Curtis (1906–90) Commander in charge, U.S. Twentieth Air Force, responsible for the strategic bombing of Japan.

MacArthur, Douglas (1880–1964) Supreme commander of Allied forces in the southwest Pacific and one of the principal movers of Allied victory against the Japanese.

Mannerheim, Carl Gustaf (1867–1951) Finnish army commander in chief against the Soviet invasion at the beginning of World War II.

Manstein, Erich von (1887–1973) German commander whose Manstein Plan enabled a rapid and overwhelming victory in the Battle of France (May 10, 1940–June 22, 1940).

Marshall, George Catlett (1880–1959) U.S. Army chief of staff who, as secretary of state after the war, was identified with the Marshall Plan of European relief.

McAuliffe, Anthony (1898–1975) Acting commander of the U.S. 101st Airborne at Bastogne, who replied to a German demand for surrender with the monosyllable "Nuts!"

Merrill, Frank (1903–55) Commander of "Merrill's Marauders," U.S. Army Rangers.

Mitscher, Marc (1887–1947) U.S. admiral and master practitioner of naval air power.

Model, Walther (1891–1945) Prominent German commander known as "Hitler's fireman" because of his brilliant performance in crises.

Molotov, Vyacheslav (1890–1986) Ruthless Soviet foreign minister during World War II.

Montgomery, Bernard Law (1887–1976) Most famous British commander of World War II, who led the British Eighth Army in North Africa and the 21st Army Group in Europe.

Mountbatten, Lord Louis (1900–79) British officer who was supreme Allied commander, China-Burma-India Theater.

Mussolini, Benito (1883–1945) Fascist dictator of Italy from 1922 until his ouster in 1943.

Nagumo, Chuichi (1887–1944) Commanded the Japanese elite carrier striking force against Pearl Harbor, December 7, 1941.

Nimitz, Chester (1885–1966) U.S. commander of the Pacific Fleet.

Oppenheimer, J. Robert (1904–67) U.S. physicist who headed the Los Alamos laboratory (1943–45), which developed atomic weapons.

Ozawa, Jisaburo (1886–1963) Last commander in charge of the Combined Fleet of the Japanese Imperial Navy.

Patch, Alexander (1889–1945) Principal U.S. commander of Operation Dragoon, the Allied invasion of the South of France (August 15, 1944).

Patton, George Smith, Jr. (1885–1945) Most celebrated, successful, and controversial U.S. field commander in Europe.

Paulus, Friedrich (1890–1957) Commander of the German Sixth Army in the invasion of the Soviet Union, defeated at the Battle of Stalingrad (August 21, 1942–February 2, 1943).

Percival, Arthur (1887–1966) British general who surrendered Singapore.

Petain, Henri-Philippe (1856–1951) French World War I hero who headed the Vichy government after the fall of France.

Quisling, Vidkun (1887–1945) Norwegian Nazi collaborator who aided the German invasion of Norway in 1940 and headed Norway's Nazi puppet government.

Raeder, Erich (1876–1960) Admiral instrumental in creating Germany's World War II navy and who led that navy early in the war.

Ribbentrop, Joachim von (1893–1946) Third Reich foreign minister from 1933 throughout the war.

Ritchie, Neil (1897–1983) British general defeated by Erwin Rommel in North Africa.

Ridgway, Matthew (1895–1993) U.S. Army general who led the airborne assault on Sicily in Operation Husky (July 9, 1943–August 17, 1943).

Rommel, Erwin (1891–1944) Germany's legendary "Desert Fox," the brilliant armor tactician who led the Afrika Korps and who later commanded Germany's "Atlantic Wall" defenses.

Roosevelt, Franklin Delano (1882–1945) President of the United States during World War II and, with Churchill and Stalin, the principal Allied leader.

Rundstedt, Gerd von (1875–1953) Brilliant German field marshal who masterminded the Ardennes Offensive (Battle of the Bulge, December 16, 1944–January 25, 1945) late in the European war.

Short, Walter (1880–1949) General in charge of U.S. Army forces at Pearl Harbor on December 7, 1941.

Skorzeny, Otto (1908–75) Austrian-born German commando leader who rescued Benito Mussolini from captivity in the mountains of Gran Sasso, Italy.

Slim, William (1891–1970) British commander in Burma who performed brilliantly on a shoestring in the China-Burma-India Theater.

Smith, Holland M. "Howlin' Mad" (1882–1967) U.S. Marine general often credited as the father of modern amphibious warfare.

Smith, Walter Bedell (1895–1961) Eisenhower's formidable chief of staff for U.S. forces in Europe.

Spaatz, Carl "Tooey" (1891–1974) Combat commander of the U.S. Army Air Forces in Europe.

Speer, Albert (1905–81) Hitler's favorite architect; as minister for armaments and war production (1942–45), administered slave labor programs.

Spruance, Raymond (1886–1969) Supremely competent deputy commander of the U.S. Pacific Fleet.

Stalin, Joseph (1879–1953) Absolute dictator of the Soviet Union from 1929 until his death in 1953 and war leader from 1941 to 1945.

Stark, Harold (1880–72) U.S. chief of naval operations from 1939–42.

Stettinius, Edward (1900–1949) As U.S. secretary of state during 1944–45, a key figure in the creation of the United Nations.

Stilwell, Joseph "Vinegar Joe" (1883–1946) Blunt and brilliant U.S. general who fought on the China-Burma-India theater.

Stimson, Henry L. (1867–1950) U.S. secretary of war during World War II.

Student, Kurt (1890–1978) German innovator in airborne assault tactics.

Szilárd, Leó (1898–1964) Hungarian-born American physicist regarded as the godfather of the Manhattan Project—the moving force that started the Manhattan Project.

Tanaka, Raizo (1892–1969) Japanese destroyer commander who fought brilliantly at the Battle of the Java Sea (February 27–March 1, 1942), Midway (June 4–June 7, 1942), and Guadalcanal (August 7, 1942–February 9, 1943).

Tedder, Arthur (1890–1967) British air marshal instrumental in planning the air component of the Normandy Landings (D-Day).

Tibbets, Paul (1915–2007) Pilot of the *Enola Gay*, the B-29 that dropped the atomic bomb on Hiroshima, Japan on August 6, 1945.

Tito, Josip Broz (1892–1980) Secretary General of the Communist Party of Yugoslavia and leader of partisan resistance during the German occupation of that country.

Togo, Shigenori (1882–1950) Japan's Minister of Foreign Affairs during World War II.

Tojo, Hideki (1884–1948) Japanese prime minister, generalissimo, and military dictator during most of World War II.

Toyoda, Soemu (1885–1957) Commander in charge of the Japanese Combined Fleet, from March 1944 to the end of the war.

Truman, Harry S. (1884–1972) Thirty-third president of the United States, succeeding Franklin D. Roosevelt on his death in April 1945; presided over victory in Europe and Japan; made the decision to use the atomic bomb on Japan.

Truscott, Lucian (1895–1965) Tough U.S. cavalryman who commanded (successively) 3rd Infantry Division; VI Corps; Fifteenth Army; and Fifth Army,

Ushijima, Mitsuru (1887–1945) Principal Japanese commander in the Okinawa Campaign.

Vandegrift, Alexander (1887–1973) Eighteenth commandant of the U.S. Marine Corps.

Voroshilov, Kliment (1881–1969) Brave but unsuccessful Red Army commander on the Leningrad front.

Wainwright, Jonathan (1883–1953) U.S. general who made a valiant but hopeless stand in defense of the Philippines and became a POW throughout virtually all of World War II.

Wavell, Archibald (1883–1950) British field marshal who defeated the Italians in the Middle East, but was himself defeated by the Germans.

Weygand, Maxime (1867–1965) Defeatist French commander in chief of the Allied armies in France during the disastrous Battle of France in 1940.

Wingate, Orde (1903–44) British organizer and commander of the famed Chindits, the legendary guerrillas who fought in Burma.

Yamada, Otozo (1881–1965) Japanese "captain general" of the Kwantung Army in Manchukuo, Japanese-occupied Manchuria.

Yamamoto, Isoruku (1884–1943) Brilliant Japanese admiral who planned the attack on Pearl Harbor and the strategy for the Battle of Midway (June 4–June 7, 1942).

Yamashita, Tomoyuki (1885–1946) Japanese general who led early triumphs, then became associated with war crimes committed in the Philippines, for which he was executed after the war.

Zhukov, Georgi Konstantinovich (1896–1974) Marshal of the Soviet Union and the most capable and celebrated Red Army commander of World War II.

AUTHOR'S NOTE

THIS BOOK IS INTENDED TO BE AN ANSWER to the question, "What's a good basic book on World War II?" The approach is purposely concise and, while authoritative, non-academic—meaning that I do not hesitate to resolve controversies with straightforward explanations of the significance of key events. *The Real History of World War II* does not go out of its way to be revisionist. The fact is that, at its core, World War II really was a titanic contest in which the forces of good warred with those of evil. But there is much more to World War II than its elemental core. Instead of taking good and evil for granted, we look for the roots and ramifications of these forces, concisely exploring the ideological, nationalistic, and economic causes of the war and probing the motivation of those involved, especially that of Adolf Hitler, Benito Mussolini, Joseph Stalin, Winston Churchill, Franklin D. Roosevelt, and Harry S. Truman. In Japan, the roots of war were associated less with an individual—contrary to American popular opinion, Hideki Tojo did not start the war—but more with a militaristic and imperialist movement that began in the middle of the nineteenth century.

Beyond the causes of war, *The Real History of World War II* provides a straightforward narrative, in concise form, of the course of the struggle. To put it bluntly, this is not easy. No other armed struggle so thoroughly engulfed the world as World War II did. This was in part due to the global ambitions of the Axis—as Germany, Italy, Japan, and their lesser allies were called—but it was also due to the state of civilization at the time. Modern ships, aircraft, armored weaponry, and electronic communication made it inevitable that the battlefield would be virtually planetary in scale. My goal has been to make a comprehensible narrative out of a war that was, in fact, a cluster of wars fought simultaneously in many places. Moreover, these wars, though separate, were intimately interrelated, action in one place affecting action in another. Add to this the fact that World War II was a total war—that is, a war waged not merely between armies, but against entire civilian populations—and the narrative task becomes even more complex. For the most numerous combatants and victims of this global cataclysm wore no uniforms at all.

In this narrative I have tried to keep time and place as distinct as possible, identifying the most significant stories in one theater of the war, then telling those stories before moving on to another theater. There is, after all, a reason that the venues of this great conflict—Asia, the Pacific, the Atlantic, North Africa, Europe—were called "theaters." Each offered its own drama, and while it would be too much of a distortion of events to present each drama complete before moving onto the next, I believe the most manageable and comprehensible narrative approach is to present at least one whole act of the drama playing out in one theater before moving on to another act in a different theater. That is the principle that has guided me in laying out the chapters that follow.

Finally, as the book begins at the roots of the war, it ends with its branches: the cost of World War II as well as its enduring political, global, social, and technological legacy. To say that the world after World War II was—and continues in many ways to be—the "postwar world" is not the simple-minded and self-evident definition it appears to be. The astounding truth is that this biggest and deadliest of all wars destroyed one world and created another.

Part One

PRELUDE AND OUTBREAK

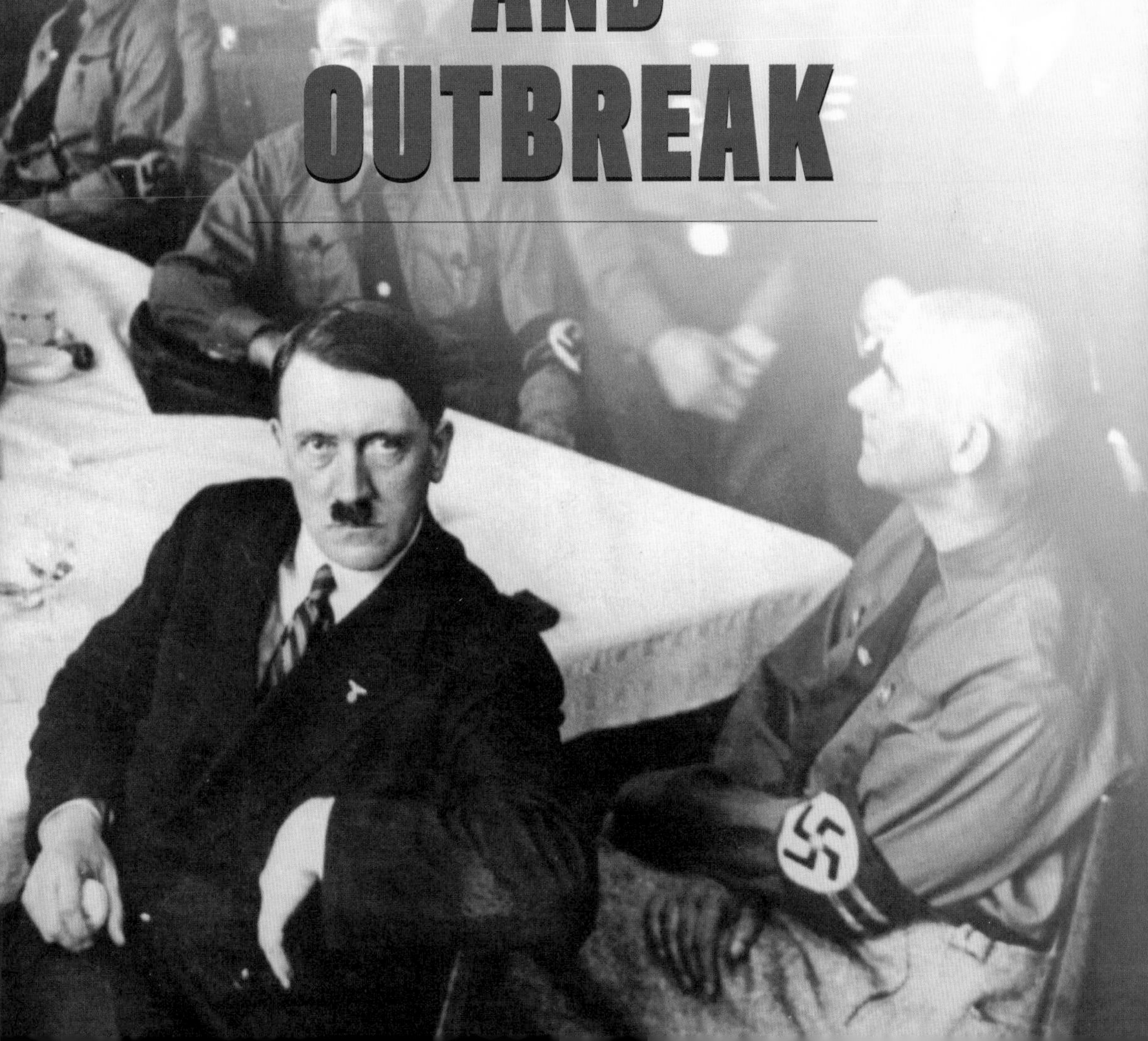

On preceding pages: Adolf Hitler poses with newly elected Nazi representatives to the Reichstag (German parliament), October 15, 1930.

CHAPTER 1

The Legacy of Versailles

How World War I Raised the Curtain on World War II

HISTORIANS KNOW THAT THINGS—laws, coronations, wars—don't just happen. They are caused, just as their causes are caused. That's why, when the American writer Washington Irving (using the pseudonym Diedrich Knickerbocker) sat down to write his satiric *A History of New York—from the beginning of the world to the end of the Dutch dynasty* in 1809 he started—tongue firmly in cheek—with the first cause, the creation of the universe. For this history of World War II, we don't need to go back nearly so far, but the beginning, the first important cause, did come earlier, much earlier, than is obvious to those who put all the blame on Hitler, Mussolini, and the Japanese militarists.

Bismarck's Europe

IN 1871, PRUSSIAN PRIME MINISTER OTTO VON BISMARCK brilliantly assembled modern Germany around the core of his home state after Prussia's lightning victory over France that year in the Franco-Prussian War. In addition to providing the impetus for the unification of the hitherto small, weak German states, the Prussian victory acquired for the new Germany the valuable coal fields of what had been the French territory of

Alsace-Lorraine. Bismarck, who became chancellor of the new Germany, well understood that German possession of the region would create a chronic sore spot between Germany and France, so he acted preemptively to isolate France from potential allies by negotiating the Three Emperors' League in 1873 with Russia and Austria-Hungary, by which the three powers pledged to aid one another in time of war. When Russia withdrew from the league in 1878, Bismarck concluded the Dual Alliance with Austria-Hungary in 1879. Next, in 1882, came the Triple Alliance, among Germany, Austria-Hungary, and Italy, followed in 1883 by Germany's agreement to adhere to a pact between Austria-Hungary and Romania. This isolated Russia as well as France—a good thing, as far as Bismarck was concerned, but he also saw it as dangerous—isolated, these two nations now had a motive to join forces. Bismarck therefore forged in 1887 a secret "Reinsurance Treaty" with Russia, by which Germany and Russia agreed to remain neutral if either became involved in a war with a third party—unless Germany attacked France, or Russia attacked Austria-Hungary. In this way, Bismarck believed he had succeeded in maneuvering Germany out of the possible trap of a two-front war against an allied France (on the west) and Russia (on the east).

"The less people know about how sausages and laws are made, the better they'll sleep at night."

Otto von Bismarck

Otto von Bismarck, shown here about 1870, created the modern German nation and, in the process, transformed Europe into an armed camp rife with alliances and enmities.

Unfortunately for Bismarck, Russia declined to renew the Reinsurance Treaty in 1890 and did just what the chancellor feared it would. Drifting toward France, by 1894 Russia concluded a formal military convention with that country in opposition to the Triple Alliance. To this, France added a secret agreement with Italy, which agreed to remain neutral if Germany attacked France or even if France—to "protect its national honor"—attacked Germany. This betrayed the Triple Alliance, of course, but Italy and France kept it secret.

Great Britain managed to stay out of this growing web by observing what its statesmen called a policy of "splendid isolation"—until 1902, when the British made an alliance with Japan, intended to block German colonial ambitions in the Pacific and Asia. Two years later, Britain concluded the Entente Cordiale with France, followed in 1907 by the Anglo-Russian Entente. Together, these pacts created the Triple Entente, binding Britain, France, and Russia. In this way, the twentieth century dawned by expanding an enduring enmity between Germany and France into the division of all the major European powers into opposed armed camps. Germany and Austria-Hungary constituted one camp; France, Russia, and Britain the other. For the time being, Italy wavered between the two.

"SOME DAMN FOOL THING"

OTTO VON BISMARCK STEPPED DOWN as German chancellor in 1890. Within little more than a decade after this, the Europe his diplomacy had created was spinning out of control—albeit very quietly, for Europe was a seemingly peaceful place up to 1914. True, the Balkan Peninsula, remote in mind and geography from western Europe, was chronically plagued by violence, which erupted into two bitter wars: the First Balkan War of 1912–13 and the Second Balkan War of 1913. These not only failed to resolve tensions in the Balkans but also left the small provinces and countries of the region burning with nationalist and ethnic zeal. Before the wars, the Balkans were perpetually torn between Turkey and Austria-Hungary, the region's major powers. After the wars, they sought national independence as well as a "pan-Slavic" ethnic identity, which Russia encouraged, pledging itself as the defender of all Slavs.

Years earlier, while he was triumphantly remaking Europe, Bismarck had a fleeting glimpse of the very thing that might demolish all he was building. "If a general war begins," he said, "it will be because of some damn fool thing in the Balkans."

A Killing in Sarajevo

Gavrilo Princip was born on his father's farm in West Bosnia in 1884 and left home as a young man to attend a business school in Belgrade, Serbia. In that city, he boarded with one Danilo Ilic, a nationalist and pan-Slav zealot, who wanted to rid the Balkans of Austro-Hungarian oppression. Inspired by Ilic, Princip tried to enlist in the Serbian army in 1912, but was rejected because, slight and frail, he was already ill with tuberculosis. Dejected, Princip lost interest in school, refused to find work, and lived as a beggar. He was befriended by nineteen-year-old Nedeljko Čabrinovič, with whom he traded fantasies of killing Archduke Franz Ferdinand, heir apparent to the Austro-Hungarian throne. In the spring of 1914, Princip heard that the archduke was coming on a state visit to Sarajevo, capital of Bosnia-Herzegovina, which had lately been made a province of the Austro-Hungarian Empire. With Čabrinovič, he recruited a boyhood friend, Trifko Grabež, and the three young men called on Milan Čabrinovič, a hero of the Balkan wars with a reputation for extreme radicalism. Čabrinovič introduced the trio to the leader of a secret organization known as the Serbian Black Hand, an ex-Serbian army colonel who called himself Apis (the "Bull"). Apis armed Čabrinovič and the three young men with revolvers and grenade-type bombs. Another three were brought into the plot, so that, on June 28, 1914, when the archduke and his wife, Grand Duchess Sophie, drove through the streets of Sarajevo in an open limousine, a total of seven assassins were poised to strike.

These young men—boys, really—were zealous, but thoroughly inept. All but one froze as the archducal motorcade passed them. Only Cabrinovic acted, hurling his bomb—but badly; it bounced off the back of the archduke's limousine, rolling in front of the car behind it and exploding with sufficient force to injure some spectators as well as members of the archduke's party. Dejected by his own failure to fire when the motorcade passed his position, Gavrilo Princip stalked off to a table at an outdoor cafe and ordered a coffee. His Browning revolver, unused but still loaded, weighed heavily in his coat pocket.

Franz Ferdinand and Sophie attended a reception at the town hall, but then changed the official itinerary in order to pay a visit to the local military hospital, where those wounded by the bomb blast were being treated. Their chauffeur was unsure of the way to the hospital, drove up a blind street, then slowly tried to turn around. Hemmed in by crowds gathered behind the car, he had to stop momentarily—as it happened, in front of the café of Moritz Schiller, where, five feet away, gloomily contemplating his coffee, sat Gavrilo Princip.

> "What is the good of your speeches? I come to Sarajevo on a visit, and I get bombs thrown at me. It is outrageous."
>
> *Archduke Franz Ferdinand, moments before his assassination, to the mayor of Sarajevo*

At 11:15 A.M., Princip took the revolver from his coat pocket, leveled it, and fired three times. One round passed through the car door, hitting the grand duchess in the stomach. The second shot entered the archduke's neck, nicking the carotid artery, then lodging in his spine. The third shot went wild.

Gavrilo Princip (seated at center), assassin of Austrian archduke Franz Ferdinand and his wife, Grand Duchess Sophie, was pictured in an Austrian magazine in 1915 as he stood trial with others implicated in the assassination conspiracy.

Sophie lived long enough to ask her blood-drenched husband, "For God's sake, what has happened to you?" She then crumpled against her husband's chest. As he cradled her head, Franz Ferdinand implored, "Sophie dear, Sophie dear, don't die! Stay alive for our children!" But she was already dead.

A certain Count Harrach, who had been sitting in the front seat, climbed into the back of the car.

"Are you suffering, your highness?"

"It is nothing, it is nothing, it is nothing."

Those were the last words of the heir apparent to the imperial throne.

History is full of murders. Most are forgotten. In this case, however, Count Leopold von Berchtold, Austria-Hungary's foreign minister, used it as an excuse for war. He accused Serbia of official complicity in the assassination and presented a list of ten

REALITY CHECK

The Impossible Plan

Many modern historians of World War I lay the blame for the failure of the Schlieffen Plan entirely at the feet of Kluck and his superior, Helmut von Moltke. It is true that Kluck made a costly tactical error and that Moltke ultimately failed in providing overall leadership, but the Schlieffen Plan was so elaborate and so inflexible that it is astounding that it worked as well as it did, carrying the German army deep into France. The realities of war—especially the necessity of maintaining supply lines over very long distances—made it doubtful that the Schlieffen Plan would have succeeded, even if fewer mistakes had been made and Moltke had been a better general.

ultimatums designed to punish that nation and thereby crush Bosnian nationalism and other Balkan bids for independence from the Austro-Hungarian Empire. The Serbs acceded to nine of Berchtold's demands, but would not allow Austrian officials wholly to usurp Serbian sovereignty by taking full charge of the investigation into the assassination. Because this single condition was not met, Austria-Hungary responded by declaring war on Serbia. This, in turn, moved Russia to mobilize, thereby bringing about war between Russia and Austria-Hungary. The entry of Russia brought Austria's ally, Germany, into the war, which declared against Russia and Russia's ally, France.

Germany's blueprint for the rapid conquest of France—the so-called Schlieffen Plan, conceived by Field Marshal Alfred Graf von Schlieffen—called for an assault on France not simply across that country's eastern border, but via a wide sweeping movement to the north, through Belgium, so that the invading force could descend on the French army from the flank and the rear. On August 2, the German government demanded free passage through Belgium. Even before King Albert I of Belgium could refuse, German divisions were already marching through Flanders. Britain, bound by treaty to France and Russia, was also treaty-bound to defend Belgian neutrality. Therefore, on August 3, it entered the war.

The Great War

On The Western Front, the German army tore through Belgium and swept into France with lightning speed. By the closing days of August 1914, it began to look as if German emperor Kaiser Wilhelm II would make good on the pledge he issued to the troops as they began their march at the start of the month: "You will be home before the leaves have fallen from the trees." But the Schlieffen Plan was complex and involved movement over great distances, as the entire German army swung around northern France to descend on Paris. Supply lines became thin. Commanders became nervous. At the very end of August, within about thirty miles of Paris, the

EYEWITNESS

It is believed that on the evening of August 3, 1914, Sir Edward Grey, Britain's foreign secretary, famously observed to a friend: "The lamps are going out all over Europe. We shall not see them lit again in our lifetime."

On the Western Front, during World War I, German soldiers advance against the village of Albert, France.

commander of the German First Army, Alexander von Kluck, thought he saw a chance to destroy what he believed was the last remnant of a crushed French army. This lured him to make a turn to the west, opposite the direction called for in the Schlieffen Plan. His target proved to be an illusion, and his turn exposed both the First Army and the German Second Army to attack by the French Sixth Army, which had been secretly built up in and around Paris. As a result, the great German advance suddenly stopped at the Marne River.

The advance would never resume. Instead, the battle—a titanic struggle involving millions of soldiers—hardened along a line of trenches that scarred Europe from the English Channel in the north to the frontier of neutral Switzerland in the south, a front of some six hundred miles that moved, by yards, east, west, east, then back again over the next four years.

By the time the First Battle of the Marne (September 6–12, 1914) began, eleven major powers were at war. Italy would join the Allies in 1915, bringing the total to twelve. But the United States, free from the treaties that bound Europe and buffered by an ocean, stayed out of what was being called the "Great War" through 1914, 1915, and 1916. Overwhelmingly, Americans were thankful for this and they reelected President Woodrow Wilson in 1916 largely on his campaign slogan, *He kept us out of war.* But through 1916 and early

REALITY CHECK

Economics of War

Doubtless, moral revulsion played a role in America's turn against the Central Powers, but high demand, an ample supply of gold, favorable shipping, and the realities of geography made dealing with the Allies far more reliable and profitable than doing business with Germany and the other Central Powers. Moreover, financial and business interests believed the Allies would win, which made them a better credit risk than the Central Powers. By 1917, American firms had done some $2 billion in business with the Allies, and U.S. banks had made $2.5 billion in loans to them. In contrast, U.S. banks had loaned by this time no more than $45 million to Germany. Politically, the United States may have been neutral, but, economically, it had already taken sides.

1917, America found it increasingly difficult to maintain neutrality. The actions of the Central Powers, as Germany and its allies were called, were morally repugnant. Germany's declarations of war on France and Russia, unprovoked, seemed impossible to justify, and its violation of Belgian neutrality was accompanied by gratuitous acts of brutality. More and more, the flow of trade and finance from the United States to the European belligerents turned away from the Central Powers and toward the Allies (as France, Britain, Italy, and Russia were called).

As the war continued, President Wilson came increasingly to believe that the United States could claim what he wanted—namely a leading voice in shaping the postwar world—only if it earned it through a commitment to the struggle. As for the attitude of the American majority, which wanted to stay out of the fray, this began to change as Germany committed outrage after outrage against American interests.

On May 7, 1915, a German U-boat torpedoed, without warning, the British liner *Lusitania,* killing 1,198 persons, including 124 Americans. In August, another British liner, the *Arabic*, was sunk, also with loss of American lives. For a time after this, Kaiser Wilhelm II, not wanting to draw America into the war, suspended unrestricted submarine warfare, but it was resumed on February 1, 1917. Two days later, a U.S. warship, the *Housatonic,* was torpedoed, prompting Wilson to sever diplomatic relations with Germany. Soon after this, British intelligence authorities turned over to Wilson a telegram they had intercepted between Germany's foreign minister, Alfred Zimmermann, and the German ambassador to Mexico. Transmitted on January 16, 1917, the "Zimmermann Telegram" authorized the ambassador to propose a German-Mexican alliance to Mexican president Venustiano Carranza. In return for a Mexican declaration of war against the United States, Mexico would receive Germany's support in a military campaign to recover its "lost territory in Texas, New Mexico, and Arizona." Zimmermann also wanted the ambassador to ask Carranza to invite Japan to join the anti-American alliance. It was an implausible, not to say hare-brained proposal, but it was quite enough to stir patriotic outrage among the American public and to move Wilson to ask Congress for a declaration of war on April 2, 1917.

A postbattle photomontage from the French magazine En Plein Feu *shows a reconstruction of German troops attacking the French village of Barcy, in a typical World War I offensive. Battle scenes such as this were often reconstructed during World War I because of the shortage of actual combat photography.*

To End All Wars

American Soldiers, Sailors, and Marines did turn the tide against Germany, bringing about its surrender in the armistice of November 11, 1918, and, as Woodrow Wilson had hoped, earning the United States—in the person of the president—a place at the peace table. Wilson had told his countrymen that he intended to fashion a peace that would make the "Great War" a "war to end all wars." As one of the "Big Four"—which included the prime minister of Britain and the premiers of France and Italy in addition to himself—Wilson took the lead in fashioning the Treaty of Versailles, which brought a formal end to the war and which included the document Wilson held most dear, the Covenant of the League of Nations. The League was to serve the world as an alternative to war by guaranteeing political independence and territorial integrity for all nations and providing a forum for the peaceful resolution of conflict. The league would fulfill Wilson's pledge to make the Great War the final war.

"The world must be made safe for democracy."

Woodrow Wilson, War Message, April 2, 1917

Although twenty-seven Allied nations participated in the creation of the Treaty of Versailles, the four major Allied powers, Britain, France, Italy, and the United States, wholly controlled the Paris Peace Conference. Germany, compelled to sign the treaty, was allowed no part in its creation. Wilson championed a conciliatory

REALITY CHECK

Unintelligence

Relations between Mexico and the United States were poor in 1917, but no historian believes that Venustiano Carranza seriously considered the proposal presented in the Zimmermann Telegram. Even with Germany's military assistance, Mexico was no match for the United States, and Carranza well knew it. The proposal was a monumentally stupid blunder on the part of the German government. With virtually no chance of provoking Mexico to war, it was diplomatic dynamite, certain to prompt the United States to a declaration of war against Germany.

settlement based on "Fourteen Points" he had enumerated before a joint session of Congress on January 8, 1918, as the basis for a just peace. Point one called for "open covenants, openly arrived at," mandating an end to the kind of secret treaties and alliances that had dragged Europe into war. Point two guaranteed freedom of the seas to all nations. Point three mandated the removal of economic barriers to international trade. Point four called for a radical reduction of armaments worldwide to the lowest levels consistent with domestic security. Point five required the modification of all colonial claims to promote the self-determination of all peoples. The next eight points addressed specific postwar territorial settlements, and the fourteenth point called for the creation of a league of nations.

An earnest, visionary, and selfless program for world peace, it was doomed. France, where the war on the Western Front had been fought for four terrible years, had made the greatest sacrifices, and Premier Georges Clemenceau was determined not only to secure France against future German attack by utterly destroying Germany's ability to make war, but also to exact vengeance. He demanded a treaty that punished Germany beyond the point of possible recovery. The two other European constituents of the Big Four, British prime minister David Lloyd George and Italy's premier, Vittorio Orlando, also had their own aims. Personally, Lloyd George favored Wilsonian moderation, but he had been elected on his pledge that Germany would be made to pay for what it had wrought. He was also worried that the Fourteen Points would interfere with British colonial policy. Orlando's concerns were more parochial. All he wanted was to ensure that Italy would receive the territories it had been promised in 1915 as an inducement to join the Allied cause.

Wilson ultimately persuaded Clemenceau to abandon his chief demand, that the left bank of the Rhine be detached from Germany and put under French military control, in exchange for British and American promises of future alliance and support. Yet most of the final Treaty of Versailles did not conform to the Fourteen Points. It was punitive and humiliating to Germany and the other Central Powers. Its main provisions included substantial German territorial cessions, German admission of guilt for the war, German disarmament, and an assessment against Germany (and other Central

Powers) of massive monetary reparations deliberately calculated to permanently cripple the German economy. Germany's overseas colonies in China, the Pacific, and Africa were taken over by Britain, France, Japan, and other Allied nations. Germany was compelled to renounce its Kaiser (who had already abdicated) and to create a new, democratic government. Similarly, the Austro-Hungarian empire was dismantled and, with it, the Hapsburg monarchy. The German army was capped at one hundred thousand men, and the General Staff (the elite military body believed to be the source of the war) was abolished. Germany was barred from manufacturing armored cars, tanks, submarines, airplanes, and poison gas. General munitions production was drastically curtailed, and German territory west of the Rhine and up to thirty miles east of that river was declared a demilitarized zone and occupied by Allied troops, the occupation to last for at least fifteen years, possibly longer.

Stars and Stripes

By and For the Soldiers of the A. E.

PRICE: 50 CENTIMES

FRANCE, FRIDAY, DECEMBER 20, 1918.

AS PARIS ROARED WELCOME

President Wilson and President Poincare setting out on the drive through the capitol last Saturday after the arrival at the Bois de Boulogne station

. CASUALTIES
VER THAN THOSE
CAMPS AT HOME

Proves Less Deadly Here Than Does In-uenza in States

PORT TOLL HEAVY

of Cases in France Third eat as Year Ago, Says hief Surgeon's Office

PRESIDENT WILL EAT HIS CHRISTMAS DINN AT A.E.F. MESS TA

BREST AND PARIS HONOR LEADER OF SISTER REPUBLIC

President Sets Foot on French Soil While Sea Guns Boom

CAPITAL ONE VAST THRONG

All Brittany Turns Out in Native Costume to Welcome Notable Addition to A.E.F.

Place Not Yet Nam Chaumont Shou on Guard

THEN TO SEE BATT

Trip Over Devastated R Precede Opening of ary Peace Confer

MAY BESTOW D.S.C.

Hope Held That Co Chief Will Award De His Soldiers in

The Stars and Stripes, *official newspaper of the U.S. Army, featured a photograph of President Woodrow Wilson riding with French president Henri Poincaré from the Bois de Boulogne railroad station through the streets of Paris, in December 1918. Wilson was visiting Paris to spend Christmas with the troops, and to attend preliminary peace talks.*

The treaty did retain important vestiges of the Fourteen Points. The disarmament of Germany, for example, was intended also to inspire voluntary disarmament by other nations, and, thanks to Wilson's efforts, his fourteenth point was embodied in the Covenant of the League of Nations, which was attached to the treaty. To accede to the Treaty of Versailles was also to accept membership in the League.

GERMANY PROTESTS—AND SIGNS

On May 7, 1919, the completed treaty was presented to a German delegation headed by German foreign minister Ulrich Graf von Brockdorff-Rantzau. It was not offered for discussion, let alone negotiation, but for signature and ratification. Had Germany refused to sign it, the war would have resumed—against an essentially disarmed Germany. Nevertheless, the delegation denounced the document, protesting that it abrogated almost every one of the Fourteen Points, which, the delegation claimed, Germany had

This December 31, 1919 rotogravure appeared in The War of the Nations, *published by the* New York Times *shortly after the armistice. The drawing depicts the signing of the armistice in a rail car at Compiègne, France.*

accepted as the basis of the armistice on November 11, 1918. Brockdorff-Rantzau further declared the obvious fact that Germany was unable to pay the reparations demanded.

Germany's chancellor, Philipp Scheidemann, likewise denounced the treaty when it was presented to him. The Allies responded to this with a naval blockade of Germany, which threatened to starve a defeated nation already desperately wanting in every essential. On June 21, 1919, Scheidemann and Brockdorff-Rantzau resigned and, on that same day, at Scapa Flow, Scotland, where the German High Seas Fleet had been interned, German sailors scuttled all fifty of the fleet's warships to prevent the vessels from becoming Allied prizes. A new German chancellor, Gustav Bauer, sent another delegation to Versailles, and, on June 28, signed the document under protest, informing the Allies that they were compelled to accept the treaty in order to end the hardships caused by the "inhuman" blockade.

WHAT IF?

Ever since World War II, historians, politicians, statesmen, and ordinary folk have repeatedly raised perhaps the greatest "What if?" of the twentieth century.

What if the Allies had made a fair, just, and generous peace with Germany instead of forcing upon it the punitive Treaty of Versailles? Would Adolf Hitler have come to power? Would there have been a World War II? Or would a reasonably stable Germany have proved fertile ground for the democracy of the post–World War I Weimar Republic? It is not easy to answer, because many Germans believed that their military had not been defeated, but had been betrayed into surrender by politicians. Moreover, although France was among the so-called victors, its territory and people had been devastated by a war fought mainly on French soil. Germany, labeled a defeated nation, had suffered very little damage to its infrastructure, and civilian suffering was minimal. Even with a just peace, there might well have been sufficient discontent in Germany to promote the rise of a Hitler. Perhaps the more relevant *what if* is what if the United States had not entered the war and Germany prevailed? Would the message of Hitler and the Nazis have found a receptive audience in a victorious Germany?

America Rejects Versailles and the League

Woodrow Wilson is pictured with his second wife, Edith Bolling Galt Wilson, in December 1919.

Woodrow Wilson was not—and could not have been—wholly satisfied with the Treaty of Versailles, but he was elated by the creation of the League of Nations. The injustices of the treaty itself, he believed, would ultimately be corrected by the League, which that flawed treaty had made possible. Therefore, he brought both the Treaty of Versailles and the Covenant of the League of Nations home in triumph.

Woodrow Wilson, a former professor of history and political science, and the former president of Princeton University, was an extremely intelligent man—who, for better or worse, had great faith in the supremacy of his intelligence. He consulted few people in government concerning Versailles and the League, and from the few he did consult he excluded all Republicans. The same elections of 1916 that had returned him, a Democrat, to the White House, brought a Republican majority to the Senate. Wilson had not sought the advice of the U.S. Senate in his negotiations and now, led by Wilson's arch-nemesis, Senator Henry Cabot Lodge, the majority of the Senate refused their consent to the Treaty of Versailles. In declining to ratify the treaty, they also necessarily rejected U.S. membership in the League of Nations—which required assent to the treaty.

Instead of attempting to reach a compromise with the Senate, Wilson high-handedly decided to take the case for the treaty and the League directly to the American people. Already exhausted by the war and by the battles at the Paris Peace Conference, he embarked on a grueling cross-country whistle-stop speaking tour. It was a desperate effort that broke his health. Wilson collapsed after speaking in Pueblo, Colorado, and was rushed back to Washington, where he soon suffered a debilitating stroke. This ended his ability to continue the crusade for ratification of the treaty, and he defiantly enjoined his colleagues to refuse all compromise with the Senate.

Without the backing and participation of the United States, the League of Nations was doomed. It came into being, but proved quite impotent. Wilson served out his term a shell of himself and was succeeded by Republican Warren G. Harding, who promised America a "return to normalcy"—by which he meant something

DETAILS, DETAILS
President Edith?

Wilson's stroke came on October 2, 1919, leaving him partially paralyzed and deeply depressed, Although his intellect was intact, his emotional state was such that he could not effectively function as president. He did not resign, however, and there is no evidence that anyone in his administration suggested that he do so. Instead, his second wife, Edith Bolling Galt Wilson, insulated him from the outside world, carefully controlling access. She participated in a cover-up of his condition, and she even made many decisions of government. Some historians have gone so far as to claim that she was virtually president by default until the inauguration of Warren G. Harding in 1921.

TAKEAWAY

Roots of the Reich

The rise of Germany under Otto von Bismarck at the end of the nineteenth century created a network of binding treaties and alliances throughout Europe, which ultimately fanned the flames of a brushfire war in the Balkans into the all-consuming conflagration that was World War I. The Treaty of Versailles, which ended the war, was so punitive to Germany, threatened by Communism and economic depression, that it provided fertile ground for the rise of Adolf Hitler and the Nazi Party, virtually ensuring that the "war to end all wars" would make a second world war inevitable.

like the "splendid isolation" Britain had claimed at the end of the nineteenth century—and, in his first speech to Congress, declared that "the League of Nations is not for us."

Germany Stews

The Treaty of Versailles is one of history's most tragic documents. Punitive, it did not punish Kaiser Wilhelm II (he lived out his life in comfortable Dutch exile) or the ministers of Germany and Austria-Hungary, but, rather, made life miserable for the people of Germany, many of whom came to believe that the German military had not been defeated, but that elements of the German government had betrayed the nation by surrendering. The illusion of betrayal was enhanced by the physical condition of Germany after the war. The fighting had taken place in France, in Russia, in northern Italy, in the Balkans, and in various colonial possessions. Germany was almost completely untouched. It did not have the appearance of a defeated nation.

With collective national discontent and a ruined economy (made worse by the worldwide depression of the late 1920s and 1930s) came political instability. Germany was threatened by the Communist revolution that had swept the Russian czar from power. Opposing this, a strong right-wing movement grew up, ultimately led by a former German corporal and failed artist named Adolf Hitler, who promised Germans a return to the greatness of which they had been cheated by the betrayal that was Versailles. Not only did the treaty create the political, economic, and emotional climate that promoted the rise of Hitler and Nazism, it also invited, under Hitler, violation. Even before Hitler became chancellor of Germany in 1932, Germany began rearming in defiance of Versailles. It did so covertly at first, but, under Hitler, began openly to build a new military. In Europe, the Allies, who had so boldly dictated the terms of the treaty, profoundly weary of war, unable even to contemplate another war, did nothing to enforce the treaty. As for America, from a self-imposed and utterly illusory isolation, it did, through the 1920s and 1930s, no more than look on with a mixture of disgust and anxiety.

CHAPTER 2

THE AGE OF DICTATORS

When People Trade Liberty for Security

IN HINDSIGHT, NO ONE SHOULD HAVE BEEN SHOCKED that Germany, defeated and humiliated, yet hardly devastated, experienced a resurgence of militarism under a ruthless dictator. More surprising was what happened in two Allied nations—who shared in the Great War victory—Italy and Japan. The rise of dictatorial militarism in these countries preceded Hitler's ascent in Germany and even helped to inspire it.

THE STRANGE JOURNEY OF BENITO MUSSOLINI

AT 2:45 P.M. ON SUNDAY, JULY 29, 1883, in the remote northeastern Italian village of Predappio, a child was born. Predappio lies within the hills of Emilia-Romagna, a region of northeastern Italy called the "Red Romagna" because it was a hotbed of radical Socialism. The child's mother, Rosa, was a schoolteacher and his father, Alessandro, a blacksmith by vocation but a radical revolutionary by mostly unfulfilled aspiration. He named his firstborn Benito Amilcare Andrea Mussolini: Benito after Benito Juárez, who had led Mexico's most important revolution; Amilcare, after Amilcare Cipriani, the right-hand man of the great Garibaldi, who surpassed Garibaldi in radicalism by embracing international Socialism; and Andrea, after Andrea Costa, an international Socialist born and bred in the Romagna.

The political journalist and agitator Benito Mussolini rose to become Italy's Duce—absolute dictator.

Benito grew up under the powerful opposing influences of his financially feckless, physically brutal, and politically strident father and his gentle, doting, and conventionally religious mother. He was a problem child who bullied the local children. At nine, he was consigned to a boarding school run by the Salesian fathers but was expelled after he stabbed a classmate with a knife. He repeated this later at another boarding school, but received a suspension rather than expulsion. As a teenager, while still in school, he added sexual aggression to his penchant for violence, frequenting brothels and engaging in sexual relationships with girls his own age as well as older, married women. If anyone criticized his behavior—which became locally notorious—a flash of the brass knuckles he habitually carried was sufficient to silence any protests.

"I was all alone and against many. I was often beaten, but I enjoyed it with that universality of enjoyment with which boys the world around make friendship by battle and arrive at affection through missiles."

Benito Mussolini, on his schooldays

Mussolini graduated from a secondary school in the small town of Forlimpopoli with an "educational diploma" that qualified him to teach school. At eighteen, then, he became a provincial schoolteacher. He also began to travel, leading the life of a vagabond in Switzerland and the Austrian Alps. As his experience broadened beyond the provinces of northern Italy, he abandoned teaching for Socialist journalism. He discovered a flair for facile expression and in 1912 became editor of *Avanti!,* the Milanese Socialist Party newspaper. As a Socialist, Mussolini was vehemently opposed to war and, in the summer of 1914, turned out articles arguing against Italy's entry into World War I. But then his already chaotic path took its most sudden—and unexplained—turn yet. In October 1914, he called for the Socialist Party to shift from "absolute neutrality" to what he called "active neutrality." When the party rejected this, Mussolini resigned from *Avanti!* and founded his own paper, *Il Popolo d'Italia* (*The Italian People*), and was promptly expelled from the Socialist Party. He now used the pages of *Il Popolo* to urge Italy's entry into the war for the purposes of defeating Austria, gaining territory, and enhancing national prestige. On the one hand, he promised that the war would be short and the sacrifices few; on the other, he warned that, should the government hesitate to declare on the side of the Allies, he would foment a civil war and a coup d'etat.

When Italy finally entered the war in May 1915, Mussolini wrote in *Il Popolo* that all factionalism had come to an end: "From today there are only Italians . . . united in a bloc of steel." At the end of August, Mussolini was drafted to fight in the war he had helped to create. He did not attempt to avoid conscription, but, on the contrary, embraced military life—much as another soldier of the Great War, young Adolf Hitler, embraced it. Like Hitler as well, Mussolini never rose above the rank of corporal. Mussolini declined his captain's offer to make him editor of the regimental newspaper—a safe desk job—and instead volunteered for combat duty. He served in combat until February 22, 1917, when a new artillery piece he was helping to test fire exploded, killing two to four men (accounts vary) and sending a shrapnel fragment into Mussolini's buttocks.

DETAILS, DETAILS

Pain in the Thigh

In later autobiographical accounts, Mussolini transformed the incident of the exploding cannon from an accident into an episode of combat, and his injury into a wound. He generally referred to it as a wound in the thigh, rather than in the buttocks.

The Birth of Fascism

Discharged from the army, Mussolini resumed publishing *Il Popolo*—this time, strangely enough, with financial help from the British. Torn by revolution and sick of disastrous war, Russia was about to make a separate peace with Germany. Italians, too, were becoming increasingly disgusted with the war. Hundreds of thousands of their sons had died—were, in fact, dying still—and Italy's military leaders had repeatedly proved themselves incompetent. Much had been lost; nothing gained. A pacifist movement was on the rise. Having given up Russia as a lost cause and fearing the defection of another ally, British officials decided that Mussolini's bellicose eloquence was just the thing to check Italian defeatism.

Italy did not plunge into World War I until 1915. This poster from 1914 was an attempt to rally the people to the Allied cause in the name of Italian self-defense. Cacciali via! runs the caption: Drive them out!

REALITY CHECK

Propaganda and Antipacifists

Officially, the British subsidized *Il Popolo* as a propaganda project. Unofficially, they also funneled money directly to Mussolini for the purpose of organizing militant opposition to pacifists. In other words, British money was used to pay thugs—as Mussolini explained to his British benefactors—to "break the heads of any pacifists who try to hold antiwar meetings in the streets." As the British saw it, this was necessary to prevail in a war against tyranny and in support of democracy.

Benito Mussolini had not been the first—or only—Socialist to favor Italy's entry into the war. Back in October 1914, a breakaway Socialist group favoring entry was formed. It called itself the *Fasci d'Azione Rivoluzionaria Interventista.* Translating this requires understanding that the *fasci* was an emblem of office carried by the lictors (bodyguards and standard bearers) of ancient Rome. It was nothing more than a bundle of sticks bound tightly together into a mace or a club, but its symbolic significance was high. The message of the *fasci* was that, although individual sticks were easily broken, bound together in a tight bundle, they were virtually unbreakable—like the Roman state—and made for a most potent weapon. Mussolini did not create this first "Fascist" group, but he was clearly attracted to it—it may even have influenced his sudden decision to become an interventionist in the war—and, by the time he accepted British subsidy of *Il Popolo d'Italia,* he exercised considerable influence over this group and other antipacifists who typically called themselves *fasci.*

By the beginning of 1918, Mussolini changed the subtitle of *Il Popolo* from "A Socialist Newspaper" to "The Newspaper of Combatants and Producers." He wrote editorials proclaiming that Karl Marx had been wrong, after all, to pronounce the death of capitalism, which, Mussolini declared, was just now entering the early stages of its development. This ideological transformation, coupled with Mussolini's highly effective journalistic efforts to keep Italy in the war, attracted attention from all the Allies. Mussolini emerged as a new voice opposed not only to the tyranny of Germany and Austria but to that other tyranny, the tyranny of Communist Russia. As the war approached its close, Mussolini praised Clemenceau of France, Lloyd George of England, and Wilson of the United States as just what the world now needed: "democratic dictators" of capitalism.

The reverse side of this 1916 U.S. dime bears the fasces—a bundle of sticks fastened to a battle-axe—an ancient Roman symbol of ruling authority. The fasces was not only adopted as an emblem of American legislative authority but was also the source of the word Fascism *in Italian politics and an important Fascist symbol.*

If Benito Mussolini emerged from World War I with enhanced prestige at home and the beginnings of an international reputation, Italy itself came out of the war broken and broken-hearted, disappointed, and angry. Some six hundred thousand young Italians had been killed, and more than a million had been wounded, with at least a quarter of these disabled for life. Mussolini seized on a single Italian victory, against the Austrians at Vittorio Veneto during October 1918, as the greatest of all victories of all the armies that fought in the Great War.

Yes, Mussolini declared in *Il Popolo* and elsewhere, this single triumph made all the sacrifice worthwhile—but—and it was a most important *but*—the Treaty of Versailles threatened to rob Italy of all that its sacrifice had gained. Britain, France, and America, allied with Italy during the fighting, betrayed Italy in hammering out the peace. The treaty gave Italy the Trentino and Trieste, but not, as had been promised in 1915, Fiume (Rijeka), the rest of Istria, Dalmatia, and the Dodecanese Islands. Nor did the treaty provide for the promised international recognition of an Italian "zone of influence" in Albania. Moreover, by the secret Treaty of London concluded with Italy, Britain had promised to cede to Italy Jubaland in Africa. Now that the war was ended, Britain did no such thing. By seizing on the "betrayal" at Versailles, Mussolini, already closely identified with having urged Italy into the war, ensured that he would not be blamed for the terrible and fruitless cost of the war. On the contrary, Italy's treatment at the hands of its allies became a new, even more compelling cause, which Mussolini joined to the fight against Communism to create a militant nationalist movement.

On March 23, 1919, in part encouraged and inspired by the poet, novelist, romantic patriot, and glamorous adventurer Gabriele d'Annunzio, he organized other Great War veterans in Milan to create the Fasci di Combattimento: the Fascists of Combat. This was the birth of the Italian Fascist Party.

LINK

From Rome to D.C.

The *fasci* (in English, *fasces*)—root symbol of Italian Fascism—is also an important symbol in American democratic government. A pair of fasces, symbolizing civic authority, flank the American flag that stands behind the Speaker's chair in the U.S. House of Representatives. Not to be outdone by the lower house, the United States Senate incorporated a pair of crossed fasces in its great seal. The famous "Mercury" dime, current in America from 1916 through 1945, features a design pairing a fasces with an olive branch.

The Rise of Mussolini

At first, the prolabor and antichurch orientation of Mussolini's Fascists was even more radical than what the Socialist Left advocated. Soon, however, the nationalism of the Fascist movement overshadowed everything else. Mussolini promised to re-create in modern Italy ancient Roman imperial grandeur. Such evocative visions recruited the support of the wildly popular d'Annunzio as well as the powerful landowners of the lower Po Valley, key Italian industrialists, and senior army officers. Mussolini's allegiance turned to these groups and away from workers and small farmers.

REALITY CHECK

The Big Lie

Adolf Hitler would famously declare the importance not merely of lying, but telling the "big lie"—a lie so big that it would, because of the sheer magnitude of its consequence, be universally believed. Well before Hitler, Mussolini had made himself master of the big lie and was especially adept at such bold oxymorons as "democratic dictators," an expression so audacious that it seems convincing. Late in 1918, Mussolini had no trouble declaring that dictatorship was the very means necessary to achieve democracy—and a growing number of Italians believed him.

Backed by the forces of capitalism, Mussolini created squads of paramilitary thugs—called Blackshirts, after the uniforms they wore—who did what the earlier Fasci d'Azione Rivoluzionaria Interventista had done back in 1914, waged a brutal street-level civil war against Socialists, Communists, Catholics, and Liberals. Except that Mussolini's Fascists did it more brutally and with greater organization than the earlier group.

> "The truth is that men are tired of liberty."
>
> *Benito Mussolini*

Cheated at Versailles and hard hit by the economic recession that swept Europe immediately after World War I, Italy seethed with revolutionary discontent. By 1922, Mussolini, having gained the support of the moneyed and powerful, had moved very far from Socialism, yet he also managed to command a vast following among the masses by promising economic recovery, jobs, and a return to imperial majesty. On October 28, 1922, he led a Fascist march on Rome. It was largely nonviolent, but intimidating nonetheless, and, by means of the march, he extorted from King Victor Emmanuel III a mandate to form a coalition government.

A defiant—and triumphant—Benito Mussolini gathers with his Fascist Blackshirts in the culmination of the 1922 March on Rome, which catapulted him to absolute power in Italy.

Like Caesar himself, Mussolini secured dictatorial powers set to last one year. He wasted no time. With remarkable speed and the backing of the rich and powerful, he did nothing less than reshape the economic structure of Italy, cutting government expenses for public services, reducing taxes on industry to stimulate production, and centralizing and consolidating government bureaucracy.

During this probationary year, Mussolini replaced the king's guard with his own Fascist squads (or *squadristi*) and a secret police force, the Ovra, both answerable to him and him alone. These forces were sufficient to suppress any domestic opposition. Although Mussolini at first avoided directly attacking labor, he brutally suppressed the strikes that traditionally hobbled the country's industry. In the sphere of foreign affairs, Mussolini significantly increased Italy's international prestige when he responded to the murder of certain Italian officials at the hands of bandits on the Greek-Albanian border by securing a huge indemnity from the Greek government and by bombarding, then seizing, the Greek island of Corfu. Mussolini also secured from Yugoslavia cession of the long-contested Fiume. With these achievements behind him, Mussolini ostensibly relinquished his dictatorial powers in 1924 and called for new elections. Many Italians and much of the world admired this apparently selfless gesture, overlooking the fact that Mussolini had taken care to secure legislation that guaranteed the Fascist Party a two-thirds parliamentary majority regardless of the popular vote.

REALITY CHECK
Feeding the Depression

By punishing Germany economically, the Allies not only created the mass national psychology that promoted the rise of Hitler, they also deprived all European nations of one of their most important markets—namely Germany—thereby exacerbating the effects of the Great Depression throughout the continent.

> "It is one thing to administer a state. The one who does this well is called statesman. It is quite another thing to make a state. Mussolini has made a state. That is superstatesmanship."
>
> *Richard Washburn Child, former U.S. ambassador to Italy, in 1928*

OPPOSITION

Not everyone was taken in by Mussolini. Among the handful of Socialists elected in 1924 was Giacomo Matteotti, a courageous campaigner who made a series of scathing speeches denouncing Mussolini and the Fascists. No mere rhetorician, Matteotti had the goods on the regime and freely exposed outrages ranging from acts of intimidation and violence, to misappropriation of public funds, to murder.

The discovery of Matteotti's own murdered body shortly after these speeches were made triggered a parliamentary crisis that emboldened the opposition press to attack Mussolini and his followers. In response, Mussolini discarded all pretense. He imposed a single-party dictatorship and a policy of strict censorship. The Ovra and Blackshirt squads visited terror on all opponents. Their techniques were brutal in the extreme. The beating death of a liberal editor was typical.

POP CULTURE

The Train Left the Station

Apologists for Mussolini observed—and some continue to observe—that, despite its evils, Fascism did indeed boost Italy's lackluster economy. The Mussolini effect came down to a catch phrase. As many saw it, the single most symbolic item of evidence that Mussolini's reforms were working was that, under his regime, the notoriously undependable Italian railroads became efficient, prompting many to observe that "Mussolini made the trains run on time." Only long after the war did a historical scholar choose to examine the validity of this pop culture mantra. By combing through old railway timetables, he discovered that Mussolini did not so much make the trains run on time—they were, in fact, often late—but he did make them *run,* which was a vast improvement.

Il Duce

Mussolini never brutalized one sector of society without rewarding another. He secured his power base among Italian capitalists by abolishing free trade unions, and he co-opted the powerful Catholic Church by concluding with it the Lateran Treaty of 1929, by which the Vatican was established under the absolute temporal sovereignty of the pope. Moreover, although the rights of ordinary citizens were curtailed and the rights of workers virtually eliminated, most Italians enjoyed an improvement in their financial condition, savored an enhanced sense of stability and security, and reveled in a rebirth of national pride. They looked to Mussolini not as a mere head of state, but as a leader, an absolute leader, whom they called "Il Duce"—quite simply, *the* Leader.

> **"This is the epitaph I want on my tomb: 'Here lies one of the most intelligent animals who ever appeared on the face of the earth.'"**
>
> *Benito Mussolini*

Il Duce promoted a cult of personality centered on himself, as he worked to become a latter-day Roman emperor. With his regime secure, he embarked on an aggressive foreign policy during the 1930s. Using as a pretext a clash over a disputed zone on the border separating Italian Somaliland from Ethiopia, Mussolini invaded Ethiopia during 1935–36 without a declaration of war, employing the instruments of modern warfare—including poison gas and aerial bombardment—against an essentially rural and tribal nation. Ethiopia's emperor, Haile Selassie, appealed to the League of Nations, which proved powerless to intervene. On May 9, 1936, Italy annexed the African nation, making it the first conquest of the new "Roman Empire."

Foot Soldier

One of the many outside Italy who looked admiringly upon the work of Il Duce was another ex-corporal in the Great War, Adolf Hitler, who had been born in the provincial Austrian town of

Braunau in 1889, the son of a minor customs officer. Whereas young Mussolini had been a bully boy driven first by violence, then by the combination of sex and violence, and, finally, by violent politics, Hitler grew up a mediocre student driven by nothing more grandiose than a frustrated desire to become an artist. In this dream, his father—like the senior Mussolini, a brute—discouraged Adolf, whereas his mother—like Rosa Mussolini, a doter—furnished nothing but praise, as extravagant as it was unfounded. In the end, neither much mattered, for the Academy of Fine Arts in Vienna twice rejected young Hitler, and, in the Austrian capital, he drifted, eking out a living painting postcards.

Like Mussolini, Hitler was a rudderless youth. But whereas Mussolini found direction in political ideas—at first, Socialism—Hitler found it in war itself. He greeted World War I with the ecstatic delirium of a boy who finds his first love. Initially spurned as unfit for military service, Hitler enlisted in the 16th Bavarian Reserve Infantry Regiment. Wounded in October 1916, he was also gassed late in the war. Like Mussolini, he failed to rise above corporal, yet, serving mainly as a front-line messenger, he proved his valor sufficiently in action to receive the Iron Cross, Second Class in 1914, and, in 1918, the Iron Cross, First Class—a rare achievement for any enlisted man.

REALITY CHECK

Dictator, Dictator

Mussolini's conquest of Ethiopia was a public relations nightmare for his regime, turning many of Il Duce's international admirers into detractors, who suddenly saw him not as a charismatic leader but a brutal tyrant. Haile Selassie, in contrast, figured in much of the world's estimation as a leader of great dignity and nobility—never mind that he himself had risen to rule Ethiopia by legislating for himself the absolute power of a dictator.

"To me those hours seemed like a release from the painful feelings of my youth . . . I fell down on my knees and thanked Heaven from an overflowing heart for granting me the good fortune of being permitted to live at this time."

Adolf Hitler, in Mein Kampf, *recalling his reaction to the news that World War I had started*

Adolf Hitler—seen here at age ten—was brutalized by an alcoholic father (a minor Austro-Hungarian customs officer) and doted on by an overindulgent mother.

The Birth of Nazism

After the war, Hitler stayed with the army, assigned as a political agent to infiltrate the fledgling German Workers' Party in Munich. He quickly converted from infiltrator to enthusiastic member of an organization that he saw as a means of overturning the humiliating

Frustrated in his dream of becoming an artist after the Academy of Fine Arts in Vienna twice rejected him, young Adolf Hitler drifted in aimless poverty until the coming of World War I suddenly shook violent meaning into his life. He never rose above the rank of corporal in the German army, but served with exceptional valor as a runner (messenger), earning the Iron Cross, First Class—a decoration rarely awarded to enlisted personnel. He is shown here, far right, with fellow members of his regiment, in France, 1916.

terms of the Treaty of Versailles. Soon, Hitler rose within the new party, which was renamed, in 1920, the Nationalsozialistische Deutsche Arbeiterpartei—the National Socialist German Workers' Party, popularly abbreviated to "Nazi" Party.

The Rise of Adolf Hitler

It was no accident that the Nazis came to maturity in the Bavarian capital. During the 1920s, the region, which never welcomed the rule of Berlin, was especially resentful toward the postwar democratic government—the Weimar Republic—which it regarded as weak and dominated by those who betrayed Germany into surrender. Munich was not only the headquarters of the new Nazi Party, it was also the center of the Freikorps, a paramilitary organization made up of German army troops who simply refused to demobilize after the world war. Prominent in the Freikorps was Ernst Röhm; Röhm and Hitler, inspired by Mussolini's Fascists, transformed the Nazi Party along paramilitary lines, including in it a private army of thugs. Whereas Mussolini's thugs wore black shirts, Hitler and Röhm clad their men in brown. These "Brownshirts" were the Sturmabteilung—storm troopers—also called the SA. Their job initially was to provide security at Nazi Party rallies, but they soon grew into a force that crushed all opposing political parties. Within a few years, the SA was larger than the official German army permitted under the Treaty of Versailles.

Like Mussolini, Hitler recognized the importance of intimidation and terror, but also like Mussolini, he understood that propaganda and the development of a cult of personality were far more important in creating a mass political movement. Physically unprepossessing, adorned with a "cookie duster" mustache that called to mind the silent film comic Charlie Chaplin, Adolf Hitler nevertheless possessed compelling charisma as a public speaker. His following grew so rapidly that, in November 1923, he joined forces with World War I generalissimo Erich Ludendorff to spark a national revolution against the hated Weimar Republic.

"In view of the primitive simplicity of their minds, [the masses] more easily fall victim to a big lie than a little one."

Adolf Hitler, Mein Kampf, *1924*

REALITY CHECK
Auxiliary Force

A bitter irony of the Treaty of Versailles was that its restriction on the size of the German army (capped at one hundred thousand men) did not apply to paramilitary organizations created outside of the official government. These included the Freikorps and, later, the SA and SS. During the interwar years, the SA and, subsequently, the SS, became larger than the German army and therefore posed a threat to that army.

On November 8, Hitler and his men burst into a right-wing political meeting in a Munich beer hall. The organizers of the meeting agreed to join Hitler's Nazis and SA in a mass march on Berlin—following the example of Mussolini's Fascist march on Rome the year before. On the next day, however, Hitler's column of three thousand Nazis were fired on by police. In the melee that followed, sixteen party members and three policemen were killed. The revolution died aborning. Both Hitler and Ludendorff were arrested and tried. Ludendorff, the war hero, was released, but Hitler was sentenced to five years imprisonment—the minimum sentence for treason.

Hitler was assigned quite comfortable quarters in Landsberg Prison. He used his sentence—of which he served but nine months before he was released—to write the first volume of a book he called *Mein Kampf*—"My Struggle." A combination memoir and political manifesto, *Mein Kampf* presented the essence of Nazism. Hitler explained that the greatness of the German people lay in their racial heritage. Like some other early twentieth-century European writers on race, Hitler believed that the original speakers of the Indo-European languages and their descendents constituted a distinctive race, a "Nordic race," superior to all others. In particular, Hitler pitted this "master race"—as he called it—against the Jewish, or Semitic, race, which, he warned, threatened the purity of Germany's Aryan heritage. Not only was there no real basis on which to conflate linguistic with racial origins in defining an "Aryan race," Hitler and his followers further twisted the term by excluding Roma (Gypsies, whom they considered inferior) from the Aryan race, even though they were of direct Indo-European descent. Yet when Japan joined the Axis—the alliance between Germany and Italy—Nazi propaganda classified the Japanese as Aryans, even

Hitler speaks at a 1923 Nazi Party rally in Nuremberg, early in his rise to power.

REALITY CHECK
Unification
The hard truth is that Hitler managed to do in Germany what the leaders of the great democracies—Franklin D. Roosevelt included—failed to do during the Great Depression. He united management and labor, capitalists and the masses, leading them to a common cause in the fate of the nation.

though the Indo-European line was utterly foreign to them. Hitler argued that the "Aryan people"—ethnically pure Germany—had been betrayed by the Weimar Republic, which, by shamelessly capitulating to the terms of the Versailles treaty, had deprived the German people of their birthright—a destiny of greatness, a destiny of dominance. As bad as Weimar was, Hitler explained, the even greater threat to the fulfillment of Germany's destiny was Marxism—by which Hitler meant both Socialism and Communism—a poisonous ideology invented by a Jew and promoted by Jews.

Anti-Semitism was hardly unique to Adolf Hitler—it was a familiar German refrain but, in *Mein Kampf*, Hitler linked all that threatened "Aryan" Germany—the Weimar betrayal and Marxism—to a great Jewish conspiracy. As Hitler portrayed them, the Jews were the very incarnation of evil: "I set the Aryan and the Jew over against each other," Hitler wrote in the early 1930s, "and if I call one of them a human being I must call the other something else. The two are as widely separated as man and beast. Not that I would call the Jew a beast. . . . He is a creature outside nature and alien to nature."

A Nazi Party election poster of 1932 urges Germans to vote the Nazi slate for the sake of the nation's future. The party gained so many seats in the Reichstag (German parliament) that Germany's aged president, Paul von Hindenburg, was forced to form a coalition government in which Hitler was made chancellor, a position he subsequently parleyed into absolute dictatorship of the nation.

The leading message of *Mein Kampf* was that Germany could be—and must be—saved, the birthright of its people restored. To do this, democratic governments such as the Weimar Republic had to be crushed and replaced by absolute rule under a single great leader. Hitler offered himself for the position: the German equivalent of Il Duce—Der Führer—*the* leader.

Nazis Triumphant

During Hitler's nine months in prison, the Nazi Party survived—but just barely. One of the biggest problems Hitler faced was an improvement in the German economy, which increased popular support for the Weimar government. Emboldened, Weimar officials barred Hitler from speaking, first in Bavaria and then almost everywhere else. Hitler managed to evade these bans, however, and not only brought the party back from the brink of dissolution but also set it on the path to growth once again. When the effects of the Great Depression triggered in the United States by the 1929 stock market crash reached Germany, Hitler and the Nazis received just the boost they needed. Bad times, misery, and helpless panic were potent fertilizer for any totalitarian regime. Whereas in the democratic countries, the Depression set management and capital against labor, Hitler directed his appeal not only to the jobless masses, but to the hard-hit industrialists and capitalists as well. This soon made the Nazis the second-largest party in the country, polling more than six million votes in the 1930 election.

Sensing that the time was now ripe, Adolf Hitler ran against Germany's war-hero incumbent, the aged and infirm Paul von Hindenburg, in the presidential election of 1932. He captured more than a third of the votes, thereby demonstrating so much popularity that Hindenburg felt compelled to create a coalition with the Nazis by appointing Hitler, whom he personally detested, chancellor. Hitler was now the equivalent of prime minister, the number two man in the Weimar government. Hitler and the Nazis were now officially entrenched in the German leadership.

REALITY CHECK

Majority Rules

Hitler's great insight was to see that he did not have to win over all of the German people—just enough of them to give him, as it were, a controlling share in the German government. With this, he could rapidly assume control of all Germany.

Der Führer

Aging and ill, Hindenburg could not prevent his new chancellor from independently building a power base that would give him dictatorial power. On February 27, 1933, fire destroyed the Reichstag, the German parliament building. Hitler immediately fixed blame on Communists, thereby securing authority to abolish the Communist Party and imprison the party's leaders. The very next month, Hitler gained passage of the Enabling Act, by which he was granted dictatorial authority for four years. It was a pattern that had been set by no less than Benito Mussolini.

LINK

Trading Rights

Today, few historians doubt that the fire was the work of Nazi arsonists, bent on creating the kind of terror that makes people pliable and willing to exchange liberty for the security offered even by a tyrant. During the American Revolution, Benjamin Franklin warned his countrymen that "A People willing to exchange liberty for security deserves neither." The perceived trade-off between these two commodities—liberty and security—frequently surfaces in history.

Hitler was not shy about exercising his new power. He banned all political parties in Germany, save the Nazi Party. With the Communists neutralized as a political threat in Germany, he turned to his other enduring scapegoat, beginning the purge of all Jews from government and from government-controlled institutions. And then he cleaned house within his own party. Ernst Röhm, the former Freikorps leader who had organized the Brownshirts—the storm troopers, or SA—had been key to Hitler's rise. Now, however, he and his Brownshirt army represented a serious threat to Hitler's enduring power. Using his own force of

SS head Heinrich Himmler (right) walks beside SA chief Ernst Röhm during a funeral procession in 1934, shortly before Röhm was executed.

Joseph Goebbels was Hitler's minister of propaganda—a master of mass media, mass persuasion, and, despite an unprepossessing appearance and lameness caused by a club foot, a charismatic personal communicator. He is seen here speaking at Zweibrücken, Germany, in May 1934.

bodyguards, the Schutzstaffel, or SS, Hitler unleashed on June 30, 1934, the so-called Night of the Long Knives, a violent purge of Röhm and the Brownshirt leadership. Hundreds of storm troopers were arrested and murdered. Röhm was quietly executed, and Hitler replaced much of the SA with the SS.

Under the command of Hitler's devoted henchman Heinrich Himmler, the SS rapidly expanded into an army parallel with but entirely separate from the regular German army. The SS controlled a secret police force, the Gestapo, which set about identifying, arresting, and eliminating all political adversaries and, as always, Jews. Some were imprisoned, others murdered, but, increasingly, "undesirables" were consigned to concentration camps, which began to appear throughout Germany. In addition to Communists and Jews, the list of undesirables came to include homosexuals and the disabled, including the mentally ill and the developmentally impaired. Eventually, individuals in these latter two categories were quietly "euthanized."

While Hitler engaged in political, ethnic, racial, and ideological terror, he assigned his minister of propaganda (such was his official title), Joseph Goebbels, to employ various mass media to bring the nation into lockstep behind him as he led Germany to an economic recovery driven by massive rearmament in defiance of the Treaty of Versailles and the League of Nations.

"That's my trade: hatred. It takes you a long way further than any other emotion."

Joseph Goebbels, 1929

As in Italy, the combination of renewed national pride and economic prosperity seemed to the majority more than a fair exchange for the loss of rational democracy, personal liberty, toleration, and simple human decency.

The Rising Sun

Immediately after the December 7, 1941, Japanese attack on Pearl Harbor thrust the United States into World War II, Americans readily demonized three dictators as the lords of war: in Italy, Mussolini; in Germany, Hitler; and in Japan, Hideki Tojo. Whereas Mussolini and Hitler were as close as human beings can come to being genuine demons and were in large measure personally responsible for the war, Tojo had become Japan's premier in October 1941, just shortly before the Pearl Harbor attack. He was more of a powerful military bureaucrat than truly a dictator. He executed national policy rather than created it. In contrast to the rise of Mussolini and Hitler, his ascendancy in the Japanese government was not something he created, but was the culmination of a national evolution that had begun in the mid-nineteenth century.

In 1867, Mutsuhito (today known as Emperor Meiji after the name of the era during which he ruled) was crowned emperor of Japan and began the modernization of his country, including opening relations with the West and setting Japan on an equal footing with the Western nations politically and economically. An important aspect of the Meiji reform movement was the expansion of the Japanese Empire, beginning in 1879 with the incorporation of the Ryukyu Islands into Japan—over the protest of China. At about this time as well, Japan began making aggressive overtures toward Korea, which resulted in the First Sino-Japanese War during 1894–95. By the treaty that ended the war both sides recognized Korean independence, but China ceded several other territories to Japan. Alarmed by Japanese expansion, France, Russia, and Germany forced the return of the Liaodong Peninsula to China, and Russia leased the peninsula from China for a naval base at Port Arthur in 1898. Russia also made overtures to extend its sphere of influence to Manchuria and Korea. This triggered the Russo-Japanese War of 1904–5, resulting in Japanese control of Korea. It also forced Russian economic and political concessions to Japan in Manchuria, including

REALITY CHECK

From Cellars to Camps of Horror

In the early 1930s, the Nazi regime confined political opponents to makeshift prisons, which ranged from cellars and the basements of large public buildings to anonymous warehouses, but soon developed into full-scale concentration camps, built on the model of facilities used by the British to contain political prisoners in South Africa during the Great Boer War at the start of twentieth century. The camps were centrally administered and set up in rural areas, somewhat shielded from public view. By the time the war began in September 1939, six major concentration camps had been established: Dachau (1933), Sachsenhausen (1936), Buchenwald (1937), Flossenbürg (1938), Mauthausen-Gusen (1938) and Ravensbrück (1939). By the end of the war, there were many more, some devoted to housing political prisoners and certain prisoners of war, others populated almost exclusively by Jews "deported" from Germany and occupied countries. Some camps were nothing more than places of confinement, others were slave-labor facilities, and still others were places of murder: death camps.

Hideki Tojo (in military uniform and wearing round spectacles) became prime minister of Japan on October 18, 1941, solidifying the military's stranglehold on the government and leading the nation into World War II. Although American propaganda portrayed him as a megalomaniacal dictator like Mussolini and Hitler, Tojo was actually a longtime military bureaucrat thrust into a position of great power. This photo was taken in front of the Diet, or Japanese parliament, in November 1941.

the return to Japan of the Liaodong Peninsula and the cession of the southern half of Sakhalin Island. Japan rapidly emerged as the most important imperialist power in East Asia and continued to extract concessions from China, especially concerning access to coal and iron resources.

The Rise of Japanese Militarism

Although many in the West persisted in viewing Japan as a quaint and backward country, there was growing recognition of the dangers of Japanese expansion. During the 1920s, a series of naval and other arms-limitation treaties were concluded among the United States, the European powers, and Japan—largely in an effort to ensure that Japanese military and naval power did not outstrip that of the Western nations. With these treaties in place by the end of the 1920s, Japan's imperialism seemed to have been curbed. The onset of the Great Depression in the 1930s, however, caused economic hardship in Japan—hardship that was exacerbated by discriminatory Western tariffs, which limited Japanese exports. A growing faction in the Japanese government advocated renewed expansion—through military conquest—to bring about economic recovery and well-being.

As the influence of this militarist faction increased, democratic politics diminished, and the Japanese government drifted toward domination by a military junta in league with civilian ultranationalists. In effect, Japan developed the equivalent of a Fascist or Nazi political philosophy, with emphasis on purity of race and nationality. Whereas in Italy and Germany dictators worked to develop about themselves an ultimately fanatical cult of personality, in Japan, such a cult was already present in the form of emperor worship. Hirohito, who became emperor in 1926, was viewed as a demigod. His ratification of the militarists' policies gave them the force of divine law.

The Second Sino-Japanese War

On September 18, 1931, charging that Chinese troops had tried to bomb a South Manchurian Railway train, Japanese army officers authorized the capture of Mukden (modern Shenyang) and the occupation of all Manchuria. The Japanese civilian government was powerless to stop this action, which emboldened elements in the Japanese military to stage a series of uprisings against the government, including a 1932 terrorist attack in Tokyo and the assassination on February 26, 1936, of a number of prominent Japanese statesmen. Although the revolt of 1936 was put down, the army remained a hotbed of aggressive imperialism, and the civilian government made repeated concessions to the military extremists, including the invasion of China for the purpose of transforming Manchuria into a Japanese puppet state called Manchukuo. Chinese Nationalists, led primarily by Chiang Kai-shek, resisted the Japanese incursion, and, on July 7, 1937, fighting broke out between Japanese and Chinese troops at the Marco Polo Bridge near Peking (Beijing). This was the beginning of a second Sino-Japanese War, and in November 1938, Japan proclaimed Manchukuo as the nucleus of a "new order" in East Asia, a "co-prosperity sphere" largely under Japanese control.

Hirohito, emperor of Japan, was regarded by his people as semidivine—theoretically all-powerful, yet politically of very limited authority.

THE AXIS FORMS

WHILE JAPAN INCREASINGLY YIELDED PARLIAMENTARY GOVERNMENT to military dictatorship and allowed its military to lead an imperial expansion in Asia, Mussolini and Hitler helped Generalissimo Francisco Franco to win the Spanish Civil War during 1936–39 and install a Fascist government in that country. Recognizing an ideological kinship with Hitler, in 1936 Japan concluded with Germany the Anti-Comintern Pact, a military alliance against Soviet Communist expansion. A year later, the pact was expanded to include Italy, and in September 1940 the Anti-Comintern Pacts were replaced by a full-scale political and military alliance among Germany, Italy, and Japan. It was officially called the Tripartite Pact, but was more usually referred to as the Axis Pact, because it created a military-political "axis" through Berlin, Rome, and Tokyo. Spain was also invited to join the Axis, but Franco, Fascist though he was, refused to take that ultimate step.

As in 1914, armed camps were being formed—the Axis on one side, and the Western democracies on the other. But, this time, the Axis camp was far more aggressive than that of the democracies, which revealed themselves as tentative, reluctant, and pitiably weak.

TAKEAWAY

Rise of the Despots

Political and especially economic conditions following World War I were conducive to the rise of military dictatorships in Italy, Germany, and Japan, putting in power leaders willing to plunge the world into a new war in order gain for themselves an empire and permanence of power.

CHAPTER 3

OUTBREAK

Slouching Toward All-Out War

BY THE MID 1930S, the planet was divided into dictatorships with rattling sabers and democracies seeking nothing but peace. The situation resembled that of 1914, except that, back then, both the Central Powers and the Allies were willing to go to war. Now, however, the democracies so feared renewing the terrors of a world war that they were inclined to do almost anything to avoid pushing the aggressors into armed conflict. Instead of averting war, this policy of avoidance—it would be called "appeasement"—virtually ensured war.

UNDOING VERSAILLES

THE TREATY OF VERSAILLES created misery, discontent, and rage in Germany. But, in the end, the Treaty of Versailles was just so much paper. It had laid down terms intended to hamstring Germany, permanently preventing its rise as a renewed threat in the world. It saddled the nation with a crippling reparations debt; it limited the German army to just one hundred thousand men; it prohibited all offensive weapons, including aircraft and submarines; and it set a fifteen-thousand-sailor limit to the navy.

Even before the rise of Hitler, the German military found ways to get around all of these limits. Under General Hans von Seeckt, the skeleton Versailles treaty army became what was termed a "Führerheer"—literally, a "leader army," consisting exclusively of the military elite. An all-volunteer force, it was highly selective, diminutive, to be sure, but designed to function as the perfectly polished core around which a new army could be rapidly formed—when the time was right.

The treaty restrictions on military hardware were even easier to circumvent. In 1922, the German government concluded the Treaty of Rapallo with the Soviet Union, which provided for military cooperation between the two countries. Whereas the Treaty of Versailles restricted development of weapons *in Germany*, the Treaty of Rapallo provided facilities *in Russia* where Germany could develop aircraft as well as advanced ground weapons. It was a loophole of momentous strategic proportions.

But Germany did not rely on loopholes alone. As support for Hitler became absolute in Germany, he led rearmament with increasing boldness in direct defiance of the Versailles. At each turn, none of the democracies offered meaningful resistance or even much in the way of objection. Indeed, the Hitler government persuaded many in the British government that a strong Germany was the West's best defense against the spread of Soviet Communism, and in 1935 the Anglo-German Naval Pact allowed Germany increased

ALTERNATE TAKE

Opposite Effect

If the Treaty of Versailles had not imposed such severe restrictions on the German military, top German commanders might never have formulated the Führerheer concept. In effect, Versailles actually forced Germany to create a super-elite military cadre, which served as the fast-growing seeds of a very formidable military in World War II.

ANGLO-GERMAN NAVAL PACT

Signed on June 18, 1935, the Anglo-German Naval Pact undid major restrictions imposed by the Treaty of Versailles on the size of the German navy.

The pact allowed Germany to increase the size of its navy to one-third the size of the Royal Navy. Additionally, Britain agreed to withdraw its navy from the Baltic Sea, effectively yielding that body of water to German control. The pact was intended to avoid friction with Germany, and while many Britons were appalled at giving Germany control of the Baltic, they were reassured by the reformulation of allowed German naval strength. It was universally believed by military theorists that when two evenly matched opponents fought, neither would win, but if one adversary possessed no more than a third of the other's armaments, it would certainly lose. Allowing the increase in German naval strength, British negotiators believed, would placate the Germans even as it continued to ensure that they would lose an armed confrontation on the sea. This crumb of comfort was, in any case, moot, since Hitler freely violated the treaty limitations.

Delegates from Great Britain, the United States, France, Japan, and Italy gather in London on December 18, 1935, for the Naval Limitation Conference—an attempt to hold in check the post–World War I rearmament of the great naval powers. The conference produced the London Naval Treaty.

REALITY CHECK
Fortified Positions

Even though their war strategy was offensive rather than defensive, Italy and Germany, like France, also built extensive fortifications, if only as a hedge against the possible failure of their aggression. Thus, what American general George S. Patton Jr. said of Italian and German fortifications in World War II applied even more strongly to the Maginot Line and the French faith in it: "The Italians and Germans spent tremendous effort in time, labor, and money, building defensive positions. I am sure that just as in the case of the walls of Troy and the Roman walls across Europe, the fact that they trusted to defensive positions reduced their power to fight. Had they spent one-third as much effort fighting as they did in building, we could never have taken the positions."

tonnage in warships. The treaty led Hitler to believe that Britain and Germany might one day—and soon—become allies.

Nor did Hitler's Germany merely rearm. It planned. It planned nothing less than the conquest of Europe, using a revolutionary new approach to war. It was called "blitzkrieg"—literally, "lightning war"—and combined tactics and weapons, especially the coordinated use of highly mobile artillery and tanks with support from massive numbers of aircraft, to invade enemy territory with speed and force that were overwhelming in their effect. The essence of blitzkrieg was to hold enemy front-line forces in check while wreaking havoc on the rear echelons, thereby preventing both retreat and reinforcement and creating chaos, panic, and debilitating demoralization. Germany's participation in the Spanish Civil War of 1936–39 was a partial dress rehearsal for blitzkrieg, with particular emphasis on aerial tactics.

Of Denial and Digging In

The rearmament of Germany was first a top secret, then an open secret, and finally a deliberate threat. As Germany clearly girded itself for an offensive war, France acted in a way that symbolized the attitude of democratic Europe.

Born in 1877, André Maginot was elected to the French Chamber of Deputies in 1910 and became undersecretary of war three years later. Intensely patriotic, he left the safety of the war department to enlist in the army as a private at the start of World War I. Severely wounded, he was discharged and returned to politics. Like so many others who had seen the horrors of the Great War firsthand, he wanted to do something—anything—that might prevent such a war from breaking out again. Maginot began campaigning to fund construction of a line of defensive fortifications along the eastern frontiers of France. If Germany was an eternal threat, lock Germany out.

Construction of the fortification line began in 1929, while Maginot was minister of war. He died early in 1932 and so did not live to see the completion, in 1938, of the system of fortifications that would bear his name. The Maginot Line was a true wonder of twentieth-century military engineering: a chain of fortresses interconnected via a network of underground tunnels through which troops and supplies could be moved by electric railroad. Whatever fortifications were above ground were built of concrete sufficiently thick to withstand bombardment by any artillery then known. Troops assigned to garrison the Maginot fortifications enjoyed quarters that were air-conditioned—which made for a life more comfortable, it was said, than that possible in most modern cities.

But the comfort of Maginot Line soldiers was nothing compared to the comfort the line gave to the citizens of France. It appealed to common sense, much as a double deadbolt appeals to an anxious homeowner. Here was a physical line of fortifications stretching along the entire Franco-German frontier, from the southern tip of Belgium down to the top of Switzerland. What could be safer than this?

The Maginot Line was born of France's militarily passive policy of static defense, which developed between the world wars. The line of elaborate hardened forts stretched from the Swiss border to Luxembourg and Belgium and was intended to stop—or at least impede—any German invasion attempt. As it turned out, the invaders simply bypassed the Maginot Line by marching through neutral Belgium. In this picture, curious U.S. troops inspect the useless defenses during the liberation of France in 1944.

The Maginot Line was a strange project for a nation victorious in war. It was, after all, a literal emblem of bunker mentality, the attitude not of one expecting victory in war but one seeking to avoid defeat. The Maginot Line was of a piece with everything else the democracies did during the 1930s, the treaties, the attempts at disarmament, the pledges of non-aggression, the averting of eyes when evidence of aggression was manifest, the hunkering down in an air-conditioned ditch. All this from the victors—even as a defeated Germany sharpened the swords of its growing armory.

Appeasement

France and the other democracies wanted to avoid defeat by avoiding war. It was a most rational aspiration, but, as national policy, it had a serious disadvantage. People rarely rally around a negative. It is hard to inspire a nation with the concept of avoidance. In contrast, Adolf Hitler hit upon a policy that, for his people, was positively intoxicating.

In 1901, the German geographer and ethnographer Friedrich Ratzel (1844–1904) wrote an essay called *Lebensraum*—literally, "living space." Ratzel declared that states expanded their boundaries according to their ability to do so. Some three decades later, Adolf Hitler appropriated the *Lebensraum* concept and twisted it to

DETAILS, DETAILS

Reich Three

The "Third Reich" (Drittes Reich) was the most popular of the names for Germany under the Nazi regime. Officially, Germany at this time was the German Reich (Deutsches Reich), until Nazi aggression annexed various nations to the Reich, transforming it into the Greater German Reich (Großdeutsches Reich). Hitler and other Nazi leaders frequently used the phrase Thousand-Year Reich (Tausendjähriges Reich) as an alternative to Third Reich. In fact, Nazi Germany would endure a mere twelve years, from 1933 to 1945. Reich is best translated as "empire," a term intended to evoke the greatness of the German Empire before its defeat in World War I. Why the Third Empire? The First German Empire or Holy Roman Empire lasted nearly a thousand years, from 843–1806. The Second Empire was established under Kaiser Wilhelm I, after the defeat of France in the 1871 Franco-Prussian War, and ended with the 1919 Treaty of Versailles, which ushered in the so-called Weimar Republic.

justify the expansion of Germany as something only right, natural, and—indeed—inevitable.

Lebensraum was highly appealing to the German people, but talk of it moved Britain, France, and even Italy to issue a joint statement opposing German expansion. Anticipating trouble, France even entered into a defensive alliance with the Soviet Union in 1935, and the Soviets concluded a similar pact with the Czechs. But among the Fascists it was Mussolini, not Hitler, who made the first aggressive move toward national expansion when Italy invaded Ethiopia in 1935. As mentioned in the previous chapter, the League of Nations proved impotent to intervene in this aggression. That was bad enough, but things were actually even worse. Sir Samuel Hoare, Britain's foreign secretary, responded to the invasion of Ethiopia with an attempt to "appease"—or, at least, buy off—Mussolini by promising no British objection to his taking most of Ethiopia provided that he agree to preserve with Britain a defensive alliance against Germany. To the credit of the British government and people, the proposal created a scandal that forced Hoare's resignation. However, neither Britain nor any other country attempted to stop the invasion of Ethiopia, and, abortive though it was, Hoare's proposal introduced the concept of "appeasement" into European politics.

> "An appeaser is one who feeds the crocodile—hoping it will eat him last."
>
> *Winston S. Churchill*

As for Hitler, Mussolini's experience with Ethiopia provided a valuable lesson, suggesting to him that neither Britain nor France possessed the will to oppose German expansion. Accordingly, on March 7, 1936, Hitler ordered twenty-two thousand German soldiers to cross the bridges of the Rhine. This was a blatant violation of the Treaty of Versailles, which mandated the demilitarization of the Rhineland. Hitler knew it, and he was prepared to withdraw what was, after all, a token force if France or Britain made any move against it. He was betting, however, that they would not. They did not.

"It's none of our business, is it? It's their own back-garden they're walking into."

London Times *editorial concerning the German remilitarization of the Rhineland*

It was the demonstrated weakness of France and Britain—first shown with regard to Ethiopia and now with regard to the Rhineland—that moved Mussolini to align Italy with Germany. He began on July 11, 1936, by agreeing that Austria, Italy's traditional enemy on its northern border, should be deemed "a German state"; then, on November 1, Mussolini coined the term by which the Fascist-Nazi alliance would become infamous. In a speech at Milan, he declared, "The Italo-German Entente forms a vertical line Berlin-Rome. This line is not a partition but is rather an axis around which all European states can collaborate." The German-Japanese Anti-Comintern Pact followed on November 25, 1936, with Italy signing on to this on November 6, 1937. In May of that year, Neville Chamberlain replaced the retiring Stanley Baldwin as prime minister of Britain. He was not one to close his eyes to German expansion and the emerging Rome-Berlin-Tokyo Axis, but neither was he prepared to oppose these developments directly. As he saw it, Italy and Japan—not Germany—represented the more serious threat of war. During the Baldwin years, Britain had extensively disarmed. Chamberlain wanted to conserve military resources and to buy time to build up the military in order to defend against the Italian and Japanese threat; therefore, to avoid a premature conflict with Germany, Chamberlain proposed a policy of what he called "active appeasement." He intended to find out just what Hitler wanted and then buy him off by giving it to him.

In 1936, Hitler boldly violated the Treaty of Versailles by sending troops across the Cologne Bridge to reoccupy the officially "demilitarized" Rhineland. The European democracies—chiefly Britain and France—offered no credible response to the violation and ultimately acquiesced in it. It was the first step in an Allied policy of "appeasement," which emboldened Hitler's march toward a cataclysmic war of conquest.

Adolf Hitler accepts the adulation of the Reichstag in March 1938 after he announced the "peaceful" annexation of Austria to the Third Reich: the Anschluss.

Had Chamberlain listened—or perhaps believed what he had heard—he would already have known what Hitler wanted. The Führer openly declared his ambition shortly after assuming the chancellorship in 1933. "Today Germany," he said. "Tomorrow, the world."

On March 13, 1938, Hitler stepped outside of Germany by invading Austria. Opposed neither by Austria nor Italy, Hitler proclaimed Austria a province of the German Reich. This annexation—in German, the "Anschluss"—put Germany in position for its next adventure across its borders. The Sudetenland was a large portion of Czechoslovakia, including major industrial areas and a region rich in iron ore and coal, populated mainly by ethnic Germans—Czech nationals who spoke German and identified themselves as Germans. Almost immediately after the Anschluss, Hitler embraced what he called the cause of the Sudeten Germans, who, he said, were a persecuted minority much abused by the Czechs. When he demanded the cession to Germany of the Sudetenland, Chamberlain intervened, warning Hitler to negotiate with the Czechs before making any aggressive move against the country. Both Chamberlain and Hitler were well aware that Britain was bound by treaty to guarantee Czech sovereignty. But, based on recent experience, Hitler stood firm. Chamberlain bowed. Hat in hand, he flew to Berchtesgaden, where Hitler maintained an Alpine chalet.

He made a proposal that exceeded even Adolf Hitler's ample dreams. He proposed to give the Führer everything he wanted.

Hitler responded by demanding the Sudetenland. Chamberlain agreed, then went off to Paris and to Prague—in that order—to persuade the French and Czech governments to go along with his plan. French officials were appalled and asked Franklin D. Roosevelt for America's support in backing Czech sovereignty. But the president would not—and, in any case, could not—shake his nation out of its isolationism. Without Britain or the United States to back it, France agreed to hand to Hitler not only the Sudetenland, but all areas of Czechoslovakia with a population more than 50 percent ethnic German.

This left only the Czechs themselves to be consulted on the matter. Initially, they proposed to fight. Chamberlain remarked privately, "How horrible, fantastic, incredible it is that we should be digging trenches and trying on gas masks here because of a quarrel in a far-away country between people of whom we know nothing," and, on September 21, he persuaded the Czech government that it really had no choice.

On September 22, Chamberlain again flew to meet with Hitler, who, having gotten what he asked for, demanded more. The Sudetenland was to be occupied by the German army, and the Czechs were to be evacuated from the area. At this, both France and Czechoslovakia began to mobilize for war. Chamberlain responded by organizing a conference at Munich on September 29–30, 1938, with Hitler, French premier Édouard Daladier, and Italy's Benito Mussolini. Mussolini proposed a plan—which had actually been written by Germany—that essentially duplicated what Hitler had demanded at his last meeting with Chamberlain. But since it came from Mussolini, making clear his solidarity with Hitler, France backed down and joined Britain in presenting the Czech government with a stark choice: stand alone against Germany or agree to being torn limb from limb. The Czechs agreed, and the Munich Conference concluded with the Munich Pact, which sold out the Czechs in exchange for Hitler's word of honor that he would make no more territorial demands in Europe.

Hitler greets British prime minister Neville Chamberlain as he arrives in Munich, September 29, 1938, for the conference in which he will appease the dictator by giving him Czechoslovakia's Sudetenland. Chamberlain returned from Munich believing he had secured "peace for our time," but Winston Churchill, fierce opponent of Chamberlain's appeasement policy, condemned the "betrayal of Czechoslovakia" as a catastrophic defeat.

"My good friends, this is the second time in our history that there has come back from Germany to Downing Street peace with honor. I believe it is peace for our time. I thank you from the bottom of our hearts And now I recommend you go home and sleep quietly in your beds."

Neville Chamberlain, speech at 10 Downing Street after returning from the Munich Conference, September 30, 1938

ALTERNATE TAKE

Vital Territory

Appeasement did not mean that Neville Chamberlain was a coward, but that he and his followers were shortsighted. Had Chamberlain understood the strategic importance of the Sudetenland, rather than viewed it as the object of a "quarrel in a far-away country between people of whom we know nothing," he might not have been so willing to yield it. The Sudetenland (and all Czechoslovakia) constituted the strategic keystone of Europe. The territory was located at the crossroads of Western and Eastern Europe, was rich in strategic ores, already contained a major arms works, and had a thirty-division army. Had the Allies taken a stand over the Sudetenland, Hitler would probably have backed down—at least for a time, which would have given the Allies more time to build forces against him.

Except for the Czechs, of course, the great majority of Europeans breathed a sigh of relief. Many, doubtless, cheered. Winston Churchill, at the time just a member of Parliament, begged to differ, warning his countrymen that Britain had just suffered its worst military defeat in history—and without a shot having been fired.

> **"England has been offered a choice between war and shame. She has chosen shame and will get war."**
>
> *Winston S. Churchill,*
> *September 1938 speech to the House of Commons*

Enter Stalin

Neville Chamberlain and the rest of the world would soon learn the awful folly of attempting to appease the very incarnation of rapacity. Despite his pledge, Hitler violated the Munich Agreement on March 16, 1939, by occupying Prague and annexing what was left of Czechoslovakia.

The democracies, which should have known better, were stunned. In the strange calculus of the late 1930s, the Soviet Union, which had figured as the common enemy of the Axis and the democracies, now emerged—in the view of Britain and France and even to aloof America—as a kind of ally. Since the onset, in 1922, of the fatal illness of Vladimir Lenin, leader of the Bolshevik Revolution, Joseph Stalin had been the ruthless dictator not only of the Soviets but also of the world Communist movement. This made him, *ex officio*, as it were, the implacable enemy of Hitler and Mussolini.

Or so it would seem. And so it should have been. But although Hitler, Mussolini, and Stalin stood on opposite sides of an ideological divide, they were, in the end, united by a tie that proved stronger—at least in 1939. They were all totalitarian tyrants. Ideology notwithstanding, that fact gave them common cause against democracy and the democratic nations.

Like everyone else, Stalin had witnessed the Western democracies cave in to Adolf Hitler, giving him whatever he wanted. Stalin wanted things, too—a piece of Poland and occupation of the Baltic states, especially Finland. Cooperation with Hitler might help him get these things. For his part, Hitler was dismayed when Britain finally showed some spine after he swallowed up all of Czechoslovakia. Prime Minister Chamberlain pledged his nation's guarantee of Polish security and sovereignty. Poland was next on Hitler's agenda, and the last thing he wanted was for the Soviets to join forces with the British in opposing him there. Stalin suddenly replaced his pro-Western—and Jewish—foreign minister Maksim Litvinov with the more pragmatic Vyacheslav Molotov and, through him, negotiated the German-Soviet Non-Aggression Pact, popularly called the Hitler-Stalin Pact. Winston Churchill described Molotov in *The Gathering Storm*, the first of his six-volume history *The Second World War*:

World War II was the culmination of an "age of great dictators," including Mussolini, Hitler, and the Soviet Union's Joseph Stalin. The poster proclaims: "Beloved Stalin—The People's Fortune."

> Vyacheslav Molotov was a man of outstanding ability and cold-blooded ruthlessness. He had survived the fearful hazards and ordeals to which all the Bolshevik leaders had been subjected in the years of triumphant revolution. He had lived and thrived in a society where ever-varying intrigue was accompanied by the constant menace of personal liquidation. His cannon-ball head, black moustache, and comprehending eyes, his slab face, his verbal adroitness and imperturbable demeanour, were appropriate manifestations of his qualities and skill. He was above all men fitted to be the agent and instrument of the policy of an incalculable machine. . . . His smile of Siberian winter, his carefully-measured and often wise words, his affable demeanour, combined to make him the perfect agent of Soviet policy in a deadly world.

Signed on August 23, 1939, the pact sent shockwaves through Europe and the world. The apostle of Communism and the avatar of Nazism—ideologically incompatible—had agreed not to make war on one another. Coupled with a trade treaty concluded days before,

Stalin, whose Communist ideology was diametrically opposed to Hitler's Nazism, stunned the world when he concluded on August 23, 1939, the German-Soviet Non-Aggression Pact, a step just short of a Nazi-Soviet military alliance. Stalin is flanked by German foreign minister Joachim von Ribbentrop (arms folded) and by his own foreign minister, Vyacheslav Molotov.

this non-aggression pact seemed to signal an outright alliance. It was unthinkable. But it was a fact. And—had the world been privy to the secret portions of the pact—the full extent of the agreement would have been seen as even more sinister. A secret protocol provided for the German-Soviet partition of Poland and cleared the way for the Soviet invasion of the Baltic. In short, Stalin gave Hitler leave to invade Poland (another Slavic nation) and, to get a piece of that country for the Soviet Union, would even assist in the invasion. For his part, Hitler agreed most immediately not to interfere with Stalin's plan to invade Finland.

The illusion of appeasement instantly evaporated. Britain formalized its Polish guarantee with an Agreement of Mutual Assistance, signed just two days after the Hitler-Stalin Pact. Maybe that would discourage Hitler and hold off war.

DAY ONE (OF 2,174)

DURING THE EVENING OF AUGUST 31, 1939, A PRISONER from one of Adolf Hitler's concentration camps, Franciszek Honiok, a German Silesian known to be a Polish sympathizer, was dressed in the uniform of a Polish soldier, transported to the German town of Gleiwitz on the Polish frontier, and shot by the Gestapo. The next day, Hitler claimed that this "Polish soldier" was cut down during a Polish attack on a German radio transmitter at Gleiwitz. It was, Hitler said, an example of Polish aggression and ample reason for the war—it would be the second world war—that began at 4:30 in the morning (local time) on September 1, 1939, as aircraft of the German Luftwaffe (air force) bombed Polish airfields, ground forces surged across the border, and a German battleship "visiting" the Polish port of Danzig (present-day Gdansk) opened fire on the port's fortifications.

REALITY CHECK

Lacking Reserves

On paper, Poland had a reserve force of nearly three million, but these men were only partially trained at best and lacked most equipment and weapons.

The invaders, which included elements of the German army as well as Soviet units, vastly outnumbered the Polish defenders.

More than one hundred active and reserve divisions, together with a cavalry brigade—a total of about two and a half million troops—opposed thirty Polish infantry divisions, eleven cavalry brigades, two mechanized brigades, and supporting units—some 280,000 men.

The numbers, lopsided as they were, tell only part of the story. After World War I and despite the Treaty of Versailles, Germany had rearmed itself as a cutting-edge military force, with advanced aircraft and tanks, whereas the Polish military, although gallant, was equipped with obsolete or obsolescent weapons, including some cavalry forces that went to war with nothing but sabers and lances.

As we will see in the next chapter, superiority of numbers and equipment was not the only element driving Germany's success in the invasion of Poland. Beginning in the 1920s, the Germany military had been perfecting blitzkrieg, the "lightning war" tactics that coordinated ground and air forces to overwhelm an enemy with a highly mobile, very swift, very violent style of warfare against which even a determined defender, using more conventional arms and tactics, stood very little chance.

NUMBERS

Air and Sea Forces

When Germany invaded Poland, the Luftwaffe had more than 3,600 operational aircraft, whereas the Polish air force had perhaps 1,900 planes of obsolescent or obsolete design, entirely outclassed by the German craft. At sea, the German Baltic fleet boasted a pair of advanced battle cruisers, 3 so-called pocket battleships, 2 heavy cruisers, 6 light cruisers, 22 destroyers, 43 submarines, and 2 older *Dreadnought*-class battleships. The entire operational Polish navy consisted of just 4 destroyers and 5 submarines.

The *Second* World War

Like the Great War—that struggle would now have to be designated the *First* World War—the Second World War began with conflicts of nationality and ideology in central-eastern Europe. Fueled by the imperialist, expansionist ambitions of dictators—above all, those of Adolf Hitler, but also of Joseph Stalin and Benito Mussolini (soon to be augmented by the militarists of Japan)—the outbreak of war was enabled by what must be described as the collective exhaustion of the democratic powers, which could not summon the strength of will to oppose the Axis.

The price of ambition on the one hand and exhaustion on the other would be apocalyptic: the deaths of forty-six million soldiers and civilians and, truly, the disruption of civilization itself. In this war, no distinction would be made between combatants and noncombatants. This war would be total war, war on a scale unimaginable at the time and, even today, almost impossible fully to comprehend.

TAKEAWAY

Failure of Appeasement

In their anxiety to avoid a second world war, the democratic powers—primarily Britain and France—repeatedly attempted to "appease" the imperial ambitions of Adolf Hitler. Appeasement succeeded only in whetting his appetite for total war.

CHAPTER 4

BLITZKRIEG

Hitler Launches a "Lightning War"

GERMANY DID NOT FORMALLY DECLARE WAR ON POLAND before it invaded it on September 1, 1939, but the world needed no declarations to go to war. It went like this: Committed by treaty to aid Poland, Great Britain and France, plus the British Commonwealth nations of Australia and New Zealand, declared war against Germany on September 3. Canada, another Commonwealth nation, followed with a declaration against Germany on September 10. The Soviets invaded Poland without a declaration of war on September 17 and then invaded Finland on November 30, also without declaration. Without declaration, Germany invaded Denmark and Norway on April 9, 1940, and Holland and Belgium—again without declaration—on May 10. The invasion of France soon followed, and, with France beleaguered, Italy declared war against France and Great Britain on June 10, then, on October 28, invaded Greece without declaration. Bulgaria declared war against the Allies on April 6, 1941. As Italy floundered in Greece, Germany invaded Greece as well as Yugoslavia on April 6, 1941. And all this was just the beginning.

OPERATION WHITE

FALL WEISS—translated as "Case" or "Operation White"—was the name of Germany's master military plan for the invasion of Poland. It was to be a massive exercise in blitzkrieg, the doctrine of lightning war that had been under development in Germany at least since the 1920s. Blitzkrieg combined tactics and strategy designed to overwhelm and overawe a defending army with a fast, violent, and highly mobile action fully coordinated among armor, mechanized infantry, massed firepower, and air power, all augmented by elite special forces units, which worked to disrupt the defenders' systems of communication and supply in order to magnify and multiply the chaos of the onslaught. Blitzkrieg always held twin, simultaneous objectives: to advance, gaining territory rapidly and rolling up the opposing army, while also paralyzing the enemy's capacity to coordinate an effective defense. Traditional invaders mounted costly campaigns to destroy all enemy defenses. In contrast, blitzkrieg called for the mere disabling of such defenses—through the disruption of supply and communication—so that major resources could be concentrated for rapid and maximum penetration of the target territory. Stab a nation quickly, violently, and deeply, and its defenses would simply be rendered useless.

As practiced against Poland, the blitzkrieg invasion thrust through a relatively narrow front with tanks, motorized artillery, and aircraft—especially the Junkers Ju-87, an airplane better known as the Stuka. Designed during the mid-1930s in defiance of the Treaty of Versailles, the Stuka was a single-engine dive-bomber, which dropped its 1,100-pound bomb load not from level flight, as a conventional bomber would, but from low altitude as it approached the end of an extreme eighty-degree dive. This ensured surgical accuracy of the attack, which meant that the Stuka could be used as "aerial artillery" in support of invading troops. Bombs could be placed

DETAILS, DETAILS

Raptor Plane

The precipitous, swooping dive made the Stuka not only an effective infantry-support weapon but also a weapon of sheer terror. Its sharp-beaked profile, its broad, gull wings, and its nonretractable, talon-like landing gear gave the aircraft the appearance of some giant bird of prey. Additionally, the Stuka was fitted with sirens—"Jericho trumpets," they were called—which emitted a terrifying scream during the high-speed dive. The scream amplified the terror and panic produced by the bombs.

The Junkers Ju-87, better known as the Stuka Sturzkampfflugzeug (dive-bomber), terrorized Poland in the blitzkrieg invasion that began World War II on September 1, 1939.

REALITY CHECK

Blitzkrieg as Neutralizer

That blitzkrieg was extremely brutal seems self-evident. To be sure, the tactic and strategy depended on extreme violence, but its great speed tended to neutralize rather than annihilate a defender, and it therefore actually spared casualties on both sides. Certainly, German military planners saw blitzkrieg as a way of avoiding the murderous stalemate that developed along the Western Front in World War I.

ALTERNATE TAKE

A Gamble on the West

Hitler committed so many troops to the invasion of Poland that he left only a light screening force to protect Germany's western frontier, thereby making the nation highly vulnerable to an attack by the Western democracies. Had Britain and France assumed the offensive immediately, Hitler might well have been obliged to withdraw from Poland. Hitler knew this, but, based on his experience thus far, he was willing to gamble that neither France nor Britain would have the capability—or the will—to mobilize rapidly enough either to come directly to the defense of Poland or to threaten Germany from the west. His gamble paid off.

accurately on target—near the invading forces as they approached but with little danger of accidentally bombing them. Victims of Stuka attacks soon learned that the initial bomb run was only the first phase of an attack. After dropping their ordnance, Stuka pilots customarily circled around to strafe scattering survivors with the plane's three 7.9 mm machine guns.

The coordination of land and air forces was intended to create a point of attack—in German a *Schwerpunkt*, or "strong point"—an open wound in the defenders' forces. As soon as this *Schwerpunkt* had been created—and before the victim nation's army could plug the breach and patch up the wound—tanks and specially trained infantry called "shock troops" would swarm through the gap, widening as well as deepening it. This tactic further disrupted the defender's line of defense, creating pockets in which the defending troops were trapped, entirely cut off from one another. For such isolated defenders, the only alternative to destruction was surrender.

Fall Weiss called for attacking Poland by way of Silesia in the south and Pomerania-East Prussia from the north in order to destroy the Polish army west of the line formed by the Vistula, Narew, and San Rivers. Most of the German forces were contained in Army Group South (Eighth, Tenth, and Fourteenth armies) under the command of General Gerd von Rundstedt. The Tenth Army headed for Warsaw, the Polish capital, while the Eighth and Fourteenth armies guarded its flanks. At the time, the total forces committed to the Polish campaign were more than sixty divisions, almost two-thirds of the entire German army.

Total Victory

Poland's armed forces fought with gallantry, but the nation lacked the military leadership, the equipment, and the trained men to offer an effective defense against the invasion. The Polish military relied on something called "Plan Z," which prescribed setting up a defensive cordon concentrated in the west to hold off the invader long enough for the arrival of aid from France and Britain. Plan Z never contemplated the utter incapacity of the Western democracies or the complicity of the Soviet Union. The Polish defensive units, strung out along the entire length of Polish frontier with Germany and Slovakia, were simply rolled over in very short order.

Air attacks achieved instant air superiority, opening the way for German bombers to penetrate deep into Polish territory. Aerial bombardment of the rear areas disrupted supply and communication before the forward echelons even became fully engaged on the ground. In other words, the Poles lost the campaign virtually before it even began.

In the first battles, the German army broke through Polish defenses. By September 3, 1939, the German Third and Fourth Armies in the north had linked up, cutting the "Polish corridor"—the country's lifeline to the west—at its base. Poland's Pomorze Army was destroyed, and its Modlin Army forced to withdraw. While this was taking place, German Army Group South, advancing from Silesia, broke through against the Polish armies defending the cities of Lódz and Kraców. By September 5, the Polish situation was for all practical purposes hopeless.

From September 6 through September 10, the Third and Fourth German armies advanced from the north while Army Group South moved up from the south, targeting Warsaw. The Poles were able to mount just one meaningful counterattack when their retreating Poznan Army suddenly launched an assault on September 9 against the flank of the advancing German Eighth Army at Kutno. In the three-day battle there, the Poznan Army decimated a full German division before air attacks and elements of the German Tenth Army struck back, ending the counterattack.

Throughout the rest of Poland, blitzkrieg was so overwhelming that forward lines melted away, the rear echelons fell into confusion, and the entire Polish command structure disintegrated. Within two weeks of the initial invasion, elements of Army Groups North and South linked up near Brest-Litovsk, thereby encircling Warsaw, which held most of the surviving Polish army.

The end of significant Polish resistance was hastened by the Soviet Red Army invasion into eastern Poland, which began on September 17. This sealed the fate of the nation. Even as Stalin commenced his invasion, however, Hitler adroitly and unilaterally altered the terms of his original secret agreement with Stalin, which had divided Poland along the Vistula River, giving the western portion to Germany and the eastern portion to the Soviets. With the invasion all but an accomplished fact, Hitler compelled

REALITY CHECK

Roots of Blitzkrieg

During World War I, General Oskar von Hutier (1857–1934) was the first to employ newly formulated German infiltration tactics—actually based on British and French tactics—in his September 3, 1917, assault on Riga, Latvia. Hutier attacked with swift violence and a high degree of coordination, entirely demoralizing and overwhelming Riga's defenders. The stunned Allies dubbed the approach "Hutier tactics." After World War I, Hans von Seeckt, head of Reichswehr (the greatly reduced German army permitted by the Treaty of Versailles), built on Hutier tactics to refine the doctrine of blitzkrieg. During World War II itself, the leading exponent of blitzkrieg was General Heinz Guderian. It should be pointed out that *Blitzkrieg*, although it is a German word, was not coined by the German military. Most likely, the term was the product of a journalist.

Victorious German troops goose-step through Warsaw in September 1939, marking the climax of the conquest of Poland.

Stalin to cede a large part of his prize to Germany and repositioned the dividing line at the Bug River.

Although diehard Poles continued to defend Warsaw and the fortress of Modlin north of the capital, the situation was now well beyond salvation. Warsaw surrendered on September 27, and Modlin the next day. The very last organized resistance was mopped up by October 5. Poland had fallen to Germany—with a small portion parceled out to the Soviet Union.

NUMBERS

Polish and German Troop Losses

In the invasion of Poland, Germany lost 8,082 killed, 27,278 wounded, and 5,029 missing. Polish losses included 70,000 killed and as many as 130,000 wounded. The Polish army was not annihilated, however. Approximately 90,000 Polish troops escaped to Hungary, Latvia, Lithuania, and Romania; about half of these eventually made their way west to France and Britain to fight on behalf of the Polish government-in-exile after the surrender of Poland.

The Winter War

Josef Stalin was one of history's most notorious paranoids. This feature of his personality made his apparent willingness to trust the likes of Adolf Hitler all the more stunning to the world. In actuality, Stalin did not trust Hitler and thought himself very clever in having negotiated the secret portions of the Non-Aggression Pact to get himself not only part of Poland, but Finland as well. For he intended both of these acquisitions as buffer zones against any possible German aggression. Stalin was keenly aware that the Russo-Finnish border was well within reach of Finnish artillery. If the Germans landed in Finland, they could easily use it as a base from which to bombard and then invade the Soviet Union. To give Stalin his due, he did try to make a military alliance with Finland before deciding simply to invade and take it. Wishing to preserve their neutrality in the developing war, the Finns rejected the Soviet overture. Russo-Finnish negotiations completely broke down on November 26, 1939, after four Soviet soldiers were killed and nine wounded by artillery fire near the Russian village of Mainila. Stalin accused the Finns of having lobbed the shells. The Finns countered that their artillery was stationed so far behind the nation's border—again, in the interest of protecting neutrality—that Mainila was far out of range. The truth was transparent: The incident had been manufactured by the Soviets as an excuse to go to war with Finland,

and the so-called Mainila shots sent the Red Army into that country on November 30, 1939. The conflict that resulted may be seen as a campaign of World War II or as a separate war, what historians call the Russo-Finnish War or the Winter War.

On the first day of the war, Soviet aircraft bombed Helsinki and launched a ground invasion with seven Red Army divisions. The Finns were outgunned and outnumbered, but they were led by skilled and committed officers, who knew how to use the snow and rugged terrain to best advantage. Everywhere the Soviets attempted to penetrate the frontier, they were repulsed. At Tolvajarvi, a Colonel Paavo Tavela led a Finnish counterattack, which cost the Soviets many casualties before it petered out by December 23.

Tolvajarvi was not a decisive battle in itself, but it gave the Finns the sense that the Soviets had lost the initiative. Encouraged, they mounted a major counterattack against the Soviet forces on the eastern border. Here the Finnish 9th Division triumphed at the battle of Suomussalmi, which began on December 8 and was fought through early January, destroying two Soviet divisions and killing about 27,500 Red Army soldiers. During this time, north of Lake Ladoga, which separates Russia and Finland, the Finns also attacked at Kitela, destroying an entire Soviet division in January 1940 with what they called "motti tactics." The Finnish word *motti* describes a pile of logs awaiting chopping or sawing. In *motti* tactics, Finnish troops surrounded an enemy column and blocked the road on which it advanced. They next launched sharp attacks against the stalled enemy, splitting the column into isolated fragments, which would be starved, frozen, and finally "chopped" to death. The Finnish triumph at Kitela is often called the "Great Motti."

NUMBERS

Battle of Tolvajarvi Stats

At the battle of Tolvajarvi, the Red Army lost 4,000 killed and 5,000 wounded, whereas the Finns lost 630 killed and 1,320 wounded. Such lopsided figures were typical of the "Winter War." Even more alarming to Soviet high command was the poor performance of the Red Air Force, which flew more than 44,000 sorties at Tolvajarvi, dropping 7,500 tons of bombs—yet without decisive effect.

The Russo-Finnish War—also known as the Winter War—coincided with the opening of World War II. Red Army ski troops are shown here advancing through the frozen Finnish countryside.

NUMBERS

Russian and Finnish Troop Losses

Of the 710,578 men the Soviets deployed to Finland, 126,875 were killed. The Finns lost 23,157 killed and 43,557 wounded out of some 350,000 engaged.

Despite staggering losses, the Soviets pressed on. Their strategy was based on a calculus as crude as it was grim. The Finns might have better commanders, better tactics, and better control of the rugged landscape of battle, but the Soviet Union had a virtually unlimited supply of men. Joseph Stalin was willing to throw those men into combat as if they were no more than cordwood to be heaped upon a pyre. As the Finns came to understand this, they sued for peace, accepting on March 12, 1940, the installation of a Soviet-controlled puppet government and ceding outright to the Soviets the Karelian Isthmus and Viipuri. And that was the end of the Winter War—for now.

The Phony War

Life was plenty perilous for the Poles and the Finns during the opening weeks and months of World War II, and the Anglo-French declaration of war against Germany came within two days of the German invasion of Poland. Yet, curiously, combat was slow to follow in the West—so slow that American newspapers coined the phrase "Phony War" to describe the inaction.

The so-called Phony War was neither more nor less than the product of continued Allied timidity, which Hitler exploited to complete the Polish conquest. While the British and French had declared war because of the invasion of Poland, they never actually came to the aid of the Poles. Not that the British were entirely inactive. The Battle of the Atlantic, which was destined to span almost all of the European war, heated up almost immediately. It will be discussed in Chapter 6.

DETAILS, DETAILS

The Pun War

What Americans called the "Phony War," British Prime Minister Winston Churchill called the "Twilight War," and the British man-on-the-street referred to it as the "Bore War," a pun on the First (1880–81) and Second (1899–1902) Boer wars in South Africa. Frenchmen referred to the period as *la drôle de guerre* ("joke war") and Germans as *Sitzkrieg* ("sitting war"), a pun on Blitzkrieg.

Denmark and Norway

On April 9, 1940, the German army made its first moves west and north, marching into Denmark and, on the very same day, invading six major ports along a thousand miles of neutral Norway's coast.

As of early 1940, the Danish army numbered fourteen thousand men, of whom eight thousand were brand-new draftees. The Danish navy consisted of two old ships. There was no air force as such, but, between them, the army and navy had fifty airplanes—all quite obsolete. Some in Denmark argued for declaring absolute neutrality in the hope that Germany would respect the nation as a neutral. Others, however, so feared Nazi aggression that they persuaded the government to conclude a non-aggression pact with Germany early in 1939. The Danes were more fortunate than the Poles in that, thanks to the secret anti-Hitler sentiments of Admiral William Canaris, chief of German intelligence, they were given several days' notice that the German army was about to invade. Canaris ensured that they were informed on April 4. Yet no one knew what to do, and military authorities did nothing to prepare until April 8—one day before the invasion. On the eighth, Copenhagen was reinforced, as was the border with Germany. These steps hardly mattered, of course, and the German army walked into Denmark at 4:15 A.M. on April 9 with almost no resistance from the Danish army and absolutely none from the navy. Two days later, Copenhagen was occupied, even as German paratroops landed south of Zealand in the North Sea. The Danish government ordered a ceasefire and meekly accepted German occupation.

As for Norway, it was not high on Hitler's hit list until some six months after the successful conclusion of the Polish invasion. At that time, it occurred to the Führer that violating Norwegian neutrality with an invasion would ensure that the Allies could not interfere with the free passage of Swedish iron ore into the German war machine.

Unlike the Danish invasion, the Norwegian operation was carried out with perfect surprise, thanks to the use of paratroops and soldiers hidden in the holds of merchant ships that sailed into Norwegian harbors. The invasion was further facilitated by a strong pro-Nazi underground operating in the country, including the chief Norwegian turncoat, Vidkun Quisling, who sold his country to Hitler in exchange for leadership of the puppet government.

In a mere forty-eight hours, Hitler seized control of the key Norwegian ports of Narvik, Trondheim, Bergen, Stavanger, Kristiansand, and Oslo. The latter was the nation's capital and chief city. It fell to a handful—fifteen hundred—German paratroops. All over the country, the Norwegian army, as if bewildered into a state of paralysis, laid down arms without even token resistance. A very small faction of the military rallied around King Haakon VII and withdrew inland, where a gallant but ineffective resistance was organized.

POP CULTURE

Traitorous Word

Vidkun Quisling's treason was so infamous that his name almost instantly entered the English language (among others) as a synonym for turncoat. In other words, Quisling was the original quisling.

WILHELM CANARIS

That Nazi Germany was a totalitarian state is self-evident, but this did not mean that its inner workings were monolithic. A significant number of highly placed individuals detested Adolf Hitler and believed Nazi policy corrupt.

Admiral Wilhelm Canaris was the leading figure in German espionage from 1935 to 1944, yet was also an agent of the anti-Nazi underground, who, from a very early period in the Nazi regime, plotted against it. On January 1, 1935, he was appointed chief of the German intelligence agency, the Abwehr, and immediately fended off attempts by Heinrich Himmler, head of the German internal security (the Reichssicherheitshauptamt), and Reinhard Heydrich, chief of political espionage (the Sicherheitsdienst), to take over the Abwehr. By way of checking them, Canaris ingratiated himself with both men, inaugurating a secret double life in which he operated to placate Nazi insiders while he fought to keep the Abwehr independent of the Nazi Party.

During the 1930s, Canaris forged the Abwehr into quite probably the best intelligence service in the world, specializing in international espionage, sabotage, and counterespionage, and earning the absolute confidence of Hitler. But when he began receiving reports of SS and Gestapo atrocities in Poland during the invasion, Canaris, appalled, confronted General Field Marshal Wilhelm Keitel, Hitler's chief of staff. Keitel blandly informed the admiral that not only was Hitler aware of what the SS and Gestapo were doing in Poland, he had personally authorized it all. From this moment, Canaris began to work covertly against the Hitler regime by deliberately compromising and distorting the intelligence he fed to the Führer. At last, on February 19, 1944, Hitler dismissed Canaris as head of the Abwehr, transferring him to head the Department of Economic Warfare in Potsdam. From this post, he continued to lead covert operations against the regime. He did not participate in the July 20, 1944, assassination attempt against Hitler, but he was among some five thousand military officers and others who were arrested as conspirators. Sentenced to death, he was given reprieve by Himmler, who sent Canaris to a concentration camp. In March 1945, however, Hitler personally ordered his execution, and, on April 9, 1945, Wilhelm Canaris was stripped naked then hanged as a traitor. His corpse, unburied, was left to rot.

Admiral Wilhelm Canaris headed the Abwehr, the German espionage agency. Secretly opposed to Hitler and Nazism, Canaris often used his position to undercut the Führer in an effort to overthrow him. He also managed to save a number of victims of Nazi persecution, including hundreds of Jews, by spiriting them out of Germany in the guise of Abwehr agents. Before the war ended, Nazi authorities arrested, tried, and then executed Canaris by slow strangulation.

A Phony War Ends

Almost immediately after securing a declaration of war against Germany, Britain's prime minister, Neville Chamberlain, took into his War Cabinet the very man who had been his most vigorous critic and opponent of the now infamous appeasement policy, Winston Churchill, making him first lord of the Admiralty—roughly equivalent to the American secretary of the navy, but a position of even greater influence. It was the very post Churchill had held during World War I. He had been aching to end the Phony War with some bold offensive action, and he now persuaded Chamberlain to authorize a counterinvasion of Norway.

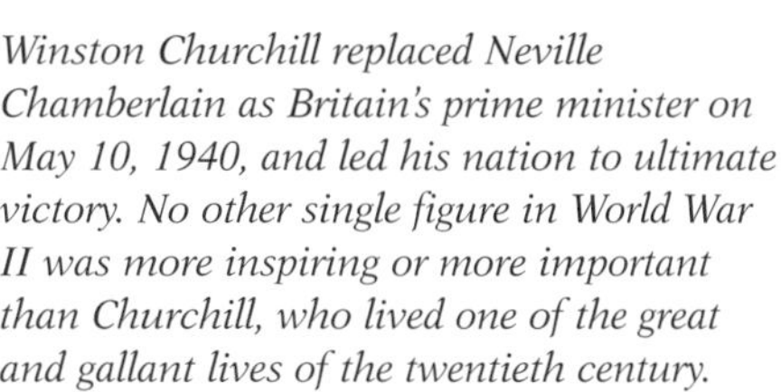

Winston Churchill replaced Neville Chamberlain as Britain's prime minister on May 10, 1940, and led his nation to ultimate victory. No other single figure in World War II was more inspiring or more important than Churchill, who lived one of the great and gallant lives of the twentieth century.

Between April 14 and 19, Allied troops landed at Namsos and Andalsnes, on either side of Trondheim, on Norway's central coast. At the same time, they launched an attack in the far north of the country in and around Narvik. Some thirty thousand troops were involved in the Trondheim-area operation, but, given inadequate logistical support, the counterinvasion rapidly collapsed, and the troops withdrew, yielding all of central Norway to the Germans by May 3.

On the sea, the Allies fared far better. Norway's large merchant fleet—about a thousand vessels—refused to be sold out to the invaders and instead joined the Allied cause. The British Royal Navy moved rapidly, sinking a German heavy cruiser, a pair of light cruisers, ten destroyers, eleven troop transports, eight submarines, and eleven auxiliary vessels, losing in these exchanges an aircraft carrier (HMS *Glorious*), two cruisers (*Effingham* and *Curlew*), nine destroyers, and six submarines. These were serious losses for the British, but not nearly so significant as the German losses were for Germany. The surface fleet of the Kriegsmarine—as the German navy was called—would never recover from them.

ALTERNATE TAKE

If the Kriegsmarine Had Prevailed

The damage inflicted on the German surface fleet in battles off the Norwegian coast certainly did not stem the tide of Nazi conquest during the early months of the war; yet, without these ships, Germany's prospects for successfully invading Britain were greatly diminished. Had the losses not occurred, Hitler would probably have launched the invasion Britons both expected and feared.

On land, at Narvik, things went better for the Allies—at least for a while—than they did in central Norway. Nevertheless, the British and French ultimately had to withdraw—not because of military failure in Norway, but because of a crisis in the Battle of France (discussed later in this chapter). The last Allied troops left Narvik on June 9, taking with them King Haakon VII, who throughout the war presided over a government-in-exile in London. Germany was left in possession of both Norway and Denmark, which served as buffers that protected the northern flank of the German armies. Even more important, possession of these northern realms assured Hitler's Reich uninterrupted access to iron ore and agricultural produce. The Germans also secured vital submarine and air bases from which they could attack Allied convoys that plied the north Atlantic.

Operation Yellow

At dawn on May 10, 1940, German army and air forces began the execution of Fall Gelb—Operation, or Case, Yellow—the incarnation of blitzkrieg on the Western Front. It started as the army invaded the three small neutral nations of Luxembourg, Belgium, and the Netherlands. As German planners knew it would, these incursions drew to the northeast the British Expeditionary Force (BEF)—the troops Britain had sent to the Continent—and French forces based in Flanders. The movement of these forces left France's more

HOW THE FORCES STACKED UP

In contrast to the contest between Germany and Poland, in which the Poles were obviously outnumbered, Allied and German forces on the Western Front looked to be matched fairly evenly.

The French army had 104 divisions available, the BEF (British Expeditionary Force) 10, Belgium 22, and the Netherlands 8, for a total of 144 divisions versus Germany's invasion force of 141. Allied artillery consisted of about 14,000 guns against 7,378 for Germany; however, much of this was outmoded, and the Allies were critically short of antitank and antiaircraft artillery. France had 3,063 tanks and the other Allies a few more, for a total of 3,384. Germany invaded with 2,445 tanks—which were superior to what the Allies had. The French air force consisted of 637 operational fighters—all obsolescent—and 242 bombers. Britain brought 262 excellent fighters and 135 bombers to France, and it had an additional 540 fighters and 310 bombers based in England. Belgium and the Netherlands contributed a few more of each, bringing the total of available Allied aircraft to 1,590 fighters and 708 bombers. Germany, which had been building a large modern air force during the interwar years, had 1,736 fighters (of which 1,220 were operational at the commencement of battle) and 2,224 bombers (of which 1,559 were operational). All of these were of advanced design and outclassed the French planes, but were more evenly matched with the British.

southerly territory exposed. French high command rationalized this exposure by reliance on the Maginot Line, the elaborate subterranean and semi-subterranean state-of-the-art chain of frontier forts that French generals considered impregnable. Never mind that prewar politicians, unwilling to offend neutral Belgium, had terminated the Maginot Line at the Franco-Belgian border, effectively leaving the door open to any invader from the east. The French generals believed that Belgium's own considerable fortifications would discourage an invasion via that small country and that the thickly wooded, rugged terrain of the Ardennes in this border region was, in any case, impassable for any large invasion force. So compelling were these beliefs, that, not only did the French allow the Maginot Line to stop short at Belgium, but they also did not even attempt to compensate by stationing large troop concentrations in the area. It was simply unreasonable to assume that an invader would brave the Ardennes. Yet that is precisely what Operation Yellow called for. Under the command of the brilliant Erich von Manstein, the Ardennes was targeted as the Schwerpunkt—the "point of concentration"—for this blitzkrieg on the Western Front.

The Allies had great faith in the French army, which was a large force of some five million men. This number said nothing, however, about the quality of French high command, which was fatally flawed. French general headquarters had a weak grasp of strategy and tactics, and the French military had failed to develop an efficient network of communications, so that it was almost impossible to coordinate action among far-flung commanders in the field. In especially vivid contrast with the Germans, who coordinated air and ground elements with great precision, the French made virtually no attempt to communicate between ground and air forces. Worst of all, the French army went into battle with all ranks—from top to bottom—pervaded by a defeatist malaise. The blame for this lay not just with the military, but also with French civilian politicians, who failed to produce a vision of the nation's war aims. Most notorious among all of its failings, the French army after World War I had embraced a doctrine of passive defense, which relied on fixed fortifications, especially those of the Maginot Line. It was a military philosophy wholly unsuited to the swift, mobile, and violent style of warfare the Germans had already introduced.

The Battle of France

Erich von Manstein saw the German campaign on the Western Front as a second chance to do what his nation's armies had almost done in World War I: win the contest decisively in its opening months. For the conquest of France, he would employ a version of the first war's celebrated Schlieffen Plan, which had called for the bulk of the invading force to sweep into France not directly from the east, but from the north in a great wheel that extended all the way to the English Channel and that hit the Allied defenders mainly on the flank and rear. Manstein knew that the tactics and technology of blitzkrieg gave him a great advantage that commanders had lacked in World War I: air support, overwhelming firepower, and tremendous mobility. He was determined to break—unexpectedly—through the thick Ardennes forest at the northeast border of France, then lead his panzers—German armored tanks—in a race across the great plain of France, clear to the Channel. The Germans would sweep across the nation like a giant scythe, a scythe that would neatly divide the British from the French forces, fragmenting them, so that they could be defeated (as military planners say) "in detail."

Belgium had a small army, but a formidable system of fortresses, the most important of which was Fort Eben Emael, which defended the bridges at Briegen, Veldwezelt, and Vroenhoven—all critical crossings for a westward-bound invasion force. Manstein and his staff understood that any traditional fortress is built to withstand and repulse a ground assault aimed at it. For this reason, it has stout walls well defended by guns. They also understood that such a fortress suffers from a single vulnerability. It is built to defeat a horizontally launched attack, not one launched vertically—that is, dropped down from the air.

On May 10, 1940, seventy-eight engineers of the Koch Assault Detachment landed on top of Fort Eben Emael and placed on its roof hollow explosive charges, specially shaped to direct the force of their blast downward. The charges were detonated, blowing up key fortress emplacements from the roof down. This did not destroy the fortress—there was no need to waste time and energy doing that—but it did neutralize it, so that paratroops could readily assault and capture the bridges Eben Emael had been built to guard.

Once these crossings into Belgium were secured, the German 223rd Infantry Division attacked the surviving portions of the fort on May 11. The fort garrison of just seven hundred men quickly capitulated, and Belgium was overrun.

The breach of Belgium allowed the principal German invading forces entry into France not *through* the vaunted Maginot Line, but *around* it. While Germany's Army Group B (commanded by Fedor von Bock) made a decoying attack in the north—drawing off Allied forces there—Gerd von Rundstedt led the much bigger Army Group A through the Ardennes for the main invasion. Simultaneously, south of this, Wilhelm Ritter von Leeb kept French forces pinned down at the Maginot Line. By threatening these fortifications, Ritter von Leeb forced the French to commit large numbers of soldiers to defend a doorway that was not even being used. The German plan thus transformed a French defensive asset into a massive liability—a drain on manpower.

Belgium's Fortress Eben Emael was considered virtually impregnable by ground assault. The Germans therefore attacked it by airborne assault. A mere handful of paratroopers—seen here crossing the Albert Canal in May 1940—breached Eben Emael through its roof, Belgium's military planners having never contemplated an attack from above.

The panzers of Rundstedt's Army Group B were commanded by Heinz Guderian—the father of German tank development, doctrine, and tactics—and Erwin Rommel, destined to become Germany's most celebrated tank commander. Leadership like this out-thought and out-moved the British and—especially—the French commanders. Maurice-Gustave Gamelin, France's commander in chief, was a competent general, but so thoroughly conventional that his every move was readily predictable. Manstein was confident that he would fall for the German decoy attack in the north, and that was precisely the case; Gamelin left the sector between Namur and Sedan—the very *Schwerpunkt* of Manstein's blitzkrieg—largely exposed and vulnerable. The sector was

NUMBERS

Belgian and German Troop Losses

The conquest of Fort Eben Emael, principal guardian of Belgium, cost the Germans six men killed and twenty wounded. Belgian losses were minimal as well, since surrender came quickly.

commanded by André Corap (French Ninth Army), a journeyman general at best, and General Charles Huntziger (French Second Army). Between the two of them, they commanded inexperienced officers and men, all of whom suffered badly from the defeatist malaise that had infected, it seemed, practically all of France.

If the French forces at the main point of the German attack were inadequate and led by inept commanders, the thirty divisions tied up along the Maginot Line were of even less use. By simply keeping them in check, German Army Group C took them out of the battle, effectively reducing French strength by a full thirty divisions.

As bad as the situation was for the French, General Gamelin managed to make it even worse by ordering the French Seventh Army, which was commanded by one of France's best generals, Henri Giraud, to rush headlong from its position as a mobile reserve force near Dunkirk—in northwestern France on the Belgian border—to Breda, Netherlands, to support the Dutch. The deeper the Germans penetrated into France, the longer their supply lines would be. That had been the Achilles heel of the Schlieffen Plan and the reason for its ultimate failure in World War I. A mobile reserve force was precisely what France needed to attack the invaders when they were most vulnerable. Gamelin, however, had moved his most important mobile reserve force out of position for any timely action. In effect, he invited the invaders to invade even more deeply.

If the Allied ground strategy was bad, its position in the air was yet more disastrous. The general inferiority of French aircraft to German aircraft was a terrible problem, to be sure, but what precipitated outright catastrophe was the manner in which the French air resources were deployed and used. On paper, General Joseph Vuillemin commanded the French air force; in reality, however, he had direct control over the air reserve only. Command of France's principal air units was shared with ground commanders. The result was almost total paralysis because air officers were torn among three or even more ground commanders, who often issued contradictory orders or none at all. Moreover, since the aircraft themselves were shared out among the ground units, they could not be dispatched by a single overall commander and therefore could not be concentrated and sent to where they were most needed. Poor to begin with, France's aircraft were simply frittered away, whereas Luftwaffe (German air force) planes, thoroughly integrated with the ground assault but commanded by air officers, flew where and when they were required.

Within forty-eight hours of neutralizing Fort Eben Emael, German invaders had overrun the Netherlands and had broken through the Ardennes into France. Beautifully orchestrated German air cover shot Allied planes out of the sky, preventing them from attacking the German armored columns. In a spectacular oversight, none of the Allied commanders had thought of mining the forest roads, which therefore served the invaders as highways.

By the night of May 12, seven panzer divisions had reached the east bank of the Meuse River from Dinant to Sedan. Seven divisions of men, tanks, and other vehicles are hardly invisible, yet, in the very face of a massive reality, the Allies persisted in using intelligence estimates that were flatly contradicted by the facts. The Allies believed that it would take five to six days for the Germans to build up sufficient force strength to cross the Meuse. That is, the Allies were confident that the river would not be crossed before May 17, giving them time to organize a resistance there. Guderian, the German panzer commander, did not wait for all of his panzers to get through the Ardennes, however, and, on May 13, supported by the Stuka dive-bombers made infamous in Poland, crossed the Meuse with what he had on hand. By that evening, Guderian had secured a Meuse bridgehead three miles wide.

Had the nearby French 3rd Armored Division responded with vigor, the advance might have been stemmed, but, persuaded that no strong German crossing was possible before May 17, the French did little. British bombers were launched in a gallant effort to destroy the pontoon bridges of the 1st Panzer Division, but these lumbering craft were blown out of the sky by German antiaircraft artillery. Not only did the British lose almost all of their bombers in this sector, not one pontoon bridge was even damaged.

With the Meuse breached at Dinant, Guderian and Rommel next rolled through the Sedan sector, crushing Huntziger's Second Army and Corap's Ninth in the process. On May 16, Prime Minister

Churchill flew across the Channel to France in the hope of rallying some sort of credible resistance. The time had come, he said, for France to use its great mobile reserve to strike at the overextended invaders, to swallow up as many of them as possible. That is when the French told Churchill that no great reserves were available. Either they had been frittered away or had been positioned, like Giraud's mobile reserve, where they were of no use. The indomitable Churchill felt his heart sink.

Defeat—and Reprieve

By this point, the middle of May 1940, French premier Paul Reynaud declared that the Battle of France had been lost. The declaration was both premature—the fighting had not stopped—and too late; for the Battle of France had been lost years earlier, when the French had built the Maginot Line and the Allies had trusted in the power of appeasement. One thing was abundantly clear. The principal German thrust was toward the French coast. The only question was whether the German objective was the English Channel, from which an invasion of England could be staged and launched, or Paris, the elusive German objective of World War I. As a result of indecision as to whether to defend the Channel or Paris, the French did neither effectively.

For the French, there would be no such thing as snatching victory from the jaws of defeat. But the Germans very nearly snatched defeat from the jaws of victory. The conquest of France had been swift beyond the German planners' wildest dreams. As a result, Guderian's panzers had moved far ahead of the slower infantry units supporting the tanks. Guderian was unbothered by this, but his superiors—including Adolf Hitler himself—were worried that, inadequately supported, the panzers were vulnerable to counterattack. Therefore, on May 15 and again on May 17, over Guderian's protests, the panzers were ordered to halt so that the infantry could catch up. Each of these pauses invited counterattack, but the Allies were so exhausted, reduced, and demoralized that they could mount nothing. Even worse, the belated replacement of General Gamelin with the aged General Maxime Weygand on May 20 hardly served to turn the French situation around but did introduce further delay in organizing any kind of counterattack. Therefore, despite the delays ordered by German high command, Guderian's 2nd Panzer Division reached the French town of Abbeville, on the English Channel, on May 19, thereby splitting the surviving Allied forces in two. The best French units, together with almost all of the BEF, were now bottled up, their backs against the Channel.

As they had demonstrated in World War I and as they would repeatedly demonstrate in this second world war, the British were at their best with their backs to the wall. The BEF now counterattacked to the south from Arras on May 21 and made remarkable headway, but a French follow-up counterattack failed to materialize, leaving the BEF with no choice but to retreat. Facing annihilation and with nowhere else to go, the BEF—which included most of Britain's prewar professional army—scrambled toward the French port town of Dunkirk on the English Channel, where it had the slimmest sliver of a hope of being evacuated to England.

But not if German general Paul Ludwig von Kleist could help it. On May 24, his tanks were arrayed against the southern perimeter of what had become the "Dunkirk pocket"—the small slice of northwestern France that contained the remnant of the BEF, together with some of the best soldiers of the French army. Kleist had his prey cornered. He burned to advance and bag it. No less a figure than Adolf Hitler intervened, ordering him to await the arrival of the infantry. The earlier halts of May 15 and May 17 had held the potential for squandering victory. This halt squandered it completely.

ALTERNATE TAKE

Delay, Defeat?

Hitler's order to Kleist on May 24, 1940, forcing him to delay his final advance against the cornered British and French armies, was one of the most momentous mistakes of World War II. To say that Hitler lost the war on that day would be an overstatement, but he did throw away an opportunity to kill or capture most of the BEF, exposing Britain to immediate invasion and compelling that nation to come to peace terms favorable to Germany; therefore, if he did not lose the war on May 24, 1940, he discarded an opportunity to win it.

MIRACLE AT DUNKIRK

Even before the war had begun, Allied code breakers had learned to read many of the German military ciphers, and they both intercepted and decrypted Hitler's halt order. This motivated one of the precious few miracles of the war's catastrophic early days, the Dunkirk evacuation. Code-named Operation Dynamo, the evacuation took place between May 26 and June 4, 1940. While a BEF and French rear guard held off the final German onslaught, a motley fleet of 693 ships, among them 39 destroyers and 36 minesweepers plus 77 civilian fishing trawlers, 26 yachts, and an assortment of other small craft, snatched from the port of Dunkirk 338,226 soldiers, including 140,000 French troops, who would otherwise

By May–June 1940, German forces had swept through France, pushing the members of the British Expeditionary Force and a large number of French soldiers up against the English Channel. They were saved from capture or annihilation by the "miracle at Dunkirk," an epic seaborne evacuation using a motley combination of warships, passenger vessels, fishing boats, and yachts—virtually anything that floated.

have been killed or captured. As it was, the British were forced to abandon most of their equipment, including tanks and other vehicles, which created a critical weapons shortage.

The Germans did not stand idly by as the Allied troops left Dunkirk. Luftwaffe aircraft, German U-boats, and E-boats (similar to Allied torpedo boats or PT boats) attacked the small craft that ferried men from shore to the larger ships. Dunkirk itself was bombed and virtually leveled during the evacuation. Fortunately for the Allies, the notoriously treacherous English Channel was calm yet the weather was overcast, greatly limiting the Luftwaffe's ability to launch attacks. Because the German advance had been so swift, there had been no time to prepare forward air bases, so the Luftwaffe fighters, limited in range, could not linger long in their attacks.

At Dunkirk, the Luftwaffe faced more than logistical problems. The British Royal Air Force (RAF) proved a formidable opponent. RAF pilots performed heroically to cover the evacuation—at the high cost of 177 precious aircraft, often with the loss of the even

DETAILS, DETAILS

Smoke Screen

Some military historians believe that the German bombing of Dunkirk actually aided the evacuation by creating a great deal of smoke, which screened operations from attack.

more precious pilots. When it was over, Winston Churchill—who had become Britain's prime minister after the resignation of Neville Chamberlain on May 10, 1940—reported to Parliament on June 4 the success of the evacuation. Always combining optimism with realism, Churchill cautioned his parliamentary colleagues that, successful as Dunkirk was, "Wars are not won by evacuations." Nevertheless, the RAF had taken a heavy toll of Luftwaffe aircraft, so that the air component of Dunkirk might well be counted a genuine British victory.

France Falls

The Dunkirk miracle gave Britain a critically needed reprieve, but there was no saving France. All that was left was for the Germans to mop up. Paris, declared an "open city"—that is, left undefended so that it would not be destroyed—fell on June 14. Almost simultaneously, the Maginot Line—useless, but still garrisoned by French troops who could have been better employed elsewhere—was captured from its undefended rear. The Maginot Line was a fixed fortification in the truest sense of the word. All of its guns and gun ports faced east, toward Germany. There was no way to turn the guns 180 degrees to the west. The designers of the line never anticipated needing to do so.

On June 10, with France prostrate, Mussolini, who had waited this long to see how Germany fared before committing his nation to the fight, declared war on France and Britain. Mussolini invaded southern France, but gained little.

> **"On this tenth day of June, 1940, the hand that held the dagger has struck it into the back of its neighbor."**
>
> *President Franklin D. Roosevelt, speaking of Italy's attack on France*

On June 22, 1940, the Battle of France was formally concluded with French signatures on an armistice agreement. With an unfailing flair for myth and drama, Hitler compelled the French to sign the armistice in the very railway car, at a siding near Compiègne, in which German representatives had signed the armistice ending World War I.

REALITY CHECK

Chaos at Dunkirk

For the British army, the Dunkirk evacuation was a reprieve from annihilation, but it nevertheless created both confusion and friction between the British and the French. At first, the French were prevented from boarding the evacuation ships. Only after the vast majority of the British troops had been evacuated were large numbers of French troops admitted onto waiting vessels. And although the evacuation involved heroism on every level—from the self-sacrificing rearguard troops, who were either evacuated at the last minute or left behind, to the thousands of mariners, both military and civilian, who risked their vessels and their lives to rescue the troops—officers also had to use small arms to control panic-stricken soldiers jostling in the evacuation lines. Sailors who managed the small boats that transferred troops from shore to waiting vessels frequently used their oars to beat away frantic evacuees who threatened to swamp their tiny craft.

NUMBERS

French and German Troop Losses

The Battle of France resulted in the deaths of 90,000 French soldiers and the wounding of 200,000. Almost 2 million French troops were taken prisoner or reported missing. German losses included 29,640 killed and 133,573 wounded.

ONE FRENCH MAN

Even as France rushed abjectly toward defeat and surrender, one French man stood tall. Born in 1890, Charles de Gaulle was a career army officer who had fought in World War I. By the start of World War II, de Gaulle was a very able tank commander; on June 6, he was elevated to undersecretary of state for defense by French premier Paul Reynaud, who sent him on several missions to Britain to explore ways in which the British might help France continue the war against Germany. De Gaulle remained in England after the Reynaud government fell and even after the capitulation of France. On June 18, 1940, he broadcast from London his first stirring appeal to the French people to resist Germany, telling them that war was not over. As a result of this and repeated broadcasts, a French military court tried de Gaulle in absentia, found him guilty of treason,

EYEWITNESS

On May 13, four days after he became prime minister, Winston Churchill met with his Cabinet and told them, "I have nothing to offer but blood, toil, tears and sweat." Later in the day, he repeated this phrase—perhaps the most unlikely battle cry in history—in an address to the House of Commons, successfully seeking a vote of confidence for his new all-party government:

> *In this crisis I hope I may be pardoned if I do not address the House at any length today. I hope that any of my friends and colleagues, or former colleagues, who are affected by the political reconstruction, will make allowance, all allowance, for any lack of ceremony with which it has been necessary to act. I would say to the House, as I said to those who have joined this government: "I have nothing to offer but blood, toil, tears and sweat." We have before us an ordeal of the most grievous kind. We have before us many, many long months of struggle and of suffering. You ask, what is our policy? I can say: It is to wage war, by sea, land and air, with all our might and with all the strength that God can give us; to wage war against a monstrous tyranny, never surpassed in the dark, lamentable catalogue of human crime. That is our policy. You ask, what is our aim? I can answer in one word: It is victory, victory at all costs, victory in spite of all terror, victory, however long and hard the road may be; for without victory, there is no survival. Let that be realised; no survival for the British Empire, no survival for all that the British Empire has stood for, no survival for the urge and impulse of the ages, that mankind will move forward towards its goal. But I take up my task with buoyancy and hope. I feel sure that our cause will not be suffered to fail among men. At this time I feel entitled to claim the aid of all, and I say, "come then, let us go forward together with our united strength."*

and sentenced him on August 2, 1940, to death, loss of military rank, and confiscation of property. De Gaulle responded by throwing himself with even greater energy and determination into organizing the Free French Forces as well as a shadow Free French government in exile.

Both of these efforts were audacious for de Gaulle was practically unknown outside of French military circles. Few French civilians knew his name, and all that sustained him in his desperate enterprise was boundless self-confidence, strength of character, and an unshakable conviction that the French nation must not be allowed to perish. He would broadcast to France until the day of its liberation, headquartered first in London and later, by 1943, in liberated French Algiers. From his exile, he also directed the action of the Free French Forces and other French resistance groups, working closely—albeit not always harmoniously—with the British secret services in this effort.

Brigadier General Charles de Gaulle, a French military maverick, rallied and led the Free French Forces and formed the Free French government in exile after the fall of France.

Fatal Seduction

As for the conqueror Adolf Hitler, gloating over the victory certified at Compiègne, he must have thought that the fate of Germany had come full circle. Yet the fall of France would prove a fatal seduction for the conquerors. Instead of following his all but total victory on the Continent with an immediate invasion of Britain—now at its most vulnerable—Hitler devoted inordinate resources to occupying and exploiting France. With Churchill's nation still in the war, the Führer—and the world—would discover that the war was very far from over.

TAKEAWAY

Darkness and Hope

Germany employed blitzkrieg tactics to conquer Poland and defeat France, both in an astoundingly short time. At this, the darkest moments of the new war, even as Britain braced for an invasion, Winston Churchill rallied his people not merely to the defense of their home but also to strike back at the Axis nations and defeat them.

PART TWO

BRITAIN ALONE

On preceding pages: The dome of London's St. Paul's Cathedral stands valiantly among the fire and smoke of burning London during the German air raid of December 29, 1940.

CHAPTER 5

Their Finest Hour

From Blitzkrieg to the Blitz

As a political organizer and manipulator of the masses, Adolf Hitler was a diabolical genius, but as a military strategist he repeatedly came up short. Never having achieved rank higher than corporal, he nevertheless saw himself as a latter-day Frederick the Great—the eighteenth-century monarch who led Prussia from one military victory to the next, beginning the consolidation of Germany around a Prussian core—and he kept a portrait of the emperor in his private quarters. But Hitler was no Frederick. And in the early summer of 1940, this was most fortunate for Great Britain, which, after the fall of France, stood alone against the Nazi conquest.

The Alliance That Never Was

As we saw in the previous chapter, Hitler personally ordered his panzer (tank) commanders to pause in their lightning advance against the Anglo-French forces so that the slower German infantry could catch up. This was a fatal error that permitted the English (along with a substantial body of French troops), their backs against the English Channel, to escape to England via the daring Dunkirk evacuation. Hitler did not lose the war at Dunkirk, but he lost an opportunity to win it. Had the British Expeditionary

REALITY CHECK

Vacillation Sealion

It was essential to the cult of personality on which the Third Reich depended that Adolf Hitler seem to the world a man of absolute decisiveness, and, to be sure, the lightning war against Poland and France surely enhanced this image. Yet the prospect of invading England tortured the Führer into dithering indecision. Instead of issuing one of his celebrated do-or-die orders, with little regard to feasibility, Hitler temporized on the subject of the invasion. On July 21, he told his commanders in chief that if they could not conclude preparations for the invasion by early September, "other plans" would have to be considered. Chief among these "other plans" was an invasion of the Soviet Union—an operation that would put Sealion on hold indefinitely. It was as if he wanted to avoid the British invasion at all costs.

Force (BEF) been wiped out, the British would either have had to ask Hitler for peace terms or have submitted to immediate invasion. The preservation of most of the BEF, however, gave Britain a fighting chance—desperately slim though it seemed—against the Germans.

What moved Hitler to sacrifice victory?

His misjudgment was due in part to his limitations as a military strategist, doubtless, and also to his unwillingness to risk his panzers, which were, after all, far ahead of infantry support units and lines of supply. Nor did Hitler imagine that the British would ever be able to mount the truly miraculous cross-Channel evacuation they instantly cobbled together. Hitler assumed that time was on his side.

There was also another reason for Hitler's fatal conservatism as his forces closed in on the British in France. He believed that, after witnessing the conquest of Poland and France, Britain would come to terms with Germany, maybe even become an ally. France had been Germany's primary enemy in World War I. Now that France had been defeated, Hitler felt that he had, for all practical purposes, won the war. His only question was, *Why didn't the British see that?*

Operation Sealion

Even though the British managed to salvage most of their expeditionary force at Dunkirk, Hitler would have done well to mount an immediate invasion of England. Instead, his forces consolidated their position in France, beginning the process of looting natural resources and production capacity and savoring the pleasures of Paris, while Hitler continued to ponder Britain's stubborn refusal to acknowledge defeat. By the middle of July 1940, Hitler reached the conclusion that Britain would not voluntarily come to terms as long as the British government believed that Russia would eventually turn against Germany. He decided, therefore, to force Britain to make peace.

On July 16, 1940, Adolf Hitler issued Directive No. 16, which outlined the preparations required for a landing operation against England. The landing operation itself—the invasion of England—was called Unternehmen Seelöwe ("Operation Sealion"). Its first preparatory phase was the destruction of the British Royal Air

Force, the RAF. Hitler and his top navy commanders were worried about British air attacks against cross-Channel troop transports.

On the one hand, Adolf Hitler failed to understand the depth of the British resolve to resist coming to terms with the Nazi regime, let alone surrendering to it, but he also failed to recognize just how vulnerable Britain was to invasion. During most of the 1930s, when appeasement had been the order of the day, the RAF had been allotted few resources, and what little it was given was devoted to developing long-range bombers as a deterrent to German attack. That is, rather than turn out fighters to defend directly against German air raids, the existence of bombers would stand as a threat of retaliation. It was a strangely indirect approach to national security, and what it meant was that the development and production of fighters were sacrificed in order to develop and build bombers. It was not until 1938 that the British government and the RAF awoke to the folly of relying on mere deterrence to discourage attacks rather than providing the means of actually defending against an attack. In this year, virtually on the eve of war, resources were allocated to fighter production and the training of fighter pilots. By the summer of 1940, however, both planes and pilots were in short supply.

The British did enjoy one significant technological advantage over the Germans in air defense. Beginning in 1934–36, a new radio technology emerged independently in France, Germany, the Netherlands, Italy, Japan, Great Britain, and the United States. It was called Radio Detection and Ranging—radar—and used radio waves to detect the presence of remote objects, such as incoming enemy aircraft, and to measure their "range" or location. For defenders, it was an invaluable early warning system. By May 1935, British physicists had developed Radar Direction Finding, a rudimentary radar system, and before the year had ended, a chain of radar stations, code-named Chain Home, or "CH," had been designed. Eighteen of these were operational on September 3, 1939, the day Britain entered the war. Between 1940 and 1943, CH was greatly expanded and improved. German scientists were certainly aware of radar, and German research in this field got under way in 1934. By 1936, the Germans had developed ship-borne radar prototypes, and by 1939, antiaircraft radar was also in use on land. Yet the

ALTERNATE TAKE

Unamphibious Warfare

Adolf Hitler and his military planners seem to have conceived conquest mainly in terms of land operations across the continent of Europe. For this reason, they developed virtually no doctrine of amphibious warfare, let alone the means of executing large-scale amphibious assaults. The lack of specialized landing craft alone would have made a cross-Channel invasion very difficult. Most military historians believe that, had he invaded England immediately after the fall of France, Hitler might have forced that nation into a negotiated settlement. However, other historians have countered that, largely unprepared for a waterborne invasion, the Germans would have suffered possibly crippling casualties in the earliest phases of Operation Sealion.

A day in the life of "Dad's Army": These British Home Guardsmen train with American Tommy guns (officially, Thompson submachine guns) in 1940, early in the war.

Germans, typically far advanced in electronic and other engineering projects, were curiously slow to recognize the potential of radar. They never developed systems as extensive as those of the British (or the Americans), and they did not fully appreciate how effective the British Chain Home system was. That failure of appreciation would prove costly.

Operation Sealion was to have used German troops from the Ninth and Sixteenth armies now based in France and Holland. They would be transported across the English Channel from the Dutch ports of Rotterdam and Antwerp and from the French ports of Dunkirk, Calais, Boulogne, Étaples, and Le Havre in every available German vessel, including military and civilian craft. Landings were planned at seven locations along the Channel coast of England. The amphibious landings would be supplemented by airborne assault—paratroop landings.

All through the planning stages, Admiral Erich Raeder, the German navy's commander in chief, piled doubt upon doubt concerning the feasibility of the landings. He cited difficulties in attaining air supremacy—that is, wiping out the RAF—clearing the English coast of mines, and, most of all, assembling and deploying so large a transport fleet. Pressed, Raeder told Hitler that the navy could not possibly be ready before September 15. Instead of protesting, Hitler merely replied that this would be the deadline for all preparations. If all elements were not ready by then, Operation Sealion would be postponed.

NUMBERS

Guarding the Home Front

The Home Guard reached its height of enlistment in June 1943, with 1,784,000 men and 4,000 women. Another auxiliary service, the Royal Observer Corps (which stood guard against the approach of enemy ships and aircraft), numbered more than 33,000 men in June 1941. By June 1944, more than 4,000 women had joined the corps as well.

Britain Braces

Having witnessed the German juggernaut in action and wholly unaware of Hitler's doubts, the British, after the fall of France, anticipated invasion at any moment. Winston Churchill, the new prime minister, called on the Royal Navy to be the first line of defense, but he did not rely exclusively on that force. He called for defense of the beaches, mainly along the east coast. Land defense would employ a combination of second- and third-line reserve troops and special "Leopard brigades," mobile elite units that could be transported rapidly to any points at which Germans made landings. Artillery and tanks would be used extensively, but the great problem was that much of this equipment—along with many of the vehicles needed to transport Leopard brigades—had been left behind at Dunkirk.

The British were critically short of rifles as well as heavy weapons, tanks, transport vehicles, and, most of all, men. War production, together with loans and purchases from the United States (see Chapter 6), would eventually make up the equipment shortfalls. More immediately, the manpower crisis was addressed by the formation of a defense force announced on May 14, 1940, officially called the Local Defence Volunteers, and later known as the Home Guard, but always informally referred to as "Dad's Army" because it consisted mainly of volunteers too old to join the regular army or to be drafted into it. Poorly equipped and inadequately trained, the Home Guard nevertheless performed important civil defense duties, manned antiaircraft artillery, and served as coast watchers and enemy aircraft observers, thereby freeing up younger men for regular army combat service.

NUMBERS

Bomber Stats

In the summer of 1940, the Luftwaffe consisted of 2,679 aircraft, including 1,015 medium bombers, 350 Stuka dive-bombers, 930 fighters, and 375 "heavy fighters" (capable of carrying heavier weapons and operating at longer ranges than conventional fighters), together with various reconnaissance aircraft. At this time, the RAF had about 900 fighters, of which approximately 600 could be launched at a given time, mainly because of a shortage of pilots, many of whom had been killed or captured in the Battle of France.

EYEWITNESS

However inadequate British land defense forces were on the eve of the anticipated invasion, the nation had in Winston Churchill a source of incalculable strength. On June 4, 1940, when he announced to the House of Commons the success of the Dunkirk evacuation, Churchill stirred the entire nation with one of history's most memorable rallying speeches, which concluded:

> *. . . Even though large tracts of Europe and many old and famous States have fallen or may fall into the grip of the Gestapo and all the odious apparatus of Nazi rule, we shall not flag or fail. We shall go on to the end, we shall fight in France, we shall fight on the seas and oceans, we shall fight with growing confidence and growing strength in the air, we shall defend our Island, whatever the cost may be, we shall fight on the beaches, we shall fight on the landing grounds, we shall fight in the fields and in the streets, we shall fight in the hills; we shall never surrender, and even if, which I do not for a moment believe, this Island or a large part of it were subjugated and starving, then our Empire beyond the seas, armed and guarded by the British Fleet, would carry on the struggle, until, in God's good time, the New World, with all its power and might, steps forth to the rescue and the liberation of the old.*

The Supermarine Spitfire was not only the most famous British fighter of World War II, it also was one of the iconic aircraft flown by all combatants throughout the entire war. Although outnumbered and outgunned, gallant RAF pilots flying Spitfires and Hurricanes defeated the Luftwaffe in the Battle of Britain.

A German combat ace in World War I, Hermann Göring had long since slipped into rotund middle age by the time he was in command of the Luftwaffe during World War II, but he managed to wedge himself into the bombardier's station in the nose of a light bomber in 1940 for this propaganda photo taken during the Battle of Britain.

The Battle of Britain Begins

When Adolf Hitler set naval readiness as a precondition for the launch of Operation Sealion, he also declared that the decision to invade would depend as well on German victory in the skies over the Channel and over England itself.

The Germans had every reason to be confident of achieving the necessary air supremacy. The German air force—the Luftwaffe—not only outnumbered the RAF in both planes and pilots, it also had so far proven itself the most successful air weapon in history and, with the fall of France, was now perfectly positioned for operations against England. Yet Germany's air marshal, Hermann Göring, delayed the commencement of the main phase of the air campaign against England—code-named Aldertag ("Eagle Day")—until August 13, 1940, seven long weeks after the fall of France. Hitler failed to press Göring, and that failure gave the British valuable time to prepare and strengthen air defenses, which were already formidable. The pacifist sentiment of the 1930s had created shortages of offensive weaponry and aircraft, but had actually encouraged the development of defensive facilities. France had fruitlessly poured its resources into the Maginot Line, but the British had devoted money and time to antiaircraft artillery emplacements and to the development of radar and the Chain Home early warning system. The delay in launching Eagle Day also gave the RAF time to marshal its fighter assets, outnumbered though they were.

Despite its geographical and numerical advantages, the Luftwaffe found itself going up against a strongly and skillfully defended target. Although the German aircraft—especially the Messerschmitt—were among the most technically advanced of the time, the RAF's mainstay fighters, the Hawker Hurricane and the Supermarine Spitfire, were also superb. Luftwaffe pilots were very well trained, but so were those of the RAF. Moreover, the British pilots were motivated by the conviction that the survival of their homeland depended on them. Although German air commanders were highly capable, Göring, the overall commander, was often erratic. His character stood in sharp contrast to that of British air chief marshall Hugh Dowding. Finally, while it is true that possession of French and Belgian air bases gave the Luftwaffe excellent positions from which to launch attacks, the fighter aircraft lacked sufficient fuel capacity to allow much time over England. British Spitfires and Hurricanes were similarly limited in range, but, based in England, they did not have to consume fuel flying across the Channel. One of the tactics RAF pilots used extensively was to lure the German fighters into extended aerial combat, forcing them to consume precious fuel, so that they would have to break off attacks prematurely, even deserting the bombers they were escorting, rendering the bombers vulnerable to British fighter attack.

Although the main phase of the Battle of Britain did not begin until Eagle Day, August 13, the entire battle was fought in three overlapping phases, starting with a heavy German bombing raid on July 10, 1940, directed against the southern ports from Dover west to Plymouth. The Germans wanted to "soften up" this area, to destroy its defenses in order to prepare it for landings. Nearly every day, German medium bombers, escorted by fighters, crossed the English Channel to bomb ships and ports. On August 15, the first phase of the Battle of Britain reached its greatest intensity as some 940 German planes attacked simultaneously in the south and the north. The RAF shot down seventy-six of the German planes, at the cost of thirty-four of its own fighters in the exchange. German attacks also destroyed twenty-one British bombers on the ground.

THE BLITZ

IN AUGUST 1940, THE LUFTWAFFE BEGAN AN AIR OPERATION carried out in parallel with the Battle of Britain. This was a series of nighttime air raids directed not against military targets—ports, port defenses, and RAF airfields—but against civilian London and other cities. The people of Britain dubbed the raids "the Blitz," shortening the German word Blitzkrieg. The Blitz would continue long after the Battle of Britain had ended, with raids staged well into May 1941.

Adolf Hitler had not built an air force suited to strategic bombing, the bombing of whole cities and elements of civilian infrastructure. Consisting of fighters and light and medium bombers, his

ALTERNATE TAKE

Seven Weeks Sooner?

Germany's air marshal, Hermann Göring, is often blamed for the delay in commencing the Battle of Britain, which thereby put off the invasion of England indefinitely. Most recent historians, however, see Hitler's failure to push unconditionally for the commencement of the air battle as the chief reason for the indefinite postponement of Operation Sealion. Had the dictator insisted on an early, all-out air battle, it is likely that the Germans would have achieved air supremacy and the invasion would have been launched. Given Germany's failure to develop adequate cross-Channel transports and specialized landing craft, and given the manifest will of the British leaders and people to resist conquest, there is no telling whether the invasion would have succeeded, but, had the RAF been defeated, the invasion almost certainly would have been attempted.

DETAILS, DETAILS

Dogfighting

The Battle of Britain was the first battle in history fought entirely in the air.

ALTERNATE TAKE

Heavier Lifting

During the 1930s, the Nazi regime devoted extensive resources to building the Luftwaffe. Acting against the advice of senior German air planners, however, Adolf Hitler concentrated exclusively on the design and production of fighters, dive-bombers, and medium bombers rather than developing any heavy bombers. As Hitler saw it, bombers were to be used tactically, mainly to prepare the way for and to support ground operations. He did not see a major role for strategic bombing, bombing apart from ground operations; therefore, he saw little need for bombers capable of long range and very heavy bomb loads. Had Hitler developed such aircraft—as both the British and the Americans had done—his air raids against Britain would have been far more destructive than they were and might well have proved decisive.

Luftwaffe was intended to play a tactical role in support of ground operations. Despite this, Hitler diverted many of his bombers from the military objectives that were targeted in the Battle of Britain and sent them on bombing missions intended to demoralize the British population, thereby undermining the nation's very will to continue to make war. The strategy proved to be another of Hitler's fatal errors. Although the Blitz brought devastation and terrible suffering on the British people, it not only failed to demoralize them, it actually galvanized their resolve, making them that much more determined to fight through to total victory. Equally bad for Germany, by diverting attacks from military targets, the Blitz gave the RAF the breathing space it needed to continue fighting the Luftwaffe in the air. The Battle of Britain and subsequent combat during the Blitz took a heavy toll on the Luftwaffe.

Although the Blitz failed to bring Germany victory, it did bring the people of Britain terror and heartbreak. Early in the Blitz, ground-based antiaircraft defenses proved woefully inadequate at night. The Chain Home radar system was incomplete, and few RAF night fighter aircraft were equipped with radar at this time. There were plenty of ground-based searchlights to go around, but the chances of catching a German bomber in a beam and then shooting it down were almost infinitesimal because the aircraft dropped their bombs from more than twelve thousand feet. More successful were the British advances in electronic warfare, which allowed defenders to jam some of the radio beams the German bombers used to find their targets at night. During the course of the Blitz, this jamming technology steadily improved, so that many German raiders, misdirected by the jamming devices, ended up dropping bombs intended for cities in fields instead.

During the early phase of the Blitz, which lasted through mid-November 1940, an average of two hundred planes (including some Italian aircraft) bombed London every night. Nor, at the height of the Blitz, were the daytime skies empty. Fighter-bombers conducted raids by day. In addition to London, Coventry, Southampton, Birmingham, Liverpool, Bristol, and Plymouth were hit hard. The Coventry raid on the night of November 14–15 was especially devastating. It made use of a new set of German radio beacon systems (the Pathfinder Force, KG 100, and X-Gerät systems), which successfully guided to their targets 449 of 509 German aircraft sent out. Only one plane was shot down. A dozen major armaments factories and most of the city's commercial center were destroyed, and the fourteenth-century Coventry Cathedral—one of Britain's great cultural treasures—was left in ruins. That night 380 residents of Coventry were killed and 865 injured. Again, however, the devastating raid failed to demoralize Britons. They regarded the ruins of the great cathedral as a symbol of heedless and barbaric German aggression, and the failure of British defense measures against the raid spurred the rapid improvement of all defensive systems.

Beginning on February 19, 1941, and continuing through May 12, the Luftwaffe once again bombed targets with greater military importance, including port cities, in an effort to disrupt British port and shipbuilding operations. Plymouth, Portsmouth, Bristol, Avonmouth, Swansea, Merseyside, Belfast, Clydeside, Hull, Sunderland, and Newcastle were all badly hit. On December 29, the Germans conducted an incendiary raid against London, using bombs intended to create fires. The raid resulted in a night of more than fifteen hundred uncontrollable blazes. On May 10, 1941, in the last—and most destructive—London raid of the Blitz, incendiary bombs started more than two thousand fires, in which more than three thousand people were killed or injured. The British did manage to shoot down sixteen of the bombers, the most ever downed in a nighttime raid.

Despite improvements in antiaircraft defenses, it was the demands of the Eastern Front (see Chapter 7), and not the RAF, that finally ended the Blitz, as Luftwaffe resources were simply stretched too thin to continue the raids.

Many of the stations of London's venerable Underground—the "Tube," or subway system—were converted into vast public air-raid shelters during the Blitz of World War II.

DETAILS, DETAILS

Not So Little Blitz

The term "Little Blitz" (or "Baby Blitz") was applied to raids the Nazis launched against London and other cities (including in Belgium and the Netherlands) in 1944 using their newly developed V-1 and V-2 rocket weapons (see Chapter 20).

DETAILS, DETAILS

Night Bombing

It is harder to hit specific targets at night than during the day. This did not matter to the Germans in the Blitz, however, because their intention was to create general terror in the cities, so precision bombing was not required. Cover of darkness gave the German bombers considerable protection from fighter attack and from ground-based antiaircraft artillery.

NUMBERS

Blitz Losses

The Blitz killed about 43,000 civilians and injured between 139,000 and 200,000. Approximately 20 percent of London's buildings were destroyed. The Luftwaffe lost about 600 bombers during the Blitz, only about 1.5 percent of the sorties flown. In relation to the number of sorties flown, this was a low loss ratio, but because these losses did not buy the hoped-for result—namely, the breaking of the British will to continue the war—the losses were in vain. Worse, by targeting cities, the Luftwaffe missed its opportunity to destroy RAF bases and RAF planes on the ground. World War II demonstrated that nations could absorb catastrophic civilian losses and keep fighting as long as they possessed the military means to do so.

EYEWITNESS

This excerpt from a December 30, 1940 piece by Ernie Pyle, a roving correspondent for Scripps Howard, vividly describes London at night during the Blitz:

Immediately above the fires the sky was red and angry, and overhead, making a ceiling in the vast heavens, there was a cloud of smoke all in pink. Up in that pink shrouding there were tiny, brilliant specks of flashing light—anti-aircraft shells bursting. After the flash you could hear the sound.

Up there, too, the barrage balloons were standing out as clearly as if it were daytime, but now they were pink instead of silver. And now and then through a hole in that pink shroud there twinkled incongruously a permanent, genuine star—the old-fashioned kind that has always been there.

Below us the Thames grew lighter, and all around below were the shadows—the dark shadows of buildings and bridges that formed the base of this dreadful masterpiece.

Later on I borrowed a tin hat and went out among the fires. That was exciting too, but the thing I shall always remember above all the other things in my life is the monstrous loveliness of that one single view of London on a holiday night—London stabbed with great fires, shaken by explosions, its dark regions along the Thames sparkling with the pinpoints of white-hot bombs, all of it roofed over with a ceiling of pink that held bursting shells, balloons, flares and the grind of vicious engines. And in yourself the excitement and anticipation and wonder in your soul that this could be happening at all.

These things all went together to make the most hateful, most beautiful single scene I have ever known.

NUMBERS

The Longest Months

In the first two months of the Blitz, raids were conducted every night for 57 nights.

The Battle of Britain: Phase Two

As mentioned, the Blitz was a departure from the Battle of Britain proper. The Blitz was a terror attack against civilian targets, whereas the Battle of Britain was both a fight for air supremacy—an attempt to wipe out the RAF—and a series of raids against military targets. Overlapping the first offensive phase of the battle was a second, which primarily targeted RAF airfields, aircraft factories, and radar installations. Between

MINISTRY of INFORMATI

BULLETIN

The following information has been prepared at the request of the Government and Local Departm

Help your Neighbours with Water.—Will all householders who now have a supply of water words WATER HERE on the door or walls so that neighbours who are less fortunate may be given sup

Advice Bureaux.—The Citizens' Advice Bureau is now open as the Rotary Club Room, Liberal C Coventry, and advice will be given free between the hours of 10.0 a.m. and 4.0 p.m. every day, Sunday Saturday a second bureau will be open during the same hours on week days but not on Sundays at Radford Avenue.

These bureaux provide information on all matters arising out of the present emergency.

Fire Equipment.—If any member of the general public sees any fire hose or any other fire equipme they please report the matter to the Central Fire Station or the Central Police Station when arrangem to collect it.

Vouchers for Evacuees.—Parents wishing to remain in Coventry, but who have relatives living ou whose company they can send their children under school age, should enquire at the Education Office, Cou travel vouchers can be issued.

Air Raid Casualties.—All air raid damage incidents and particularly public shelters have been thorou and there is no ground for believing that large numbers of bodies remain to be recovered. It is pure rumo it is playing Hitler's game.

To Motorists.—Will motorists please park their cars off the streets wherever possible. Vehicles sho into the centre of the City if it can be avoided, and they must NOT be parked in this area unless urgently rec duties. Your co-operation in this matter is urgently requested.

Emergency Petrol.—Applicants for emergency petrol obtainable at the Council House, Hay Lane, produce their registration books or insurance certificates, or road fund licences.

This office will be closed on Monday the 25th inst., at 3.0 p.m., and all subsequent applications for eme persons employed by firms engaged on work of national importance must be made to the Divisional Pe Birmingham, through their employers.

Tips to Shelter Users.—If you use a shelter, you can help largely in preventing illness within it. Here

Help keep the shelter and sanitary accommodation clean.
Provide yourself with warm covering as far as you can.
Do not overcrowd sleeping space.
Gargle daily night and morning.

On November 14, 1940, 509 German bombers pounded the English industrial city of Coventry, killing 380 residents and destroying sixty thousand buildings, including the city's majestic medieval cathedral. Britain's Ministry of Information issued an information and instruction bulletin on November 22 intended to control panic, bring relief, and get the city back on its feet. Like everything the Churchill government published, the bulletin was replete with practical information and made no attempt to minimize the magnitude of the losses or rally the people with hollow propaganda.

August 24 and September 6, 1940, the Luftwaffe destroyed or severely damaged 466 Hurricane and Spitfire aircraft, many of them on the ground, and killed 103 British pilots, wounding an additional 128. These casualties represented one-fourth of the RAF's fighter pilot strength. But achieving this cost the Luftwaffe so heavily that the result can best be described as a Pyrrhic victory—if not a German defeat. The Luftwaffe lost more than twice the number of planes and pilots as the British.

Beginning on September 7, the Battle of Britain was turned away from RAF targets and war-production factories to military objectives more closely related to the Blitz. On September 7, some three hundred German airplanes made a daylight raid against London's antiaircraft defenses. On the fifteenth, more than four hundred bombers hit London in the war's biggest daylight raid on the capital. Fifty-six of the medium bombers were shot down by RAF fighters or ground-based antiaircraft artillery.

The Battle of Britain: Phase Three

The Luftwaffe bomber losses suffered on September 15 shook Hermann Göring to the core. He decided then and there to abandon daylight bombing raids and opened the third and final phase of the Battle of Britain with night bombing. This third phase of the battle is difficult to distinguish from the Blitz; some military historians cite October 31 as the end of the Battle of Britain, others consider the London raid of November 3 as the concluding event of the Battle of Britain, and the rest of the German raids as part of the Blitz.

NUMBERS

RAF and German Losses

Between July and November 1940, the RAF lost 915 fighters, 481 pilots killed or missing, and 422 pilots wounded. The RAF claimed to have downed 2,698 Luftwaffe aircraft, although fully documented German aircraft losses amounted to 1,733—a devastating number nevertheless.

"London Can Take It"

Throughout the Battle of Britain and the Blitz, the motto "London can take it" was on every British lip. It was not merely a defiant declaration of a willingness to absorb punishment, but a recognition that London itself had become a key combatant in this terrible war. To bomb London, the Germans had to spend aircraft and pilots. By May 1941, Hitler realized that he could no longer afford the expense. His efforts to beat England into surrender were destroying his air arm. The Battle of Britain had been lost back in November 1940, when Hitler failed to achieve air supremacy, and the Blitz rapidly petered out after May 12, 1941. Battered, Britain was unbowed and undefeated. Worse, Operation Sealion had become a lost cause—the most momentous Axis operation of World War II that would never be carried out.

Victory

In a speech to the House of Commons on June 18, 1940, with France irretrievably lost and Britain apparently laid open to invasion, Winston Churchill observed that the Battle of France was indeed over. "I expect that the Battle of Britain is about to begin," he said.

> "The gratitude of every home in our Island, in our Empire, and indeed throughout the world, except in the abodes of the guilty, goes out to the British airmen. . . . Never in the field of human conflict was so much owed by so many to so few."
>
> *Winston Churchill, Speech to the House of Commons, August 20, 1940*

> Upon this battle depends the survival of Christian civilization. Upon it depends our own British life, and the long continuity of our institutions and our Empire. The whole fury and might of the enemy must very soon be turned on us. Hitler knows that he will have to break us in this Island or lose the war. If we can stand up to him, all Europe may be free and the life of the world may move forward into broad, sunlit uplands. But if we fail, then the whole world, including the United States, including all that we have known and cared for, will sink into the abyss of a new Dark Age made more sinister, and perhaps more protracted, by the lights of perverted science. Let us therefore brace ourselves to our duties, and so bear ourselves that, if the British Empire and its Commonwealth last for a thousand years, men will still say, "This was their finest hour."

RUDOLF HESS

Bombs were not the only commodity dropped on England. On May 10, 1941, Rudolf Hess, one of the earliest members of the Nazi Party—a man whose loyalty to Hitler was legendary, earning him the number three post in the party—parachuted into Scotland.

Hess was bearing a proposal that Britain give Germany leave to pursue its war aims on the Continent and to return all former German colonies to the Reich in exchange for Germany's pledge to keep hands off the British Empire. It was a bizarre mission, undertaken entirely on Hess's own initiative and without Hitler's knowledge, let alone authorization. Not a single official of the British government responded to the proposal. Instead, Hess was arrested and deemed a prisoner of war. Held throughout the war, he was turned over to the Nuremberg War Crime Tribunal after the war. Found guilty of war crimes, he was sentenced to life imprisonment and was incarcerated in Berlin's Spandau Prison. From 1966 until his death in 1987, he was the prison's only inmate.

Rudolf Hess parachuted into Scotland on May 10, 1941, hoping to persuade Britain to withdraw from the war. Arrested and imprisoned, he was tried at the Nuremberg War Crimes Tribunal after the defeat of Germany and spent the rest of his life behind bars. He is pictured here during the tribunal. To his left is another accused war criminal, German foreign minister Joachim von Ribbentrop.

Having prevailed in the Battle of Britain, Churchill and his countrymen knew all too well that victory in World War II was still far from having been won. Yet out of the ashes of the British capital and so many of its other cities, a great victory had unquestionably emerged. Adolf Hitler had been stopped by the free people of a small island nation on Europe's very edge.

TAKEAWAY

The Stand

The fall of France left Britain as Europe's only democracy unconquered by Hitler. When he delayed his invasion of England and then failed to gain air supremacy in the Battle of Britain, Hitler lost the initiative against this nation, creating in it a determination, against all odds, to strike back and defeat the German war machine.

CHAPTER 6

The Atlantic Front

Combat on the World's Biggest Battlefield

At the edge of Europe, the island nation of Great Britain had stopped Adolf Hitler. For now. For the moment. The fact was that Hitler's Germany had swallowed up most of the European continent, and it was doubtful that, standing alone, Britain could hold off a determined assault for long. Its ally to the southeast, France, now fallen—divided by the terms of a humiliating armistice into a German occupied northern zone and a nominally unoccupied southern zone administered by a puppet government headquartered in the town of Vichy—Britain turned west, to the United States. At this point, however, the sweet land of liberty was neutral, the vast majority of its people—at least 80 percent—wanting no part of the second "European war" in little more than two decades.

Neutrality

President Woodrow Wilson had led the United States into World War I largely because he saw an opportunity for the nation to play a major role in reshaping the world—he hoped—into a place in which war would be forever obsolete. Although Americans felt justifiably proud of what their military had accomplished in that war, the vast majority of them, after the armistice of November 11, 1918, wanted no more to do with "foreign" wars, which meant that they wanted little to do with international affairs. In the elections of 1920, voters spurned the Democratic Party of Woodrow Wilson and embraced the isolationist, America-first Republican Party, sending Warren G. Harding into the White House.

The national mood of isolation endured through the Republican administrations of Harding, Calvin Coolidge, and Herbert Hoover, and even well into the presidency of Democrat Franklin Delano Roosevelt. During the first Roosevelt term, in 1935, as war in Europe loomed, Congress passed the first of a series of Neutrality Acts. Despite their name, these successive acts actually marked the evolution of American foreign policy away from neutrality.

The Neutrality Act of 1935 and those that followed in 1936 and 1937 departed sharply from the definition of neutrality that had applied in earlier wars. Instead of proclaiming the nation's right as a neutral—especially its right to ply the seas and to trade freely—the acts cautiously sought to preserve neutrality by imposing self-limitations on the exercise of neutrality rights, especially with regard to trading with belligerents—whether aggressors or victims. In previous conflicts—especially World War I (see Chapter 1)—the bold proclamations of neutrality had actually served to draw the United States into the war. Congress wanted to avoid repeating this pattern.

The Neutrality Acts of 1935 and 1936 had been passed in response to Italy's May 1935 invasion of Ethiopia. They gave the president authority to embargo arms shipments to belligerent nations and to issue warnings to U.S. citizens that travel on vessels belonging to the belligerents was undertaken at their own risk. The act did not restrict trade in non-arms goods, even goods of strategic importance, such as oil, steel, and copper.

A new crisis beginning in 1936, the Spanish Civil War, moved Congress to pass in January and May 1937 two new Neutrality Acts. These explicitly included civil wars among the conflicts to which neutrality restrictions would apply, and they also empowered the president to add strategic goods to the embargo list and even to bar

REALITY CHECK

Neutral Zone

During the early nineteenth century—the War of 1812 is the prime example—and during World War I, the concept of U.S. neutrality was less a means of keeping the nation out of war than it was a cause for war. Neutrality entailed certain rights—mainly freedom and security of international trade—which, as Americans saw it, went to the heart of their nation's sovereignty. Any nation that threatened these rights would be spoiling for a fight. After World War I, however, most Americans so dreaded the prospect of a new war that they were willing to accept a new definition of neutrality, one which sought to avoid conflict by imposing limitations on trade and political affiliations. The first two Neutrality Acts of the 1930s were by no means attempts to appease belligerents, but they did represent an effort to avoid giving any nation an excuse for going to war with the United States.

DETAILS, DETAILS

Lessons of *Lusitania*

In giving the president authority to forbid American citizens from traveling on vessels belonging to nations at war, a wary Congress in 1937 was mindful that the sinking of the British liner *Lusitania* in 1915, in which American lives were lost, became one of the causes for America's entry into World War I.

U.S. citizens from traveling on vessels belonging to the belligerents. In an effort to prevent provocative incidents at sea, the 1937 acts also prohibited the arming of American merchant vessels.

On November 4, 1939, after the outbreak of war following the September invasion of Poland, President Roosevelt signed into law the Neutrality Act of 1939. For the most part, the new law merely recapitulated the 1937 legislation, with the key exception that it now permitted the sale of arms and strategic materials to those belligerents the president did not specifically exclude. Such sales, however, were to be made on a strict cash-and-carry basis. Congress was anxious to prevent the United States from being drawn into a war because its financial and business interests held the debt of a belligerent country. Nor did Congress want a U.S.-flagged ship provoking an incident by an attempt to run a blockade in order to deliver goods. The 1939 act authorized the president to designate "combat areas," through which travel by U.S. citizens and vessels would be prohibited. Retained was the earlier prohibition against the arming of merchant vessels. On November 17, 1941, during what must be described as an undeclared naval war between the United States and Germany on the Atlantic, Congress amended the act to permit the arming of merchant vessels and also to permit those vessels to carry cargoes into belligerent ports.

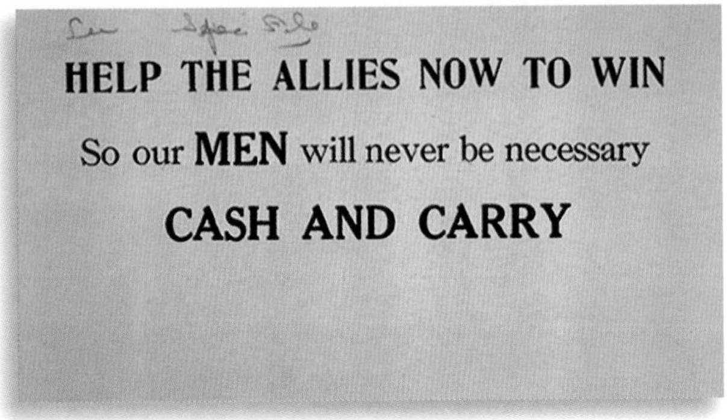

Roosevelt understood and appreciated the American public's desire keep their sons out of a new war, but he was also aware that the nation's long policy of disengagement from world affairs had led Adolf Hitler to dismiss the United States as of no military concern. When Hitler finally went to war in September 1939, FDR came to the conclusion that had the United States been more engaged with Britain and France, its former allies of the Great War,

During the late 1930s, the U.S. Congress passed a series of neutrality acts and amendments. Originally designed to keep America out of the war at all costs, the legislation evolved into an alliance with the British and other Allied nations just short of entering into outright combat. Late in 1939, President Roosevelt lobbied for an amendment to allow the United States to sell arms to the Allies on a "cash and carry" basis, which would furnish the Allied nations with the weapons they needed without involving U.S. businesses and banks in the kind of financial entanglements that had helped propel America into World War I. This postcard touts "cash and carry" as an alternative to declaring war.

Chamberlain's appeasement policy would have been rejected, and Hitler's aggression might have been stopped. The president shared this conclusion only with his inner circle, withholding public comment. But he believed that America's isolationism had helped to make this second world war inevitable. Through the late 1930s, Roosevelt also believed that the United States would ultimately be compelled to enter the war, and he therefore conducted a quiet policy of preparedness.

Churchill and Roosevelt

Roosevelt's inclination to prepare for war was encouraged by Winston Churchill. Vast as it was, World War II was dramatically defined by the larger-than-life personalities of its leaders: Hitler, Stalin, and even Japan's Hideki Tojo. Even more vivid were the two principal Allied leaders, Winston Churchill and Franklin Roosevelt.

In many ways, they were opposites by political orientation and by upbringing. Churchill had been born of a distinguished yet somewhat disreputable family and had led an early life of high adventure as a soldier and a journalist-author before entering politics. He was by turns a conservative (Tory), then a liberal (Labor Party), then a conservative again. Roosevelt had been raised in wealth and genteel privilege on his family's estate at Hyde Park, New York, then joined a Wall Street law firm. Despite his upper-crust background and moneyed profession, he developed a deep concern for the plight of the poor—the growth of his social consciousness nurtured by marriage to a distant cousin, Eleanor Roosevelt, who was a committed social activist. This led to FDR's involvement in liberal Democratic politics. In 1921, when he was thirty-nine years old, Roosevelt was stricken with polio, which left him a paraplegic. Confined to a wheelchair or, when he wished to be seen standing, forced to endure heavy leg braces, Roosevelt's disability contrasted with the intense physicality of Churchill's early life. Yet, as Churchill—and many others—came to recognize, FDR's personal burden had given him great strength of character and boundless sympathy for the suffering of others.

On September 11, 1939, days after Britain declared war on Germany following the Polish invasion, Roosevelt wrote to Churchill, who was then serving as first lord of the Admiralty, the

On April 14, 1939, when this picture was taken at Mount Vernon, Virginia, much of the world and the United States were still at peace—barely—but rapidly drifting toward war. President Franklin D. Roosevelt (center) stands beside his military aide (in uniform), General Edwin "Pa" Watson.

same post he had held during part of World War I. During that same war, FDR had been assistant secretary of the Navy, and he wrote:

> It is because you and I occupied similar positions in the World War that I want you to know how glad I am that you are back again in the Admiralty. . . . What I want you and the Prime Minister [Neville Chamberlain] to know is that I shall at all times welcome it if you will keep me in touch personally with anything you want me to know about.

Churchill understood that the United States was strictly neutral, but he took the president's letter as an invitation. Shortly after he replaced Chamberlain as prime minister, Churchill cabled Roosevelt on May 15, 1940. Air attacks, he wrote, are "making a deep impression upon the French":

> . . . small countries are simply smashed up, one by one, like matchwood. . . . We expect to be attacked here ourselves, both from the air and by parachute and air-borne troops. . . . If necessary, we shall continue the war alone and we are not afraid of that. But I trust you realize, Mr. President, that the voice and force of the United States may count for nothing if they are withheld too long. You may have a completely subjugated, Nazified Europe established with astonishing swiftness, and the weight may be more than we can bear.

To Roosevelt, Churchill neither wept with despair nor bellowed in bellicose optimism. His leading message was simply this: *We are not afraid.* And he continued: "All I ask now is that you should proclaim non-belligerency, which would mean that you would help us with everything short of actually engaging armed forces." From absolute neutrality, Churchill wanted America to move to non-belligerency—in effect, non-combatant support of Britain—and he then asked for forty or fifty obsolescent World War I-vintage American destroyers (desperately needed to escort British convoys), several hundred new aircraft, antiaircraft defense equipment, and steel. He asked, too, that a U.S. Navy squadron be sent to make a "prolonged" visit to an Irish port to discourage what was believed to be an impending landing in neutral Ireland by German paratroopers. He also asked that FDR send warships to call at the port of Singapore, "to keep that Japanese dog quiet in the Pacific." Japan, an ally of Germany, had yet to declare war on Britain. Churchill concluded by unabashedly putting out his hand as if to take America's generosity for granted: "We shall go on paying dollars for as long as we can, but I should like to feel reasonably sure that when we can pay no more, you will give us the stuff all the same."

On May 17, 1940, Roosevelt replied, demurring on the request for destroyers and planes: "As you know a step of that kind could not be taken except with the specific authorization of Congress and I am not certain that it would be wise for that suggestion to be made to the Congress at this moment." He was more encouraging about the antiaircraft equipment and the steel, and he promised to think about sending ships to Ireland, though he resolved to keep the Pacific Fleet safe in Pearl Harbor "for the time being." On the very next day, Churchill turned up the heat: "Many thanks for your message for which I am grateful. . . . We must expect . . . to be attacked here . . . before very long and we hope to give a good account of ourselves. But if American assistance is to play any part it must be available [soon]."

Even as Churchill was promising Roosevelt that, against all odds, Britain would prevail, the U.S. ambassador to Britain, Joseph P. Kennedy Sr. (father of the future president and senators) cabled FDR on May 27, 1940: "Only a miracle can save the BEF [British Expeditionary Force] from being wiped out [in France] or, as I said yesterday, surrender." He went on to say that the possibility, even the desirability, of British surrender was in the air. Whereas Churchill and a few others "want to fight to the death . . . other members [of the Cabinet] realize that physical destruction of men and property in England will not be a proper offset to a loss of pride."

Fortunately for Britain—and the future of the free world—President Roosevelt knew that his ambassador was a defeatist, yet, given the scale of desperation in Europe, how could he possibly credit Churchill's perception of reality more than Kennedy's? Besides, at this point, America had no end of isolationist voices, including that

REALITY CHECK
The IRA and the Abwehr

By the time of World War II, Ireland was still nominally a member of the British Commonwealth but, in fact, acted as an entirely independent nation after having suffered centuries of bitter oppression under the English yoke. Many in England feared that the Irish would make a deal with Germany, thereby squeezing Britain between the occupied Continent to the east and a German-allied Ireland to the west. Instead, the Irish government steered a neutral course throughout the war, but the radically militant Irish Republican Army (IRA), which aimed for total independence from Britain and reunification with Northern Ireland (still wholly under English administration), did approach Germany's international espionage organization, the Abwehr, for arms and funding. Because most German government officials believed that promoting IRA subversion would be ineffective, little came of the IRA-Abwehr relationship.

of its most revered hero, Charles A. Lindbergh, who warned against "meddling with affairs abroad." In the thick of battle, Churchill continued to beseech Roosevelt for destroyers and aircraft, but polls showed that only 7.7 percent of Americans favored entering the war now and a scant 19 percent thought entry would be justified if Allied defeat seemed certain. The vast majority of Americans wanted to stay out of the war, and FDR continued to hold off seeking congressional authorization for the release of ships and planes. Clearly chagrined, Churchill nevertheless refused to waiver or to scold, and Roosevelt, for his part, continued to hold out hope to Churchill. Responding to Churchill's narration of a rare British victory, in the naval battle of the River Plate, which had taken place in the South Atlantic off the coast of South America on December 13, 1939, FDR wrote, "You are much in my thoughts. I need not tell you that."

To the surprise of everyone—except Churchill—the Dunkirk evacuation (Chapter 4) saved the British army, and, on June 10, 1940, the very day Italy declared war on Britain and France, FDR gave the commencement address to the University of Virginia Law School Class of 1940, pledging "in our American unity" to

> pursue two obvious and simultaneous courses: we will extend to the opponents of force the material resources of this nation; and, at the same time, we will harness and speed up the use of those resources in order that we ourselves in the Americas may have equipment and training equal to the task of any emergency and every defense. Signs and signals call for speed—full speed ahead.

The speech was broadcast, and Churchill heard it. He cabled the president on June 11: "Your statement that the material aid of the United States will be given to the Allies in their struggle is a strong encouragement in a dark but not unhopeful hour."

America's Undeclared War

As the evolving neutrality acts suggest, President Roosevelt gradually prepared an unwilling nation for war. On January 3, 1940, he asked Congress to provide $1.8 billion for national defense, including new appropriations of almost $1.2 billion and a program to produce

CHARLES LINDBERGH

America loves its heroes, and it also has a passion for tearing them down. After his 1927 solo trans-Atlantic flight, Charles A. Lindbergh was the most celebrated man in America.

He went on to become an aviation executive and promoter, and in 1936, after visiting Germany, he warned his fellow Americans against that nation's growing air power. For their part, the Nazis courted Lindbergh and gave him an official decoration in 1938—his acceptance of which many Americans found appalling. Worse, he became an outspoken advocate of absolute American neutrality well into 1940–41. This drew bitter criticism from no less than President Franklin D. Roosevelt, prompting Lindbergh to resign his Air Corps Reserve commission in April 1941. Lindbergh's public reputation was at low ebb, and, in many quarters, he was even seen as a crypto-Nazi. For many Americans, he was forever tainted—despite the fact that, once America entered the war, Lindbergh, a civilian, committed himself quietly but wholeheartedly to the struggle. As a consultant to the Ford Motor Company and to the United Aircraft Corporation, he contributed to aircraft design and manufacture, going to the front lines to observe aircraft performance. Secretly, in the Pacific, he even flew fifty combat missions. Had this been widely known, Lindbergh's reputation would certainly have been rehabilitated.

As was the case on the eve of America's entry into World War I, there was a strong U.S. pacifist movement during the 1930s. "America First," it was called, and one of its most prominent advocates was Lindbergh, the "Lone Eagle." Lindbergh is seen here speaking at an America First rally in April 1941. The Japanese attack on Pearl Harbor, December 7, 1941, instantly ended the antiwar efforts of "America First"and others.

fifty thousand aircraft—what seemed a staggering number. On May 16, with France clearly in collapse, the president returned to Congress to request an additional $2.5 billion to expand the army and the navy. On May 31, Roosevelt introduced the Accelerated U.S. Defense Plan, along with a request for an additional $1.3 billion to enable the army and navy to meet expansion requirements.

More legislation followed. On June 22, 1940, Congress passed the National Defense Act, which was intended to generate $994 million annually, and to make room for anticipated wartime expenditures,

REALITY CHECK

Laying the Groundwork

Contrary to popular and enduring mythology, the Japanese attack on Pearl Harbor, December 7, 1941, did not catch the United States wholly unprepared. Indeed, thanks to FDR's persistent advocacy of rearmament and preparedness, the nation was thrust into World War II more adequately prepared than it had ever been for any war in its history.

Congress raised the national debt ceiling by what was then an astounding $4 billion, to $49 billion. The next month, on July 19 1940, the president signed the "Two-Ocean Navy Act" in order to fund adequate naval coverage of the Atlantic and the Pacific in anticipation of being faced with a two-front war, against Germany in the Atlantic and against Japan in the Pacific. Some $5.2 billion was appropriated to increase the size of the navy by 70 percent, including the construction of 201 new warships, among them seven new mammoth battleships, displacing fifty-five thousand tons each.

Also on June 20, the Burke-Wadsworth Bill was brought before Congress to reactivate the Selective Service System, which had drafted men into the army during World War I. Passed on September 16 as the Selective Training and Service Act of 1940, the law created the first peacetime draft in United States history, requiring men between the ages of twenty-one and thirty to register with local draft boards. Selection from among this pool of registered men was made by lottery, and each man drafted was obligated to serve for one year. The law specified that no more than nine hundred thousand men were to be in training at any one time, so that 1.2 million regular army soldiers and eight hundred thousand reservists would be available for service in any twelve-month period. By October 16, 1940, 16.4 million American men had registered, and early in the summer of 1941, the president asked Congress to extend the term of duty for the conscripts beyond twelve months. Passed by just a single vote in the House of Representatives (and by a wider margin in the Senate), the extension was controversial, provoking a number of draftees to threaten desertion. Very few made good on their threats.

Lend-Lease

On June 3, 1940, as the Dunkirk evacuation drew to a close, Prime Minister Churchill appealed to President Roosevelt for weapons and equipment to replace those abandoned in France. The president responded by immediately shipping to Britain vast quantities of obsolescent but still serviceable rifles, machine guns, field artillery pieces, and ammunition. Days later, on June 16, Congress passed the Pittman Act, authorizing the sale of munitions to any North or South American republic.

One of America's most momentous prewar moves came on September 3 1940, when FDR and Churchill agreed that the U.S. Navy would transfer fifty World War I–era destroyers to the British Royal Navy in exchange for ninety-nine-year leases on British naval and air stations in Antigua, the Bahamas, Bermuda, British Guiana, Jamaica, Newfoundland, St. Lucia, and Trinidad. The destroyers were obsolescent, but they were adequate to serve as escorts for the British Atlantic convoys that were otherwise easy prey for German U-boats (submarines).

The "Destroyers-for-Bases Deal" not only helped to ensure the survival of Britain's Atlantic lifeline, it was also the de facto end of U.S. neutrality. It was followed by another step toward an outright Anglo-American military alliance with the November 20 Stimson-Layton Agreement, in which U.S. secretary of war Henry Stimson and British minister of supply Sir Walter Layton agreed to standardize certain British and American weapons, thereby enabling their free exchange. Beyond this, the agreement pooled U.S. and British technical know-how, including weapons patents.

The acts of 1940 culminated in passage of "An Act to Promote the Defense of the United States," better known as the Lend-Lease Act, which FDR signed on March 11, 1941. Lend-lease came in response to Churchill's warning that Britain would soon be unable to purchase matériel from the United States on the cash-and-carry basis mandated by the U.S. neutrality law. The lend-lease legislation authorized the president to give aid to any nation whose defense he deemed critical to that of the United States. Beyond this, it empowered the government to accept payment "in kind or property, or any other direct or indirect benefit which the President deems satisfactory."

The Atlantic Charter

Lend-lease took the United States to the verge of a formal alliance with Britain. The next step came during August 9–12, 1941, when President Roosevelt and Prime Minister Churchill met aboard naval vessels of the United States and Great Britain in Placentia Bay, off the coast of Newfoundland. Here they drafted the Atlantic Charter, which set forth eight principles of American and British policy in war as well as peace.

NUMBERS

Uncle Sam Wants You

After the United States entered the war on December 8, 1941, a new selective service act expanded the liability for service to men between the ages of eighteen and forty-five and required all men between eighteen and sixty-five to register. The new law redefined the term of service as the duration of the war plus six months. Between 1940 and 1947 (the year in which the wartime selective service act expired, after a series of extensions by Congress), more than ten million men had been inducted into the armed forces.

DETAILS, DETAILS

Pittman Act Expanded

On September 26, the Pittman Act was expanded to authorize the U.S. Export-Import Bank to lend American republics up to $500 million and to permit these countries to acquire munitions up to a total value of $400 million for their defenses.

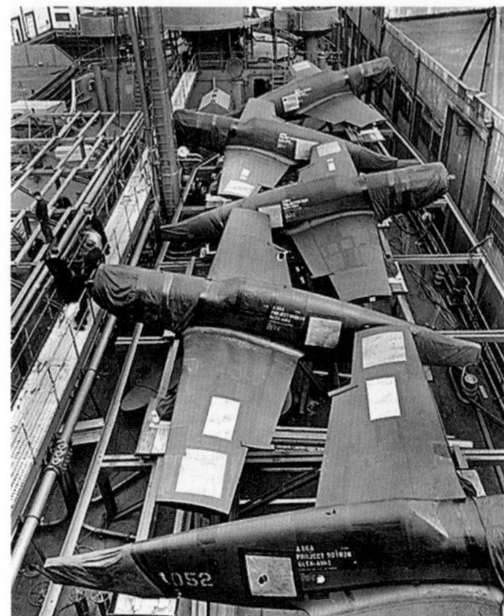

These U.S.-built fighter aircraft—partly dismantled for shipping—have been loaded aboard a cargo ship for transport to Britain as part of FDR's lend-lease program, which authorized the president to give military aid, free of cash payment, to any nation whose security he deemed vital to America's own. Lend-lease began before American entered World War II and continued throughout the war.

COURTING WAR

As early as October 3, 1939, with the Declaration of Panama, the United States created with twenty-one Latin American countries a three-hundred-mile "neutrality zone" in the waters of the Americas, which was declared to be off limits to all belligerents. The U.S. Navy assumed responsibility for patrolling these waters. Early in 1941, the so-called neutrality patrol was pushed farther out, to a distance of two thousand miles from the U.S. coast. In August of 1941, following the issuance of the Atlantic Charter, American naval vessels began escorting fast convoys partway to Britain. The navy provided cover in the sea-lanes of the western Atlantic, including the area adjacent to Iceland. By mid-September, navy ships were escorting convoys between Newfoundland's Grand Banks and Iceland. These escort operations provoked an undeclared naval war between the United States and Germany. On September 4, 1941, the destroyer USS *Greer* was attacked by a German submarine. On October 15, the USS *Kearny* was attacked, and on October 31, the *Reuben James* was sunk. The sinking prompted Congress, on November 17, 1941, to permit merchant vessels to be armed and to carry cargoes into belligerent ports.

"When you see a rattlesnake poised to strike you, you do not wait until he has struck before you crush him"

Franklin D. Roosevelt, September 11, 1941, in a speech justifying the undeclared naval war against Germany

NUMBERS

World Lender

By the time World War II ended, more than forty nations had participated in U.S. lend-lease programs, representing total American aid valued at $49.1 billion.

THE LONGEST BATTLE

AMERICA'S UNDECLARED NAVAL WAR in the western Atlantic was part of what historians of World War II call the Battle of the Atlantic, effectively the longest battle of the war, spanning all six years of the conflict, from 1939 to 1945. For the Allies, it was a struggle to defend the convoy routes, which were under unrelenting attack by German U-boats, and it was also an endeavor to maintain a full naval blockade of Axis Europe. Finally, for the United States in particular, the contest for control of the Atlantic had to be won in order to secure and maintain the ability to project military force overseas.

President Franklin D. Roosevelt (second from right, assisted by his son, Army Air Corps captain Elliot Roosevelt) poses with Prime Minister Winston Churchill aboard the USS Augusta *riding at anchor in Placentia Bay, Newfoundland, during the Atlantic Conference of August 1941. The conference produced the Atlantic Charter, a document amounting to an Anglo-American alliance months before the United States actually entered World War II.*

Of the three objectives of the Battle of the Atlantic, blockading Axis Europe was the most attainable. The Allied navies greatly outnumbered the combined German and Italian naval forces, and the Allied naval blockade proved effective so far as seaborne traffic was concerned. The European Axis had conquered so much of Europe, however, that it did not have to rely solely on the Atlantic for its sustenance. Much that came into Germany and Italy traveled overland.

Attaining the third objective, the ability to project military strength overseas, required the development of amphibious warfare tactics and equipment. These were not fully available until Operation Overlord, the "D-Day" invasion of Normandy in June 1944 (see Chapter 20). By this time, the Allies had come a long way in attaining the number one objective as well, securing the convoys against attack. However, that objective proved by far the most difficult. Although Germany's surface fleet was not large, the Kriegsmarine (the German navy) had an extensive and technologically advanced fleet of U-boats, which, in the hands of skilled and courageous commanders and crews, took a devastating toll on Allied shipping. Churchill rarely confessed to being afraid, but he freely confided to Roosevelt and to his own staff that the U-boat menace terrified him. It was a knife at Britain's throat.

> "The only thing that ever really frightened me during the war was the U-boat peril."
>
> *Winston Churchill*

During the first months of the war, the German navy operated against Allied shipping mainly with their surface fleet rather than submarines. They employed what the Allies called "pocket battleships"—which were smaller than conventional battleships, but often packed even greater firepower—and cruisers, also referred to

DETAILS, DETAILS

Q-Ships

The German navy also made use of what the Allies dubbed "Q-ships." These were merchant raiders, heavily armed warships disguised as civilian freighters, their guns hidden. Q-ships made a close approach to Allied merchant vessels, then suddenly opened fire.

DETAILS, DETAILS

Sound Sonar

Sonar uses reflected sound to detect submarines. During World War II, *active* sonar systems employed an acoustic projector to generate a sound wave into the water, which was reflected or echoed back by a target. The reflected sound waves were detected by a sonar receiver, which incorporated electronics that analyzed the signal to determine the range, bearing, and relative motion of the target. Passive sonar systems used only receiving sensors, which detected the noise of a submarine's engines, its rotating screw, or even the sound of its movement through the water. These sound waves were electronically analyzed for direction and distance.

as "surface raiders." These were supplemented by light, or auxiliary, cruisers. The fall of France and Norway in 1940 gave the Germans French and Norwegian bases from which they could launch submarines. From this point on, German operations in the Atlantic became chiefly a U-boat war, and whereas the surface raiders had randomly harassed British convoys, the U-boats operated more intensively with the object of strangling the island nation by cutting off all Atlantic communication and supply routes.

Early in the war, Admiral Karl Dönitz, Germany's principal U-boat tactician and advocate (he would eventually replace Erich Raeder as commander in chief of the entire navy), developed the Rudeltaktik, which the Allies called the "wolf pack." The destroyers and other ships that escorted convoys made it difficult for individual U-boats to attack and sink isolated ships. By massing several U-boats into a "wolf pack" and stealthily delaying the attack until the pack was assembled and in position, the submarines could overwhelm convoy escorts, effectively disrupting the defense of the transport ships. Typically, one submarine acted as the "shadower," making contact with a convoy, following ("shadowing") it, and continuously reporting its position to the other boats as they gathered into a pack. Combined with technological advances that gave U-boats greater and greater range, the wolf-pack tactics proved devastating.

Throughout the first months and years of the war, the Allies desperately sought to conduct more effective antisubmarine warfare. Fully practical sonar (Sound-Navigation and Ranging), enabling surface ships to detect submerged U-boats, did not become widely available until 1943. By this time, too, long-range bombers were increasingly used for anti-submarine patrol. Developments in radar technology greatly increased their effectiveness. These technological developments were supplemented by tactical improvements in the convoy system and in the use of escorts. As all of these means were developed, the tide began to turn against the U-boats, and the hunters became the hunted.

The Course of the Battle

The Battle of the Atlantic began on the very first day of the war, September 1, 1939, when U-boats sank the British passenger liner *Athena*. To chronicle all of the engagements of this six-year "battle" would require more than a single volume, but some of the major fights deserve attention here. The first British warship to be sunk on the Atlantic was HMS *Courageous* on September 14. That same day, the British sank their first U-boat. During September, Germany sent out two formidable surface raiders, the *Admiral Graf Spee* and *Deutschland*. In November, two more surface raiders, the mighty *Gneisenau* and *Scharnhorst*, followed.

On October 14, 1939, in a spectacular raid on the Royal Navy's "Home Fleet" harbor, Scapa Flow, off the northeastern coast of Scotland, a German U-boat skippered by Captain Günther Prien torpedoed and sank the British aircraft carrier HMS Royal Oak. *Prien (at the center of the conning tower) is pictured with some of his victorious crew as they return from the raid.*

On October 12, the Royal Navy suffered a stunning blow when German raiders sank the aircraft carrier *Royal Oak* while it was "safe" at Scapa Flow, the main home base of the British fleet. However, on December 13, 1939, off the coast of Uruguay in the South Atlantic, the British cruisers *Ajax*, *Exeter*, and *Achilles* trapped the *Admiral Graf Spee* in the battle of the River Plate, forcing the commander of the *Graf Spee* to scuttle his ship rather than let it be captured. It was, during these early days of the war, a rare triumph that was much relished by the Royal Navy and the British people.

In March 1940, the German surface raider *Atlantis* made its maiden voyage. Although far less celebrated than the great pocket battleships, the *Atlantis* would sink 145,697 tons of Allied shipping, more than any other surface raider, before it was itself sunk in November 1941 by HMS *Devonshire*. The British fleet enjoyed success during April 9–13, 1940, off the coast of Narvik, Norway, when the battleship *Warspite*, operating along with the destroyers *Hardy*, *Hotspur*, *Havock*, *Hunter*, and *Hostile*, fell upon a ten-ship German destroyer flotilla and either sank or forced the scuttling of all ten ships. On June 8, however, the British carrier *Glorious* and her two escorts were sunk by *Scharnhorst* and *Gneisenau*.

These sea duels between warships took place against the relentless background of attacks against convoys. One of the worst occurred on the night of October 17/18, 1940, dubbed by distraught Allies the "Night of the Long Knives." A wolf pack sunk twenty out of the thirty-four ships of Convoy SC 7. In January 1941, *Scharnhorst* and *Gneisenau* renewed their attacks on convoys, and in February a new tactic debuted, as the Germans launched the first combined air-surface-underwater convoy attack using aircraft, surface ships, and U-boats, which sank nine of the sixteen ships of convoy HG 53. On one terrible day, February 22, *Scharnhorst* and *Gneisenau* sank five British vessels. Amid this devastation, the Royal Navy achieved a great victory at the battle of Cape Matapan, off the Peloponnesian coast on March 27/28, 1941, sinking the Italian cruisers *Pola*, *Fiume*, and *Zara* as well as two destroyers. More than twenty-four hundred Italian sailors perished in this terrible blow against the Italian fleet, delivered without the loss of a single British ship or sailor.

Still, the convoy ships sank. In March, forty-three British ships were lost. The newly enacted American lend-lease policy promised to make up some of the losses, but the toll for April climbed to forty-five ships sunk. Then, in May, came another blow as the German pocket battleship *Bismarck* and its companion, the cruiser *Prinz Eugen*, sank the British battle cruiser *Hood* with the loss of virtually all hands. At forty-two thousand tons, *Bismarck* was the fastest and most powerful battleship in the German fleet. After the loss of the *Hood*, Prime Minister Churchill made sinking this symbol of the Nazi war machine a top priority. At ten-thirty on the morning of May 26, 1941, British aircraft sighted the elusive *Bismarck*, and the carrier HMS *Ark Royal* launched torpedo bombers. The air attack damaged *Bismarck*'s steering gear. Without the ability to maneuver, the pride of the German fleet was a sitting duck, and, on May 27, the battleships HMS *Rodney* and *King George V* opened fire on her. Reeling under the onslaught, *Bismarck* was in a hopeless situation when the cruiser *Dorchester* closed in with a torpedo attack. Out of a crew of 2,222 only 115 survived.

The 41,673-ton battleship Bismarck, *commissioned in August 1940, was the pride of the German High Seas Fleet. When she was launched,* Bismarck *was the most formidable battleship in the Atlantic, and on May 24, 1941, sunk HMS* Hood, *one of the Royal Navy's greatest battle cruisers. After this, Prime Minister Winston Churchill proclaimed the sinking of* Bismarck *the Royal Navy's number one priority, and on May 27, she was sunk—with the loss of all but 115 of her 2,222-man crew.*

The loss of *Bismarck* moved Adolf Hitler to command that the rest of the German surface fleet be recalled and confined to home waters. He did not think that German morale could sustain another such sinking. From this point forward, virtually all German actions in the Battle of the Atlantic were carried out by U-boat.

As mentioned, the United States joined the Battle of the Atlantic even before it formally entered World War II. In the months before Pearl Harbor, U.S. Navy destroyers escorted convoys through waters adjacent to the North American continent. Eager to avoid pushing America into the war, Admiral Dönitz ordered his U-boats to avoid attacking U.S. ships, but on September 4, 1941, U-boat U-652 attacked the USS *Greer*, and, on October 16, a U-boat sank the destroyer *Reuben James* with the loss of 115 American seamen. When Germany declared war on the United States on December 11, 1941, Dönitz instantly sent U-boats to patrol the waters off the American East Coast. This gave rise to Operation Drumbeat, beginning on January 13, 1942, an intensive U-boat campaign against Allied shipping in U.S. waters. Before the month was out, thirty-five ships had been sunk close to American shores.

The U-boats enjoyed great success in American waters, but American industry built transport ships faster than the U-boats could sink them. The Allies also became more aggressive and more adept at defending against attacks on convoys—as the battle of Barents Sea demonstrated on December 31, 1942. The Royal Navy cruisers *Jamaica* and *Sheffield* and the destroyers *Obdurate*, *Onslow*, and *Achates* attacked the German pocket battleship *Lützow*, the cruiser *Hipper*, and seven destroyers, sinking one destroyer and driving off the assault on a convoy—although the *Achates* was lost. In the end, the battered convoys got through, delivering weapons, ammunition, supplies, and, ultimately, American troops.

LIBERTY SHIPS

The Battle of the Atlantic was fought by brave men on both sides, but, in the last analysis, Allied victory was mostly a question of numbers. The Allies had to find a way to build transport ships faster than they were being sunk—and to replace lost crews.

In September 1940, before the United States entered the war, Britain ordered sixty transports from U.S. shipyards. British naval

REALITY CHECK

Sunk or Scuttled?

The *Bismarck* survivors claimed that the British had not sunk their ship, but that the captain had ordered it scuttled to prevent capture. The British Admiralty vigorously disputed this, but evidence from a 1989 salvage dive suggests that this was indeed the case.

REALITY CHECK

Lights On

The bright lights of America's East Coast cities vividly silhouetted Allied ships operating off the coast. As a result, U-boats, operating at night, often had very clear targets at which to aim. Despite insistent pleas and, later, laws, America's cities refused to adopt a blackout policy, even though this would have greatly reduced casualties among Allied shipping.

architects supplied the yards with a radically simple design intended to speed construction. The most important innovation was the use of welded rather than riveted plates. Welding took far less time than riveting, and although it produced a less durable ship, the designers realistically observed that very few vessels would survive the U-boat menace long enough to make durability an issue. Led by the U.S. industrialist Henry J. Kaiser, American shipyards adapted and modified the British plans, building vessels even more rapidly than the British had hoped possible. In January 1941, preparing for war, the United States launched a crash building program of its own, calling for two hundred ships dubbed the "Liberty Fleet." From this time on, the name "liberty ship" was used to describe these rough-and-ready transports, which were built with prefabricated subassemblies put together at shipyards on the west and east coasts. Sailors said that they were "built by the mile and chopped off by the yard." A total of 2,710 liberty ships were launched, and Kaiser competed with other shipyard owners to prove who could turn out liberty ships the fastest. The record was an astounding four days, 15.5 hours from the laying of the keel to launch.

Manning the liberty ships were officers and sailors of the U.S. Merchant Marine. The United States entered the war with 55,000 experienced civilian mariners. Special training programs increased this number to more than 215,000 before the war ended. The Merchant Marine suffered the highest rate of casualties of any service in World War II. The official toll was 1,554 U.S. merchant ships sunk by enemy attack; many more were damaged. About 8,300 Merchant Mariners were killed in battle, and another 12,000 wounded (of whom at least 1,100 died from their wounds). One of every twenty-six Merchant Mariners was killed in action.

Last Gasp

By 1943, Hitler began pouring all funding earmarked for the navy into the increased production of U-boats. Yet by spring of that year, Allied losses—although heavy—were clearly leveling off. In May, Dönitz avoided attacks on North Atlantic convoys because his U-boat losses had become catastrophic. Fighting continued elsewhere in the Atlantic, but some military historians believe that the Battle of the

Atlantic effectively ended with this withdrawal—not that anyone actually sailing the Atlantic would have accepted this interpretation. In September 1943, commandos of the Royal Navy attempted to plant special explosive mines—called "limpets"—to sink the battleship *Tirpitz*. They succeeded only in damaging the ship, which was finally sunk by RAF bombers in November 1944. On December 26, 1943, Royal Navy ships attacked the *Scharnhorst*, which was sunk with the loss of 1,927 sailors—all but thirty-six of the vessel's crew.

NUMBERS

The U-boat War in the Atlantic

Year	Allied Losses*	U-Boat Losses*	German Surface Ship Losses*
1939	755,392	421,156	61,337
1940	7,805,360	3,801,095	277,028
1941	4,921,792	3,111,051	205,966
1942	7,790,697	6,546,271	325,086
1943	3,220,137	1,189,833	7,040
1944	1,045,629	NA	NA
1945	438,821	NA	NA

* figures in tons

In terms of actual numbers of ships lost, the battle looks like this:

Year	Allied Losses to U-boats	U-boats Sunk
1939	50	9
1940	225	24
1941	288	35
1942	452	87
1943	203	237
1944	67	242
1945	30	151
Total	1,315	785

It is undeniable that the intensity of the Battle of the Atlantic diminished during 1944 and the opening months of 1945, and although fighting continued right up to the German surrender in May 1945, the role of the Atlantic fleets of the U.S. Navy and Royal Navy were largely refocused during and after June 1944 on supporting the D-Day invasion of France and the ongoing build-up of forces in Europe. After that invasion was well under way, most Allied ships in the Atlantic were assigned to continue escorting convoys—a mission that remained hazardous, but that became easier with each passing week as the U-boat fleet was worn away.

TAKEAWAY

The Atlantic Theater

The Battle of the Atlantic spanned the European phase of World War II and was mainly a contest between German U-boats and Allied supply convoys (and their escorts). The U.S. Navy pitched into this battle even before America officially declared war.

Part Three

INFAMY

On preceding pages: Sailors battle the flames on USS West Virginia, *a victim of the Japanese attack on Pearl Harbor, December 7, 1941. Although severely damaged by seven torpedo and two bomb hits, the* West Virginia *was refloated on May 17, 1942, and rejoined the fleet on September 14, 1944. Most of the major ships damaged and even sunk in the attack were eventually restored to service.*

CHAPTER 7

BARBAROSSA

Hitler Betrays His Ally

JOSEPH STALIN WAS ONE OF THE FOUNDING FATHERS OF SOVIET COMMUNISM and was heir to the mantle of Lenin himself, assuming absolute control of the Communist Party—and, by virtue of this, the Soviet state—in 1922, when Lenin fell seriously ill. In sharp contrast to Lenin, Stalin was far less a Marxist ideologue than he was a ruthless pragmatist. This meant that he was less interested in creating a purely Communist state than he was in ensuring the survival of the Soviet Union and his own total control of it. In Nazism he recognized the ideological antithesis of Communism, but in Adolf Hitler he saw a kindred spirit: a leader far more interested in power than in politics. He trusted that this would be a sufficient basis on which to conclude an agreement just short of an alliance, a non-aggression pact. It was a fatal error.

PARANOIA

STALIN'S NON-AGGRESSION PACT WITH HITLER was not unlike British prime minister Neville Chamberlain's efforts to appease the dictator. On the face of it, both of these moves were rational, pragmatic attempts to avoid war—or, at least, stave off war—but, in the end, there can be no rational bargain with the devil. That Stalin should have failed to realize this is surprising, because, by his very nature, he trusted no one. To be part of Stalin's political circle could bring great power, but it could just as easily bring sudden death. The dictator was infamous for promoting a subordinate one day and ordering his execution the next. He seemed to believe that he ruled over a den of assassins and was determined to wring all he could out of them, only to end their power—or even their lives—before they could turn against him.

> "When Stalin kissed me, he said in my ear, 'If you're a traitor, I'll kill you.'"
>
> *Politburo member Alexander Kosarev, remark after a Kremlin banquet, 1938*

With Joseph Stalin, paranoia was a matter of policy. Nowhere did this policy have graver consequences than in the case of the Red Army. During 1937 and 1938, Stalin conducted highly public mass purges of the Red Army officer corps. There was no objective evidence of disloyalty, let alone any overt military plot against him. Yet, in a series of show trials, Stalin subjected nearly half of his officer corps to prosecution, relief from command, and, in many cases, death by execution. By 1938, some 35,000 officers out of a total corps of 80,000 had been purged, including 3 of 5 marshals of the Soviet Union—the Red Army's most senior commanders. In addition, all 11 deputies of the Commissar for War—the top executives of the Soviet war ministry—were removed and/or killed. Of 85 corps commanders, 75 were "relieved," some by execution. Of 195 divisional commanders, 110 were removed—and, in many instances, subsequently executed.

No enemy could have been more destructive to the Red Army than Joseph Stalin. With so many of its senior commanders liquidated, this formidable force of some 5.37 million soldiers was largely leaderless and therefore vulnerable.

HITLER'S PLAN

WHEN OPERATION BARBAROSSA—the code name for the German invasion of the Soviet Union—was launched on June 22, 1941, Stalin was stunned into a state of paralysis and collapse. Yet as early as 1924, in his autobiographical political manifesto *Mein Kampf*, Hitler had openly called for the conquest of the Soviet Union, both to wipe out Communism and to acquire for Germany the *Lebensraum*—living space—that Hitler believed was the birthright of the German people. Operationally, Hitler ordered his generals to study the requirements of a Soviet invasion as early as the summer of 1940. There seems never to have been a question of whether or not to invade, but whether to strike primarily against Moscow or divide forces between north and south flanks. Always fancying himself a strategic genius, Hitler wanted his armies to wheel north and south from the center after breaking through Soviet defenses. German army brass thought it far more effective to hit Moscow first in a decapitating blow. On December 18, 1940, Hitler issued Directive No. 21, which outlined Operation Barbarossa, and on January 31, 1941, the army produced the Army High Command Deployment Directive, which detailed a "swift campaign" to crush the Soviet Union through offensive operations focused on the destruction of Red Army forces in the western part of the country. This was something of a compromise between Hitler's and the army's approaches. The objective was to defeat the Red Army west of the Dvina and Dnieper rivers, then capture the entire industrialized Donets basin, including Moscow.

DETAILS, DETAILS

Emperor Frederick I

Operation Barbarossa was named after the twelfth-century German king and Holy Roman emperor Frederick I—known as "Barbarossa"—who stood as a symbol of national conquest and unity to modern Germans.

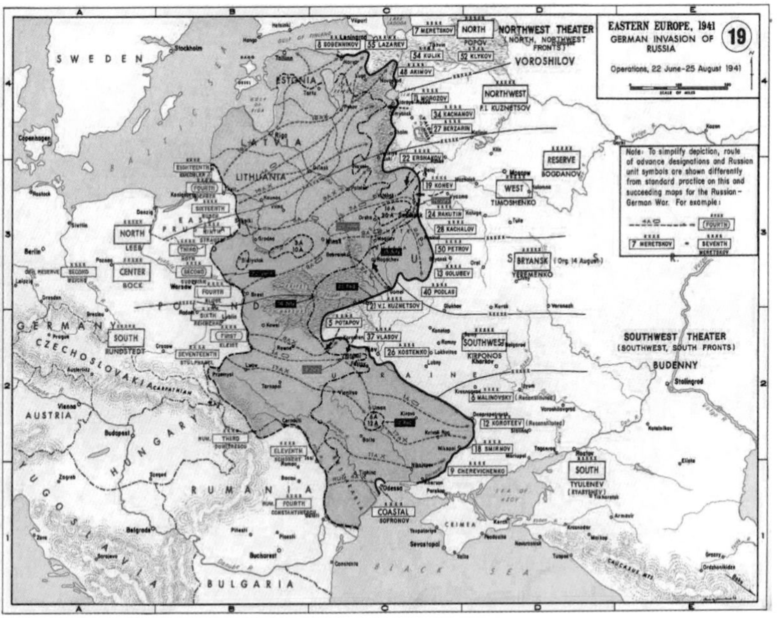

Operation Barbarossa. The dashed line at the left shows German positions on June 22, 1941. The solid line at the right represents the positions on August 25. The vast area between was devastated.

REALITY CHECK

Commissar Order

The invasion of the Soviet Union had military, political, and genocidal dimensions. The political dimension included the infamous Commissar Order (Kommissarbefehl), issued on June 6, 1941, about two weeks before the invasion, which was aimed at destroying Soviet Communism by physically liquidating all who transmitted the ideology of the Communist Party. The Red Army included a corps of commissars, whose function was to indoctrinate troops politically and ensure that the Communist Party always had direct control over the military. In violation of international law, the Commissar Order commanded that all commissars "captured during combat or while offering resistance . . . must on principle be shot immediately. . . . Protection granted to prisoners of war . . . will not apply to them. After having been segregated they are to be liquidated."

Invasion

On June 20, 1941, Hitler issued the single code word "Dortmund" (after the German city built by Emperor Barbarossa), authorizing the invasion in complete violation of the non-aggression pact he had concluded with Stalin. The two dictators had not clashed, and Hitler had given no hint that he intended to abrogate the pact. The invasion was an act of treachery, neither more nor less. It was launched across a broad 930-mile front between 3:00 and 3:30 A.M. on June 22 with a force of almost 3.6 million German and other Axis soldiers. A blitzkrieg operation, Barbarossa used thirty-six hundred tanks and more than twenty-seven hundred aircraft. It was, in fact, the largest invasion force in European military history.

The men and machines were organized into three army groups under Field Marshal Walther von Brauchitsch, commander in chief of the regular German army. He was a highly competent commander, but that is not the only reason Field Marshal Wilhelm Keitel, head of the German Armed Forces high command, had chosen him overall commander of the army. He knew that Brauchitsch was politically naïve and would raise no serious objections to whatever Adolf Hitler ordered. Walther von Brauchitsch said and did nothing when Hitler invaded Poland in September 1939, igniting World War II; yet, in November 1939, he did meet with him in an effort to talk him out of fighting a long war, telling him that he did not believe Germany could win a protracted conflict. Hitler turned on Brauchitsch, who emerged from the meeting thoroughly cowed. He swallowed his doubts and did a brilliant job of managing the logistics of the Battle of France. This earned from Hitler the baton of a field marshal, but it did not earn the Führer's respect. He made it his business to ignore all military advice Brauchitsch offered, including a wrenching plea to lift the order halting the panzer advance against Dunkirk (see Chapter 4).

Brauchitsch had been appalled by Hitler's error at Dunkirk, but he could not deny that victory over France had been swift and total. He managed to convince himself that victory over the Soviet Union would also be rapid and complete—just as Hitler said it would be. Besides, Brauchitsch knew that he had superb commanders at the head of each of his army groups. The North Army Group was commanded by Field Marshal Wilhelm von Leeb. A distinguished commander in World War I, Leeb was the outstanding theorist of

...NOR A BORROWER BE

Like many senior officers in the regular army, Brauchitsch cordially despised the Nazi Party and was appalled by Hitler's naked aggression. The Führer had the proverbial ace up his sleeve, however, which made Brauchitsch's reservations irrelevant and enabled Hitler to ensure that the army and its top commander would be answerable directly to him.

Before the war, Brauchitsch had wanted a divorce in order to remarry. As for his wife, she was willing to give him a divorce—for a price, which the general could not meet. Adolf Hitler was more than happy to help. He loaned Brauchitsch eighty thousand deutschemarks, a sum that forever bound Brauchitsch to the Führer. When Hitler presented him with his plans for the Anschluss, the invasion and annexation of Austria, Brauchitsch voiced objections, but offered no resistance. Shortly after this, in 1938, as Hitler pressed for the annexation of Czechoslovakia, General Ludwig Beck appealed to Brauchitsch to arrest Hitler's headlong rush to war by using his influence to persuade the entire General Staff to resign. Brauchitsch figuratively threw up his hands and replied that he would simply let events take their course. In September 1938, a number of officers asked Brauchitsch to take charge of a military coup against Hitler. He replied with his customary passivity, declining to participate, but pledging that he would not stop anyone else from acting.

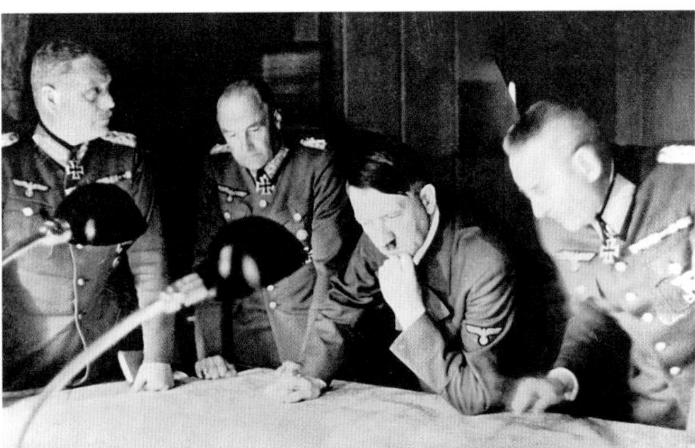

Adolf Hitler monitors the invasion of the Soviet Union at his headquarters in Rastenberg, June 1941. At the far left is the German army chief of staff, Wilhelm Keitel. Beside him is General Walther von Brauchitsch. To Hitler's left is General Franz Halder.

defensive warfare. He was a committed opponent of Hitler and the Nazi regime and was for this reason forced into retirement in January 1938, but was soon recalled to command the Twelfth Army in the occupation of the Czech Sudetenland. When this crisis passed, he returned to retirement, but was again recalled to fight in the Battle of France. He opposed the western invasion, arguing that to violate Belgian neutrality for the second time in the century would turn the entire world against Germany. So strongly did he

NUMBERS

Upping the Troops

During the ten days following the start of the invasion, the Soviets mobilized an additional five million men.

REALITY CHECK

Stalin as Savior

Like the other dictators of the World War II era, Stalin developed about himself a cult of personality. This cult intensified during the Soviet struggle against the invasion, and masses of Soviet people looked to Stalin as their savior. There is no question that he did emerge as a highly effective wartime leader; however, Stalin did not succeed in totally unifying the ethnically and nationally diverse Soviet Union in opposition to the Germans. In some areas, thousands voluntarily enlisted in special German military units, including the infamous SS, to aid in the invasion. Their purpose was to gain independence from Stalin and the USSR.

feel about this that, in contrast to Brauchitsch, he threw his active support behind General Franz Halder's proposed coup d'etat against Hitler in 1939. But when the coup came to nothing, Leeb led Army Group C against France, earning a promotion to field marshal in July 1940.

Army Group Center was to be led by Field Marshal Fedor von Bock. Like Leeb, he had served well in World War I, and although he was not opposed to Hitler, he was thoroughly shocked by the criminal brutality of the SS against the Jews during the invasion of Poland (see Chapter 8). This did not move him to lodge any official protest, however, and he went on to fight in France, earning promotion to field marshal. Finally, Army Group South was under the command of Field Marshal Gerd von Rundstedt, who had been instrumental in the covert rearmament of Germany after World War I.

Opposing the Germans were all the Red Army formations available in the west—140 divisions and forty brigades, about 2.9 million men, with perhaps fifteen thousand tanks and eight thousand aircraft. The troops were often poorly trained and, thanks to Stalin's purges, inadequately led. The tanks and aircraft, though numerous, were mostly obsolescent and far inferior to the German equipment.

Hitler wanted to do to the Soviets what he had done to the Poles and the French: overwhelm and crush them with a devastating blitzkrieg. Added to this was the outright motive of genocide. As the invaders encountered them, Jews (see Chapter 8) were to be murdered, along with local Soviet political leaders. This was total warfare—war against soldiers, war against civilians. In the opening hours of the invasion, German bombers demolished sixty-six Soviet airfields, destroying huge numbers of aircraft on the ground. Simultaneously, bombers struck the cities of Kovno (present-day Kaunas), Minsk, Rovno (Rivne), Odessa, and Sevastopol as well as Libava (Liepaja), the principal Soviet naval base on the Baltic.

During the opening days and weeks of the invasion, the German army and air forces rolled over the Soviet defenders, consuming them. Stalin seemed dazed and unable to act—at least at first. His naïve trust of the non-aggression pact and his paranoid purges of the Red Army High Command had brought disaster. Yet, somehow, Stalin found a deep reserve of strength within himself and proved to be an effective and inspiring leader, who rallied the civilian population and the military to make great sacrifices in resisting the invaders. In a radio broadcast of July 3, he defined the struggle against the invaders as a "great patriotic war" and called for boundless sacrifice, including a scorched-earth policy and partisan resistance behind the rapidly moving German lines. He even ended official Soviet opposition to the Russian Orthodox Church—which had been effectively forced underground by the Communist regime—and enlisted the aid of priests to rally the people.

Hitler paid little attention to Stalin's attempts to organize the defense of his nation. If the Soviets wanted to fight to the death, let them. Hitler believed that the Russian Slavs, like the Jews, were an inferior race that deserved either enslavement or death. Intoxicated with the speed of the invasion's opening weeks, Hitler began planning a victory parade through Moscow for the end of August. After the parade, he planned to level Moscow as well as Leningrad (today St. Petersburg) and to kill or forcibly resettle the residents of these cities. Ultimately, he planned to move some thirty million Russians to the east in order to make room for German and Germanic peoples. Here would be plenty of *Lebensraum*, as vast tracts of the Soviet Union would become permanent additions to the Third Reich—the German state.

Hitler and his generals underestimated the determination and the capability of the Red Army. Like other invaders before them—most notably Napoleon—they also underestimated the effect of the Russian land itself. Both sides employed a scorched-earth policy. The invaders destroyed everything they saw, their purpose to deprive Soviet troops and civilians of every source of sustenance. But, in obedience to Stalin, the Soviets themselves burned their own crops and villages in order to prevent the invaders from living off the land. This situation became increasingly critical as German supply lines stretched thin across the Russian vastness, and Red Army forces repeatedly attacked those fragile lines of supply and communication.

Initially overrun and overwhelmingly defeated, the Soviet army exhibited an extraordinary capacity for absorbing loss. The troops retreated, rallied, retreated, and rallied again. Although Hitler's forces penetrated more and more deeply into Russia, the Red Army refused simply to melt away. The invader began to suspect that *he* was being swallowed up by the land itself.

"We have only to kick in the door and the whole rotten structure will come crashing down."

Adolf Hitler to General Alfred Jodl, just before the Soviet invasion

Before the onset of winter, the invasion of the Soviet Union was marked by the high-speed advance of heavy armor supported from the air and backed up by infantry. These German tanks charge past a burning village on the Eastern Front.

Despite spectacular German successes at the early major battles of Bialystok and Minsk (June 22–mid July) and Smolensk (July 10–19), it became increasingly apparent to German field commanders that they had underrated the Red Army, especially its sheer will to resist. German commanders almost always outgeneraled their Soviet counterparts, forcing the Red Army to withdraw. But then, apparently undeterred, the Soviets repeatedly regrouped and resumed the fight. Worse for the Germans, the Red Army never fell back on an exclusively defensive mode. Battered—like a boxer down for the count—the army shook it off and counterattacked. To be sure, such tactics were costly to the Red Army, but they were costly as well to the Germans, whose vision of a quick conquest began to fade.

"It is hardly too much to say that the campaign against Russia has been won in fourteen days."

General Franz Halder, diary entry for July 7, 1941

The army plan had been to wipe out Soviet industrial capacity, which would deprive the Red Army of the weapons of war. Stalin, however, had ordered the mass evacuation of Soviet industry far to the east. It was a miraculous exodus that preserved the nation's ability to turn out tanks and planes at an astounding pace. The first weeks of the invasion had brought massive destruction of matériel—but most of the tanks and planes that had been destroyed were obsolescent or obsolete. Now Soviet industry was turning out aircraft and tanks—including the T-34, which historians generally agree was the finest tank of World War II—of a quality that stunned the Germans.

Operation Barbarossa called for the lightning occupation of both Leningrad and Moscow, as well as the destruction of the entire industrial Donets basin. The Red Army would succeed in depriving the invaders of all three of these objectives, but at a cost that to this day has never been accurately calculated.

Hitler Falters

In the summer of 1941, the German army achieved a great victory at the battle of Smolensk, killing or capturing more than one hundred thousand Soviet troops. This accomplished, Hitler suddenly decided to divert his armies from direct assaults on Moscow and Leningrad, ordering them instead to concentrate in the south on the invasion of the Ukraine and, in the north, on seizing the industrial and mining region outside of Leningrad. This shifted the momentum of the invasion from the center to its wings, a change that proved disastrous. German Army Group Center, poised offensively to take Moscow, was now forced to assume the defensive because of the diversion of resources north and south. The Soviets were thus given a rare gift: time—time to organize counterattacks and to develop stronger defensive positions. Hitler closed his eyes to this because, in the south, the Ukraine was indeed overrun. By the end of September, Kiev was encircled. Feeling triumphant, Hitler ignored the problems developing at the center of the German invasion. He was conquering the Ukraine!

Emboldened by what amounted to a local success, Hitler mistakenly concluded that the Soviet army was on the ropes, that it had (in the military parlance of the times) been "bled white." He believed he could now capture Moscow—and do so before the onset of winter.

Launched late in September, the advance on Moscow by a depleted Army Group Center made early progress, defeating no fewer than eight Soviet armies. The fall of the capital seemed inevitable, but then the Red Army dug in and seemed to draw on an inexhaustible reservoir of reinforcements. The German advance was stalled. Then came heavy autumn rains, which churned the battlefield into a quagmire, preventing the passage of vehicles, including tanks, and thereby defeating the blitzkrieg. In the most literal sense, the advance against Moscow bogged down—within sight of the Kremlin's onion-shaped domes.

Stalin made the defense of Moscow a national crusade. With great drama, he proclaimed the capital a fortress, and although much of the government withdrew from the city, he refused his own evacuation—although a special train stood ready at the station. Playing to the hilt the role of the war leader, Stalin personally rallied soldiers as well as civilians to Moscow's defense. In November, the Germans mounted an all-out assault that brought them to within eighteen miles of the Kremlin, but the advance again stalled, and, by the beginning of December, the panzers had broken off the attack.

REALITY CHECK

Nazism vs. Communism

Americans watched the struggle between the people of Hitler and the people of Stalin with mixed emotions. Many American intellectuals were Left-leaning and saw the fight as a desperate contest between evil Fascism and progressive Communism. The response of the more typical American man-on-the-street, however, was probably closer to what Harry S. Truman, at the time a Missouri senator, told the *New York Times* on July 24, 1941: "If we see that Germany is winning the war, we ought to help Russia, and if Russia is winning we ought to help Germany; and in that way let them kill as many as possible." As most Americans saw it, both Nazism and Communism were totalitarian tyrannies, and neither was good for democracy.

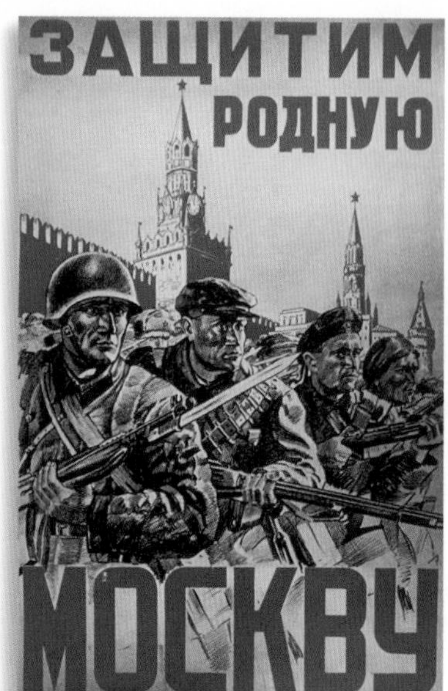

"Defend our beloved Moscow from German attack," this Soviet poster of 1941 implores Russian citizens.

The Tide Turns

After the failure of the assault on Moscow, German commanders looked for comfort in the hope that the Red Army was as exhausted as their own forces. In their arrogance, the Germans had not prepared for a winter war; they did not expect the invasion to require that much time. The idea now was to withdraw and regroup for a fresh assault in the spring. The Soviets well knew, however, that winter was their great ally, and, to prevent a German withdrawal, the Red Army launched a massive counterattack on December 5–6 that penetrated and shredded German lines already stretched thin.

The German generals frantically sought Hitler's permission to give ground in an effort to preserve their forces. The Führer refused. Some commanders objected. They were summarily relieved, and, seeking to stave off a defection within the military, Adolf Hitler assumed personal command of the invasion forces on December 19, 1941. The Soviets could not have hoped for a more favorable development. By the end of December, the Red Army had defeated, once and for all, the German assault on Moscow. Operation Barbarossa had failed and, with it, the compelling myth of German invincibility dissolved.

NUMBERS

German and Russian Troop Losses

By January 31, 1942, the German army had lost approximately 918,000 men killed, wounded, or captured in the invasion of the Soviet Union. This represented 28.7 percent of the invasion force. The German military as a whole would never recover. Red Army losses were 3.35 million killed, wounded, or captured. Yet that army would fight on.

Stalingrad

Hitler's decision to concentrate the invasion in the north and south rather than the center cost him more than Moscow. Shifting the momentum put the southern city of Stalingrad in the crosshairs. An important industrial center, Stalingrad was also significant—for both dictators—because of its very name. Just as Hitler wanted to seize the place named for Stalin, Stalin was determined that the city would not fall.

The Battle of Stalingrad was an epic spanning July 17, 1942 to February 2, 1943. In the initial German attack on the seventeenth, Field Marshal Fedor von Bock led Army Group B against the city as, on his south, Army Group A attacked the precious oil fields of the Caucasus. Bock's left wing reached the Don River at Voronezh on July 1 but proved unable to hold that town. Hitler ordered Bock's relief by Field Marshal Maximilian von Weichs on July 13. In the meantime, Hermann Hoth's Fourth Panzer Army made a spectacular one-hundred-mile run to the Don, then wheeled southeast to push on between the Donets and the Don rivers in support of General Paul von Kleist's First Panzer Army, which crossed the lower Don River en route to the Caucasus oil fields. Coordinated with these movements was the advance of Friedrich von Paulus's Sixth Army east from the Don toward Stalingrad, on the west bank of the Volga. All of these movements positioned German forces at the western rim of Stalingrad by August 24. In the city, the Sixty-second Red Army, stiffened by thousands of local civilian volunteers, mounted a tenacious urban warfare defense. They fought the Germans block by block, street by street, and house by house. The German Sixth Army fought through, reaching central Stalingrad on September 22, but having suffered severe casualties. As for the city, it was a city in name only, ceaseless artillery fire having reduced it to rubble. Even as a ruin, however, Stalingrad had value, and the Soviets were determined to make it the place of Paulus's destruction.

Georgi Zhukov, the Red Army's most capable general, reinforced the Stalingrad garrison in a bid to keep the Germans from crossing the Volga. As he held the Germans, Zhukov built up his forces north and south of the city. Then, with the German Sixth Army in Stalingrad, and the city itself between the jaws of the great Red Army pincer, Zhukov ordered a counterattack under Konstantin Rokossovski. On November 19, Rokossovski descended from the north, crossing the Don with his tanks on November 21 and breaching the German lines there. Into this gap General Nikolai Vatutin led his forces, which routed three armies allied with the Germans: the Third Romanian, Eighth Italian, and Second Hungarian. Panzer Corps H counterattacked but was beaten off.

As this pitched battle raged north of the city, General Andrei Yeremenko came up from the south on November 20 and, during the course of the next five days, defeated the Romanian Fourth Army. This allowed him to link up with Rokossovski west of the city, thereby completing the envelopment of the German Sixth Army. Its situation hopeless, Paulus asked Hitler for permission to withdraw in order to save what he could. The Führer refused to allow it, and, on November 23, Paulus and his men were totally cut

MEDICAL ISSUES

Dying of Thirst in the Snow

Cut off from supplies, the men of the German Sixth Army starved. Horses were slaughtered; strands of the stringy meat made a watery soup. A ration box of potatoes weighing about two pounds was divided among every fifteen men. The bread ration—one pound a day at the siege's start—fell to under three ounces by the first week in January. As fuel supplies dwindled, so did fires for warmth, cooking, and for melting snow to produce drinking water. The result was widespread dehydration. While men starved and literally froze, lice and flies flourished. Rats survived and multiplied. During one Soviet counterattack, many German tanks could not be started because infesting rats had chewed through cables. Those who survived often succumbed to other diseases endemic to the Stalingrad siege, including dysentery, typhus, diphtheria, tuberculosis, and jaundice. The latter, often treatable, became a nearly coveted fate, since diagnosis resulted in a stint in the relative warmth of a field hospital.

Red Army soldiers fight in the streets of Stalingrad, October 1942. Both Hitler and Stalin saw Stalingrad as the make-or-break battle of the Russian Front. In the end, Stalingrad was devastated, but the entire German Sixth Army was killed or captured, and the German victory in Russia was transformed into a long, catastrophic defeat.

off within the rubble of Stalingrad. Hermann Göring, head of the Luftwaffe, promised that he would airlift three hundred tons of supplies daily, but severe weather and vigorous Soviet antiaircraft defenses kept his planes on the ground. The isolated German army starved and froze.

Belatedly waking to the reality of the crisis, Hitler ordered Erich von Manstein to lead Army Group Don to break through the Soviet envelopment and relieve the Sixth Army. Starting from sixty miles southwest of Stalingrad, Manstein's subordinate, Hoth, led the Fourth Panzer Army as the vanguard of Army Group Don's counterattack beginning on December 12. Hoth came within thirty miles of Paulus's besieged Sixth Army by December 21, but was met with overwhelming Red Army resistance and broke off his attack, withdrawing altogether on December 23. Paulus was on his own.

The Red Army commanders issued a surrender demand on January 8, 1943. By this time, Paulus had lost 300,000 men, 2,000 tanks, and 4,000 artillery pieces. None of this mattered to Hitler, who refused permission for the surrender. In response, on January 10, the Soviets let loose a massive artillery attack, then charged in from three sides. On January 16, the last German airfield was captured, and on the twenty-fourth, the Soviets issued another demand for surrender. Hitler shot back: Paulus was to fight to the last man.

But even the Führer's orders no longer meant much. Part of the Sixth Army surrendered on January 31; the rest followed two days later. By this time, there were only ninety-one thousand survivors.

TAKEAWAY

Red Winter

Like Napoleon before him, Adolf Hitler grossly underestimated the task of conquering Russia. After making early spectacular inroads into the vast nation, his armies (like those of the earlier would-be conqueror) were swallowed up—both by the opposing Red Army and by the land itself, the unspeakably harsh Russian winter proving to be the invader's most terrible enemy.

Catastrophe and Triumph

The Battle of Stalingrad was a catastrophe for the German army—although, horrific as it was, it could have been yet worse. The long delay in surrender had tied down so many Red Army troops that Kleist was able to withdraw from the Caucasus, thereby saving Army Group A from annihilation. But the German invasion of the Soviet Union had definitively failed, and from this point on, it was the Germans who were forced to assume the defense, as they fought their way *out* of Soviet territory, into eastern Europe, and, ultimately, through eastern Germany to the very gates of Berlin.

CHAPTER 8

HOLOCAUST

An Empire of Death

THE GERMAN INVASION OF THE SOVIET UNION brought war to an unprecedented level of destruction and terror. It also introduced a ghastly new dimension to war. "Total war" had been defined by the German military theorist Carl von Clausewitz in 1830 as war directed not only against an enemy army but also against the enemy civilian population. Virtually every major German operation was an example of total war, but the Soviet invasion particularly targeted for death the Soviet commissars, Gypsies, and—above all—Jews. Members of these groups were not simply killed when the invading soldiers encountered them, they were murdered systematically. Approximately three thousand men of special SS units called Einsatzgruppen (deployment groups) followed just behind the lead troops of the invasion force. Their assigned mission was to round up and murder individuals in the targeted groups, Jews especially. Wherever feasible, the Einsatzgruppen secured the cooperation of local police and local anti-Semitic activists to aid in accomplishing their mission.

The work of the Einsatzgruppen extended to eastern Poland, Lithuania, Latvia, and Estonia, as well as western Russia. It was the first manifestation of the "Final Solution" to what the Nazi leadership called the "Jewish question." It was the start of the major phase of the Holocaust.

"If, at the beginning of [World War I] and during the war, twelve or fifteen thousand of these Hebrew corrupters of the people had been held under poison gas, as happened to hundreds of thousands of our best German brothers in the field, the sacrifice of millions at the front would not have been in vain."

Adolf Hitler, Mein Kampf, *1924*

NEW MEANING FOR AN ANCIENT WORD

HOLOCAUST DERIVES FROM THE GREEK WORD *holokauston,* which is, in turn, a translation from the Hebrew *olah*, meaning "burnt sacrifice." It is an ancient word resurrected by historians and survivors to describe a horror of World War II unparalleled in history and for which no truly adequate word could be found. Indeed, since the origin of *holocaust,* in the word for burnt sacrifice, puts the emphasis on the ultimate fate that befell most victims—mass cremation—some modern scholars use the Hebrew word *shoah*, meaning "catastrophic upheaval."

While the events surrounding Hitler's programs of genocide required a new language, the foundation of the Holocaust was not new. Anti-Semitism and the scapegoating of Jews for a host of economic and other problems had been routine features of European and

During the invasion of the Ukraine, a member of an SS Einsatzgruppe prepares to murder a Jew in Vinnitsa. The mass grave was dug by the victims who already lie in it. The murderers forced their victims to kneel at the edge of the grave, so that they would fall into it when they were shot. Waffen-SS troops and soldiers of the Reich Labor Service look on passively. Most likely, the photograph was taken by another Einsatzgruppe member, perhaps as documentation of the mission, but more likely as a souvenir.

German life since at least the Dark Ages. In *Mein Kampf*, Adolf Hitler voiced his own condemnation of the Jews, equating them with Bolshevism (Communism) and an international conspiracy to destroy what he called the German race. As Nazi Party doctrine developed, the familiar themes of anti-Semitism became a political and cultural crusade. When the Nazi Party gained control of the government of Germany, anti-Semitism figured in virtually every law, government activity, and administrative policy.

NUMBERS

Babi Yar

The most infamous of the Einsatzgruppen massacres during the Soviet invasion occurred at Babi Yar, near Kiev, Ukraine, where, on September 29–30, 1941, 33,771 Jews were executed at a ravine. In all, historians believe that Einsatzgruppen personnel killed more than one million people, mostly Jews, during a six-month period in the Soviet Union, eastern Poland, Lithuania, Latvia, and Estonia, all by shooting.

THE JEWISH QUESTION

HITLER DID NOT RISE TO POWER advocating the extermination of the Jews. Initially, he and the Nazi Party called for merely "purging" Jews from what they termed "German" life. Hitler did not define "Jewishness" as chiefly a matter of religion, but of "blood" or "race." He and his followers also purposely confounded "Jewishness" with Marxism and Bolshevism/Communism, as if they were all one and the same. Thus, Jews were depicted as a biological menace—a racial pollution—as well as enemies of German culture, economics, and government. In parallel with his racial depiction of the Jews, Hitler created a mythology of German racial purity by conflating German nationalism with the doctrine of "Aryanism" (see Chapter 2, "The Rise of Adolf Hitler"), the idea that Germany was the inheritor of an ancient heritage of racial superiority and purity. In short, the German birthright was to be the "master race," but the Jews posed a continual threat to that birthright.

Russian-born Helena Blavatsky—better known as Madame Blavatsky—started the Theosophic movement in the late nineteenth century. Soon after, Theosophy took root in the United States and in Europe, especially in Germany, where Blavatsky's racial theories—including her assertion that the Aryans were the "root race" of modern humanity—found many enthusiastic adherents. Blavatsky's writings on race probably influenced Adolf Hitler as well as Alfred Rosenberg, chief racial ideologist of the Nazi Party, bolstering Nazi claims to German racial superiority and Jewish and Slavic "racial" inferiority.

Having developed the mythology of German racial purity and Jewish racial pollution, Hitler pledged to the German people that he would free the nation of Jews and Jewish influence. In conjunction with this pledge, he posed to the German people what he called the "Jewish Question" (Judenfrage), which was *What was to be done to make Germany "Jew-free" (Judenrein)?*

One of the first answers, beginning in 1933, was a kind of internal exile, by which the Jews of rural Germany were driven out of their villages and small towns and left to find new homes either in the larger German cities or outside of Germany altogether. The policy of internal exile overlapped the encouragement of voluntary

NUMBERS

Forced Emigration

Between 1933 and 1938, more than 50 percent of Germany's 500,000 Jewish citizens voluntarily emigrated, despite the staggering economic losses involved. Of this number, some 100,000 settled in the United States, 63,000 in Argentina, 52,000 in Great Britain, and 33,000 in Palestine, which, shortly after the war, became the state of Israel.

emigration abroad. Officially, the policy of the Third Reich from 1933 to 1939 was to encourage—but not require—the departure of the Jews. The catch was that, although the emigration was voluntary, new German laws barred Jews from leaving the country with their property (including financial proceeds from the sale of homes and businesses) and with most of their money. Virtually everything belonging to the émigré was confiscated by the government. Jewish emigration therefore became a profitable growth industry for the German state during the 1930s.

Crystal Night

About half of Germany's Jews accepted voluntary emigration, willingly sacrificing livelihood and property because, increasingly, they were persecuted at home. Both unofficially and officially, the Reich fostered and supported programs of organized discrimination and persecution, including many economic restrictions and almost total exclusion from all professions (especially teaching positions). The first phase of organized persecution culminated in Crystal Night (Kristallnacht) during November 9/10, 1938.

Jewish shop owners in Berlin survey the wreckage of Kristallnacht, the government-sanctioned "spontaneous" anti-Jewish riots that marked the beginning of the program of persecution that culminated in the "Final Solution" and the Holocaust.

The "Night of Broken Glass," as it was also known, was a nationwide pogrom, a collective act of anti-Semitic terrorism both instigated and led by Nazis. During this night, more than one thousand synagogues were burned and some seventy-five hundred Jewish businesses were looted, their windows smashed. It is known for certain that ninety-one Jews fell victim to mob violence during Crystal Night, and more died over the next two days. Jewish homes, hospitals, schools, and even cemeteries were vandalized. The spasm of national violence was touched off by the November 7 shooting, in Paris, of German diplomat Ernst von Rath by Herschel Grynszpan, a Jewish student from Poland. Hitler and his minister of propaganda, Joseph Goebbels, seized on the incident as an excuse for mass reprisal. Goebbels secretly called on the storm troopers—the SA—to organize violent "spontaneous demonstrations," and Gestapo chief Heinrich Müller broadcast telegrams to police officials throughout the Reich, not only telling them that the "spontaneous" demonstrations were about to begin but also warning them not to interfere—except, of course, to arrest Jews.

In the wake of Crystal Night, some thirty thousand Jews were arrested and sent to concentration camps, which had been built to house political prisoners and other "undesirables." Government officials also acted to seize any insurance settlements that Jewish victims obtained as a result of the vandalism committed against them. Government officials fined the Jewish community approximately one billion Reichsmarks, assessed to defray the cost of cleaning up after the riots—even though the Jewish victims were themselves forced to do the cleaning.

DETAILS, DETAILS

Kristallnacht

The name "Crystal Night" was a cruelly ironic reference to the vast amount of broken glass after rioters smashed the windows of synagogues, Jewish businesses, and Jewish homes. It was typical of the Nazi propaganda machine to put a poetic name to the most brutal of actions.

The Nuremberg Laws

As mentioned, Nazi anti-Semitism was not religious persecution, but virulent racism. Even if a Jew converted to Christianity, he or she was still—"racially"—a Jew. On September 15, 1935, the Reichstag (German parliament) enacted the first of several laws collectively known as the "Nuremberg Laws" or, in full, the "Nuremberg Laws on Citizenship and Race." The first major law, called the "Law for the Protection of German Blood and German Honor," barred marriages (and extramarital sexual intercourse) between Jews and Germans. Additionally, German females under forty-five years of age were prohibited from working in Jewish households. The second major law, the Reich Citizenship Law, stripped Jews of German citizenship by creating a distinction between "Reich citizens" and "Reich nationals"—the Jewish Germans to be included in the latter category. Subsequent laws provided a complex definition of what constituted "Jewish blood"; essentially, anyone with at least one Jewish grandparent was defined as a Jew—regardless of religious belief or cultural practice.

Toward the Final Solution

After the Anschluss, the German annexation of Austria in 1938, the German government created the Central Office for Jewish Emigration, which was headed by an SS officer named Adolf Eichmann. He was soon transferred to the leadership of a newly created SS agency, the Race and Resettlement Office, and assigned to create more efficient answers to the Jewish question. In 1941, Eichmann coined a new term for his answer, "Endlösung," the "Final Solution."

The Final Solution, mass murder, was neither openly nor officially discussed before the war began. No one even knows if it was actually contemplated before 1939. It is true that, between 1933 and 1938, several thousands of German citizens were murdered in concentration camps. Most of these victims were not Jews, but opponents of the Nazi regime. That some were Jewish had nothing to do with their dire fate. As for the camps, such facilities had been established as early as 1933 to hold those who posed a threat to Hitler's power. The first places of confinement were little more than improvised basements and cellars, but by March 1933, the

ADOLF EICHMANN

Like virtually all other prominent Nazis, including those who perpetrated the most monstrous acts, Adolf Eichmann was hardly a man of extraordinary background or abilities.

He had been born in Solingen, Germany, but grew up in Linz, Austria, and aspired to become an engineer. Failing his engineering course work, he found work as a common laborer in his father's modest mining enterprise, then moved on to become a salesman for an Austrian electrical contractor. From 1927 to 1933 he was a traveling salesman for the Vacuum Oil Company. He joined the Austrian Nazi Party on April 1, 1932, and when he lost his sales job in July 1933, he emigrated to Bavaria, where he killed time with involvement in a paramilitary political organization called the "Austrian Legion." This made him attractive enough to Heinrich Himmler, chief of the SS, to earn him an appointment to the Sicherheitsdienst (SD), the Nazi security and intelligence service, in which Himmler assigned him to investigate "Jewish questions." Eichmann responded with great enthusiasm, learned basic Hebrew and Yiddish, and even traveled to Palestine in 1937 to investigate the Zionist movement. Thus an ordinary man, distinguished only by the thoroughness of his mediocrity, began to drift into the profession of mass murderer. It was, in fact, a typical Nazi résumé.

A failed engineer and mechanic, Adolf Eichmann became a clerk and a machine oil salesman before joining the Nazi Party and, subsequently, the SS. In these organizations, he discovered his talent for bureaucratic organization and logistics, which, under orders from Reinhard Heydrich, he applied to the mass murder of six million Jews in the Holocaust.

storm troopers (SA) built camps at Nohra in Thuringia, and in Oranienburg, Prussia. At about this time, the SS, in concert with the Bavarian Political Police, built Dachau in southern Germany, usually considered the first concentration camp of the Nazi regime.

Before the end of 1933, Sonnenburg, Lichtenburg, Börgermoor, Esterwegen, and Brandenburg, all in Prussia, were added to the list of camps, followed in 1934 by Sachsenburg in Saxony. By May of 1934, the camps held about eighty thousand inmates. Heinrich Himmler took over responsibility for all of the camps and assigned Theodor Eicke, commandant of Dachau, to reorganize them. He temporarily reduced the number of camps and the number of prisoners, retaining only Communists and those judged undesirable or "antisocial," including Gypsies and habitual criminals. It was November 1938 before substantial numbers of Jews began to be incarcerated. By this time, the camps were no longer simple holding pens, but were now slave labor facilities managed by the SS, which derived a significant portion of its funding from the prisoners' labor.

The Anschluss and the annexation of the Czech Sudetenland (followed by the annexation of Bohemia and Moravia) during 1938 brought a total of 250,000 Austrian and Czech Jews under German control. Perhaps one thousand Jews were murdered in concentration camps during 1939. Of Austria's 160,000 Jews, some 100,000 managed to emigrate, but by this time many nations had enacted policies restricting Jewish immigration. The 1939 invasion of Poland brought under Reich control another three million Jews—the largest Jewish community in Europe—along with a massive influx of new prisoners into the concentration camps. Of the ten thousand Polish civilians killed during the initial phases of the Polish invasion, three thousand were Jews, many of them herded into synagogues and burned alive.

By the winter of 1939, a third answer to the Jewish Question—after internal exile and emigration—was instituted on a large scale: the concentration of Polish Jews not merely within cities, but inside of ghettos within those cities. Walled off from the non-Jewish portions of the Polish cities, the ghettos were severely overcrowded. Food was rationed at starvation levels. Anyone who attempted to leave the ghetto or to smuggle food into it was shot on the spot.

Death was not incidental to ghetto life. It was precisely the outcome the Nazis wanted. By the early summer of 1941, half a

REALITY CHECK

Persecution

The Holocaust was unprecedented in scale, scope, and basis. Various European nations had persecuted and expelled Jews, especially during the Middle Ages and culminating in the Spanish Inquisition, which began, in 1492, with the expulsion of some three hundred thousand Jews from Spain. Yet even in these cases, "Jewishness" was not defined racially, but was a matter of belief. Jews who sincerely converted to Christianity were freely integrated into Christian society and subjected to no further persecution. In Hitler's Germany—and in the countries conquered by Hitler—a Jew was a Jew by birth, and nothing could alter that fact or the doom dictated by that fact.

"In spite of everything I still believe people are really good at heart."

Anne Frank, Diary (published 1952)

DETAILS, DETAILS

Jewish Ghettos

Ghetto is derived from medieval Italian and was originally applied to urban neighborhoods in Venice in which Jews were traditionally concentrated and in which they practiced their trades and arts. The Nazi occupiers of Poland used the term to label small neighborhoods to which Jews were restricted by law in Warsaw, Łódz, and other cities. These ghettos were walled off from the gentile (non-Jewish) quarters of the city.

A PEOPLE MARKED

Shortly after Kristallnacht, on November 12, 1938, Reinhard Heydrich, a principal architect of the Final Solution, suggested requiring that all Jews be distinguished by a badge. The first actual use of the Star of David badge came shortly after the start of World War II, in a November 16, 1939 order decreed for German-occupied Łódz, Poland.

It was not until September 1, 1941, that all Jews in Germany as well as occupied and incorporated Poland were ordered to wear a yellow Star of David with the word *Jude* ("Jew") on their clothing. The idea of the badge did not originate with Nazis, but may be traced at least as far back as 807, when the Abbassid caliph Haroun al-Raschid ordered all Jews to wear a yellow belt and a tall, cone-like hat.

In Europe, during the Middle Ages, Jews—as well as Muslims—were often required to distinguish themselves from Christians with legally prescribed items of dress. In a bitter twist of irony, it was a German Jew and Zionist leader, Robert Weltsch, who first suggested—in an April 4, 1933 article—that German Jews proudly wear a Star of David badge as a token of defiance of a Nazi boycott of Jewish businesses—on whose windows Nazi Party members had painted yellow Stars of David.

Mendel Grosman covertly photographed life, death, and impending death in the Jewish ghetto of Łódz, Poland during World War II. Here, dispossessed Jews haul their belongings to a ghetto hovel. His images are among a precious few that document the beginnings of Hitler's "Final Solution."

million Jews were confined in the Warsaw ghetto, starvation and disease claiming about two thousand persons per month. Yet German authorities estimated that twenty years would be required for the total starvation of the population. This rate was deemed too slow, especially as German conquests in Western Europe brought even more Jews under Reich control. In such occupied lands as Norway, Denmark, France, the Netherlands, Luxembourg, Belgium, Greece, and Poland—and in Germany—the Jews were identified and forced to wear a yellow Star of David on their clothing. This would ensure that they were excluded from all professions and any desirable jobs. The badges would also identify them when it came time to round them up for incarceration in concentration camps.

But identification, segregation, persecution, and concentration were, as the Nazis saw it, only halfway measures. The deaths that occurred in the Polish ghettos clearly pointed the way to the Final Solution, which the Einsatzgruppen during the invasion of the Soviet Union began to carry out on a large scale.

Death Factories

In the space of half a year, the Einsatzgruppen managed to kill perhaps a million Jews. For those in the inner circles of the Nazi regime, even this was hardly enough. Shooting Jews wherever they were found was slow, inefficient, and costly work. It also took an emotional toll on the soldiers assigned to the Einsatzgruppen. Adolf Eichmann began a program of locating and arresting all Jews living in the conquered countries. Those rounded up would be held locally until they could be shipped, via rail, in boxcars and cattle cars, to the multiplying concentration camps. Here, some were selected to serve as slave labor until either the labor (along with starvation and disease) killed them or they were executed. Others, too young, old, or sick to be useful as slaves, were killed immediately.

Eichmann's version of this Final Solution to the Jewish Question was well under way when, on January 20, 1942, Reinhard Heydrich, head of the Reichssicherheitshauptamt (Reich Security Central Office)—the very man who had faked the "Polish" attack on a German radio transmitter in the frontier town of Gleiwitz that was the pretext for the invasion of Poland and the start of World War II—convened a secret conference at Wannsee, a villa on the Wannsee in southwestern Berlin. Here SS officials and administrators of the German civilian government agreed to cooperate in carrying out the Final Solution—the genocide of the Jews of Europe. Heydrich's lieutenant, Adolf Eichmann, drew up minutes

REALITY CHECK

Secret Genocide

It is not an easy matter to keep genocide secret, yet that is precisely what the Nazis sought to do—and apparently thought they could do. Alfred Rosenberg, Reich minister for the Occupied Eastern Territories, wrote on November 18, 1941: "There are still about six million Jews living in Russia, and the problem can only be resolved by a biological elimination of the entire Jewish population of Europe. . . . It is self-evident that we should neither speak nor write about the setting of political goals. In the delicate situation in which Germany finds itself, it would be extremely harmful if the public got to know about these things."

"The Jews are to blame for this war. The treatment we give them does them no wrong. They have more than deserved it."

Nazi propaganda minister Joseph Goebbels, from an editorial in the magazine Das Reich, *November 16, 1941*

Land	Zahl
A. Altreich	131.800
Ostmark	43.700
Ostgebiete	420.000
Generalgouvernement	2.284.000
Bialystok	400.000
Protektorat Böhmen und Mähren	74.200
Estland - judenfrei -	
Lettland	3.500
Litauen	34.000
Belgien	43.000
Dänemark	5.600
Frankreich / Besetztes Gebiet	165.000
Unbesetztes Gebiet	700.000
Griechenland	69.600
Niederlande	160.800
Norwegen	1.300
B. Bulgarien	48.000
England	330.000
Finnland	2.300
Irland	4.000
Italien einschl. Sardinien	58.000
Albanien	200
Kroatien	40.000
Portugal	3.000
Rumänien einschl. Bessarabien	342.000
Schweden	8.000
Schweiz	18.000
Serbien	10.000
Slowakei	88.000
Spanien	6.000
Türkei (europ. Teil)	55.500
Ungarn	742.800
UdSSR	5.000.000
Ukraine 2.994.684	
Weißrußland ausschl. Bialystok 446.484	
Zusammen: über	11.000.000

This page from the January 20, 1942 Wannsee Conference document inventories the "roughly eleven million Jews [who] will have to be taken into consideration . . . [in] connection with this final solution of the Jewish question." In the manner of an accountant, Heydrich's henchman Adolf Eichmann broke the number down by country.

of the conference, which historians call the "Wannsee Protocol." The document officially outlined the shift in policy from emigration to deportation, forced labor, and outright genocide. "Deportation" meant exile to concentration camps. Forced labor extracted work needed for the war effort, and it also represented a deferred means of execution. The labor was grueling and working conditions inhumane; almost inevitably, they led to the death of the laborers. The third policy objective, outright murder, would increasingly become the fate of Europe's Jews under the Nazi regime.

The Wannsee Protocol made it clear that the extermination of the Jews was not an objective incidental to the war, but was a top national priority, a major war aim. It also necessitated the development of efficient means of mass murder. Shooting was inefficient. Death would be brought about by asphyxiation, either using carbon monoxide generated by the redirected exhaust of prisoner transport vans or, increasingly, in specially designed gas chambers built to accommodate scores of victims at a time and typically disguised as shower or delousing facilities. Because generating carbon monoxide was somewhat inefficient, a new substance was introduced, Zyklon-B, a pesticide agent consisting of prussic acid crystals that produced deadly cyanide gas when dissolved.

An efficient mode of murder was only half of the mechanical means of genocide. Death produced corpses—hundreds, thousands, ultimately millions of them. Burial, even in mass graves,

REALITY CHECK

Inner Circle Order

Heydrich's directive came straight from Göring, who occupied the innermost circle around Hitler. On July 31, 1941, he issued to Heydrich the following order: "I hereby charge you with making all necessary organizational, functional and material preparations for a complete solution of the Jewish question in the German sphere of influence in Europe." If any single surviving document may be identified as the order for genocide, this is it.

THE WHITE ANGEL

Born in Günzburg, Germany, in 1911, Josef Mengele was the son of a prosperous farm-machinery manufacturer. As a philosophy student at the University of Munich during the 1920s, Mengele fell under the spell of the anti-Semitic ideology of the racist Alfred Rosenberg.

After graduating, he earned a degree in medicine at the University of Frankfurt am Main. Moved by Rosenberg's philosophy, he joined the SA (storm troopers) in 1933 and became a committed Nazi as well as, in 1934, a researcher in the newly founded Institute for Hereditary Biology and Racial Hygiene.

At the beginning of World War II, Mengele joined the Waffen SS as a medical officer, serving in France and Russia until May 1943, when SS chief Heinrich Himmler appointed him chief physician at Birkenau, an extermination camp attached to the Auschwitz concentration camp. Here Mengele and his staff conducted a daily "selection," choosing which of the incoming Jews would be murdered immediately and which would be used as slave laborers. He also selected some prisoners as the involuntary subjects of bizarre, grotesque, and almost always horrific medical experiments, including some intended to devise means of increasing fertility in order to accelerate the growth of the German "race." Mengele had a particular fascination with twins, on whom he conducted experiments ostensibly related to his search for various means of increasing the German birth rate; however, it is clear that most of his experiments were neither more nor less than exercises in extreme sadism. In several cases, he injected twins with varying concentrations of poisons and pathogens to study their effects. In one instance, he supervised an operation in which two Gypsy children were sutured together to artificially create conjoined twins. Untold thousands died by Mengele's hand, and many others suffered permanent injury or disfigurement.

Mengele always attired himself in an immaculate white lab coat and was therefore dubbed by inmates the "White Angel" or the "Angel of Death." Although he made himself notorious at Birkenau-Auschwitz, he managed to evade capture by the Allies after the war and lived in obscurity for four years near Rosenheim in Bavaria, working as a stable hand. It is believed that he escaped to South America in 1949, and it is known that he married—it was his second marriage—under his own name in Uruguay in 1958. Under the name José Mengele, he was granted Paraguayan citizenship in 1959, and it is believed that he moved to Brazil in 1961, apparently assuming the identity of Wolfgang Gerhard, a former Nazi who had also found refuge in Brazil. Never brought to justice, Mengele's fate remained a mystery until 1985, when a team of Brazilian, West German, and American forensic specialists determined that he had died of a stroke in 1979 while swimming and was buried under Gerhard's name.

The always white-coated SS physician Josef Mengele, the "Angel of Death," performed grotesque, gratuitously sadistic, and typically lethal medical and genetic "experiments" primarily at the Auschwitz-Birkenau concentration camp. He is pictured here shortly before the war, at Verschuer's Institute for Hereditary Biology and Racial Hygiene, Frankfurt.

POP CULTURE

Schindler's List

The story of Oskar Schindler, a notorious lady's man and war profiteer whose conscience and essential humanity were nevertheless profoundly moved by the plight of the Jews, was the subject of a 1982 novel by the Australian writer Thomas Keneally, published in Australia as *Schindler's Ark* and in the United States as *Schindler's List*. In 1993, the novel was transformed into a successful and important motion picture by director Steven Spielberg.

was impractical. The death camps, therefore, were equipped with large-scale crematoriums in which the bodies were burned.

The Nazi death factories were built far from the areas from which the Jews had been "deported," but they were not remote from German or Polish towns and villages. To be sure, the Nazi inner circle did not make the genocide policy public. In fact, certain camps were maintained as public show places, to demonstrate that the Jews and other inmates were treated humanely. Yet the business of mass murder required many willing hands, and although, after the war, soldiers and civilians alike, including residents of towns adjacent to the death camps, claimed ignorance of the genocide, it is apparent that a large segment of the German people knew that Jews were being murdered. They raised no objections.

THE SCOPE OF THE HOLOCAUST

GERMANY AND TWENTY-ONE GERMAN-OCCUPIED COUNTRIES were engulfed in the Holocaust. Most of the occupied territories were helpless to defend their Jewish populations, and, in some, governments and local populations, themselves infected by anti-Semitism, willingly collaborated with German occupation authorities in identifying, arresting, and even murdering Jews.

Hungary entered World War II as a German ally and instituted various programs of persecution against Jews, but, as a matter of national sovereignty, the Hungarian government refused to allow the Jews to be deported to camps. When Hungary turned against Germany and was subsequently invaded by Germany on March 19, 1944, occupation forces quickly confined Jews to ghettos and, beginning on May 15, 1944, deported them to Auschwitz, sending out 438,000 in fifty-five days.

"I was the accuser, God the accused. My eyes were open and I was alone—terribly alone in a world without God and without man."

Elie Wiesel, Night *(1958)*

Like Hungary, Romania started the war as a German ally, but, in contrast to Hungary, willingly conducted genocide on its own. Bulgaria, yet another ally, permitted the deportation of Macedonian and Thracian Jews, but when the government attempted to deport the Jews of Bulgaria proper, it was met with strong popular resistance, which delayed deportation. Throughout Vichy France—essentially a puppet of the Third Reich—officials and even members of the public were notoriously eager to expel

EYEWITNESS

On December 8, 1942, Rabbi Stephen Wise and other Jewish leaders met with President Franklin D. Roosevelt, presenting him with a document outlining the Nazi plan to annihilate European Jews. Wise appealed to the president "as head of our government, to do all in [his] power to bring [the extermination program] to the attention of the world and to do all in [his] power to make an effort to stop it." The president replied:

> *The government of the United States is very well acquainted with most of the facts you are now bringing to our attention. Unfortunately we have received confirmation from many sources. Representatives of the United States government in Switzerland and other neutral countries have given up proof that confirm the horrors discussed by you. We cannot treat these matters in normal ways. We are dealing with an insane man—Hitler, and the group that surrounds him represent an example of a national psychopathic case. We cannot act toward them by normal means. That is why the problem is very difficult. At the same time it is not in the best interest of the Allied cause to make it appear that the entire German people are murderers or are in agreement with what Hitler is doing. There must be in Germany elements, now thoroughly subdued, but who at the proper time will, I am sure, rise, and protest against the atrocities, against the whole Hitler system. . . . As to your proposal, I shall certainly be glad to issue another statement, such as you request.*

FDR asked the delegation for suggestions. Wise suggested getting some representatives from neutral nations into Germany to intercede in behalf of the Jews. Wise reported:

> *The President took notice of that but made no direct replies to the suggestions. The entire conversation on the part of the delegation lasted only a minute or two. As a matter of fact, of the 29 minutes spent with the President, he addressed the delegation for 23 minutes. . . .*

their Jewish citizens. In occupied France, officials and the public were also highly complicit in the Holocaust.

A few occupied countries resisted collaborating in the Holocaust. Italians largely refused to persecute, arrest, or deport Jews until Germany occupied northern Italy after the overthrow of Benito Mussolini in 1943. Denmark, occupied early in the war, developed active and effective resistance to the Holocaust. In October 1943, the Danish government managed to evacuate many Jews by covertly sending them by sea to neutral Sweden. Despite these instances of courageous humanity, the story of the

THE COURSE OF THE CRIME

The biggest intermediate step on the road to genocide was the creation of approximately four hundred ghettos throughout occupied Poland, in which all of the nation's Jews were confined. The overcrowded ghettos began the process of mass murder, and they provided a means by which Poland's Jews could be easily controlled, policed, and, when the time came, removed to death camps.

The Germans used overcrowding, with consequent starvation and disease, as a more-or-less passive means of mass murder. The largest of the Polish ghettos, in Warsaw, occupied just 2.4 percent of the city's area, but held 30 percent of the city's population.

As mentioned, the next step was the summary execution of Jews (and others) as part of the invasion of the Soviet Union. Then, pursuant to the Wannsee Protocol, death camps were built, mostly in Poland, to which Jews and others were transported by rail. The first camp expressly dedicated to mass murder was at Chelmno, Poland, and used mobile gas vans to kill victims. Soon, in other camps, permanent gas chambers were built, typically adjoining crematoriums.

The most notorious of the Nazi death camps was Auschwitz, in Poland. The size of a small city, it was actually a complex of three camps. "Auschwitz I" was the prison camp, where prisoners were received. As they left the incoming trains—a significant number did not survive the journey in unventilated, unheated boxcars, without water or food—camp physicians (all members of the SS) conducted *Selektion* (selection). Pregnant women, young children, the old, the feeble, the disabled, and the sick were sent directly to Auschwitz II–Birkenau, the death camp, where they were immediately gassed and cremated. Others were selected to be held at Auschwitz I as simple prisoners, while still others were sent to Auschwitz III–Buna-Monowitz, the slave-labor camp (Auschwitz III also included approximately forty satellite camps located outside the main camps). In the vast majority of cases, selection for Auschwitz I or III merely deferred death. Inmates either starved, succumbed to disease, were worked to death, or were

At Auschwitz-Birkenau, which combined slave labor facilities with a death camp, reception began with "selection." SS physicians would survey the arriving Jews, consigning most of the able-bodied to slave labor and the others to immediate murder in the camp's gas chambers. In this photograph from the so-called Auschwitz Album, a collection produced by SS-Hauptscharführer Bernhardt Walter, head of the camp's photo lab (Erkennungsdienst, "Identification Service"), newly arrived Jews from Subcarpathian Rus (in the Ukraine) await selection.

summarily executed. Those who did not were subject at any time to further selection—and consignment to the death camp. Some camps, including Auschwitz and Majdanek, combined the holding, slave labor, and extermination functions, while others, including Belzec, Treblinka, and Sobibor, were devoted exclusively to mass murder. Still others, such as Buchenwald, were primarily slave labor camps that also incarcerated political prisoners and POWs in addition to Jews.

Escape from the camps was almost impossible. Jack Werber, a Polish Jew, spent five and a half years in Buchenwald, a notorious labor camp. Werber bore witness to the futility of trying to escape from the camps (toward the last days of the war the Buchenwald Underground liberated the camp themselves, after managing to save seven hundred boys from transport to death camps). In his book, *Saving Children: Diary of a Buchenwald Survivor and Rescuer* (co-written with William Helmreich), he recalls that even if one got past the electrified barbed-wire fences and the watch-tower guards, there was nowhere to escape to. Most escapees were captured and killed.

This photograph of a gas chamber at the Majdanek death camp was made after the liberation. The stains visible on the wall are cyan blue deposits created by the chemical action of Zyklon-B cyanide gas.

Private First Class W. Chichersky took this photograph of the cremation ovens at the Buchenwald concentration camp on April 14, 1945, after Patton's Third U.S. Army liberated the camp. In a comment on the photograph, Chichersky particularly noted that bones remained in the ovens. Cremation proceeded round the clock in the Nazi death factories, but the pace became most frenetic as the Allies closed in. Those who ran the camps worked frantically to commit the evidence of their crimes to the flames.

> **REALITY CHECK**
> **Justice**
> Some of the most notorious perpetrators of the Final Solution managed to escape prosecution (some settling in South American countries with Fascist regimes sympathetic to the former Nazi Germany) or to evade it for many years. For example, Adolf Eichmann was not tracked down until 1961. Tried and convicted by an Israeli court, he was hanged. Klaus Barbie, infamous as the "butcher of Lyon," was located and brought to justice in 1987. Likewise, most of the Jewish property and money looted by the Nazi regime or by German officials in occupied countries was never restored—neither to the survivors nor to their heirs. However, some lawsuits did prevail, and various governments offered compensation, as did some German corporations that had used slave labor during the war. Various legal attempts at recovery of stolen assets continue into the twenty-first century.

Holocaust presents a mostly dismal picture of apathy or outright collaboration in mass murder. Heroic governments and heroic individuals are few and far between. The Swedish diplomat Raoul Wallenberg, for example, worked successfully in Hungary to prevent the deportation of the last of that nation's Jews. In Poland, which had a long history of anti-Semitism before World War II, the Zegota (Council for Aid to Jews) was financed by the London-based Polish government-in-exile. The members of this covert organization risked their lives by hiding Jews and providing them with food as well as forged identity documents. Even in France, some rose to protect Jews. The Huguenot (French Protestant) village of Le Chambon-sur-Lignon became a refuge for some five thousand Jews; a history of religious persecution had made the Huguenots sympathetic to the plight of the Jews. Finally, in Germany itself there were those who resisted the Final Solution. Oskar Schindler, a Nazi Party member, sheltered several thousand Jews by pretending to employ them as slave labor.

Liberation

As Allied forces closed in on the German homeland late in 1944 and during early 1945, word of imminent liberation began to circulate through the camps. For the first time in years, there was a glimmer of hope. But, now desperate to conceal their crimes against humanity, German camp officials worked feverishly to dispose of the evidence against them—that is, the Jewish survivors. The pace of killing and cremation was accelerated. As the Soviets broke into Poland, prisoners were also evacuated from the Polish camps and marched—under the worst possible conditions—into Germany. Many died on these forced marches.

Despite all the German efforts to kill surviving prisoners, the Allied armies began to liberate the camps early in 1945. Soldiers discovered realms of the walking dead, and, indeed, many prisoners were so malnourished and sick that liberation could not restore them. At Bergen-Belsen, for instance, twenty-eight thousand prisoners died *after* the camp was liberated and despite the efforts of U.S. Army medical personnel.

The Nazi regime murdered approximately 12 million civilians for political, cultural, social, or racial reasons:

RESISTANCE

In the years following the war, questions were raised as to why the Jews themselves did not mount an effective resistance against the Holocaust. The fact was that Jewish communities did resist, in the ghettos—most notably in an uprising in the Warsaw ghetto—in rural areas, and even in some concentration and death camps.

Could the Jews have ended the Holocaust through mass resistance? The most probable answer is that resistance on a mass scale was almost certainly impossible. Jews, like most other civilians, had little or no access to arms. They were, in any given population, a minority, often subject to anti-Semitism at the hands of their neighbors. And they, like everyone else, were slow to perceive the enormity of the Nazi policy of the Final Solution. It seemed, quite simply, too horrible to be believed. For their part, the German authorities instituted a ruthless system of collective reprisal, whereby any individual act of resistance was met by massively disproportionate reprisal in the form of the random killing of perhaps hundreds.

The Jews of Eastern Europe had been persecuted for so long that, when the Nazi pogroms began, it was almost impossible to organize effective armed resistance. Nevertheless, a number of resistance groups did come into existence, including in Poland's Warsaw Ghetto and, pictured here, in the Nalibocka Forest of Belorussia (present-day Belarus). This unit of Jewish partisans was led by Tuvia Bielski (1906–87) and functioned not only as military resistance group but also as a Jewish community, harboring families and including a clinic, a lay court, a synagogue, a tannery, and a machine shop for weapons repair.

An American soldier of the 80th Division took this photograph of Buchenwald slave laborers in their barracks during the liberation of the camp. It became one of the iconic images of the Holocaust.

The Nazi regime murdered approximately twelve million civilians for political, cultural, social, or racial reasons; six million were Jews. Those who survived had little to return to. Their wealth and property had been looted, their communities physically destroyed. Many lived among other refugees for extended periods after the war in displaced-persons camps. The Holocaust did provide a major impetus to the Zionist movement, culminating in the creation of a Jewish homeland in what, after the war, was British-administered Palestine. The state of Israel was officially founded in May 1948 and was open to all Jews. The government of the United States, which had done virtually nothing to rescue Jews during the war, now liberalized immigration laws to allow the admission of Jews and other refugees. As a result, many Holocaust survivors settled in America.

Before the end of the war, with the liberation of the concentration and death camps, the full horror of the Holocaust became internationally known. There was widespread support for the Nuremberg War Crimes Tribunal, which tried SS members and other Nazi officials not merely for war crimes but—for the very first time in history—for what tribunal indictments called "crimes against humanity."

TAKEAWAY

Genocide

Hitler and his Nazi Party exploited and amplified traditional anti-Semitism into a myth of the Jewish pollution of the German race, nation, and culture. They made the total extermination of the Jews—throughout Europe and, it can only be assumed, the world—a top-priority objective of the war they had begun. The result was the mass murder of at least six million European Jews.

"For me was the Holocaust not only a Jewish tragedy, but also a human tragedy. After the war, when I saw that the Jews were talking only about the tragedy of six million Jews, I sent letters to Jewish organizations asking them to talk also about the millions of others who were persecuted with us together—many of them only because they helped Jews."

Nazi hunter Simon Wiesenthal

CHAPTER 9

PEARL HARBOR

The Tactical Triumph That Doomed Japan

THE BERLIN-ROME-TOKYO AXIS formally created by the Tripartite—or Axis—Pact of September 27, 1940, was, at the time, bewildering to most Americans. It was difficult to see what Japan had in common with the two European nations. Italian Fascism and German Nazism were clearly cut from the same cloth, but Japan did not seem to be motivated by anything resembling these ideologies. True, the Sino-Japanese War, which began in 1937, made it abundantly clear that Japan, like the European dictatorships, was hungry to expand its empire and influence, to possess or control territories offering resources unavailable in the homeland. It was also apparent that the Japanese government, like the governments of Italy and Germany, was strongly anti-Communist—so the Anti-Comintern Pact signed with Germany (1936) and Italy (1937) also made sense. Yet Italy and, even more, Germany were moved by racially based ideologies, including talk of a "master race" and of "supermen," that seemed to have no counterpart in Japan. Or was it that America was blind to this very dimension of Japan, a nation preparing to go to war?

POP CULTURE

Mr. Moto

On the eve of World War II, few Americans had ever actually met a Japanese person; a fraction of 1 percent of the U.S. population was of Japanese descent. Many Americans identified the Japanese persona with a fictional secret agent invented by American author John P. Marquand: Mr. Moto. Marquand capitalized on the Asian detective vogue started by novelist Earl Derr Biggers and his Charlie Chan series. Moto embodied the popularly held image of the bland, consummately polite Japanese character—with a hidden edge. The insipid agent was a judo master who, though not rapacious, was willing to kill if necessary. Marquand wrote several Mr. Moto stories for *The Saturday Evening Post* and a number or novels, but even better known were the eight films turned out in the late 1930s, starring Peter Lorre as Mr. Moto. The character was "retired" during the war, but briefly revived in the late 1950s.

Race War

Like the people of most other Western nations, Americans generally held a racist view of Japan and other Asian nations. U.S. immigration law had long placed limits on Asian immigration, and, in the days before World War II, if Americans thought much at all about Japan, it was as a country of small, polite, quaint people, whose men typically wore Coke-bottle eyeglasses and whose women dressed like porcelain dolls.

The truth was that, by the beginning of the twentieth century, Japan had become a formidable industrial nation, as its stunning victories over the czarist navy and army during the Russo-Japanese War of 1904–5 dramatically demonstrated. As the century progressed, the twinned issues of race and national destiny became increasingly important to the Japanese. Since virtually the first significant socioeconomic contact between the Western powers and the nations of Asia, Asians had been largely treated as the economic, political, and cultural vassals of Euro-American civilization. Europeans—and, later, Americans as well—rationalized Western imperialism in Asia by asserting the West's "self-evident" cultural, moral, religious, political, and racial superiority. By the end of the nineteenth century, Asia had been extensively subjugated and colonized. While it was true that Japan found itself compelled to make compromises with the Western powers, especially following the intimidating "visit" of the U.S. Navy's Matthew C. Perry in 1854, the Japanese were never conquered or colonized. Indeed, through thousands of years of history, Japan, though frequently torn by civil strife, had never been successfully invaded by any foreign power.

Although the Japanese resented Western imperialism and pretensions of racial superiority, Japan, more than any other Asian nation, seemed determined to benefit from contact with the West. While holding close a wealth of traditional beliefs and values, the Japanese proved eager students of what they considered the best that the West had to offer, particularly in the areas of military doctrine, tactics, and equipment—which were uniquely adopted by the Japanese warrior—and technology. The Russo-Japanese War was the first dramatic evidence of this synthesis, and, after that war, the Japanese military assumed an increasingly important role in Japanese government. Both militarization and industrialization proceeded rapidly.

BUSHIDO

It has often been observed that the Japanese soldier in World War II was motivated by *Bushido*, a word meaning the "way of the warrior," and, as popularly understood in the West, a word describing a fanatical martial code used to justify all manner of brutality in war and dictating death as the only alternative to victory—surrender being so dishonorable as to be unthinkable.

In fact, Japanese soldiers were highly dedicated, and it is true that career Japanese officers were guided by a sense of themselves as warriors in service to the emperor. It is also true that Japan had no historical tradition of surrender, and, in military doctrine, surrender was never presented as a viable option. Yet the Japanese militarist's willingness to die and unwillingness (perhaps even cultural inability) to surrender cannot simply be reduced to the influence of *bushido,* which was not merely a military code, but a way of life, a concept roughly similar to the medieval European notion of chivalry. *Bushido* developed between the eleventh and fourteenth centuries, an era of chronic instability in Japan, and was, like chivalry in Europe, an alternative to anarchy. What the *bushido* tradition did influence during World War II and the period leading up to it was the widespread Japanese perception that the military represented Japan's greatest hope for enduring and productive stability as well as greatness, which depended on the expansion of Japanese empire.

The ukiyo-e *(Japanese woodcut) artist Kuniyoshi Utagawa (1798–1861) produced this well-known image of a traditional Japanese warrior—the embodiment of* bushido.

Americans tend to associate modernization with democratization, as if the two trends were inextricably linked. Such was certainly not the case in Japan. As the nation became more formidable economically and militarily, it did not seek to install the blessings of liberty, but to expand its empire in search of the equivalent of what Adolf Hitler would call *Lebensraum*—living space. On a pragmatic, practical level, expansion was needed to acquire both the resources (oil, steel, foodstuffs, and so on) and the markets to fuel industrialization. On a racially based nationalistic level, imperial expansion was a campaign to redeem Japan—and all Asia—from the long oppression of white Western Christian imperialism.

The Emperor's Place

Americans of the 1930s could be forgiven if they had a hard time understanding the Japanese government. The Meiji Restoration and Constitution of 1889 created a constitutional monarchy in which the emperor was a sovereign who had extensive executive, legislative, and military power and who was, moreover, revered as a semi-divinity, the direct descendant of a god. Nevertheless, the emperor's authority was far from absolute; the 1889 constitution assigned the actual exercise of royal prerogatives variously to the emperor's Cabinet, to the Diet (a bicameral parliament), and to the military. Hirohito, emperor during the period of World War II, was certainly not a mere figurehead (in contrast to the British king, for example), but neither was he the unambiguous head of the Japanese state. Although he reigned, he did not rule. Politically, the emperor ratified policy decisions made by the Cabinet, Diet, and military. He was both guided and insulated by his most intimate advisers, the lord keeper of the privy seal and the grand chamberlain. The emperor's place was to remain above day-to-day politics and serve mainly as a symbol of national destiny.

Subtle, often ambiguous, the Japanese government fostered cliques, secret deals, and power struggles. Because factions and politicians approached the emperor individually and separately, Hirohito sometimes ratified contradictory policies. Despite this, broadly speaking, Japanese national policy was made by the Cabinet, which reported to the emperor (who appointed a prime minister) rather than the Diet. In practice, the power of the Cabinet was inferior to that of the military, and the power of the Diet was almost exclusively limited to budgetary review. Moreover, although the lower house of the Diet consisted of elected representatives, the upper house was made up of hereditary nobles and royally appointed officials, who had authority to check the actions of the lower house. Added to this complex picture was the influence of civilian and military institutions, including business and labor interest groups, various military organizations, and the Supreme War Council, among others.

Poised for Empire

On the eve of World War II, Japan was a thriving industrialized power of about seventy million people. The nation had become a major manufacturer of consumer goods, but, by the early 1930s, the military-dominated central government was increasingly replacing the market economy with features of a totalitarian command economy, including strong government control and planning of production. A growing sector of production was being devoted to war-related industries. Additionally, during 1934–36, the electric power and oil industries were nationalized, and in 1939 rice rationing was introduced. By the end of the decade, Japan was on a war footing driven by a wartime economy.

Launched a week after the commencement of World War II in the Pacific, the Imperial Japanese Navy's Yamato, *at sixty-five thousand tons the biggest battleship in the world, was the pride of a militaristic empire.*

Japan's militarists well understood that their nation was strategically located between Asia and the Pacific, which put Japan in an ideal position for launching a war of imperial conquest, and also exposed it to attack on at least two fronts—from the continent and from the sea. Expansion, the militarists determined, was necessary to the survival and growth of Japan as a great industrial power. To some extent, expansion might be achieved by persuading the other nations of Asia to participate in a kind of pan-Asian movement opposed to the West. But, realistically, the militarists understood that imperial expansion would require more than persuasion. It would mean war.

During the 1930s, Japan's military planners outlined a blueprint for a rapid offensive war—roughly the equivalent of what Germany would call blitzkrieg, "lightning war," but with the added dimension of significant naval conquest. The need for a strong navy prompted Japan to withdraw in 1936 from the London Naval Treaty of 1930, a post–World War I disarmament agreement that placed limits on the signatories' naval tonnage. Freed of treaty restrictions, the Imperial Japanese Navy embarked on an ambitious program of shipbuilding, creating (among other vessels) a mighty fleet of aircraft carriers and battleships, including the *Yamato*, the largest battleship ever built by any nation. The navy planned to use its new fleet to carry out what it called the "Southern Strategy," a plan by which Japan would aggressively expand into Southeast Asia.

The militarists were keen to acquire control over what they called the "Southern Resources Area," which encompassed

NUMBERS

Great Warship

Launched on August 8, 1940, the *Yamato* was a truly awesome ship of war. Empty, it displaced 65,027 tons (fully loaded, 72,800 tons), compared with 45,000 tons for the U.S. *Iowa*-class battleships. It was more than 800 feet long at the waterline with a beam (width) of 121 feet. The ship carried a crew of 2,750 officers and men and bristled with nine 18.1-inch guns (the biggest of any battleship, ever) in addition to a dozen each of 6.1-inch and 12.7-centimeter guns, twenty-four 25-mm antiaircraft guns, and four 13-mm antiaircraft guns.

Malaya, the Philippines, Indochina, and the Dutch East Indies. To make this program of expansion palatable to the people of Southeast Asia—and to put the best face on it as far as the rest of the world was concerned—Japanese politicians and statesmen called the Southern Resources Area the "Greater East Asia Co-Prosperity Sphere." They attempted to sell the program as a campaign to reclaim, for the benefit of Asians, territories that had been usurped by the colonial powers of the West. Inasmuch as the Japanese were Asians, the acquisition of Southeast Asia would benefit Asians—but not really Asia as a whole. Japanese rulers and militarists believed the Southern Resources Area was Japan's by divine right. On a more pragmatic level, they recognized that the region offered most of the raw materials required by industry and the military, as well as an abundant supply of food and labor. To possess the area would make Japan autonomous and inordinately powerful.

Even as the Imperial Navy, during the 1930s, promoted the idea of the Southern Strategy, the Imperial Japanese Army—a rival force in Japanese politics—was more concerned about Soviet threats to Manchuria, which, since 1931, had been occupied by the Japanese as the state of Manchukuo, nominally ruled by Puyi, China's last emperor and now a Japanese puppet. Pressing for a stronger military presence in Manchukuo, junior army officers staged a coup d'etat after the Japanese elections of 1936 in which they assassinated the home secretary and the finance minister, then occupied government offices in Tokyo. The coup was suppressed, but it brought both the army and the navy more deeply into the government, and in April 1936 the two services agreed on the need for the Southern Strategy and absolute control over Manchukuo. The army and navy secured from Emperor Hirohito approval of an offensively based "defense" policy, which quickly evolved into a policy that called for aggressive expansion on the continent as well as toward the south.

Military Dictatorship

On October 12, 1940, Imperial Japanese Army leaders and a group of civilian supporters formed the Imperial Rule Assistance Association (IRAA), with the prime minister, Prince Fumimaro

Konoe, as its president. The IRAA resembled the Nazi Party in Germany, at least insofar as it succeeded in forcing Japan's other political parties to dissolve themselves and be absorbed into the IRAA. In addition, the IRAA controlled a variety of labor unions and management organizations to create the IRAA-controlled Industrial Patriotic League. In this way, a single political party centralized government authority and gave the military yet more control over the government—but it by no means ended the many personal rivalries in the corridors of power. Nor did the IRAA succeed in totally streamlining the government. An attempt to do this was the Liaison Conference, created to coordinate military and civilian branches of government in decision-making. Dominated by the military, the Conference became an extra-constitutional body that entirely usurped the role of the Cabinet. This led to a dispute with Prince Konoe, who resigned as prime minister in October 1941 and was replaced by Hideki Tojo, an army general and, before succeeding Konoe, the war minister.

Tojo's sudden elevation virtually ensured war because his mandate was to make all final preparations for war with the British and Americans in anticipation of what the government now deemed the near certainty that ongoing negotiations between Japan and the United States would break down. In contrast to Mussolini and Hitler, Tojo was not a head of state, but a tremendously powerful bureaucrat who assumed dictatorial powers within the constraints of his mandate to prepare for war and, once that war began, to prosecute it. In a nation now focused narrowly on war, Tojo served as prime minister, army minister, and home secretary.

Lieutenant general and new Japanese prime minister Hideki Tojo poses with his cabinet members after their first cabinet meeting on October 18, 1941. Tojo was a military bureaucrat, not an egocentric dictator like Hitler or Mussolini, but he was convinced that the U.S. military had to be eliminated as a threat to Japan, and he rapidly led his nation into war with America.

The March to War

By the summer of 1941, the empire of Japan consisted of the home islands plus Sakhalin Island south of the 50th parallel, Korea (a Japanese colony since

1910), Formosa (acquired in 1895 and today called Taiwan), and Manchukuo (only nominally independent). In February 1939, Japan occupied the Chinese-owned island of Hainan and, as of March, the Spratly Islands as well. Japan also secured important air bases and naval stations in Thailand.

During that summer of 1941, Japanese diplomats engaged in a protracted negotiation with the American government, which had demanded that Japan withdraw its military forces from China and French Indochina (Vietnam). The Japanese government had no intention of doing this, but, not wishing to provoke the Americans outright, its diplomats stalled to give their nation more time to make war preparations. The United States was Japan's principal supplier of oil, steel, and other strategic materials, and the Japanese government was torn, on the one hand, between the fear that its aggressive policy in China would provoke a U.S. embargo and, on the other, by an intense desire to end reliance on America by acquiring alternative sources of strategic materials. The policy of the United States was, therefore, both an incentive to restrain aggression and an incentive to intensify it.

DETAILS, DETAILS

Tojo's Edge

Whereas European dictators took on muscular titles—Il Duce, for Mussolini, and Der Führer, for Hitler, both meaning "absolute leader"—Tojo's colleagues called him the "Razor" because of his talent for cutting through bureaucratic tangles. It was intended as a high compliment.

President Franklin D. Roosevelt believed that trade pressure would serve as an economic alternative by coaxing Japan into ending its aggression against China. Many in the U.S. government and the military believed that FDR's policy of sanctions on Japan and, ultimately, embargoes on strategic exports—the very materials Japan needed to continue its war against China—were less an alternative to war than a provocation of it. As the 1930s drew to a close and Japan became increasingly prepared for war, then joined the Axis, Japan emerged as a very real threat to the United States. The Roosevelt administration decided to take a new tack, developing what it called a policy of "moral embargo" against Japan. On June 11, 1938, Secretary of State Cordell Hull condemned not only Japan's aggression against China but also as what he called the "material encouragement" of Japanese aggression. The next month, on July 1, 1938, the Department of State sent letters to U.S. aircraft manufacturers and exporters expressing opposition to the sale of aircraft to countries that were using the planes to attack civilian populations. Although these letters did not carry the force of law, they conveyed the moral sense of the government. This "moral embargo" was extended in 1939 to raw materials essential to airplane manufacture as well as to plans, plants, and technical information for the production of aviation gasoline. The moral embargo proved highly effective, as U.S. firms suspended export to Japan of aircraft, aeronautical equipment, and other materials. Encouraged, the U.S. government applied moral pressure to discourage U.S. financial firms from extending credit to Japan.

The moral embargo proceeded in an ever-deteriorating climate between Japan and the United States. As 1938 came to a close, Japanese authorities and Japanese-sponsored agents repeatedly interfered in the interests of U.S. nationals and companies in China, provoking a formal diplomatic protest from the U.S. State Department on December 31, 1938. When this proved ineffective, the Roosevelt administration decided that the 1911 commercial treaty between the United States and Japan no longer afforded adequate protection to American commerce either in Japan or in Japanese-occupied portions of China. In July 1939, the administration informed Japan of its intention to terminate the treaty—a clear signal that a full embargo was in the offing.

During 1939 and 1940, Japanese and American officials repeatedly met, ostensibly with the object of improving relations and averting war. As France tottered on the brink of defeat in the summer of 1940, Japan began to demand an agreement for the use of three airfields in French Indochina and for the right of Japanese troops to transit Indochina in order to facilitate operations against China. Fearing war with Japan in its colonies, the French agreed to the demands. No sooner was this done than Japanese forces attacked French Indochina and occupied several strategic points. Secretary of State Hull's protests fell on deaf ears, and Japan went on, at the end of September 1940, to conclude the Tripartite (Axis) Treaty with Germany and Italy.

As the threat of Japan loomed larger, U.S. rearmament accelerated, putting increasing demands on strategic materials for domestic use. This brought formal legislative and executive limits on exports. The Export Control Act of July 2, 1940, authorized the president to curtail or entirely prohibit the export of war materials. Under this act, licenses were refused for the export to Japan of aviation gasoline and most types of machine tools. When this was followed in September by a ban on the export of iron and scrap steel, Japan lodged a formal protest on October 8, 1940, condemning the prohibition as an "unfriendly act." Secretary Hull rejected the protest, and the embargo on iron and scrap steel was extended on October 16, 1940 to all countries other than those of the Western Hemisphere and Great Britain. By the winter of 1940–41, U.S. shipment to Japan of virtually all strategic commodities had completely stopped.

Far from deterring Japanese aggression, the U.S. embargo made the Japanese militarists all the more determined to seize sources in Asia and the Pacific, then, by means of war, force the United States into accepting this policy. FDR rubbed salt into the Japanese wound on July 26, 1941 with an executive order freezing Japanese assets in the United States. Diplomatic discussions continued, but were increasingly perceived as doomed.

The Japanese Plan

Like the Germans, the Japanese had no desire to start a protracted war and therefore created a plan to strike a blow so devastating that the United States would sue for peace on terms favorable to Japan. Japan's objective seemed much more attainable than Germany's; for whereas Hitler sought to conquer his principal opponents, Japan wanted no more than to extort American acquiescence in Japan's program to conquer others. By no means did Japanese dreams of conquest extend to America itself. To attain this limited objective, Japan's top admiral, Isoroku Yamamoto, proposed an all-out attack on the U.S. Navy's Pacific Fleet anchored at Pearl Harbor, Hawaii Territory. Yamamoto reasoned that the United States would almost inevitably be drawn into war against Hitler and Mussolini. Under the best of circumstances, the Americans would not want to fight a two-front war, against the European Axis and Japan. Destroy the U.S. Pacific Fleet, and a two-front war would become not merely undesirable, but impossible. Combine the attack on the Pacific Fleet with overwhelming assaults on other U.S. and Allied possessions in the Pacific and Asia—including the Philippines, Guam, and Wake Island (all U.S. held) and British-held Singapore and Hong Kong, the Dutch East Indies, and Australia—and America would have to come to terms favorable to Japan.

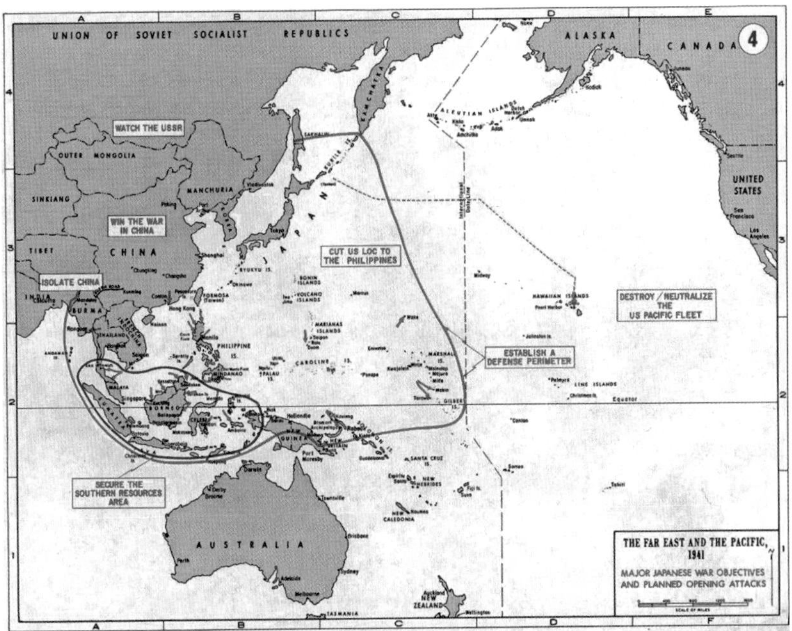

This map illustrates the overall Japanese strategy in the Pacific: control the Southern Resources Area (source of raw materials and food), defeat China, keep the Soviets neutral, and simultaneously capture the U.S.-held Philippines, destroy the U.S. Pacific Fleet, and push out into the Pacific a vast defensive perimeter.

The key, Yamamoto emphasized, was the totality of the attack on Pearl Harbor. The fleet had to be destroyed, not merely crippled. If the United States saw any way to recover from the attack, Yamamoto warned, it would find a way to retaliate until Japan was defeated—no matter how long that took. Indeed, having proposed a massive attack on Pearl Harbor as the only hope Japan had for forcing a favorable peace with the United States, Yamamoto went on to declare that the consequences of failing to deliver a sufficiently devastating blow were so dire that Japan should simply find a way of avoiding war with the United States altogether.

Ignoring Yamamoto's reservations, the militarists approved his Pearl Harbor plan. In addition to delivering total devastation, they all recognized that two additional requirements had to be met. The first was to achieve total surprise. The intention was to launch the attack before a formal declaration of war was made, but to make the declaration before the bombers, launched from aircraft carriers, actually began the attack. This would require very careful timing. It was anticipated that last-ditch negotiations would fail, whereupon the bombers would be launched, then the declaration would be delivered to the American secretary of state—about a half hour before Pearl Harbor actually fell under attack. Yamamoto and others

"It is significant that despite the claims of air enthusiasts no battleship has yet been sunk by bombs."

Caption beneath an official U.S. Navy photograph of the battleship Arizona, *November 29, 1941; the ship was bombed and sunk at Pearl Harbor eight days later*

REALITY CHECK
American History

Yamamoto knew the United States well. He admired and quite liked the Americans he had met when, as a young staff officer, he had been sent to the United States to study at Harvard University from 1919 to 1921. From 1925 to 1928, he served in Washington, D.C., as Japanese naval attaché. Contrary to what many of his Japanese colleagues believed, he thought the American character essentially noble, honorable, and determined. He had also seen the magnitude of American industry, and he warned his colleagues that, on the basis of industrial capacity alone, the United States would defeat Japan in a protracted war.

warned that attacking before a declaration was delivered would so enrage the American people that, no matter how devastating the attack, they would never allow a negotiated peace. Apart from this matter of timing, total secrecy would be maintained by moving the Japanese fleets into position swiftly but under complete radio silence.

The second issue that had to be resolved was the problem of Pearl Harbor's shallow waters. They were too shallow for torpedoes normally dropped by torpedo bombers. Instead of traveling through the water to their targets after they were dropped, the torpedoes would bury themselves in the sand at the bottom of the harbor and detonate harmlessly. Yamamoto and his staff had an answer to this problem. Japanese naval observers had witnessed the battle of Taranto the British had mounted on November 11, 1940, against the Italian fleet anchored at the Taranto naval base in southern Italy. British torpedo bombers badly damaged two Italian battleships and a cruiser, forcing the fleet to evacuate to Italy's west coast, thereby eliminating a major threat to British convoys. Like Pearl Harbor, the harbor at Taranto was shallow—too shallow for conventional torpedoes. British technicians had modified the torpedoes to function in shallower water, and the pilots had practiced techniques for dropping the torpedoes in a way that reduced the depth to which they descended below the surface of the water. For the Pearl Harbor attack, the Japanese modified their torpedoes similarly and developed similar maneuvers for dropping them. Not only did this solve the chief technical problem of the planned attack, it also greatly enhanced the element of surprise. For most

An American sailor stationed at Pearl Harbor snapped this tranquil photo on the eve of World War II. Note that the ship rides high in the water, having jettisoned ballast in order to clear the harbor's shallow depths. U.S. naval planners mistakenly believed that the shallowness of Pearl Harbor would preclude torpedo attacks launched from the air.

American naval planners believed that Pearl Harbor was essentially immune to airborne torpedo attack because of its shallow waters. U.S. Navy commanders were so confident that torpedoes could not be successfully dropped there that they did not employ the torpedo nets commonly used to protect the fleet.

Unprepared

It is one of the most persistent myths surrounding World War II that the United States was thrust into the conflict unprepared. As discussed in Chapter 6, the Roosevelt administration had been girding the nation for war, and, as a result, the United States entered the conflagration better prepared than it had been for any previous war. Nevertheless, the nation and its military were woefully unprepared for a first strike against Pearl Harbor.

As just mentioned, most American naval officers believed Pearl's shallow harbor waters offered immunity from airborne torpedo attack. They also believed that an air assault was highly unlikely because of the great distances involved. Surely, the approach of a large Japanese carrier fleet could not go undetected. Virtually everyone agreed that if Japan attacked—and many U.S. military planners and politicians believed it would attack—the first assault would come in the Philippines, which were much closer to Japan than was Hawaii, or would be directed against U.S. outposts at Wake and Midway islands—again, much closer to Japan. In fact, Lieutenant General Walter Short, commander of the army facilities at Pearl Harbor, transferred many of his P-40 fighters—aircraft designed to intercept incoming attackers—to Wake and Midway, specifically to provide escort cover for bombers that were being flown to reinforce the Philippines.

On November 27, 1941, U.S. Army chief of staff George C. Marshall issued to all commanders a "war warning," a message indicating that, based on the continued failure of negotiations, war with Japan was imminent. Admiral Husband E. Kimmel, commander of the Pearl Harbor naval base, and General Short, his army counterpart, interpreted the war warning mainly as a reason to take precautions against sabotage. Hawaii had a substantial Japanese population, including American citizens of Japanese descent, recent Japanese immigrants, and even many Japanese

REALITY CHECK

Hindsight: Tragic Errors

The attack on Pearl Harbor abruptly ended the distinguished careers of Kimmel and Short. These two local commanders absorbed most of the blame for the vulnerability of Pearl Harbor. In significant part, the blame was justified. As members of "rival" services, Kimmel and Short did not meet to plan the defense of Pearl Harbor, nor did they regularly share information. But the failure of communication extended far beyond Kimmel and Short. The politicians failed to communicate adequately with top military command in Washington, and Washington did not communicate effectively with its local commanders. At every level, there were failures of initiative and imagination, as well as arrogance and sophomoric interservice rivalry. Even though U.S. intelligence analysts had broken key Japanese diplomatic and military codes, there was a breakdown in channels that prevented intelligence from being disseminated. The stunning failures would continue even as the attack began to unfold.

DETAILS, DETAILS

A Plane by Any Other Name

The names of Japanese aircraft were either bewildering or simply unknown to Allied pilots and other military men; therefore, Allied intelligence made up code names for each of the aircraft, such as Kate, Val, George, Betty, and even Irving. The most celebrated Japanese fighter was something of an exception to this code-name rule. Officially designated the Mitsubishi A6M Type 00 Fighter, it was popularly known in Japan as the Zero-Sen. Although it was code-named by the Allies "Zeke," it was universally known among American, British, and Commonwealth pilots as the "Zero."

nationals. Espionage and sabotage were considered virtually inevitable. Kimmel deployed his ships close together within the mooring places, so that they could be more easily guarded against saboteurs. Moreover, only every fourth machine gun aboard the moored ships was manned and all ammunition was securely locked up to keep it out of the hands of saboteurs. Because no threat was expected from the air, Kimmel decided not to waste personnel by continuously manning antiaircraft batteries. On the fateful morning of the attack, December 7, 1941, the batteries were, as they had been for days before, unmanned. Nor did Kimmel order any special air reconnaissance. Indeed, the admiral saw no reason to keep his officers on a war alert, standing by on board their ships. On December 7, about a third of the fleet's captains were ashore, along with many other officers.

Like Kimmel, Short made preparations against saboteurs rather than against air attack. He took the precaution of communicating the nature of his preparations to Washington, and when he received no reply, he assumed that army high command concurred with his interpretation that sabotage was the only real threat. This prompted Short to follow the example of Kimmel and keep ammunition closely guarded under lock and key rather than loading his antiaircraft batteries. Short also ordered all U.S. Army Air Forces fighters and bombers to be grouped together on the airfields, wingtip-to-wingtip, so that they could be more easily guarded.

Launch

On November 22, the Japanese striking force rallied at Etorofu in the Kuril Islands, then sailed on November 26 toward Pearl Harbor. Vice Admiral Chuichi Nagumo was in charge of the elite force and, with consummate seamanship, used a weather front, which moved at about the same speed as the fleet, to cover the movement of six aircraft carriers—the *Akagi,* Nagumo's flagship, the *Hiryu, Kaga, Shokaku, Soryu,* and *Zuikaku*—two battleships, two heavy cruisers, a light cruiser, nine destroyers, and three fleet submarines. On board the carriers were 423 aircraft, including Mitsubishi A6M Type 00 ("Zero") fighters, Nakajima Type 97 ("Kate") torpedo bombers, and Aichi Type 99 ("Val") dive-bombers. In addition to the principal ships, there were eight tankers for refueling. Associated with the striking force was an Advanced Expeditionary Force, which included twenty fleet submarines and 5 two-man Ko-Hyoteki-class midget submarines. The submarines were to gather last-minute intelligence on Pearl Harbor and, during the attack, attempt to track and sink any American ships that might flee.

Japanese sailors cheer pilots as they take off from one of the aircraft carriers poised to attack Pearl Harbor, December 7, 1941.

Moving with stealth and maintaining radio silence, Nagumo's fleet took up its attack position 275 miles north of Hawaii without being detected. At 6:00 A.M. local time, Sunday morning, December 7, 1941, Nagumo launched his first wave of aircraft: 49 bombers, 40 torpedo bombers, 51 dive-bombers, and 43 fighters. This was followed by a second wave, consisting of 54 horizontal bombers, 78 dive-bombers, and 36 fighters.

In the meantime, in Washington, where it was already afternoon, time consumed in decrypting and transcribing lengthy communications from Tokyo meant that the Japanese ambassador did not have his complete instructions prior to the attack. He was therefore late delivering to U.S. secretary of state Cordell Hull his nation's note formally breaking off peace talks. By the time Hull had the note, the attack was nearly an hour old.

The result, unintended by the Japanese, was that Pearl Harbor constituted a "sneak attack" in time of peace. It was, therefore, precisely what President Roosevelt would call it when, on December 8, he asked Congress for a declaration of war against Japan. It was an act of "infamy."

"I have never seen a document that was more crowded with infamous falsehoods and distortions on a scale so huge that I never imagined until today that any government on this planet was capable of uttering them."

U.S. secretary of state Cordell Hull,
responding to the Japanese notee breaking off peace talks, received an hour after the commencement of the attack on Pearl Harbor

Attack

For the Japanese, making a "sneak attack" would prove a fatal strategic blunder that ensured their eventual total defeat. On December 7, 1941, however, none of this was apparent. Just as the weather had served to cloak the approach the attackers, the clouds that shrouded Honolulu and Pearl Harbor that morning suddenly parted as the Japanese pilots closed in, revealing the target with perfect clarity. To the attackers, it seemed nothing less than evidence of divine intervention and approval.

At 6:45 A.M., an American destroyer on patrol sank one of the Japanese midget submarines as it tried to enter Pearl Harbor. The vessel had been sighted three hours earlier, but the destroyer skipper shadowed it rather than reporting its presence. Even when he did report the sinking, navy officers at Pearl Harbor did not pass the report to the army and even delayed sending it to the attention of Admiral Kimmel. In this way, a final opportunity for advance warning was lost.

Similarly, data from a newly installed mobile radar unit at Opana, which tracked a reconnaissance floatplane between 6:45 and 7:00 A.M., though duly reported, was not acted upon. Despite tracking the aircraft, two of the three radar units were shut down at 7:00 A.M. so that the operators could eat breakfast. The truck delivering breakfast to the third set of operators was late, so they continued working their radar, which detected the approach of the carrier aircraft of Nagumo's first wave. Once again, the operators reported the contact, but, inexperienced, they did not specify the number of aircraft detected. This led the duty officer who received the report to assume the targets were a flight of U.S. Army Air Forces B-17 bombers, which were due from the mainland. Once more, warning of the imminent attack was ignored.

As for the Japanese aircraft, they found it extraordinarily easy to locate their target on that sleepy Sunday morning. They homed in flawlessly on Pearl Harbor by following the signal of commercial radio broadcasts from Honolulu, as if it were a military radio beacon. As they approached Pearl Harbor, each of the pilots took out copies of a bombing grid, which had been drawn up by the Japanese consul general stationed in Honolulu.

In the harbor on December 7 were seventy warships, including eight battleships and twenty-four other major vessels. So far, every-

DETAILS, DETAILS
Disconnected

American military cryptanalysts intercepted and decoded the fourteenth and final part of the message Tokyo sent to the Japanese embassy in Washington, announcing an end to peace talks, well *before* the Japanese ambassador's staff decoded it. U.S. Army chief of staff George C. Marshall acted on the decrypted message by issuing a "war warning" message to the forces in Hawaii. But Marshall's warning was dogged by delays: first, Marshall himself could not be quickly found (he was out on his morning horseback ride), then there were snags in the army's long-distance communication network (interservice rivalry apparently dissuaded army technicians from using the U.S. Navy's communication facilities), and, finally, a delay in delivering the message from the commercial telegraph office in Honolulu to General Short's headquarters. Short received it hours after the attack had ended. It was delivered to him by a youthful Japanese-American bicycle messenger.

thing had gone right for the attackers and everything wrong for unsuspecting Americans—except for one crucial stroke of luck. The U.S. heavy cruisers and fleet carriers were not in port, but out at sea.

The first wave of torpedo and dive-bombers descended on the ships of the U.S. battle fleet and also bombed and strafed the airfields from 7:55 to 8:25. Within fifteen minutes of these attacks, the high-level bombers dropped their ordnance. At 9:15, the dive-bombers of the second wave attacked, withdrawing at 9:45 after a half-hour run. About 360 of Nagumo's airplanes participated in the attack, and they took a terrible toll: the battleship *Arizona* was destroyed, and the battleship *Oklahoma* capsized; the battleships *California*, *Nevada*, and *West Virginia* were sunk in shallow water. In addition, three cruisers, three destroyers, and four other vessels were either damaged or sunk. On the airfields, 188 aircraft were destroyed and another 155 were badly damaged. The human toll was 2,388 army and navy personnel and civilians killed and 1,174 wounded. Japanese losses were a mere 29 aircraft and 6 submarines—1 I-Type standard submarine and 5 "midget" subs. Of the Japanese, 64 died, and 1 was captured.

REALITY CHECK

The Giant Awakens

As Yamamoto had warned, the fact that the attack came without a declaration of war—creating the impression of infinite Japanese treachery—did more than any other aspect of the Pearl Harbor attack to galvanize American political and popular resolve to strike back at Japan and bring about its total defeat. It was widely reported (but never confirmed) that Yamamoto observed just after the attack, "I feel all we have done is to awake a sleeping giant and fill him with a terrible resolve."

EFFECTS

Initial reports of the battle of Pearl Harbor thrilled Nagumo. The results had exceeded his wildest expectations. Nevertheless, a cautious commander, he decided against launching a third wave of

The attack on Pearl Harbor took a toll: 2,388 Americans killed and 1,174 wounded. One hundred eighty-eight aircraft were destroyed, almost all of them on the ground, and five battleships, three cruisers, one minelayer, and three destroyers were sunk or badly damaged. Most of the ships, including four of the great battleships, were repaired and even refloated before the end of the war. The battleship Arizona, *however, seen here, was a total loss and remains at the bottom of the harbor, todays a solemn monument to Pearl Harbor.*

aircraft, lest he provoke a counterattack by American submarines, which he thought were in the area. The third wave was to have targeted the base's repair facilities and fuel installations. Had this been done, Pearl Harbor would probably have been knocked out of the war for a very long time, if not permanently. As it was, the facility was quickly repaired and back in service almost immediately. Losses to the U.S. Pacific Fleet were severe, but they were not fatal. The battleships that had been damaged were quickly repaired and even those that had been sunk in shallow water were refloated. Six of the eight battleships attacked at Pearl Harbor returned to service, along with all but one of the other ships sunk or damaged. Moreover, Nagumo did not appreciate the consequences of the survival of the aircraft carriers and heavy cruisers, which were out at sea. These would become the core of a resurrected U.S. Pacific Fleet. Pearl Harbor was a devastating attack, but it was not pushed to the point of ultimate decisiveness. From the perspective of history, assessing the effect of the battle of Pearl Harbor is easy. A great tactical triumph for Japan, it was a monumental strategic blunder, because it provoked a great industrial power to a massive and united war effort that ensured Japan's ultimate defeat.

"A military man can scarcely pride himself on having 'smitten a sleeping enemy'; in fact, to have it pointed out is more a matter of shame."

Admiral Isoroku Yamamoto, January 9, 1942

TAKEAWAY

Imperialism, Embargo, War

President Franklin D. Roosevelt used embargoes and other economic measures in an attempt to curb Japan's grand program of imperial expansion throughout Asia and the Pacific. He saw these as alternatives to war, but Japan, determined not to be thwarted, took them as a provocation to war and thus launched a preemptive attack on the U.S. fleet at Pearl Harbor, hoping to destroy the American naval presence in the Pacific and force the United States to come to favorable terms that would permit Japan to complete the realization of its imperial ambitions.

Admiral Isoroku Yamamoto made the cover of Time *on December 22, 1941, portrayed as the architect of the attack on Pearl Harbor. In fact, he had argued against going to war with the United States, whose industrial might, he believed, would ultimately defeat Japan.*

CHAPTER 10

BANZAI!

In the Path of a Pacific Juggernaut

THE MONTH OF DECEMBER 1941 resounded with *banzai!* It was the Japanese battle cry. On December 7, British-held Malaya (Malaysia) was invaded. On the night following this, the Philippines, U.S. territory since the end of the Spanish-American War in 1898, fell under attack, as did Hong Kong, the bustling British Crown colony.

On December 8, President Franklin Delano Roosevelt addressed a joint session of the United States Congress. "Yesterday, December 7, 1941," he began, "a date which will live in infamy—the United States of America was suddenly and deliberately attacked by naval and air forces of the Empire of Japan." The president pointed out that the "United States was at peace with that nation, and, at the solicitation of Japan, was still in conversation with its government and its Emperor looking toward the maintenance of peace in the Pacific." Never one to sugar-coat bad news, FDR reported the facts frankly and straightforwardly: "The attack yesterday on the Hawaiian Islands has caused severe damage to American naval and military forces. I regret to tell you that very many American lives have been lost. In addition, American ships have been reported torpedoed on the high seas between San Francisco and Honolulu." He continued:

> Yesterday the Japanese Government also launched an attack against Malaya.
> Last night Japanese forces attacked Hong Kong.
> Last night Japanese forces attacked Guam.
> Last night Japanese forces attacked the Philippine Islands.
> Last night the Japanese attacked Wake Island.
> And this morning the Japanese attacked Midway Island.

"There is no blinking at the fact that our people, our territory and our interests are in grave danger," the president told Congress, and then, on behalf of the government and the people, he made a pledge and a prediction: "With confidence in our armed forces, with the unbounding determination of our people, we will gain the inevitable triumph. So help us God." It would, however, be a very long journey, with no end of terror and an abundance of heartbreak.

MALAYA AND THAILAND

JAPANESE FORCES MADE ATTACKS throughout Asia and the Pacific. Their success was far beyond what even the most optimistic planners had anticipated. Americans think of Pearl Harbor as the beginning of the Pacific war, but the Malayan campaign began early on the morning of December 7, even before the Pearl Harbor operation got under way. With sixty thousand men, supported by 158 naval aircraft and 459 aircraft of 3rd Air Division, General Tomoyuki Yamashita took the peninsula's Anglo-Indian garrison completely by surprise. Yamashita's first landings, at Singora (Songkhla) and Pattani in southern Thailand, were entirely unopposed, and his next landings, during the night of December 7/8, on the northern Malayan coast, were met with inadequate resistance that was quickly brushed aside.

While Yamashita pounded the garrison on Malaya, Japanese naval forces engaged and sank the British battleship *Prince of Wales* and the battlecruiser *Repulse* on December 10. Yamashita then proceeded with blitzkrieg-like speed, quickly taking and occupying Bangkok in Thailand and, in Malaya, securing the aid of natives who were weary of British imperial rule. On January 11, 1942, Yamashita took Kuala Lumpur, forcing a British retreat. All attempts to check the advance of the Japanese were defeated, and, by January 31, 1942, all British, Indian, and Australian forces had withdrawn to Singapore, where they could do nothing but await invasion.

HONG KONG

IN 1941, THE BRITISH CROWN COLONY OF HONG KONG—measuring approximately 426 square miles—was packed with a population of about 1.4 million, mostly Chinese. The British had long recognized

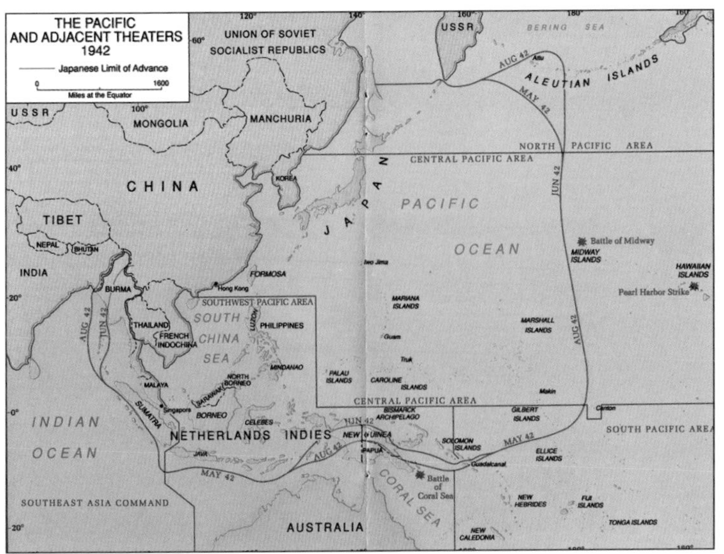

The Pacific theater through the summer of 1942: The line shows the extent of Japan's "defensive perimeter" in May and August. Japan's failure to capture the Midway Islands in the Battle of Midway (June 4–7, 1942) marked the moment at which the Pacific war turned against the empire. From that point on, the Japanese fought a long and bloody retreat.

that Hong Kong was vulnerable to invasion from Japanese-occupied China, but, during the months preceding the outbreak of the Pacific war, British military planners had only so many soldiers to spare. The island was defended by a garrison of twelve thousand, whose standing order was, if attacked, to hold out as long as possible in order to buy time for the arrival of a Chinese army under Generalissimo Chiang Kai-shek.

The British set up a main defensive line three miles north of Kowloon in the so-called Leased Territories on the Chinese mainland. Along this line, a small force of Scottish and Indian troops was thinly deployed. On Hong Kong itself, three battalions, two of them Canadian, were stationed. There was also a poorly equipped home guard, which manned artillery and antiaircraft defenses. As for naval support, it consisted of a single destroyer, eight motor torpedo boats (small craft similar to U.S. Navy PT boats), and four very old gunboats. If anything, the island's air force was even more feeble, consisting of just seven ancient aircraft.

When it came—one day after Pearl Harbor—the attack on Hong Kong was swift and violent. It began with an air attack that destroyed all seven available British planes before they could even take off. The overland invasion followed, initially into the mainland Leased Territories. The British were forced to withdraw from Kowloon and hunker down on Hong Kong Island itself. The

REALITY CHECK
Wishing, Hoping

The British plan for the defense of Hong Kong was not so much a plan as it was wishful thinking. First, Japanese spies had been active in Hong Kong for years and had furnished Japanese high command with extensive details concerning the island's fortifications and troop dispositions. Second, there was never much chance that Chiang Kai-shek would be able to raise and equip an army sufficient for the defense of Hong Kong, especially with the Chinese mainland under varying degrees of Japanese occupation.

Japanese commander unleashed relentless air attacks against Victoria City, the island's British business district, and also against the few British vessels in port. Finally, on December 15, the Japanese commander ordered his men to cross to the island—but, to his great astonishment, they were repulsed. He mounted a larger attack on the eighteenth and soon made headway, albeit at a slower rate than had been anticipated. Nevertheless, the final outcome was never seriously in question, and on Christmas Eve the vastly outnumbered British surrendered. Hong Kong was now in Japanese hands.

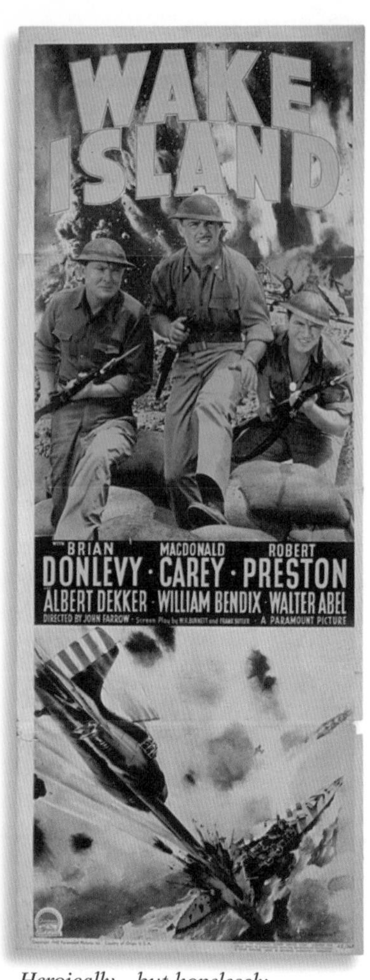

Heroically—but hopelessly—defended by a tiny band of U.S. Marines and civilian contractors, Wake Island became the Alamo of the Pacific war. On August 11, 1942, months after the fall of the island to overwhelming Japanese forces, Hollywood released an Oscar-winning patriotic, exuberantly fictitious depiction of the battle.

Wake Island Epic

Although Hong Kong was a triumph for the Japanese, it offered stiffer resistance than anticipated. This should have served the imperial aggressors as a warning. Pacific conquest would not be as easy or as swift as top military command had predicted. Wake Island was a case in point.

"Wake Island" is a somewhat misleading name because it applies not to a single body of land, but a group of three remote coral islets in the Pacific, twenty-three hundred miles west of Hawaii. This collection of land was claimed by the United States after the Spanish-American War, to provide a way station for the U.S. Pacific Fleet. By World War II, it was mainly an airfield, servicing Pan American World Airways and military aircraft. It was defended at the outbreak of the war by the 1st Defense Battalion, which consisted of just 449 marines and a dozen marine F4F Wildcat fighters. Along with the marines were sixty-nine sailors, five army signalmen, and 1,216 civilians, most of them construction workers contracted to build fortifications. The marines were commanded by Major James Devereux, who reported to U.S. Navy commander Winfield S. Cunningham, the overall commander of Wake.

The Japanese anticipated having to make little effort to take Wake Island, which they wanted as an air base. Since Wake Island is located west of the International Dateline with respect to the United States, it was December 8 there—but still December 7 in Honolulu and Washington—when thirty-four carrier-based bombers raided their objective, destroying eight of the F4Fs on the ground. On December 11 (local time), Japanese troops stormed ashore, only to be repulsed by the marines. Indeed, the greatly outnumbered defenders of Wake Island exacted a heavy toll on the invaders, not only killing troops but also sinking two destroyers and damaging a third, while also causing damage to a pair of Japanese cruisers. The invaders were shocked by the ferocity and effectiveness of the resistance, and the marines were heartened, especially because they anticipated reinforcements from the United States at virtually any moment.

In fact, no reinforcements were being sent. After the Pearl Harbor attack, U.S. Navy high command was reluctant to risk precious remaining ships to relieve a small garrison on a remote outpost. The marines and the others were left to fend for themselves.

The Japanese regrouped for a new assault on December 22, sending against the marines two thousand specially trained amphibious assault troops. This force was sufficient to overwhelm the garrison, and, late on the twenty-second, Cunningham surrendered to General Sadamichi Kajioka.

NUMBERS

Remember the Alamo

Sometimes called "the Alamo of the Pacific," the battle of Wake Island cost the lives of 50 marines and 70 civilians. In addition to the ships lost, the Japanese gave up 820 killed and 335 wounded. All of the surviving Americans were captured and spent the rest of the war as prisoners, except two Marines who managed to escape in May 1945 while being held in occupied China.

GUAM

GUAM, THE LARGEST OF THE MARIANA ISLANDS, was ceded to the United States after the Spanish-American War. At the outbreak of World War II in the Pacific, the island was entirely unfortified and was defended by just 430 U.S. Marines and 180 native Chamorro guards, all under the command of navy captain George McMillin, who served as the military governor of the island. Like Wake Island, Guam lay west of the International Dateline. It was hit by an air raid on December 8, local time, which was December 7 for Hawaii and the mainland United States. On December 10 (local time), fifty-four hundred Japanese troops landed on Guam, fighting McMillan's outnumbered command for three hours before the captain surrendered. Seventeen marines and Chamorros were killed, and one of the Japanese invaders died.

The consequences of losing Guam were out of proportion to the small battle fought to take it. In 1941, the island had the only adequate fresh water supply in all the Marianas, and it provided

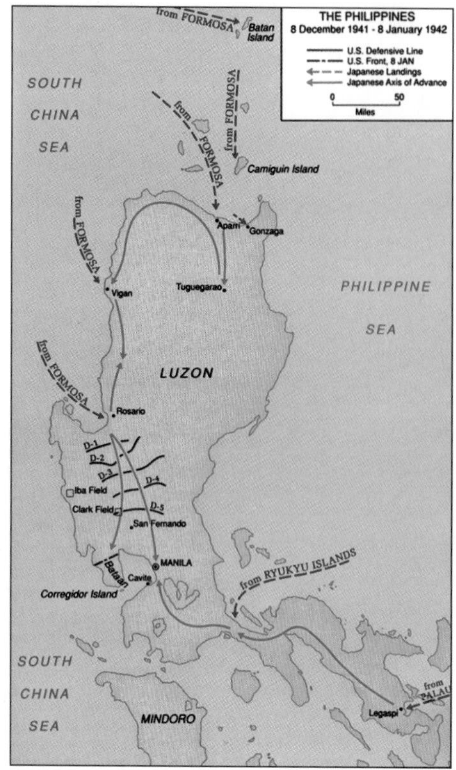

The Philippines were attacked and invaded by Japanese landing from Formosa (modern-day Taiwan), the Ryukyu Islands, and Palau. MacArthur organized a defense that exacted a heavy toll on the invaders, buying time for the arrival of U.S. reinforcements—which, however, were never dispatched. MacArthur was evacuated from the islands, which were completely overrun by the Japanese by May 8, 1942—well behind the Japanese commanders' planned schedule.

excellent harborage. Whoever possessed Guam would have a superb advance base. The Japanese wasted no time in garrisoning their prize with some nineteen thousand troops.

THE PHILIPPINES

THE JAPANESE STRATEGY was to possess all of the principal Pacific and Asian outposts in order to create a vast cordon around the Japanese home islands, a buffer zone thousands of miles in extent. The greatest prize in the Pacific was the Philippines, the defenses of which were commanded by Douglas MacArthur, who had charge of what were called the "U.S. Far East Forces." These consisted of about eleven thousand U.S. soldiers and marines, eight thousand U.S. Army Air Forces personnel, twelve thousand Philippine Scouts—Filipinos trained by and incorporated into the regular U.S. Army—and more than one hundred thousand other Filipino troops. The latter were hardly organized and were inadequately equipped, many lacking weapons entirely. The air force on the Philippines was commanded by Major General Lewis Brereton, subordinate to MacArthur, and consisted of about 275 aircraft, many of which were outmoded, except for 35 B-17 bombers and 107 P-40 fighters. Anchored in Manila Bay was the U.S. Asiatic Fleet under Admiral Thomas Hart.

MacArthur received the "war warning" message from U.S. Army chief of staff George Marshall and, in response, put his command on alert. Despite this, the Americans were surprised by the swift intensity of the Japanese air attack on Clark Field, the main air base, about noon on December 8 (local time—December 7 in Hawaii and the U.S. mainland). Fifteen of the seventeen B-17s parked on the field were destroyed. When night fell, Admiral Hart stealthily steamed out of Manila Bay, sailing south to Borneo. This saved the fleet, but it left the Philippines with almost no naval protection.

Two days after the opening air raid, on December 10, the invasion began as four thousand Japanese soldiers landed at Aparri and

Vigan, at the northern end of Luzon, the principal island of the Philippine archipelago. On the fourteenth, a second landing was made on the island's southern end. Both of these were nothing more than probing attacks to assess the nature and extent of American defenses. The main invasion assault came on December 22, when General Masaharu Homma led forty-three thousand men of the Fourteenth Japanese Army in landings at Lingayen Gulf on Luzon's west coast, 125 miles north of Manila, the nation's capital. This main force linked up with the earlier invaders, then marched south toward Manila.

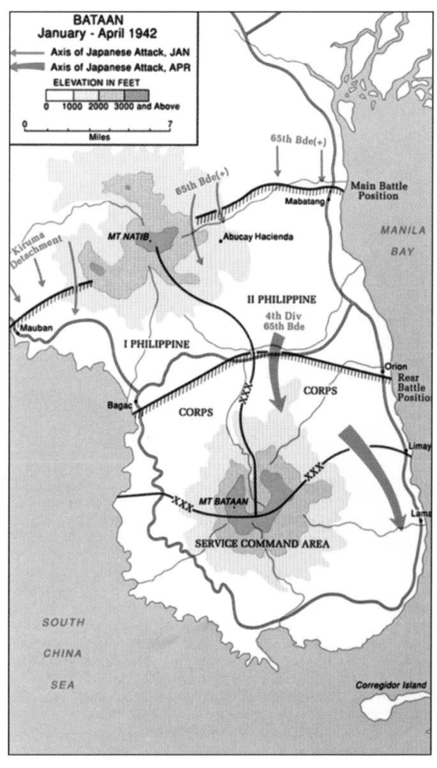

American and American-led Filipino forces made their last stand against the Japanese on the Bataan Peninsula, conducting a fighting withdrawal that cost the invaders heavily.

MacArthur ordered his troops, overrun, to withdraw on December 23 to the Bataan Peninsula, on the west coast of Luzon, between Manila Bay and the South China Sea. It was the most defensible position on Luzon. In the meantime, however, on December 24, an additional ninety-five hundred Japanese soldiers landed at Lamon Bay, sixty miles southeast of Manila. The capital was now within the jaws of a great pincer, Homma's main force bearing down from the north, this second wave pushing up from the south.

Not without reason did the Japanese planners think the conquest of the Philippines would proceed speedily. To Homma's great chagrin, however, MacArthur's American and Filipino troops staged a gallant fighting withdrawal, calculated to take a toll on the invaders and buy time for a general withdrawal—intact—to Bataan. MacArthur assumed that, if he could hold out long enough, reinforcements would be sent from the States.

But it would be supremely difficult to hold out. Over Christmas, from December 24 to December 26, the Japanese bombed Manila so ferociously that MacArthur called off any attempt to defend the city and instead declared it "open," hoping that this would spare it from further destruction. It did not. The Japanese stormed into Manila on January 2, 1942, and, perhaps in

The Bataan Death March, in which American and Filipino prisoners were sent on foot from Bataan to incarceration in remote Japanese-held Camp O'Donnell, came to symbolize Japanese atrocity. This photograph was taken near the end of the march, the men bearing their fallen comrades on stretchers improvised from blankets and bamboo poles.

revenge for the fierceness of the defense of the island as a whole, treated the people of Manila most brutally.

By January 1, 1942, the main U.S.-Filipino force, commanded in the field by MacArthur's principal subordinate, Lieutenant General Jonathan Wainwright, and the smaller southern force unit (under George Parker, who was later replaced by Albert Jones) completed the withdrawal to Bataan. MacArthur then demolished the bridges over the Pampanga River, to retard the Japanese advance. With Philippine president Manuel Quezon, MacArthur established a headquarters on Corregidor Island, a hardened natural fortress off the southern coast of Bataan nicknamed "the Rock."

As MacArthur and his men continued to resist from Bataan, the invasion progressed. On December 20, five thousand of the invaders were diverted to Mindanao, at the southern end of the Philippine archipelago. This detachment took Davao, a key port, then moved on to Jolo Island and North Borneo, thereby severing the Philippines from communication with Australia. Even cut off, however, the Bataan defenders held fast.

Then MacArthur received a message that no reinforcements could be sent, and President Roosevelt personally ordered him to evacuate with his family to Australia. MacArthur was profoundly shaken by the order, but, on March 11, obeyed, leaving Wainwright in command and instructing him not to surrender. For MacArthur still held out hope that reinforcements would, eventually, materialize.

Wainwright remained at Bataan for another month, until, on April 10, judging the U.S.-Filipino position there untenable, he evacuated his remaining troops to Corregidor, leaving Bataan to be overrun. The Japanese occupied all of the strategic coastal positions in the central Philippines, and, from these, mounted a ceaseless bombardment of the Rock.

POP CULTURE

Bastards of Bataan

The embattered defenders of Bataan adopted a sardonic battle song, by war correspondent Frank Hewlett: "We're the battling bastards of Bataan; No mama, no papa, no Uncle Sam; No aunts, no uncles, no cousins, no nieces; No pills, no planes, no artillery pieces. And nobody gives a damn."

Corregidor's underground tunnels made for a formidable defensive fortress, but, in the end, cut off from all supplies, the last defenders of the Philippines, under Lieutenant General Jonathan Wainwright's command, were forced to surrender. Survivors spent the rest of the war as prisoners under the most inhumane conditions.

Starvation, more than the Japanese shells, was the real enemy. Wainwright held Corregidor until May 6 before surrendering. On May 10, Major General William Sharp surrendered his troops on Mindanao. A small guerrilla force under Colonel John Horan, which had withdrawn to the mountains of northern Luzon, gave up on May 18. The Japanese now possessed the Philippine Islands.

It was a grievous blow, both to the Philippine people and to the Americans, who were not accustomed to accepting defeat. All that sustained the war effort with regard to these islands was the pledge General MacArthur made when he stepped ashore in Australia, having endured a harrowing Pacific voyage on a tiny PT boat. Before an array of microphones, he broadcast to the world: "I shall return."

BORNEO

AMERICANS AND OTHERS WOULD, in the course of World War II, become intimately familiar with some of the most remote places on Earth. Borneo, the world's third largest island, was one of these. Remote, it was nevertheless strategically situated across the principal sea-lanes of the region. Possession of Borneo would provide a broad platform from which the Japanese could mount an invasion of Australia.

Borneo fell under attack in December 1941. The small number of Anglo-Indian troops there defended only a single objective, Kuching airfield in Sarawak. However, they set about destroying oil fields in Sarawak and in Seria, Brunei, thereby depriving the Japanese of these valuable resources when they landed on December 15. The Anglo-Indian forces conducted a fighting withdrawal into Dutch Borneo before finally surrendering.

SINGAPORE

AFTER THE FALL OF MALAYA, British general Arthur Percival withdrew his soldiers across the Johore Strait to the island of Singapore. After the last troops were across, on January 31, 1942, Percival ordered the

REALITY CHECK

Epic Withdrawal

Some military historians and others have criticized MacArthur for preparing inadequately for the invasion, yet no one can deny that the epic withdrawal of the Filipino and U.S. forces was brilliantly led. It cost the Japanese men and time. As for the Americans and Filipinos, combat losses and desertions (mainly from the Philippine army) amounted to 13,000 men, which left about 80,000 troops on Bataan.

causeway connecting Johore and Singapore destroyed. Unfortunately, the job was never fully completed.

Percival had an army of about eighty-five thousand British, Indian, and Australian troops—although, of these, perhaps only seventy thousand were fully armed combat soldiers. Defending Singapore required sealing a thirty-mile perimeter. Singapore was a formidable naval fortress, but its artillery was permanently fixed to fire toward the sea and in a flat trajectory intended to destroy attacking ships. Against an attack by land, the guns were virtually useless.

General Tomoyuki Yamashita, having earned the sobriquet of the "Tiger of Malaya," now turned his attention on Singapore. Yamashita positioned heavy siege artillery at the southern tip of the Malay Peninsula and commenced firing on Singapore on February 5. After this artillery preparation, during the nights of February 8 and 9, he landed about five thousand men on the island, who quickly captured bridgeheads on the northwest and northern sides. Seeing that the great causeway was still intact, Japanese engineers made hasty repairs, and twenty-five thousand more troops, with tanks, rolled across.

As the Japanese ground forces moved toward Singapore City, artillery and aircraft kept up a steady bombardment. On February 13, Percival ordered the evacuation of three thousand British noncombatants in small boats. Japanese patrols intercepted them, killing or capturing most.

The ground assault drove a wedge between the defenders' various positions. Yamashita out-generaled Percival, defeating his forces in detail. By mid February, Singapore was completely cut off, running critically short of food, water, ammunition, and fuel. Percival therefore surrendered on February 15, 1942, turning over to the Japanese an island of great strategic and economic value, along with the thirty-two thousand Indian, sixteen thousand British, and fourteen thousand Australian troops under his command.

REALITY CHECK

Occupation Impossible

Occupying the Philippines turned out to be a full-time job for the Japanese. A significant number of Filipino and American troops refused to surrender and, fighting as guerrillas, continually harassed the occupation forces, their activities tying down many troops. In addition, guerrillas supplied the Allied commanders with a stream of behind-the-lines intelligence, which greatly aided the Pacific campaign.

NUMBERS

British Troop Losses

Combined, the British defeats at Malaya and Singapore cost the Allies 138,000 soldiers, 130,000 of whom became prisoners of war. They were especially humiliating defeats.

"If the army can't fight better than it is doing at the present we shall deserve to lose our empire!"

British general Sir Alan Brooke, writing in his diary on February 18, 1942

REVENGE

DELUGED BY DISASTER ON THE PACIFIC FRONT, President Franklin Roosevelt was desperate to buy time for the buildup of American forces. During this build-up period, he knew that the news was certain to continue being all bad. He wanted the military to come up with an operation that would lift morale *now*, even as it shook the confidence of the triumphant Japanese. The official U.S. Army Air Forces account of the operation that soon took shape credits the president with the idea, but U.S. fleet commander Admiral Ernest J. King reported after the war that the first he had heard of a daring plan to attack Tokyo and other Japanese cities was in the form of a casual remark by his operations officer, who off-handedly observed that it was probably possible to launch twin-engine bombers from an aircraft carrier—even though these aircraft were designed to take off from runways that were much longer than an aircraft carrier deck. Why would you want to fly a bomber off the deck of a carrier? The Japanese had deprived the Allies of every piece of land close enough to Japan to launch an air attack. Only an aircraft carrier could get close enough. If you could fly bombers off of a carrier deck, you could bomb Japan.

King took fire from the idea. He met with Air Forces chief Henry "Hap" Arnold, proposed it, and was met with high enthusiasm. Arnold turned to Colonel James H. "Jimmy" Doolittle, a daring pilot who also had an advanced degree in aerodynamics. He asked him to organize and to lead an air group to execute the mission—to launch bombers from an aircraft carrier in order to raid Tokyo and other cities.

Doolittle chose the B-25B "Mitchell" medium bomber for the job. An advanced aircraft, it was also sturdy and combat proven. He quickly made tests to demonstrate that it could be launched from a carrier even while hauling a militarily useful bomb load—one ton—and enough fuel to get it to targets in Japan and then continue to airstrips in China.

After Doolittle established the technical feasibility of the mission and honed the maneuvers necessary for lifting off a short deck, he recruited volunteers, telling them only that the mission was top secret and that it was extremely dangerous. Doolittle took on crews and back-up crews for sixteen aircraft—the most that could possibly be jammed onto a flight deck (the planes were too big to fit on the elevators that would have taken them to the hangar deck below the flight deck). He then conducted an intensive training program for the recruits while also supervising technical modifications to their aircraft.

REALITY CHECK

One Way to China

Landing in China was the only hope of recovering the aircraft and the crews. Although, with plenty of practice, the B-25s could be launched from a carrier, there was no way to land them on one. The plan was to turn the bombers over to the Chinese air force and to get the crews home by whatever roundabout routes could be found.

REALITY CHECK

To Midway Island

The Doolittle Raid had another effect that the planners could not have anticipated. It lifted all official objection in Japanese military circles to a plan proposed by Admiral Isoroku Yamamoto to lure the American fleet to the vicinity of Midway Island so that the Japanese fleet could deliver a fatal blow, finishing the job left incomplete by the attack on Pearl Harbor. As it turned out, the Battle of Midway would bring a hard-fought American victory that turned the tide of the war in the Pacific.

A sailor aboard the aircraft carrier USS Hornet *snapped this photo of one of Jimmy Doolittle's B-25 bombers lifting off en route to raid Japan for the first time in the war.*

Chosen to carry the aircraft into battle was the USS *Hornet*, a brand-new aircraft carrier; however, the mission was kept so tightly under wraps that the *Hornet*'s skipper, Captain Marc A. Mitscher, was not even briefed until just before the bombers were loaded onto the flight deck. He sailed his ship out of harbor on April 2, 1942; en route, it was joined by the carrier *Enterprise*, flagship of Admiral William F. "Bull" Halsey. The mission of the *Enterprise* was to provide air cover as the ships approached the launching point, just four hundred miles off the Japanese mainland, scheduled to be reached on April 18.

Just before dawn on the eighteenth, Japanese picket (patrol) craft were sighted much farther east than expected. The *Hornet* task force evaded some of the pickets and sank others, but Doolittle had to assume that they had already transmitted radio warnings. If Japanese warships attacked, at the very least the element of surprise would be lost—at worst, the B-25s would be lost. Doolittle therefore decided to launch his raid, not four hundred miles off the Japanese coast, but right now, seven hundred miles from the coast. Fuel was already tight. Launching from this distance would mean that at least some of the aircraft would be unable to reach Chinese airfields. Extremely dangerous from its inception, the raid was now virtually a suicide mission. Doolittle was undeterred.

At about 8:00 A.M. on the eighteenth, the raiders took off, sixteen five-man crews. They reached their targets undetected and unopposed, one bomber attacking Kobe, another Nagoya, and a third, slated to bomb Osaka, opting instead to drop its bombs on the Yokosuka naval yard and on Yokohama. Engine trouble forced one plane to divert to Vladivostok, but the twelve other raiders bombed Tokyo at noon.

Coincidentally, the citizens of Tokyo were conducting an air raid drill at precisely this time. Almost certainly this blunted the psychological impact of the raid, but the drill also provided a diversion that probably helped the bombers escape pursuit by fighters. Not a single B-25 was lost over Japan.

Sixteen bombers carrying a total of sixteen tons of explosives do not inflict extensive damage. About fifty people were killed and one hundred houses damaged or destroyed. But strategic destruction was never the objective of the raid. It was, rather, to shatter the Japanese aura of invincibility, to show the people of Japan that they were vulnerable to attack, and to force the Japanese air forces to divert significant numbers of aircraft to defend the home islands. Additionally, as President Roosevelt had wanted, the raid on the Japanese heartland would be felt by Americans as some measure of vengeance for Pearl Harbor and all the rest.

Their bombs dropped, the raiders, all critically short of fuel, either crash-landed as best they could on Chinese soil or bailed out. That Doolittle and seventy other mission members survived to find their way back home is very nearly miraculous.

NUMBERS

Consequences

One airman was killed when he parachuted from his plane, and eight more were captured by the Japanese. Of these eight, three were executed and one died in prison. The others survived the war and were liberated. Far more horrific were the reprisals Japanese occupation authorities took against the Chinese because some had aided crews who had landed or ditched in China. In the wake of the Doolittle mission, Japanese soldiers murdered some 250,000 Chinese civilians.

BURMA

THE DOOLITTLE RAID ON TOKYO and the other cities was a major psychological victory—but wars are not won by psychological victories alone. The reality, after some four months of war in the Pacific, was that Japan had seized major strong points and was poised to take others. Burma, through which China could be supplied, was attacked by Japanese forces on December 14, 1941. Victoria Point and its airfield at the southern tip of Burma fell, preventing the British from flying reinforcements from India to Malaya. During January 1942, Tavoy, Kawkareik, and Moulmein, all north of Victoria Point, were captured, and on March 8, Rangoon, Burma's capital city, fell to Japan.

Combined British and Chinese attempts to retake Burma failed, forcing the Chinese and the British to retreat into India as the Japanese continued a relentless advance. By April 1942, the Imperial Japanese Army had reached the Chinese-Burmese frontier. Months of fighting in Burma had cost the Anglo-Indian forces dearly and had gained the Allies nothing.

TAKEAWAY

Onslaught and Reprisal

In the weeks and months following the attack on Pearl Harbor, Japanese forces overran most important Allied outposts in Asia and the Pacific, suffering a single, mostly psychological and symbolic, defeat at the hands of Jimmy Doolittle and his daring B-25 raiders.

PART FOUR

UNDERBELLY

On preceding pages: Yugoslavia falls to German invaders. Many in this crowd were happy to greet the victory of Fascism over Communism, but Communist partisans, chiefly led by Josip Broz—known as "Tito"—resisted the German occupation throughout the war and were an invaluable aid to the Allied war effort in the Balkans.

CHAPTER 11

GREECE AND THE BALKANS

War at the Fringes of Europe

THE STORY OF WORLD WAR II IS HARDLY NEW. It has been told in books hundreds, probably thousands, of times. But that doesn't make the telling any easier. The magnitude and simultaneity of the conflict—it was, really, a collection of many wars in many places—defies simple narrative. While the titanic events of Western Europe and the Soviet invasion were unfolding, along with the fierce war engulfing Asia and the Pacific, the struggle also raged along the margins of what most participants in and observers of the combat considered the main battlefields. From even before the beginning of the war, the Mediterranean and southern Europe, especially the Balkans, were troubled. It was the region Prime Minister Winston Churchill included in what he called the "soft underbelly of Europe," the region he would target as the best way for the Western Allies to begin chipping away at the Axis conquest.

INVADING ALBANIA

BEFORE WORLD WAR I, WHICH BEGAN THERE, the countries and peoples of the Balkan Peninsula were little known to most Americans and even to most Western Europeans. Among the most obscure of the obscure Balkan nations, even as late as the eve of World War II, was Albania, on the western portion of the peninsula at the Strait of Otranto, the southern entry into the Adriatic Sea. In 1939, Albania was ruled by King Zog, who had devoted much of his reign to forging closer relations with Italy. Under Zog, in fact, Italian influence had become so pervasive that, on April 7, 1939, when the armies of Benito Mussolini invaded, Albanians offered little resistance—although a pair of government battalions and a handful of irregulars managed to slow the Italian advance for some thirty-six hours, giving Zog, his queen, and their infant son time to flee to Britain.

Victor Emmanuel II, king of Italy, was proclaimed king of Albania as the nation was annexed to Italy, but the real government was a Fascist regime installed at Tirana, the national capital. A diehard core of Albanian nationalists mounted a revolt against the new government early in 1940, which the British—now that war was under way—covertly supported. The revolt was led from Kosovo, a province of Yugoslavia, but when Germany invaded Yugoslavia in April 1941, Kosovo was delivered to Albanian control, and the revolt promptly dissolved.

The Communist partisan Enver Hoxha—at left—led the Albanian resistance to the German occupation. He is seen here on December 29, 1944, reviewing troops celebrating the liberation of Tirana, Albania's capital.

Nationalism did not die, however. The revolt against Italian occupation was renewed during late 1942 and into 1943 under the leadership of a college professor and committed Communist named Enver Hoxha, who worked in cooperation with Yugoslavia's Communist nationalist leader, Josip Broz ("Tito"), to form a partisan movement, a campaign of guerrilla warfare against the occupiers. Beginning in 1943, British SOE (Special Operations Executive) agents worked in cooperation with the Albanian partisans. This put a strong resistance movement in place when, later in the year, Mussolini was overthrown as leader of Italy. That triggered a general insurrection throughout Albania. Of the five Italian divisions occupying the country, two obeyed the orders of the new

Italian head of state, Marshal Pietro Badoglio, and joined the partisans. With the overthrow of Mussolini, Badoglio had agreed to a separate peace with the Allies, breaking away from the Axis. He now faced the task of persuading the army to turn 180 degrees against the nation's former ally. The other three divisions either cooperated with German units or simply dispersed. In any case, by the fall of 1943, the Albanian partisans had seized most of the equipment of the Italian garrison and liberated their country from Italian occupation.

"I think you will agree that there is a vast difference, in ethics, between the time honoured operation of the dropping of a spy from the air and this entirely new scheme for dropping what one can only call assassins."

British air chief marshal Charles Portal, an early opponent to the formation of the SOE

Almost immediately after the partisan liberation, Albania was overrun by German invaders. They set about crushing the partisan movement through a regime of reprisals, killing disproportionate numbers of civilians in response to every act of partisan resistance. Thoroughly terrorized, most Albanians withdrew any support for the partisan movement. For their part, their hands full at this point in the war, the Germans were less interested in conquering Albania than in merely neutralizing it. The Third Reich supported Mehdi Frasheri, a former Ottoman governor of Jerusalem, to form a neutral government. Frasheri controlled the major cities and the nation's coastal plain, but the rest of Albania was torn among rival warlords and guerrilla leaders. The ensuing chaos gave Enver Hoxha the opportunity he wanted to assert his own dominance by suppressing a militant anti-Communist activist organization resistance known as the Balli Kombëtar. The German government aided Frasheri in supporting the Balli Kombëtar with equipment and weapons, thereby prompting the partisans to accuse the Ballists of collaborating with Germany. This brought Albania to civil war—in the midst of the greater war swirling around it—and the country was so destabilized that, by early 1944, Germany was able to regain complete control over the coast and the major cities.

DETAILS, DETAILS

Stealth Agents

SOE, Special Operations Executive, was formed by the British in July 1940 as a secret service to foster and support subversive warfare in enemy-occupied countries. SOE agents—whose ranks included many women—braved great danger to infiltrate far behind enemy lines to coordinate the activities of resistance fighters, partisans, and guerrillas, as well as undertake commando missions.

REALITY CHECK

Zog in Britain

The British government had no love for Mussolini, and it welcomed Zog and his family—as refugees. Fearful of pushing the Italian dictator into the arms of Germany, however, Britain refused to recognize Zog as head of the Albanian state and even went so far as to recognize Italy's annexation of Albania.

At this late point in the war, the Allies recognized that the chief value of Albania to Hitler was as a route of retreat from Greece. Hoping to destroy the German army rather than let it retreat intact, the British SOE again supplied Albanian partisans, urging the nation to abandon civil war and turn against the common enemy, Germany. Tragically, the weapons supplied by the British were used not against the German invaders, but were turned by one faction against the other. The civil war intensified.

In September 1944, just as the British had feared, the German army withdrew from Greece and retreated through Albania. Aided by the Balli Kombëtar, on the run from Communist forces, the tribal leader Abas Kupi led hit-and-run attacks against the German columns, but the civil war, continuing unabated, prevented British agents from inciting all of northern Albania against the Germans.

GREEK EPIC

WHEN HE INVADED ALBANIA IN APRIL 1939, Mussolini emulated Adolf Hitler by giving assurances that his territorial ambitions extended no farther than that country. He assured Britain and France that Italy would not go on to invade Greece, but, despite this pledge, Britain and France promised to defend the sovereignty of Greece as well as Romania. Although Britain recognized Italy's annexation of Albania, its promise to stand by Greece and Romania propelled Italy directly into the German camp as Mussolini and Hitler concluded the Pact of Steel on May 22, 1939, formalizing the Rome-Berlin "Axis."

In contrast to Hitler, Mussolini wavered in his aggression, promising not to invade Greece—even after Italy declared war against the Allies on June 10, 1940. Ultimately, the promise was not worth much. On October 28, 1940, asserting that Greece had forfeited its status as a neutral because of its friendship with Britain, Benito Mussolini marched Italian troops from Albania into Greece. The Italian dictator made it a practice to choose his fights carefully, targeting nations from which he expected no resistance—or just enough to make the conquest that much more glorious. By the time Italy moved against Greece, France had fallen and Britain was fighting for its life. Mussolini reasoned that Greece was therefore essentially defenseless, and he invaded on the cheap, with an under-

REALITY CHECK

Churchill Retaliates

Seeing an opportunity to cause Germany pain and loss, Winston Churchill sent considerable RAF forces to Greece, even though homeland defense was obviously the top British priority. Five RAF fighter squadrons were sent to the region, and long-range British bombers were dispatched to drop ordnance on Italian port facilities and communications outposts as the Greeks advanced against the Albanian town of Valona. It was a bold move by a determined war leader who did not relish staying on the defensive.

strength force that—to his great chagrin and humiliation—was easily brushed aside by Greek resistance, which was shored up by five Royal Air Force (RAF) squadrons that provided close air support. Worse for Mussolini, on November 14, the Greeks mounted a counteroffensive that pushed the Italians out of the country and deep into Albania.

Hitler watched Mussolini falter. He had no great desire to bail out his Italian ally, but he desperately wanted to secure the Romanian oil fields and to provide protection for what would be the southern flank of the Soviet invasion he was planning. He decided, therefore, that he could not let Greece be lost, and, in January 1941, Germany built up a troop concentration in Romania, which had recently joined the Axis. Luftwaffe units were sent to another new Axis member, Bulgaria. Both ground and air forces were poised on the borders of Greece even as German diplomats made a show of mediating between Greece and Italy.

On March 9, 1941, Mussolini decided to redeem the honor of Italian arms by launching a new invasion into Greece, this time using twenty-eight divisions. Despite the greatly enlarged force, however, the Italians were again pushed out of Greece. Nevertheless, the Greeks were in a desperate situation, especially now that, for political reasons, the Anglo-Greek alliance was beginning to falter. Fortunately for the Greeks, the announcement by the Yugoslav government, on March 25, that it was joining the Axis provoked an anti-Fascist coup in Yugoslavia, which had the effect of reinvigorating the Greek-British alliance. Seeing weakness in the hold of the Axis over the Balkans, the British government rushed troops to Greece, along with yet more RAF units. This would have been quite sufficient to crush the Italians once and for all, but, on April 6, 1941, the Germans entered the fray by bombing Belgrade, Yugoslavia, and, simultaneously, invading both Yugoslavia and Greece with its Twelfth Army, under General Siegmund List. On April 8 and April 10, a combination of German, Italian, and Hungarian troops marched into Yugoslavia, taking Belgrade on April 12 and forcing the anti-Fascist coup leaders to surrender on the seventeenth.

The rapid collapse of Yugoslav resistance allowed List to send his army directly into Greece in a lightning movement that

REALITY CHECK

Rail Resistance

All too often, national resistance movements were largely symbolic in nature. The Greek resistance fighters, however, took a very realistic and pragmatic approach to their work. They never engaged in resistance or sabotage for its own sake, but focused on what they identified as the most vulnerable aspect of the German occupation: the rail lines, which were essential for transporting German troops and keeping them supplied. Greece's rail network was meager to begin with, and the guerrillas continually attacked it, quite effectively disrupting the daily business of occupation.

After the diminutive and poorly equipped Greek army repelled an Italian invasion, Adolf Hitler came to the aid of his ally Mussolini by staging a new invasion. The Germans succeeded where the Italians had failed, as this photograph of German vehicles rolling southward through Greece in April 1941 attests.

outflanked the Greek troops who held the defensive Aliakmon Line. At the same time, he dispatched his XVIII Corps against the so-called Metaxas Line (a chain of fortifications along Greece's border with Bulgaria), taking the key Greek port of Salonika on April 9. Maitland Wilson, the general in charge of British ground forces aiding the Greeks, pulled his men back to a new defensive line on April 10, but on the fourteenth, withdrew all the way to Thermopylae. Fearing the complete collapse of Greek army morale, General Alexandros Papagos delayed leaving the Albanian Front as long as possible. By the time he finally began to withdraw, on April 12, List had been able to drive a wedge between the Greek forces and their British and Commonwealth allies. A New Zealand unit defeated List's XVIII Corps at Olympus Pass on April 14, but this furnished a mere reprieve for the Allies. On April 21, deciding it was time to cut losses, British high command pulled all British and Commonwealth units out of Greece, and the Greek army, instantly overwhelmed, surrendered.

The Germans did their best to disrupt the British and Commonwealth evacuation, but it was successfully completed during the night of April 30/May 1. The Greek Communist Party (KKE) parted company with the Greek government and quickly organized guerrilla bands into a coordinated anti-Nazi resistance that became, in September 1941, the National Liberation Front (EAM). Although the core of the EAM was Communist, the organization attracted Greek nationalists of every stripe. In December, EAM established the National People's Liberation Army (ELAS), which deployed in the country's rugged mountains, where it was joined by other, smaller resistance groups, most notably the National Republican League (EDES). Recognizing a viable partisan movement, the British SOE parachuted operatives into the country to work with the guerrillas, who specialized in sabotage, persisting in acts of destruction despite drastic German reprisals.

The Battle for Crete

Although the British had withdrawn from the Greek mainland on April 30/May 1, they wanted desperately to hold on to the Greek island of Crete to use as a base for bombers flying against Romania's Ploesti oil fields, which were critical to Germany's vast war machine. At this point in the war, however, the demands of so many other fronts left few resources to spare for the Crete garrison. Just thirty-five thousand soldiers—a mixture of British, Commonwealth, and Greek troops—were expected to defend the island. As if their weak numbers were not problem enough, the mountainous topography of the rugged island impeded mobility, making defense that much more difficult.

"At first it was impressive, but after half an hour deadly monotonous. It was like everything German—overdone."

British novelist Evelyn Waugh, diary entry on the bombing of Crete, May 26, 1941

The Germans decided to take Crete by means of an airborne assault, and on May 20, German paratroops of Fliegerkorps XI, under General Kurt Student, landed at both ends of the island. It was a tactic calculated to strain the already inadequate defense forces, and the Allies did just what Student hoped they would: They spread their forces very thin in an effort to cover attacks from both sides. Nevertheless, the defense forces were larger than Student had anticipated, and he was forced to call for reinforcements from the island of Milos. British aircraft descended on the troop transports, which were either sunk or dispersed. Left on their own, the elite paratroops succeeded in taking the airfield at Maleme, which was sufficient to turn the tide against the defenders.

NUMBERS

Crete Troop Losses

Losses in the battle of Crete were heavy and included 1,742 British, Greek, and Commonwealth troops killed, 2,225 wounded, and 11,370 captured. The Royal Navy lost nearly 2,000 men killed and 183 wounded. Yet German fatalities were even greater: 7,000 of Student's elite paratroops were killed. These losses stunned Hitler, who deemed the battle of Crete a Pyrrhic victory and personally forbade airborne assaults for the rest of the war. The German army never again launched a major paratroop operation.

On May 26, Lieutenant General Sir Bernard Freyberg, overall commander of the Allied garrison, radioed British command that he could no longer defend Crete and secured permission to evacuate. Yet another British withdrawal began on May 27, to Sphakia in southwestern Crete and Heraklion, the capital in the north-central part of the island. From Heraklion, troops were quickly removed by British warships. However, several battalions, mostly Australian soldiers, left behind to defend Retimo airfield were soon cut off and surrendered, and the troops who had withdrawn to Sphakia found themselves targeted by a massive air attack, that sank three of the British cruisers and six of the destroyers that had come to fetch the troops. Seventeen other vessels of the evacuation fleet were badly damaged, and on May 30, the entire evacuation had to be aborted, leaving five thousand men stranded on Crete.

The German airborne assault on Crete in May 1941 succeeded in defeating the British defenders of the island, but at such a high cost that Hitler barred any further major airborne operations for the rest of the war. The photograph shows the demise of a German transport plane.

The majority of these were taken by the Germans, but a significant number managed to evade capture and joined the small but valiant Cretan resistance, which harassed the German occupiers of the island until the Germans withdrew from Crete in 1944.

The Yugoslav Front

Yugoslavia was a new nation at the outbreak of World War II, having been created on December 1, 1918, following World War I (at first called the Kingdom of the Serbs, Croats, and Slovenes). Its founding was an attempt to stabilize the Balkans by uniting the disparate southern Slavic lands, which had been possessions of the Austro-Hungarian Empire, with Serbia and Montenegro, which were already independent. The hope was that the new country would reduce the likelihood that the Balkans would once again prove a tinderbox to ignite war.

It was, of course, a forlorn hope. With a population of nearly sixteen million and a territory of some ninety-five thousand square miles, Yugoslavia was, between the wars, a nation in name only. Tensions were especially great between the country's Catholic Croat and Orthodox Serb populations. When World War II broke out in September 1939, Yugoslavia declared itself neutral, but the religious and ethnic gulf dividing Croat and Serb was greatly widened by the war. The Serbs, who made up the majority of the armed forces, were pro-Allied, but the Croats and others, although not opposed to the Allies, were quite unwilling to challenge the Axis. Ultimately, the issue of Yugoslav neutrality was moot because Germany not only dominated the country's foreign trade but also owned a controlling share of its important nonferrous mines. Early in the war, Yugoslavia's head of state, Prince Paul (who served as regent to the underage King Peter), repeatedly and increasingly gave in to German demands for the cheap export of agricultural produce and raw materials. Even more ominously, Yugoslavia yielded to Germany on the matter of

LINK

Croat vs. Serb

In World War II, Hitler avidly exploited the age-old enmity between the Croats and Serbs. After the war, Tito managed to create a state of peaceful coexistence, but after he died in 1980, the nation began to fall apart. With the general collapse of Eastern European Communism in the early 1990s, Yugoslavia became a loose federation, which Bosnia voted to leave in 1992. The Bosnian Orthodox Serbs, however, refused to secede, triggering a genocidal civil war (1992–95) between the Bosnian Catholic Croats, who wanted independence, and the Serbs, who did not.

Jewish policy by instituting a program of organized anti-Semitic discrimination and persecution.

Prince Paul, regent of Yugoslavia, stands next to Adolf Hitler on a lavishly decorated dais on June 1, 1939, during a parade in Berlin given in the prince's honor. The prince made a series of concessions to the Nazis in the vain hope of appeasing Hitler.

It was, in fact, very difficult for Yugoslavia to resist the Axis machine. Each of its neighbors, Hungary, Romania, and Bulgaria, entered the Axis orbit, whereas the Allies were staggered under the repeated blows of Hitler's armies and air force. Neither Britain nor France was in any position to bolster a Yugoslav stance against Hitler and Mussolini. And, as for the Soviet Union, having signed the 1939 Non-Aggression Pact with Hitler, Joseph Stalin was in no humor to suddenly defy him. Thus, very early in the war, Yugoslavia found itself surrounded by Axis powers and existing entirely at the mercy of Italy and Germany.

To Hitler, Yugoslavia represented a rich source of agricultural produce and important ores—copper, chrome, lead, zinc, and bauxite (aluminum ore), all of which were of great strategic value. Equally important, the sprawling nation was strategically situated, offering a ready means for traversing the entire Balkan region. Surrounded by potential enemies and invaders, Prince Paul at length yielded to Hitler and added his signature to the Tripartite (Axis) Pact on March 25, 1941.

Now Yugoslavia was a German ally—but that did not bring the stability Paul had hoped for. Signing onto the Axis Pact immediately ignited demonstrations by Serbian nationalists, leading them to join forces with various elements of the military to stage a coup on the twenty-seventh. Prince Paul was overthrown—that is, his regency over King Peter was dissolved—and a new government was formed under the presidency of General Dušan Simoviç.

Yet the overthrow of Paul did not end the alliance with Germany. The Croats who formed part of the new government insisted that Yugoslavia continue to adhere to the Axis Pact. Suddenly fearful of a German invasion—and having no desire to alienate the Croats—the Serb majority folded, agreeing to retain membership in the Axis. But now it was Hitler who rejected the pact. He issued Directive 25, an order for nothing less than the obliteration of Yugoslavia as a sovereign entity.

Josip Broz, "Tito," (center) presides over a meeting of Communist partisans in a Yugoslav cave or dugout near Vis. The price of supporting Tito was the creation of Communist Yugoslavia after the war. Under Tito, Yugoslavia steered a course of independence from both the West and the Soviet Union.

On April 6, 1941, simultaneously with the German assault on Greece, Hitler's legions invaded Yugoslavia, starting with the bombing of Belgrade and followed by ground operations. Government-organized resistance crumbled under blitzkrieg tactics, and Yugoslavia surrendered on April 17. Hitler tapped General Milan Nediç to head a puppet government, then promptly instituted a policy intended to "Germanize" Yugoslavia, beginning with a campaign of genocide against Croatia's Serb minority as well as Jews, Gypsies, and others the Nazis branded as undesirable. The invaders made use of Croat henchmen, who willingly acted as Hitler's executioners. This, however, proved to be a grave error on the part of the Nazis. As nothing else could have done, the Nazi-Croat reign of genocide galvanized the Serbian will to resist the Axis. A Serb uprising erupted, which was soon organized into a widespread and quite effective partisan movement.

In the meantime, during June 1941, King Peter—now of an age that freed him from Prince Paul's regency—established a government in exile in London. Yet neither Peter nor his government proved a dynamic force, and the Allies decided to support not the king but the far more charismatic leader, the Communist partisan Tito. Prime Minister Winston Churchill intervened to create a coalition between Tito and King Peter by broadly hinting to the Communist leader that this would put him into position to take control of most of Yugoslavia after the Germans had been ousted. Churchill had no love for Communism, but he knew an effective leader when he encountered one, and he was quite willing to buy Tito's cooperation. It was a good bargain. Tito led perhaps the most militarily successful partisan campaign of the war. By the end of 1943, his forces—about two hundred thousand in number—had succeeded in pinning down thirty-five Axis divisions—approximately three-quarters of a million soldiers—who would otherwise be fighting the Western Allies in Italy or the Soviets on the Eastern Front.

TAKEAWAY

Strategic Territory

Greece and the Balkans were at the margins of the war in Europe, but were coveted by the Axis as important sources of strategic raw materials and as territory essential to maneuver, especially between Germany and the Soviet Front. Churchill saw the region as an important back door into the Continent, part of what he called the vulnerable "soft underbelly" of Europe.

CHAPTER 12

AFRICA AND THE MIDDLE EAST

The End of the Beginning

WHAT DID IT MEAN TO FIGHT a *world* war? In large part, it meant learning that no region of the world was safely insulated from another. It meant fighting close to home and also very far away. It meant thinking, planning, and acting strategically, controlling apparently remote regions that held vital raw materials or that figured as a means of access to vital supply and transportation routes. It also meant finding and exploiting weaknesses in the enemy, identifying his isolated colonial garrisons and attacking them.

In the early months of the Pacific struggle, the Japanese excelled at fighting a world war. For them, no place was too remote. For them, all regions offering strategic war materials were valuable. For them, the weakness of the enemy was a magnet, not to be resisted. But even before the Japanese opened the Pacific theater of the war, the English also strove to master the meaning of world war. Even as they reeled under the Blitz assault on their homeland and braced to fight a defensive war against what they thought was the inevitable—a German invasion—the British fought an offensive war at the margins of what had once been their empire. It was at these margins, too, that America, when it finally entered the war, would strike its first offensive blows.

EARLY TRIUMPHS IN THE DESERT

AS THE WAR IN EUROPE BEGAN, Libya—a major part of which had been colonized by Italy in 1912 and completely pacified by 1934—was the nation with the principal North African ports supplying the Axis war effort via the Mediterranean. As a long-established Italian stronghold, Libya was also the ideal staging area from which to launch an invasion of British-controlled Egypt, an even more strategically valuable prize than Libya. Since 1869, the Suez Canal had run north-south across the Egyptian Isthmus of Suez, joining the Mediterranean and the Red seas, both separating and uniting Africa and Asia, and providing the shortest sea route between Europe and the lands of the Indian and western Pacific oceans. Since its opening, it had become one of the world's most heavily traveled shipping lanes. Whoever controlled the canal controlled much of the globe's shipping. Possession of the Suez Canal could both provide a lifeline and furnish a stranglehold.

Only after Italy's absolute dictator, Benito Mussolini, believed that the German juggernaut had virtually ensured Axis victory did he bring Italy into the war, on June 10, 1940, attacking a prostrate France. He was, however, fatally slow in ordering his marshal in Libya, Rodolfo Graziani, to strike out against British-held Egypt. Italian forces in Italy far outnumbered British forces in Egypt, and a timely attack might have seized the Suez Canal for the Axis, but Mussolini did not order an invasion until September 17, 1940. The odds were overwhelmingly with the Italians. The invading force, the Italian Tenth Army, under General Mario Berti, consisted of five (later augmented to nine) divisions; it was opposed by the British Western Desert Force, with just two divisions commanded by Archibald Wavell.

> "I think he (Benito Mussolini) must do something, if he cannot make a graceful dive he will at least have to jump in somehow; he can hardly put on his dressing-gown and walk down the stairs again."
>
> *General Sir Archibald Wavell, writing in a letter to a colleague about Mussolini's hesitation to enter the war*

By World War II, Egypt was no longer a part of the British Empire, but it was no more than nominally independent of British control. The key document was the 1936 Anglo-Egyptian Treaty, which gave Britain the right to defend the Suez Canal and obliged the Egyptian government, in time of emergency, to turn over to British forces control of almost everything of military value in the country. For all practical purposes, Egypt was under British occupation throughout the war. Its capital, Cairo, was headquarters for the British Middle East Command. Yet it was also the case that Egypt's King Farouk and his prime minister, Ali Mahir, were anti-British and pro-Fascist. Neither leader actively opposed the British, but they consistently withheld full cooperation by tolerating German and Italian nationals in the country, despite British orders that these individuals be placed under arrest. (Later in the war, they were, in fact, rounded up by British authorities.) In June 1940, British pressure finally prompted Farouk to remove Ali Mahir as prime minister, but when the Italian invasion came on September 17, Farouk refused to declare war on Italy, even though the 1936 treaty obligated him to do so if Italy invaded. He proclaimed instead a state of non-belligerency, leaving Wavell and his troops to manage against the Italians as best they could.

REALITY CHECK

Hidden Black Gold

With its ports, Libya was of great strategic significance during World War II. Had its rich reserves of oil been discovered by this time, it would have been an even greater prize; however, Libya's oil remained unknown until postwar exploration.

Despite the odds against him, Wavell staged a counterattack against the invaders on December 9, 1940, stunning the Italians and inflicting heavy losses. The British penetrated Libya and, in January, took the Libyan Mediterranean port of Bardia, forcing the Italians to withdraw northwest, into Tripolitania. Unwilling to lose Libya to the Allies, Adolf Hitler ordered the German 5th Light Division (part of the Afrika Korps, soon to become one of the German army's most celebrated units) to reinforce the Italians. Despite the addition of the German troops—who were far superior to the Italians, in equipment, training, and leadership—one of Wavell's key field commanders, General Richard O'Connor, advanced against Tobruk, a major port in northeastern Libya, on January 7, 1941. His British XIII Corps—known as the "Western Desert Force"—laid siege to the city, and, on January 21, the 6th Australian Division and the 7th (British) Armored Division attacked the fortress there, which was heavily garrisoned by thirty-two thousand Italian troops of Graziani's Tenth Army under the immediate command of

A pair of British tanks patrols Tobruk, Libya.

General Petassi Manella. The attack was brilliantly executed, dividing the perimeter defenses, bringing Tobruk to its knees by the night of January 22. Manella and twenty-five thousand of his men were made prisoners of war, whereas British and Commonwealth losses were light. It was a signal triumph.

With Tobruk in hand, O'Connor marched across the desert to cut off the retreat of the Italian Tenth Army at Beda Fomm. This achieved, Wavell and O'Connor were now prepared to drive the Italians out of Libya altogether. It was at this point, however, that British high command ordered them to send troops to Greece to help drive off a combined German-Italian invasion there (see Chapter 11, "Greek Epic").

ALTERNATE TAKE

Win Some, Lose Some

The order diverting troops from North Africa to Greece was a mistake of grave consequence. Had Wavell and O'Connor been permitted to focus on the Italians, the North African campaign would have ended more quickly than it did—and with less loss of life. Yet the order illustrates the great problem of fighting a world war. Churchill did not want to lose Greece in order to conquer Libya, and he hoped he could avoid the former while still achieving the latter. But to win victory in one area often requires neglecting another, and that was the hard lesson the Allies would learn—repeatedly.

Enter Rommel

The British order to divert troops to Greece unwittingly gave the Axis forces just the opening they needed for a counterattack. That operation was led by Erwin Rommel, one of Germany's most highly respected commanders. In the 1930s, he had led the Führerbegleitbataillon, Hitler's personal bodyguard, and, during the Battle of France (Chapter 4), he commanded the 7th Panzer Division. One of Germany's leading exponents of armored warfare, Rommel was a master tank tactician. At the beginning of February 1941, he assumed command of the Afrika Korps in Libya.

On March 24, Rommel hit the British and Commonwealth forces—diminished in number by the troops sent to Greece—at El Agheila, which quickly fell, followed by Mersa Brega, which he captured on April 1. Rommel rolled over thinned-out British resistance to recapture Benghazi on April 4. Four days later, he was at Tobruk, which was garrisoned principally by the 9th Australian Division. Instead of laying siege, the relentlessly aggressive Rommel led a storming attack that spanned April 10 to April 14. Repulsed,

Rommel regrouped, then renewed the attack on April 30, only to be driven back again. He now detached a portion of his Afrika Korps to lay siege to Tobruk, which lasted an astounding 240 days, during which the Royal Navy somehow managed to keep the garrison supplied and also to replace the Australians with the 70th (British) Infantry. It would be November 29 before the British Eighth Army broke through to Tobruk to lift the siege.

General Erwin Rommel—the celebrated Desert Fox—rides in his scout car with two staff officers and a driver somewhere between Tobruk and Sidi Omar, Libya, during operations in 1941.

While part of his corps battered Tobruk, Rommel led the remainder in an advance to Sollum, an action that took back every gain Wavell and O'Connor had made. Worst of all, Rommel captured key airfields from which the Luftwaffe launched raids in support of the siege of Malta.

DETAILS, DETAILS

General POW

Astoundingly, Rommel's forces managed to capture no less a figure than General Richard O'Connor himself. During a night reconnaissance mission on April 7, 1941, O'Connor and General Philip Neame were spotted by a German patrol, which took them prisoner. One of the best fighting generals in the British army, O'Connor was idled for the next two and a half years as a prisoner of war, held mainly in Florence, Italy. Repeatedly, he attempted to escape, but was recaptured each time until, in September 1943, with the help of the Italian resistance, he finally succeeded and went on to serve with further distinction.

MALTA

THE MEDITERRANEAN ISLAND OF MALTA was a British colony with a population of about 270,000. Its airfields were of great military importance, and its capital Valletta's harbor was the only British port between Gibraltar, off the coast of Spain, and Alexandria, Egypt. Malta was the base from which the Royal Navy launched attacks against Axis convoys supplying forces in North Africa. Its strategic location also made Malta supremely vulnerable to attack. It was close to Axis-held Sicily, and distant from any other British base.

The island was first attacked by Italian bombers on June 11, 1940. From January through April 1941, the German Luftwaffe, operating from Sicily, staged additional raids, and during July 1941, Italy's 10th Light Flotilla attacked the island's major port, Valletta Harbor. By this time, however, most of the Luftwaffe had been sent to the East to support operations in the Soviet Union. This gave the Maltese a breather, until the Luftwaffe raids resumed in December. From January 1 to July 24, 1942, the Maltese sky rained fire almost every day. During this siege, the Maltese took to living in underground

NUMBERS

Deadly Convoy

Sending convoys to Malta was a grim business indeed. Of eighty-six convoy ships dispatched to the island between August 1940 and August 1942, thirty-one were sunk and others were damaged.

shelters. They suffered from semistarvation and great privation, including epidemic disease. The bombing itself killed 1,493 civilians and wounded 3,764 more.

British high command did what it could to provide relief for Malta, sending RAF fighters to duel with the Luftwaffe and dispatching fast convoys to deliver as much food and other provisions as possible. At last, during the spring of 1942, the Axis sowed the waters off Malta so thickly with mines that resupply became suicidal and nearly impossible, prompting German general Albert Kesselring to report Malta "neutralized" on May 10, 1942. This premature assessment gave the island another respite, which opened a narrow window through which supplies were delivered and fighter reinforcements put in place. In October 1942, Kesselring realized that Malta was still active, and he ordered new air raids. By this time, however, Axis losses in North Africa had deprived the Luftwaffe of key airfields, and the raids had to be stopped. The siege of Malta ended, however, only after the Axis had been pushed out of Africa in May 1943.

The Desert Fox

Erwin Rommel was a great tactician, whose ability to move armor across the desert, uncannily appearing precisely where his adversary was weakest, earned him the nickname the "Desert Fox." His British adversaries both feared and admired him. Unfortunately for Rommel—and quite fortunately for the British—the Desert Fox received remarkably little support from the German high command. Hitler admired Rommel personally, but his attention was increasingly focused on the invasion of the Soviet Union. Through high command, Hitler ordered Rommel to make do with whatever resources he had, not to act aggressively in the Western Desert, but merely to defend it.

Rommel Falters . . .

Mobile warfare is hungry warfare. Tanks need fuel, their guns need ammunition, and troops—especially in the harsh conditions of desert warfare—need plenty of food and water. Mobility depends on logistics—a reliable flow of supplies—and that is precisely what dwindled away with each passing day. The Desert Fox began to go lame.

In contrast to German high command, Winston Churchill, who took a strong hand in conducting the war, was thoroughly convinced that North Africa was the key to victory—especially after he had realized the folly of diverting troops to Greece, a lost cause. Control North Africa, Churchill now believed, and the entire Mediterranean would open up. Control the Mediterranean, and what he often called the "soft underbelly of Europe" would be exposed. Accordingly, Churchill expedited quantities of tanks and fighter aircraft to Wavell and spurred him unsparingly to make use of them in mounting an offensive against Rommel.

. . . And Rommel Recovers

Churchill was a great war leader in large part because of his unerring ability to infuse others with his own boundless will and confidence. Sometimes, however, his zeal outran the realities of war, and such was the case now. Mercilessly prodded and inspired by Churchill, Wavell launched a premature offensive, was defeated, and was replaced as theater commander by Claude John Ayre Auchinleck on July 1. Auchinleck well understood that Wavell was a fine general who had fallen victim to Churchill's zeal, and he was determined not to let the same thing happen to him. Resisting pressure from on high, he patiently built what he considered a force sufficient to mount a successful offensive.

Auchinleck had at his disposal a new army, the British Eighth Army, commanded by Lieutenant General Alan Cunningham, which included the XIII Corps and XXX Corps. On November 18, Auchinleck launched Cunningham on Operation Crusader, an all-out offensive against Rommel's Panzer Group Afrika (consisting of the Afrika Korps plus the Italian XXI Corps). The principal action of Operation Crusader was the battle of Sidi Rezegh, the taking of which was essential to the relief of nearby besieged Tobruk. On November 19, Rommel parried the initial attack by pushing back the British XXX Corps, preventing its link-up with the Tobruk garrison. Having done this, Rommel counterattacked on November 22 and drove clear through to the British rear at the frontier of Egypt on November 25. Greatly alarmed, Cunningham radioed Auchinleck for permission to withdraw to

Sir Claude John Ayre Auchinleck succeeded Archibald Wavell as commander in chief of British forces operating in North Africa in July 1941.

General Italo Gariboldi (left), Italy's military governor of Libya, and Erwin Rommel review troops of Rommel's vaunted Afrika Korps, in 1941.

Mersa Matruh, in northwestern Egypt. The theater commander responded by instantly removing Cunningham and replacing him with Neil Ritchie. Over the next two weeks, Ritchie held fast against Rommel, even opening a passage to Tobruk on November 29.

Chronically starved for logistics, Rommel knew that he could not sustain another prolonged assault against Tobruk. He broke off his attack and withdrew across Cyrenaica during the night of December 7/8. Ritchie gave chase, occupying Gazala, just west of Tobruk, on the fifteenth. Benghazi fell to the Eighth Army on Christmas Day. Finally, on January 6, 1942, the Eighth Army paused at El Agheila, having, over seven weeks, killed more than thirty-three thousand of the enemy while incurring 17,700 casualties.

Ritchie had achieved a fine victory over one of Germany's greatest commanders, but, having done so, he made the fatal mistake of failing to follow up. Given a respite, Rommel was reinforced and, even more important, resupplied. On January 12, he attacked Mersa Brega, spoiling Auchinleck's plan to invade Tripolitania. By the twenty-second, Rommel had forced Ritchie to retreat. With Benghazi laid bare, Rommel rushed in, and then confronted Ritchie at the battle of Gazala.

At Gazala, Ritchie deployed his forces in what he called "boxes," defensive strong points strung across the desert and designed to defend Tobruk. This deployment showed Ritchie to be what he was: a determined journeyman commander facing, in Rommel, a military genius. Whereas Rommel exploited to the maximum the mobility of his tanks, Ritchie used his in a static line of defense. The "box" concept hobbled him, making it difficult to mass the tanks quickly where and when they were most needed.

Ritchie had access to excellent intelligence—decoded intercepts of much of Rommel's radio traffic. Despite this, he did not know precisely where Rommel's attack would come. When it came, it did so with lightning speed. Rommel hurled his Italian troops against the Gazala Line in a head-on assault even as his German panzers wheeled wide around Bir Hakeim, which was at the southern end of the Gazala Line. With the Italians occupying the British from the front, the panzers were in position to roll up the line from the flank. As usual, however, Rommel moved so far so fast that his logistics failed him. His supply lines stretched to the breaking point, and, worse yet, his intelligence had badly underestimated British strength. On May 29, 1942, therefore, Rommel's flanking attack was defeated, and he was forced to pull back to an area the British dubbed the "Cauldron." Now it was Ritchie's turn to make a mistake. He could not believe that Rommel had withdrawn, but assumed that he had merely temporarily disengaged. He therefore delayed mounting a counterattack—and that gave Rommel a most valuable gift: time. The German commander used the lull to regroup and to reestablish his supply lines. This done, he made a new assault at Bir Hakeim, forcing a breach in the Gazala Line at this point on June 10.

Ritchie counterattacked, pushing Rommel back to the Cauldron. This done, Ritchie began an encirclement. His back to the wall, Rommel responded with the unexpected. He refused to mount a defense, but instead counterattacked, pushing a great bulge—or salient—into the Gazala Line at a "box" the British codenamed "Knightsbridge." Stunned by this development, the British faltered, and Gazala Line began to disintegrate sufficiently to open a corridor into Tobruk.

"The prime minister wins debate after debate and loses battle after battle. The country is beginning to say that he fights debates like a war and the war like a debate."

Labour Party member Aneurin Bevin,
speaking in Parliament in support of a motion to censure
Churchill's government after the fall of Tobruk

Seeing these developments, Auchinleck hurriedly ordered Ritchie to establish a new defensive line. It was, however, too little too late. Rommel barreled through to Tobruk on June 21. This stunning defeat laid Egypt bare to invasion. Auchinleck's first reaction was to fire Ritchie and assume personal command of the Eighth Army. He pulled it back to Mersa Matruh, where, at the end of June, he was defeated by Rommel and forced to withdraw all the way to El Alamein, on Egypt's northwest coast, there to await the arrival of reserves from Syria and Egypt.

Two Battles at El Alamein

Like so many other landmarks and objectives in the Western Desert campaign, El Alamein was hardly big enough or developed enough to be called a *village*. It was a tiny Egyptian settlement scratched out some sixty miles west of Alexandria along a rail line that followed the coastline of the Mediterranean Sea.

Auchinleck made a defensive stand here with the Eighth Army during July 1–4, 1942, checking Rommel's advance at a rise of sand called Ruweisat Ridge and therefore bringing the first battle of El Alamein to a successful close for the British.

Rommel was little deterred, however. His aim was to seize the Suez Canal, and he decided to strike at the British Eighth Army again. By the time he did, in September 1942, Auchinleck had been replaced by Sir Harold Alexander, and the Eighth Army was also given a new commander, Bernard Law Montgomery. He met Rommel at Alam Halfa and drove him back. This done, Montgomery determined to seize the initiative, turn the tables, and go after Rommel.

Montgomery observed that Rommel had temporarily assumed a defensive position west of El Alamein due to his chronic shortage of fuel and other supplies. Montgomery understood that, in motion, the Desert Fox was virtually unbeatable. In camp, however, he was as vulnerable as anyone else. What Montgomery did not know was that Rommel had been stricken with acute nasal diphtheria and, on September 23, had taken sicken leave, trusting his 15th Panzer Division to other hands—although not before overseeing the preparation of formidable defenses, including thick minefields. Aware, too, of the inherent weakness of the Italian forces, Rommel took care to stiffen the Italians by lacing their ranks with some German units.

As for Montgomery, he enjoyed superiority of numbers: 195,000 troops versus 104,000—of which more than half were

Italians. He drew up Operation Lightfoot, a plan to break through Rommel's defenses from the north with four infantry divisions marching across a ten-mile front. These divisions would also clear a route through the minefield to accommodate the next wave, the armored divisions of X Corps, which would set up a defensive line at a place called Kidney Ridge, facing the panzers. The idea was to hold this position in order to fend off any counterattack while the infantry completed its offensive. Only after the infantry had completed its mission—Montgomery referred to it as a "crumbling" process—would X Corps shift from defensive to offensive operations.

British Eighth Army commander General Bernard Law Montgomery watches his tanks move into position for the second battle of El Alamein, November 1942, a sharp defeat for Germany's Desert Fox.

Montgomery's plan was prudent rather than bold, but it was charged with a certain genius in that it was pointed directly where it was least expected—not against the weakly held Italian Front, but against the most strongly defended German sector. To enhance the surprise, Montgomery made several diversionary attacks in the more-likely sectors. He conceived the battle as a three-stage combat, starting with what he termed the "break-in," followed by a "dogfight," and then the "break-out." The break-in, he believed, would be swift, but the dogfight would, he thought, be a week-long struggle.

Montgomery was wrong. The break-in attack, which began on the night of October 23/24, nearly bogged down within the depths of Rommel's defenses. The armor of X Corps stopped well short of Kidney Ridge, but other units, including the 9th Australian Division and the 1st Armored Division, did get farther, the 1st Armored even flanking the Kidney Ridge position.

"Let no man surrender so long as he is unwounded and can fight."

Montgomery's order to the Eighth Army on the eve of the second battle of El Alamein

The Germans responded with ruthless counterattacks, especially when Rommel returned to the front during the second day of the battle. Each of the German jabs was contained, albeit at a high cost in British casualties. Instead of neatly progressing from break-in to dogfight, the two phases of battle overlapped, more or less,

> **NUMBERS**
> **El Alamein Arsenals**
>
> In addition to outnumbering Rommel in terms of manpower, Montgomery also had more tanks—1,029 medium tanks versus 496—and more antitank guns: 1,451 versus 800. The British Eighth Army carried 908 mobile artillery weapons, whereas Rommel controlled just 500. In terms of close air support, the RAF furnished Montgomery with 530 aircraft versus 350 Luftwaffe planes—with an additional 150 available from some distance.

in one long and arduous "crumbling" action—a relentless combination of Allied aerial and artillery bombardment with infantry action. The Australians moved about the battlefield, drawing off Rommel's best forces and leaving the weaker Italian units exposed. On the night of November 1/2, behind schedule, Montgomery launched a second attack, code-named "Supercharge," which finally pierced through Rommel's lines. It was in a much-reduced condition that the Germans took the full offensive thrust of the British armored units.

Recognizing that the battle had been lost, Rommel sent a coded message to Adolf Hitler on November 2. He told the Führer that he was nearly out of fuel, which meant that the entire force was vulnerable to destruction. For what is more vulnerable than a mobile force that has lost its ability to move? He told Hitler that he intended to withdraw to Fûka. Thanks to Operation Ultra—a major Allied code-breaking effort—Montgomery was able to read intercepts of Rommel's communications. He sent units to cut off the retreat, but was stunned by the next decrypt delivered to him. Hitler had refused Rommel permission to withdraw. Responding to this, Rommel tried to organize a stand, but there was no time to stop all of the retreating units. It was the worst possible situation for the Desert Fox. Part of his army had withdrawn; part was attempting a stand. Early on the morning of November 4, the 51st Highland Division overran this disorderly mix of retreat and defense. Too late now, Hitler gave his permission for the withdrawal, and Rommel struggled to preserve his army in retreat.

The second battle of El Alamein closed with an epic pursuit across the desert as Montgomery chased the Desert Fox, capturing thirty thousand prisoners of war and all but breaking the German's celebrated Afrika Korps. Rommel did succeed in keeping a significant portion of his forces intact, but he was forced to withdraw from Libya and hole up in Tunisia. The Italians were entirely smashed and effectively taken out of the war.

Operation Torch

The second battle of El Alamein was the turning point of the Western Desert campaign, and the beginning of the end of the Axis hold on North Africa. Its most important immediate effect was to persuade the Vichy administration of French North Africa to cooperate with Allies. That would make the Americans' baptism of fire, in Operation Torch, significantly easier—not that it would be easy.

Pearl Harbor had thrust the United States into World War II, and the American people thirsted for vengeance against the Japanese. To most, the war in Europe and the European fringes was very much a secondary priority. Churchill, of course, urgently wanted American help in fighting Hitler and Mussolini. President Roosevelt, as well as the American military, agreed with the prime minister. The United States—the free world—could not afford to allow Britain, with its great navy, to be lost to the Axis. Therefore, the first major American offensive push would be against Hitler and Mussolini.

What the Allies were not entirely agreed upon was where the action should take place. Top U.S. military planners, including army chief of staff George C. Marshall and the relatively junior officer he had chosen above many more senior men as a top War Department planner, Dwight D. Eisenhower, wanted to mount an immediate invasion across the English Channel. Prime Minister Churchill and most of his military advisers believed this would be very premature. Fresh in their minds was the disastrous Battle of France and the hair's-breadth escape via Dunkirk. Much more recently was the modest Dieppe Raid, launched on August 19, 1942, against the German-occupied French port. Too small and inadequately coordinated, it had ended in disaster and futility.

Instead of attempting another cross-Channel operation, Churchill proposed intensifying the campaign in North Africa, with the object of destroying all Axis forces there, then using the African Mediterranean coast as a staging area for an invasion of southern Europe—what he called the "soft underbelly of Europe"—targeting Greece, the Balkans, and, especially, Italy, beginning with Sicily, then landing on the Italian Peninsula and working northward. This, Churchill argued, would force the Germans to divert forces from the Soviet Front, thereby enabling Stalin to mount a successful counteroffensive. Facing offensives from the east and the south, the Germans would be hard pressed to defend their western front, which, at a later date, would become the object of a very large-scale Allied invasion. The war, Churchill argued, would be won by

REALITY CHECK

Ultra Secret

"Ultra," one of the most important Allied weapons, was the name that the British intelligence service initially applied to its decrypts of German coded communications; eventually the name was applied by the Allies to all intelligence derived from any Axis code-breaking operation. From quite early in the war—and even before—Allied cryptanalysts had broken key German and Japanese codes. Naturally, this information was of tremendous value; however, it had to be exploited sparingly in order to keep the enemy from realizing that its codes had been compromised. Thus, Ultra intelligence was sometimes deliberately withheld from field commanders. Doubtless, Allied lives were lost because of this practice. Yet the Ultra secret was so well kept that neither the Germans nor the Japanese discovered that their codes had been broken—the Allies enjoyed access to top-secret enemy communications throughout the war. "It was thanks to Ultra that we won the war," Churchill once declared.

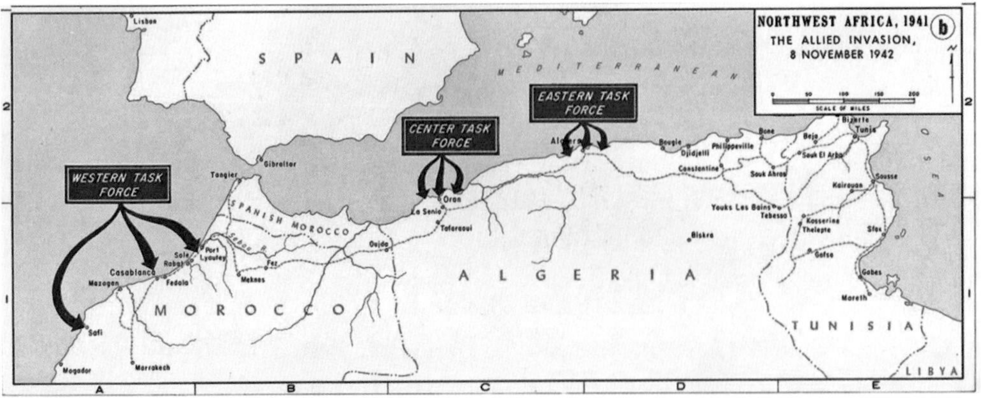

Operation Torch, the Allied invasion of northwest Africa, November 8, 1942, consisted of landings by three units, designated the Western, Center, and Eastern Tasks Forces.

pressing Germany not on one or two, but on three fronts. Only grudgingly, the U.S. military agreed, and, in collaboration with British commanders, drew up Operation Torch, a plan to land in North Africa as a prelude to invading the Continent.

Although it was the brainchild of Churchill, Operation Torch was primarily an American operation, planned under the supervision of and directed by Dwight D. Eisenhower, whom General Marshall tapped as commander in charge of the Allied Expeditionary Force. Morocco and Algeria were administered by the Vichy government, which existed at the sufferance of Germany. Eisenhower and his British colleagues were prepared to fight the Vichy French in North Africa, if need be, but they hoped that the Vichy administrators would either side outright with the invading Allies or, at least, put up no substantial resistance. In either case, it would be a great boon not to have to fight the French as well as the Germans and Italians.

Eisenhower's chief operational lieutenants were U.S. major general Mark W. Clark (deputy commander of Operation Torch and a dashing figure whom Churchill dubbed the "American Eagle"), U.S. brigadier general James Doolittle (who, as a lieutenant colonel, had led the heroic Tokyo Raid and who served in Torch as Western Air Commander), British lieutenant general Kenneth Anderson (operational ground commander), British admiral Andrew Cunningham (commander in charge of naval

DIEPPE RAID

The Dieppe Raid is generally counted as one of the great Allied blunders of World War II. Originally intended as a hit-and-run raid on a key German-held French port, it was transformed by British general Bernard Law Montgomery into a full-scale frontal assault—planned by the British but primarily executed by Canadian troops of the 2nd Canadian Division (in response to the Canadian government's plea for a greater role in the war).

At the last minute, when bad weather postponed the operation on July 7, 1942, Montgomery, stricken with second thoughts, recommended canceling the mission altogether—and Dieppe might never have been attempted, if Montgomery had not been transferred just then to command the British Eighth Army in North Africa, leaving the decision to Vice Admiral Lord Louis Mountbatten, who decided to proceed.

Launched from five English ports between Southampton and Newhaven on August 19, the operation involved 4,963 Canadians, 1,075 British, and 50 U.S. Army Rangers. It was a force too large for a hit-and-run raid and far too small for a frontal assault on a major port. Moreover, although 237 warships and landing craft were assembled for the mission, no battleships were used—and thus no heavy artillery bombardment of enemy defenses was possible. Nor did the Allies provide much air cover, since British bombers were being used against Germany. Aerial reconnaissance was also inadequate, limited to a survey of coastal defenses. The fact that great German gun emplacements were nestled in the cliffs of the headlands was entirely unknown. In fact, knowledge of the inland terrain was gathered not from spies or other eyewitnesses, but from an examination of miscellaneous holiday snapshots.

For some four hours during the principal assault, German artillery fire took a terrible toll. Of 4,963 Canadians committed to battle, 3,367 were killed, wounded, or taken prisoner. The British lost 275 men, a Royal Navy destroyer, and 33 landing craft, along with 550 sailors killed or wounded. The RAF lost 106 aircraft. German casualties were virtually negligible: 48 of 945 aircraft, and 591 men killed or wounded. Potentially the most catastrophic casualty of Dieppe was Winston Churchill, who nevertheless weathered a storm of criticism.

By any tactical measure, the Dieppe Raid was a tragic waste of life; however, it also served as a set of hard-learned lessons about how to conduct a major cross-Channel assault. They were lessons that would contribute to the success of the Normandy invasion—D-Day—on June 6, 1944.

The ill-conceived Allied raid on the German-fortified French port of Dieppe, August 19, 1942, was too small to succeed and resulted in very heavy casualties. Here, survivors of the debacle wearily march along a British dockside.

support), and Air Marshal William Welsh of the RAF (Eastern Air Commander). Whatever else it would be, Operation Torch would serve as the first great Allied experiment in what was called unified or single command—the command of British and American forces under the absolute authority of one supreme commander: in this case, Eisenhower.

The first step in the conquest of Axis-occupied North Africa, Operation Torch was to consist of three amphibious landings: at Casablanca (the Western Force, under U.S. major general George S. Patton Jr.), at Oran (the Central Force, under U.S. major general Lloyd Fredendall), and at Algiers (the Eastern Force, under U.S. major general Charles Ryder). Air support would be provided for the two western landings by the Western Air Command, while the Eastern Air Command would cover the vicinity of Algiers. Prior to the main landings, General Clark made a daring covert pre-invasion landing near Algiers on October 22, 1942, to meet with French major general Charles Mast, chief of staff of the French XIX Corps, an officer believed to be sympathetic to the Allies. Clark managed to secure from Mast a promise that, given four days' notice of the landings, he would see to it that the French army and air force offered nothing more than token resistance—in effect, a "demonstration" merely to satisfy French military honor. Mast could not speak for the attitude and actions of the French navy, however.

ALTERNATE TAKE

Too Many Chefs . . .

Single, or unified, command remained controversial throughout the war. Eisenhower believed in it absolutely, but other commanders, both British and American, often complained—and some even believed that the war would have been won more quickly if the concept of national autonomy had not been entirely abandoned. On balance, this does not seem very likely, based on the experience of the Germans and Italians, who failed to develop unified command and who were often at destructive odds during the war.

> "Have been giving everyone a simplified directive of war. Use steamroller strategy; that is, make up your mind on course and direction of action, and stick to it. But in tactics, do not steamroller. Attack weakness. Hold them by the nose and kick them in the pants."
>
> *George S. Patton Jr., diary entry, November 2, 1942, while sailing to North Africa*

The Allied landing forces consisted of sixty-five thousand men, just over half the strength of the Vichy forces stationed in North Africa. Some 650 warships supported the landings, which took place early on November 8, 1942. The first to fall was Algiers, which capitulated immediately. Oran fell two days later. At Casablanca, Patton encountered more serious resistance, but, on November 10, Admiral Jean-François Darlan, the top Vichy authority in North Africa, agreed to a ceasefire, which prompted the surrender of Casablanca.

Once the landings had been made and the major French North African objectives taken, Operation Torch opened into the North African campaign.

North African Campaign

After Darlan agreed to the ceasefire, the Germans responded by marching into unoccupied Vichy France, the Italians moved into Corsica, and combined German and Italian forces invaded Tunisia. Darlan, in turn, responded by deciding that the German occupation of Vichy (in violation of the Franco-German armistice that followed the Battle of France) released him from affiliation with the Vichy government, and he now agreed not merely to a ceasefire, but to total cooperation with the Allies. All he asked was that Eisenhower appoint him high commissioner for French North Africa. Eisenhower agreed.

Although Darlan's cooperation certainly saved Allied lives, he proved unable to persuade the French fleet at Toulon to join him in the Allied cause—the fleet was scuttled instead—and Darlan himself fell to an assassin's bullet on December 24, 1942. He was replaced as high commissioner by General Henri Giraud, who, in any case, was more palatable to the Free French. Eisenhower's remarks on the subject were noted by his aide, Henry C. Butcher, in his November 9, 1942 diary entry:

> Usually we pity the soldier of history that had to work with Allies. But we don't now, and through months of work we've rather successfully integrated the forces and the commands and staffs of British and American contingents—now we have to get together with the North African French!! Just how the French angle will develop only the future can tell.

By the end of November 1942, the Vichy were entirely out of the picture as adversaries, but Luftwaffe and Axis ground forces fought fiercely. By December, those ground forces had been consolidated as

DETAILS, DETAILS

Risky Position

Eisenhower's decision to appoint Darlan high commissioner was very controversial. Darlan was despised as a Nazi collaborator by the Free French under Charles de Gaulle, and Eisenhower understood that the appointment might jeopardize his own job. Both Roosevelt and Churchill, however, recognized the wisdom of what Ike had done, and they backed him fully.

REALITY CHECK

Auxiliary Force

A bitter irony of the Treaty of Versailles was that its restriction on the size of the German army (capped at one hundred thousand men) did not apply to paramilitary organizations created outside of the official government. These included the Freikorps and, later, the SA and SS. During the interwar years, the SA and, subsequently, the SS, became larger than the German army and therefore posed a threat to that army.

Eisenhower struck a controversial agreement with the Vichy French leaders in the region to ensure that the Allies would not face French bullets along with German and Italian ones. With General Henri Honoré Giraud, commander of French forces, Eisenhower salutes the French and American colors in 1943.

the Fifth Panzer Army, with the 10th Panzer Division as its principal striking force, under General Hans-Jürgen von Arnim, whose mission was to keep the Allies from capturing Tunisia and advancing to the central Tunisian coast—a move that would divide Arnim's forces and those of Rommel.

At first, Arnim was quite successful. Toward the middle of January 1943, the U.S. 1st Armored Division and part of the U.S. 1st Infantry organized a fresh assault on him, only to be counterattacked on January 18 before it could be launched. By the end of January, the Germans controlled all Eastern Dorsale mountain passes, and in mid-February launched an offensive of their own, taking the towns of Sidi Bou Said and Sbeitla even as Rommel captured Gafsa, forcing the Allies to withdraw into the mountains of the Western Dorsale. The withdrawal was completed successfully on February 19, 1943, but General Fredendall's U.S. II Corps was badly chewed up by Arnim and then, at the Battle of Kasserine Pass on February 19–25, suffered a humiliating defeat.

The first major one-on-one engagement between the Germans and the Americans, Kasserine was profoundly demoralizing to the U.S. Army, and it created a grave crisis of confidence in the Americans' British allies, who referred derisively to the U.S. Army as "our Italians." Yet the defeat, stinging as it was, could have been far worse, and it prompted Eisenhower, who had misplaced his faith in the mediocre Fredendall, to replace that general with the dynamic Patton. In a masterpiece of leadership, Patton rapidly rehabilitated II Corps, restoring its pride and hammering it into a highly effective unit, before turning over command to Omar Bradley.

If Rommel had been given a free hand, he would have boldly outflanked the Allied forces in northern Tunisia. Instead, he was compelled to yield to Italian high command, which ordered him to attack Allied reinforcements at Le Kef instead, thereby passing up an opportunity to exploit his victory with a truly major blow.

NUMBERS

Allied Troop Losses, Axis POWs

Together, Operation Torch and the North African campaign cost the Allies 76,000 casualties, killed or wounded. For their part, the Allies took more than 238,000 Axis prisoners of war.

While Rommel was preoccupied at Le Kef, the Allies reorganized their forces into the 18th Army Group and established a thoroughly unified air command under British air chief marshal Arthur Tedder. General Harold Alexander now became Eisenhower's deputy as well as the commander in charge of the army group (including the First U.S. and the British Eighth armies) dispatched to Tunisia.

U.S. troops of Battery B, 33rd Field Artillery, serve a 105-mm howitzer positioned in a mud-block house at Kasserine Pass, Tunisia. This first major battle between American and German forces resulted in a humiliating defeat for the Americans.

Alexander was a vigorous commander, who extensively reorganized the front, so that, by April 1, the Allies had retaken Kasserine and the other ground they had earlier yielded. In the meantime, on March 6, the British Eighth Army had bested Rommel at Medenine in southern Tunisia. Montgomery then led the Eighth Army against the Italians at a defensive position known as the Mareth Line, ultimately pushing them—and the Germans—into a smaller and smaller pocket around Tunis, capital of Tunisia. Operation Vulcan was launched on April 22, in which the First U.S. Army attacked toward Tunis as Bradley, commanding II Corps, struck Bizerte and the Free French IXX Corps marched on Pont du Fahs. This was followed rapidly by Operation Strike, which brought additional pressure on the Axis forces, rolling up Arnim's defenses so thoroughly that all three Allied objectives—Tunis, Bizerte, and Pont du Fahs—simply collapsed. On May 13, the Axis forces, disorganized, depleted, and dispirited, surrendered. North Africa was in the hands of the Allies.

Jumping Off

Control of North Africa secured extraordinarily valuable Mediterranean ports, saved Malta, and ensured control of the Suez Canal, in addition to costing many German and Italian military assets. Most of all, it put the Allies in position for the next step, Operation Husky, the invasion and conquest of Sicily, which would be followed by the invasion of Italy—bold entry into Europe via its "soft underbelly." What Churchill said of the El Alamein victory applied as well more generally to the triumph in North Africa: "Now this is not the end. It is not the beginning of the end. But it is, perhaps, the end of the beginning."

TAKEAWAY

The Tide Turns

Acting in accordance with a plan enthusiastically endorsed by Winston Churchill, the Allies mounted their first major offensive campaign against Hitler and Mussolini not in Europe, but in North Africa, seeking not only to destroy Axis forces here but also to ensure Allied control of the Suez Canal and the strategically vital Mediterranean coast. Once taken, North Africa became a stepping-off point for the invasion of Sicily and mainland Italy.

CHAPTER 13

The Italian Campaign

The Long Allied Advance

THE AXIS POWERS WANTED TO BECOME INVINCIBLE. Japan expanded outward from its home islands in an effort not merely to create an empire, but to fashion a vast protective cordon in Asia and the Pacific, a kind of hemispherical picket line no enemy could cross. As for Germany, Adolf Hitler liked to speak of "Festung Europa"—Fortress Europe—an armed camp protecting the Fatherland on all sides. We will see in Chapters 14 and 15 how Japan's cordon was breached. In this chapter, Fortress Europe is penetrated, albeit tentatively and at great cost.

Operation Husky

THE TWO GREAT ALLIED WAR LEADERS, Franklin Roosevelt and Winston Churchill, took the bold step of meeting in freshly conquered French North Africa, in the Moroccan city of Casablanca, from January 14 to January 24, 1943. They each brought with them their top military aides and advisers with the objective of jointly planning the next steps in the war against the Axis. One of the most important decisions the leaders made was to jump off from North Africa to Sicily. This confirmed acceptance of Churchill's "soft underbelly" approach.

The decision having been reached, it was now up to Dwight Eisenhower and his Anglo-American staff to plan the conquest of the large, rugged island off the southwestern coast of the Italian Peninsula. What they came up with was code-named "Operation Husky." As with the action in North Africa, overall unified command fell to Eisenhower, with British general Harold Alexander as the top commander in the field, leading the newly formed 15th Army Group, consisting of the British Eighth Army (under Bernard Law Montgomery) and the U.S. I Armored Corps (commanded by George S. Patton Jr.). For technical reasons, Patton's command would be redesignated the Seventh U.S. Army once it had landed on Sicily. The 15th Army Group consisted of eight divisions, including elite airborne, commando, and Ranger units. The landings would be supported by U.S. and Royal Navy contingents under British admiral Andrew Cunningham, with air support directed by British air marshal Arthur Tedder. Top command, therefore, was the same as in the successfully concluded North African campaign—yet all through the process of planning Operation Husky, American and British officers argued bitterly. Ike Eisenhower—celebrated for his ability to make the most egocentric and argumentative prima donna generals work harmoniously—was sorely tried by the disputes, which greatly impeded progress on the plan.

It its original version, Operation Husky called for Montgomery and Patton to land on opposite sides of Sicily in order to carry out, on

REALITY CHECK

Cross Purposes

Some American commanders, including Eisenhower, complained about wasting time and resources on an Italian campaign, time and resources that could be better invested in a cross-Channel invasion of France. As it was, however, Churchill got less than he asked for. His desire was not only to invade Italy, but also to recapture the other parts of the European underbelly, including Greece and the Balkans. The Americans held fast in their objection to this, arguing that concentrating here would delay the cross-Channel invasion far too long.

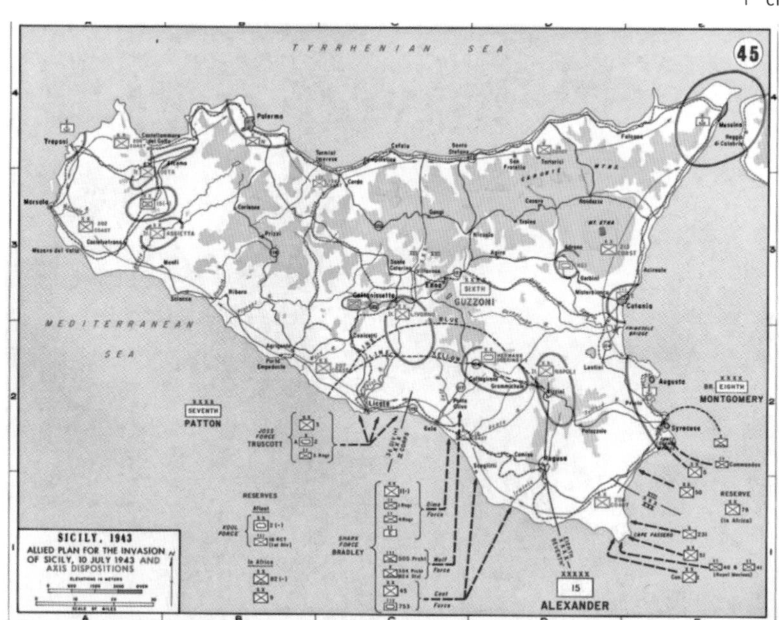

The final plan for Operation Husky had the British Eighth Army making the principal assault on the southeast coast of the island while the Seventh U.S. Army, commanded by Patton, was relegated to a supporting role, landing at three positions along the southern coast, then covering Montgomery's left flank.

REALITY CHECK

A Driven Man

Patton was notoriously hostile to his British colleagues and was especially competitive with Montgomery, whom he tended to view as more of a personal enemy than the Germans. Yet, in contrast to Eisenhower and other U.S. commanders, he was not opposed to the Sicilian invasion and the Italian campaign, because he believed these would get him back into the fight sooner than the cross-Channel invasion would. Patton was driven by a hunger to engage the enemy—any enemy, anywhere. Sicily also appealed to his profound sense of military history. He was thrilled by the idea of walking in the footsteps of the great Roman conquerors.

a large scale, a pincer movement, which would crush the Italian and German forces within its jaws. The famously audacious Patton enthusiastically endorsed the plan, but Montgomery, always cautious, thought it risky and ill-conceived, dismissing it contemptuously as a "dog's breakfast"—a mess. He insisted on drastically revising the plan, casting Patton and his Seventh Army in a subordinate role as mere protection for the flank of the British Eighth Army as it advanced to the port town of Messina, which was to be the stepping-off place for an invasion of the Italian mainland. Patton objected bitterly, but accepted his orders—as it turned out, strictly for the time being.

Landings

The landings of Operation Husky were launched before dawn on July 10, 1943. They constituted an operation more than twice the size of the Torch landings on North Africa, involving the movement of 180,000 Allied troops and 2,590 ships. It was a complex and highly risky affair, hampered by inadequate air support and adverse wind conditions, both of which rendered the landings highly vulnerable to German and Italian counterattack. What prevented this was Operation Mincemeat, an elaborate program of deceptions and decoys, which worked so well in the run-up to the invasion that the Germans deployed their men in all the wrong places, leaving the entry points thinly defended. Just two German divisions were available to oppose the landings.

The two corps of Montgomery's Eighth Army—X and XIII Corps—landed between Pozzallo and Syracuse on the east coast of Sicily. XIII Corps easily captured Syracuse on the very day of the landings. The three American divisions that hit the beach between Cape Scaramia and Licata on the southwest coast were bedeviled by bad weather and a greater concentration of Germans, but, despite this, established their beachhead by the

Ever the leader, George S. Patton Jr. points the way in Sicily, July 1943. Note the spit-and-polish exquisitely tailored combat uniform.

end of the first day. German tanks unleashed a vicious counterattack at Gela on July 11, but American warships responded with an artillery bombardment of their own, thereby saving Patton's landings.

Per the revised plan, British general Harold Alexander, Ike's man on the ground, ordered Patton and the Seventh Army to cover Montgomery's left flank as the XIII Corps of his Eighth Army marched against Catania and his XXX Corps advanced on the towns of Leonforte and Enna. The supremely egocentric Patton was frustrated by this enforced subordination, but so was Omar Bradley, a much more modest officer by nature. His American II Corps found itself in an excellent position from which to trap the German 15th Panzer Grenadiers by simply cutting the island in half. The orders to play second fiddle to Montgomery prevented this.

It was not in Patton's nature to remain passive, and, on July 15, 1943, he formed a provisional corps under Lieutenant General Geoffrey Keyes, ordering it to advance against Palermo, the principal city of Sicily. When Alexander reiterated that Patton was to do no more than cover Montgomery's flank, the American commander met personally with Alexander and explained that Keyes could take Palermo even as the rest of Seventh Army continued to cover Montgomery. Alexander capitulated—as did Palermo, on July 22.

By July 17, the Germans had established a triple line of defense, stretching from south of Catania across to San Stefano on the north coast of the island. The defenders took great advantage of the rugged Sicilian landscape, which gave them plenty of places to hide while also impeding the advance of British tanks. While the contest for Sicily was ongoing, on July 25, Benito Mussolini was quietly removed from power—not by some anti-Fascist resistance, but by the Grand Council of Fascism itself. Shaken, Adolf Hitler authorized preparations for the evacuation of German forces. In Sicily, on July 27, the Germans started their withdrawal from the first of their three defensive lines, making a fighting retreat that exploited the rugged terrain of Sicily to slow Allied progress. His advance reduced to a crawl, Montgomery did not capture Catania until August 5.

Despite Montgomery's frustration, the U.S. 1st Division won a five-day battle to capture Troina, and British units took Adrano. The fall of these two towns prompted the German commander, Albert

DETAILS, DETAILS

Massive Landings

The landings of Operation Husky were second only to those of Operation Overlord, the D-Day invasion of Normandy on June 6, 1944, and the days following.

REALITY CHECK

Ego Boost

The capture of Palermo thrilled Americans at home and gave the American army a substantial morale boost. Moreover, Keyes bagged a bounty of Italian POWs in the process. But none of this was really essential to the conquest of Sicily. At most, the taking of Palermo was a magnificent sideshow.

Allied air and naval forces coordinated with the landings on Sicily, destroying Italian warships anchored in the harbors.

Kesselring, to evacuate his forces from Sicily during the night of August 11/12. This ensured Allied victory in Sicily, but it also meant that approximately forty thousand German and sixty-two thousand Italian troops had evaded capture. In some desperation, the Allies launched amphibious assaults in a bid to cut off the retreat to the Italian mainland. But it was too little, much too late.

That Patton and Montgomery allowed so many of the enemy to slip out of their grasp was a major failure of the Sicilian campaign. Nevertheless,

THE FALL OF MUSSOLINI

The downfall of Benito Mussolini was strangely anticlimactic. The leading avatar of Fascism, a role model for Adolf Hitler during his rise, and the longest-serving Axis dictator (he came to absolute power in 1922), Mussolini was not overthrown in some terrific coup d'etat, but, on July 25, 1943, by a simple vote of the Grand Council of Fascism.

Nor did he, Napoleon-like, raise a great army to oppose his downfall. Instead, he meekly submitted when King Victor Emmanuel dismissed him as premier and allowed himself to be held under house arrest in Gran Sasso, in the Abruzzi. It was Adolf Hitler, not any of Il Duce's former followers, who found this intolerable. He ordered Mussolini's rescue, which was accomplished on September 12, 1943, in a brilliant commando raid planned and led by Otto Skorzeny, the dean of Germany's airborne assault commanders. Skorzeny landed ninety men in gliders and light aircraft on the remote mountaintop where Mussolini was being held. They transported him in a single-engine "Stork" aircraft to Germany. There Hitler greeted him and reinstalled him in northern Italy—still held by the Germans—as a puppet rival to Marshal Pietro Badoglio, whom Victor Emmanuel had appointed interim head of the Italian state.

As a puppet dictator, Mussolini exercised no influence on Italian affairs. When the Allies closed in on him in April 1945, he and his mistress, Clara Petacci, fled, only to be captured by Italian partisans near Lake Como. Despite Allied orders that Mussolini was not to be harmed, the partisans executed him, Petacci, and other former Fascist leaders by firing squad on April 28. The half-naked bodies of Il Duce and Clara Petacci were strung up by the heels from a fence at a square in Milan, where they were mocked and desecrated by a mob.

the conquest of Sicily hardly felt to the Allies like a failure, especially after Patton made a spectacular drive to Messina, which he triumphantly liberated on August 17. With the seizure of the stepping-off place for the invasion of the Italian mainland, the Sicily campaign ended.

> **REALITY CHECK**
>
> **Sicily vs. Montgomery**
>
> The conquest of Sicily was a flawed Allied victory. Patton well understood that Allied soldiers would have to fight, on the mainland, those Axis troops who had been allowed to escape. He was, in fact, more delighted with having beaten his British rival, Montgomery, to Messina than he was with having defeated the Germans in Sicily. In fairness to Patton, virtually everyone who was obliged to work with Montgomery found him supremely difficult. Winston Churchill, a sublime master of the one-liner, summed him up: "In defeat unbeatable; in victory unbearable."

RAISING AN ORPHAN

EVEN AS THE ALLIES PREVAILED IN NORTH AFRICA AND SICILY, the American commanders—George C. Marshall in Washington and Dwight D. Eisenhower in theater—continued to view the "soft underbelly" approach as something of a diversion, which drew off precious resources better used for the far more difficult invasion across the English Channel and into France. As Winston Churchill and his top planners saw it, however, the way was now open to mainland Italy, which, they believed, would fall quickly, providing a rather smooth inroad into Hitler's vaunted Fortress Europe. From the American point of view, then, the entire Italian campaign was something of an orphan—more or less unwanted—whereas the British saw it as an easy approach to the European heartland.

There was one thing on which the British and Americans absolutely agreed: the need for speed and surprise. Yet it was these very elements that were lost as the Allies dithered, delaying the invasion of the mainland while they pondered whether or not the surrender terms offered by Marshal Pietro Badoglio's provisional Italian government—which had replaced the Mussolini regime on July 24—were consistent with what had been decided at the Casablanca Conference: to accept nothing less than unconditional surrender from any member of the Axis. While the debate raged through the late summer of 1943, the Germans had sent sixteen new divisions to bolster the defense of Italy. The delay therefore had tragic consequences.

Salerno

At last, on September 3 and 4—two weeks after the fall of Messina—the British Eighth Army crossed the Strait of Messina to land at Reggio di Calabria, on the toe of the Italian boot. To Montgomery's surprise, the landing was virtually unopposed, and, a few days later, on September 8, Badoglio announced the surrender of Italy. At dawn on the very next day, the Fifth Army (which included U.S. and British elements) made an amphibious landing at Salerno.

Whereas the British had encountered no resistance at Reggio di Calabria, the Americans were stunned by the ferocity of the Germans at Salerno. Code-named Operation Avalanche and led by Fifth Army commander Lieutenant General Mark Clark, the U.S. Salerno landings were divided into southern and northern flanks. The southern—or right—flank consisted of the U.S. VI Corps under Ernest Dawley, who was subsequently relieved by John Lucas. The 36th and 45th Infantry Divisions of this corps took the town of Paestum within seventy-two hours, then marched inland ten miles. On the northern (or left) flank, the British X Corps,

THE SLAPPING INCIDENTS

George S. Patton Jr., hailed as the conqueror of Sicily and widely regarded, by the Allies as well as the Germans, as the best of America's field commanders, was assigned no part in the assault on the Italian mainland. Indeed, throughout the campaign and even into the next year, as D-Day came and went, Patton found himself on the brink of being relieved from command.

On August 3, 1943, Patton, who believed that top commanders should personally visit the wounded whenever possible, called at the 15th Evacuation Hospital near Nicosia. Among the injured, he encountered Private Charles H. Kuhl. Because Kuhl appeared unhurt, Patton asked him what his problem was. Kuhl replied, "I guess I can't take it." It was as if a match had been put to a fuse. Patton exploded, cursed Kuhl, slapped him across the face with his gloves, then, grabbing him by the scruff of his neck, booted him out of the hospital tent. This incident—a flagrant violation of military law—was largely kept from the public, but, astoundingly, on August 10, while touring the 93rd Evacuation Hospital, Patton came across Private Paul G. Bennett. To Patton's question concerning what ailed him, Bennett replied, "It's my nerves," and began to sob. Patton once again exploded: "What did you say?" Bennett replied, "It's my nerves, I can't stand the shelling any more." The general screamed: "Your nerves, hell; you are just a goddamned coward, you yellow son of a bitch." Patton slapped Bennett, told him to "Shut up that goddamned crying" and exclaimed that he "won't have these brave men here who have been shot at seeing a yellow bastard sitting here crying." With that, he struck Bennett again and turned to the admitting officer, ordering him not to "admit this yellow bastard; there's nothing the matter with him. I won't have the hospitals cluttered up with these sons of bitches who haven't got the guts to fight." Turning back to Bennett, Patton told him, "You're going back to the front lines and you may get shot and killed, but you're going to fight. If you don't, I'll stand you up against a wall and have a firing squad kill you on purpose. In fact"—now reaching for his consisting of the 56th and 46th divisions under Richard McCreery, captured Battipaglia as well as Salerno. It was not until September 12 that the Germans counterattacked with great force, quickly retaking Battipaglia, then rolling up the Allies all along the line of their advance. In some places, the Fifth Army retreated to within two miles of the coast. On September 14, Allied aircraft were sortied in an effort to break the counterattack. Strafing and aerial bombardment were augmented by heavy naval gunfire. British general Sir Harold Alexander, who had overall command of Allied ground forces in Italy, rushed the U.S. 82nd Airborne and the British 7th Armored divisions to buck up the Fifth Army landing forces. This timely action arrested the counterattack by the night of

trademark sidearm, an ivory-handled revolver—"I ought to shoot you myself, you goddamned whimpering coward."

This second incident was duly reported to upper command, including Dwight D. Eisenhower himself. Eisenhower wrote Patton a personal letter of reprimand, but he also prevailed upon journalists not to report the incident. Patton made apologies to soldiers throughout his command, including personal apologies to Kuhl and Bennett (both of whom, it turned out, were suffering from debilitating fevers and not just battle fatigue), but major command was withheld from him. Mark Clark, not he, was put at the head of Fifth Army invading the Italian mainland, and Omar Bradley, not he, was tapped to organize forces for the planned cross-Channel invasion. Patton was stuck in Sicily, overseeing the dissolution of the Seventh Army, whose troops were parceled out to other commands. Worse, late in November 1943, during a Sunday-evening radio broadcast, the popular columnist Drew Pearson made the slapping incidents public, touching off a firestorm of popular outrage and widespread calls for Patton's immediate dismissal not just from major command, but from the United States Army.

The slapping incidents and their consequences raise some of the war's greatest "what-ifs." What if the incidents had not occurred? Would Eisenhower have tapped Patton for top command in the Italian campaign? If Patton had been in command, would that campaign have proceeded more aggressively and more successfully instead of getting bogged down, as it did under Mark Clark? But if Patton had been consigned to Italy, would he have been unavailable to command the Third Army in its phenomenal advance across Europe in the months following D-Day? And what if, after Drew Pearson's radio broadcast, Eisenhower had yielded to public pressure and sent Patton home? Would the American push across Europe have been so swift and so successful as it was under Patton's command? The scandal kept Patton from major command from September 1943 to July 1944. Eisenhower did make use of him, but only as a decoy to keep the Germans guessing as to where the Allies would next attack. It was a humiliating role, although it did succeed in forcing the Germans to squander many of their precious resources in a vain effort to defend against attacks that would never come. Yet how much more useful might Patton have been, during those months of decoy duty, as a field commander? The answer will never be known.

The Allied conquest of Sicily was a hard-fought, if flawed, triumph, but the invasion of mainland Italy that followed, although ultimately successful, was one bloody heartbreak after another. On the shingle beach at Paestum, south of Salerno, U.S. Navy beach battalion personnel and U.S. Coast Guardsmen hug the sand as German bombs explode around them.

September 15 and forced German general Kesselring to retreat. On the next day, Montgomery arrived from the south with his Eighth Army and tied in with the Fifth Army. This secured the Salerno landings, so that, reinforced by the U.S. 3rd Division, the Fifth Army made a breakout toward Naples, which fell on October 1. In all, it was a costly and unnerving start to the invasion.

The Agony of Cassino

Adolf Hitler was never easily pleased with his generals, but he was justifiably impressed by what Albert Kesselring had managed at the battle of Salerno. This prompted the Führer to make a fateful decision. He authorized Kesselring to mount a full-scale defense against the invasion of Italy with the object not so much of holding Italy as of inflicting on the Allies a maximum of casualties. For the American, British, and Commonwealth troops who fought in Italy—their top commanders anticipating a rapid blitzkrieg-style invasion—the bitter and bloody lesson would be that as destructive as the German military was in offensive operations, it was equally effective on the defense.

> "Abbey at Monte Cassino was the creation of one of man's noblest dreams . . . but this morning the tired infantrymen, fighting for their lives near its slopes, were to cry for joy as bomb after bomb crumbled it into dust."
>
> *From* Return to Cassino,
> *the 1964 memoir by U.S. infantryman Harold L. Bond*

The Allies did not so much march up the Italian Peninsula as they clawed their way up, paying in blood for every inch. All too representative of Italian combat was the battle of Monte Cassino, a series of four battles that spanned January 17 to May 18, 1944. Located about eighty miles south of Rome, the town of Cassino was a mile west of Monte Cassino, a rocky hill atop which was a medieval Benedictine monastery. The Germans fortified not only the town, but the hill as well, creating a formidable defensive position, which served as a strong point in the German defensive line known as the Gustav Line, which stretched across the Italian Peninsula. To reach Rome, Mark Clark and his Fifth Army needed to penetrate the Gustav Line, and Cassino was the place to do it.

Hoping to deny the Germans a fortress, the Allies bombed the monastery of Monte Cassino into rubble. Not only was a priceless landmark destroyed, but the ruins gave the Germans even more effective defensive cover than the intact building had provided.

The first battle commenced on January 17, 1944. Assuming that the Germans were holed up in the monastery, Allied bombers were called in on February 15 to reduce the ancient edifice to rubble. Tragically, as it turned out, German troops had not occupied the monastery—and would not do so, until it had been destroyed. The defenders found that the ruins made for more effective defensive positions than the intact building would have. On March 15, more Allied bombing missions were ordered, this time to pulverize the rubble in an effort to kill or drive out the Germans.

The first three battles of Cassino—January 17–25, February 15–18, and March 15–25—involving U.S., British, Indian, Canadian, Australian, South African, Polish, Belorussian, and New Zealand troops—failed to take either the town or the hill. The fourth battle of Monte Cassino was fought by the Polish II Corps under General Wladyslaw Anders on May 11–19. The first assault of this battle, on May 11–12, produced very heavy Polish losses, but opened the way for the British Eighth Army, now under Sir Oliver Leese, to break through German defenses in the Liri River Valley below the monastery. This accomplished, the Polish II Corps launched a second assault in cooperation with French Moroccan troops during May 17–19. The Moroccans, expert in mountain warfare, boldly scaled the hill and were instrumental in dislodging the German 1st Parachute Division. Although successful, this operation exhausted both the Poles and Moroccans, who nevertheless made a valiant effort to cut off the retreat of the German paratroops. Most, however, were able to escape.

REALITY CHECK

Procrastination?

Joseph Stalin pulled no punches when it came to expressing his opinion of the Italian campaign. He believed it was nothing more than an excuse to avoid a major invasion of Europe. Churchill and others countered that fighting in Italy would force the Germans to take troops off of the Soviet Front. This certainly proved to be the case, but progress in the Italian campaign was so slow that it certainly delayed the great cross-Channel invasion.

NUMBERS

A Costly Victory

Because it opened the way forward in the invasion of Italy, the Cassino battles must be counted as an Allied strategic victory. Tactically, however, they were a defeat; for whereas the Germans suffered some twenty thousand killed or wounded, the Allied forces incurred fifty-four thousand casualties in the taking of Cassino. Throughout the war and for years afterward, Allied officials and former officials refused to admit that the bombing of the monastery—which was not occupied by German troops—had been a mistake. At last, in 1969, the error was admitted.

On the morning of May 18, elements of the Polish 12th Podolian Uhlans Regiment occupied the ruins of Monte Cassino's monastery and raised above them the Polish national flag. At tremendous cost, this major obstacle to the advance on Rome had been cleared.

Anzio

The battles of Monte Cassino revealed grave shortcomings in the Allies' Italian strategy. British general Harold Alexander, overall commander of ground forces, repeatedly underestimated the capacity and will of the Germans to resist the Allied advance, and, at places like Cassino—indeed, all along the Gustav Line and the Hitler Line (running from Terracina on Italy's west coast, to Monte Cairo), which together formed what was called the "Winter Line"—combat closely resembled the trench warfare of the Western Front in World War I. It was static rather than mobile, a grinding kind of combat that resulted in heavy losses with little movement.

Mark Clark wanted to break the stalemate at all costs. He was driven by two motives. First was the lure of Rome. With Berlin and Tokyo, it was one of the three great Axis capitals, which made it a most seductive objective, although (as we will see) one of dubious strategic value. Second, he needed to break through in order to effect a linkup with the U.S. VI Corps, which was cut off and pinned down in desperate battle at Anzio.

Ironically, the Anzio assault had been conceived as a means of accelerating the Italian campaign after it had stalled unexpectedly during the Salerno landings. Anzio, along Italy's west coast, looked to be an ideal spot for a second landing to accelerate penetration of the Winter Line and the capture of Rome. The Allies formulated Operation Shingle, which sent Major General John Lucas at the head of elements of the VI Corps, Fifth Army, to land along a fifteen-mile beach near Anzio, a popular resort town thirty miles south of Rome. On January 22, 1944, the VI Corps units made textbook landings followed by encouragingly rapid progress inland. By noon of day one, British and American units had attained their first day's objectives, and, before day's end, they had advanced three to four miles inland.

"We hoped to land a wild cat that would tear out the bowels of the Boche. Instead we have stranded a vast whale with its tail flopping about in the water."

Winston Churchill, on Anzio operations, February 29, 1944

Luck was with the Allies. Kesselring had not expected an amphibious assault at Anzio, and this presented a golden opportunity—which, however, the conservative Lucas failed to exploit.

Instead of moving rapidly and aggressively, he spent the next week consolidating his position. This afforded the enemy ample time to move forces into place. Because of Lucas's delay, what had begun as a cinch landing bogged down into what became a horrific four-month campaign.

Tall, handsome, and courageous, commanding the Fifth Army in the Italian campaign, Mark Wayne Clark was dubbed by Winston Churchill the "American eagle."

REALITY CHECK

A Stubborn Leader

Mark Clark was a courageous and energetic commander, yet the frustration caused by combat along the Winter Line seemed to bring out the worst in him. He stubbornly and repeatedly resorted to frontal attacks against the Winter Line, despite their high cost and slight profit. Some military historians have praised his persistent valor, whereas others have condemned a lack of imagination.

Kesselring's subordinate, Eberhard von Mackensen, commanding the German Fourteenth Army, had a force of seventy thousand, which he used to envelop Lucas before that commander finally began his major inland advance. Colonel William O. Darby led some of his celebrated Rangers—elite American troops modeled on the British commandos—in an attempt to infiltrate the German lines and break the stranglehold, but they fell victim to an ambush at Cisterna.

Surrounded, Lucas gave up the idea of an offensive and settled in to mount a stern defense. In this he was highly effective, costing many German casualties. But Lucas's superiors believed that wars were not won by defensive actions, no matter how successful, and on February 22, General Lucas was replaced by his deputy commander, Major General Lucian Truscott, an aggressive cavalry officer much admired by Patton. Truscott wasted no time in beating back a new attack on February 29, but he was unable to break out of Kesselring's encirclement until the spring, after he had received reinforcements. It was not until May 25 that elements of Truscott's

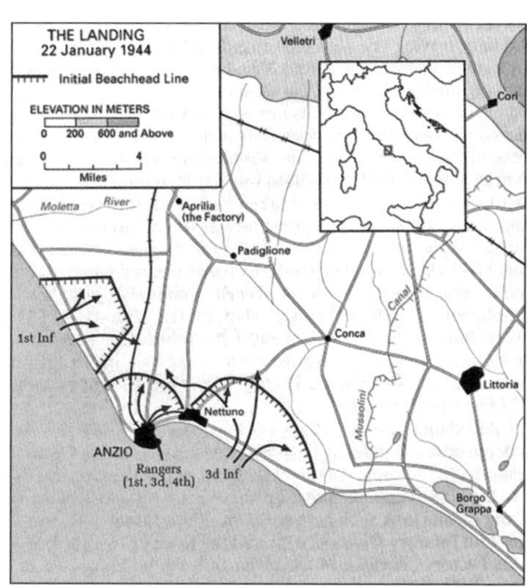

The Anzio landings, seen here, began very promisingly, but the Allies' failure to advance aggressively set up the conditions for a bloody stalemate.

DUKWs ferried supplies from cargo ships to Allied troops pinned down at Anzio. Pronounced "duck," the designation of this ubiquitous amphibious vehicle came from letters signifying its specifications: D denoted a vehicle designed in 1942; U stood for "utility (amphibious)"; K was the designation for all-wheel drive vehicles; and W indicated two powered rear axles.

VI Corps started to link up with the main body of the Fifth Army, effecting the union that had been scheduled to take place months earlier, no more than a week after the Anzio landings.

Like the Monte Cassino battles, Anzio was bloody and heartbreaking. Certainly it failed to speed the capture of Rome, but it did tie down the German Fourteenth Army for four months, which prevented this large force from being used elsewhere, either in Italy or in the Soviet campaign. In a real sense, therefore, Anzio was an Allied victory in what had become—in Italy, at least—a war of attrition.

REALITY CHECK

Lost Opportunity

Lucas absorbed most of the blame for the problems at Anzio, and he was undeniably too cautious in this campaign; however, he was also operating from his understanding of Mark Clark's orders, which were to lead VI Corps in an effort to divert enemy strength from the south and to prepare defensive positions in anticipation of a strong German counterattack. Lucas did not see his mission as immediately capturing territory. Yet in adhering to the letter of his orders, he lost a precious opportunity for rapid progress and gave the enemy time to mount a terribly destructive defense.

On to Rome, and the Bloody Anticlimax

In May, breakthroughs were achieved at both Monte Cassino and Anzio, so that, by the end of the month, all elements of Mark Clark's Fifth Army were in position to strike Kesselring at Valmontone. This was an opportunity to destroy the best part of the German army in Italy. Instead of devoting his forces to this task, however, Clark decided to advance on and capture Rome. It was one of the most controversial decisions of World War II.

Ironically, when Rome fell to the Allies on June 4, 1944, the Allied triumph—which also gave Kesselring the breathing space he needed to withdraw his army intact and to continue the fight in Italy—was quickly eclipsed by news of D-Day, June 6, the great Allied invasion of Europe at Normandy (see Chapter 20).

For himself and on behalf of his men who had sacrificed so much, Mark Clark was bitter that the conquest of the first of the great Axis capitals had been overshadowed by the Normandy invasion. Yet, overshadowed as it was, the capture of Rome was widely seen—by the Allied public as well as by top Allied commanders—as the culmination of the Italian campaign. The result was that Italy came to be regarded as a secondary front, and six divisions were immediately withdrawn from the country to be used in landings in the French Riviera, which followed the Normandy landings by about a month.

The reduced Allied forces continued to fight their way north, impeded by Kesselring as well as by the landscape of Italy, which was traversed by river after river. With autumn 1944 came heavy rains and floods. In September, even after it breached the last great German defensive line, the Gothic Line, running through the Apennine Mountains, from north of Lucca on the west coast to south of Pesaro on the east, the British Eighth Army wallowed in a muddy bog.

> "Looking round the mountains, in the mud and rain,
> There's lots of little crosses, some which bear no name,
> Blood, sweat and tears and toil are gone,
> The boys beneath them slumber on.
> These are your D-Day dodgers, who'll stay in Italy."
>
> *Allied soldiers' song in response to Lady Astor's reckless allegation that the troops in Italy sat out the "real fighting" in Normandy*

Delayed in the Romagna, in northern Italy, Alexander was about to make a final, long-delayed push into Austria when the Combined Chiefs of Staff (CCS)—Allied high command—ordered him instead to focus on pinning down within Italy as many German divisions as possible. It was an important mission, but decidedly one secondary to the ongoing invasion from the west. The soldiers of the Fifth Army and the British Eighth did what they were told, but "pinning down" Germans in Italy was hardly the triumphant breakthrough they had been promised and they had sought.

There was much heroism but little glory in the Italian campaign. Conceived as a relatively "easy" alternative to an immediate cross-Channel invasion, it became instead a contest of attrition that did not end until the war in Europe ended. To be sure, the campaign did draw off German forces from the Soviet and Western fronts, but it also kept numbers of Allied troops from fighting in France. It was an Allied victory, but hardly the most efficient way to win a war.

NUMBERS

Total Troop Losses

The Italian campaign cost the Fifth Army 188,746 men killed or wounded, and, in the British Eighth Army, 123,254 killed or wounded. The Germans lost 434,646 killed, wounded, or missing.

TAKEAWAY

A Long, Bloody Victory

The Allies began the European offensive via the Continent's underbelly, leaving North Africa to take Sicily, then using Sicily as a staging area for the invasion of the Italian mainland. Planned as a rapid and relatively easy invasion, the Italian campaign turned out to be an epic of blood and heartbreak that lasted until the very end of the war in Europe.

Part Five

THE PACIFIC WAR

On preceding pages: During the opening months of the Pacific war, the Imperial Japanese Navy carried the empire's flag to the far reaches of Asia and the ocean islands.

CHAPTER 14

TURNING POINTS

America Fights Back—Hard

EVEN AS THE UNITED STATES AND BRITAIN REELED UNDER one Japanese land conquest after another, a major series of sea battles was fought between Allied warships and the Imperial Japanese Navy off the coast of Java. Collectively called the battle of the Java Sea, the first encounter took place on February 27, 1942, after the Japanese had already captured much of the Netherlands East Indies and had cut off Java. Vice Admiral Ibo Takahashi commanded two invasion forces against Java. The eastern force, consisting of forty-one transports escorted by four cruisers and fourteen destroyers, was intercepted by a fleet of five American, British, Dutch, and Australian cruisers and nine destroyers, all under the tactical command of Dutch rear admiral Karel Doorman.

On paper, the forces were evenly matched, but, in reality, the Allies were a mixed and inexperienced lot, sailing ships with significantly less firepower than the Japanese had. Worst of all, the Allied fleet, cobbled together, had virtually no ship-to-ship communication, nor was fire control—the timing, aiming, and duration of firepower—centralized. As for the tactical commander, Rear Admiral Doorman had never commanded a fleet in action. The battle of the Java Sea had all the makings of another humiliating defeat.

REALITY CHECK
Colonial Yoke

The islands and lands of the Pacific and Southeast Asia were valued outposts of the British and Dutch empires, but their status as imperial possessions was also their weakness and vulnerability. In many of these places, people longed to free themselves of the colonial yoke, and they saw the Japanese not as conquerors but as liberators. Segments of the native populations of the various colonies collaborated with the Japanese. In some cases, however, the indigenous people resisted the Japanese onslaught, not out of loyalty to colonial masters but because they recognized the rapacity of the Japanese.

Doorman assumed that the battle would commence after nightfall and therefore left all reconnaissance aircraft ashore, rendering himself blind. Without air reconnaissance or air cover, the Allied fleet fell easy victim to the Japanese. In the initial encounter, the British cruiser *Exeter* was so badly hit that it had to withdraw to Surabaya, on the north shore of East Java, while two Dutch cruisers and three destroyers were sunk. The hapless Doorman was killed in combat. Japanese losses were one destroyer—damaged but not sunk.

On the night of February 28, two Allied cruisers that survived the battle, the Australian ship *Perth* and the American *Houston*, were withdrawing from the encounter when they stumbled across the second Japanese invasion fleet, riding at anchor forty miles west of Batavia (present-day Jakarta). Although outnumbered, they attacked, sinking two Japanese ships and damaging three others before three Japanese cruisers and nine destroyers appeared over the horizon, counterattacked, and sank both Allied cruisers. In the meantime, also on the night of the twenty-eighth, the *Exeter* and two Allied destroyers attempted to slip out to Ceylon (Sri Lanka), but, on the morning of March 1, they were all sunk, leaving only four American destroyers as the survivors of the disastrous battle series.

On sea as on land, the Japanese seemed unstoppable. But they would be stopped.

Duel on the Coral Sea

In the early months of the Pacific war, as one Allied stronghold after another crumbled, Australia stood alone as the great bastion, the principal Allied base, and the prize that Japan most jealously eyed. If Australia were conquered, the Allied presence in Asia and the southern Pacific would be, for all practical purposes, eliminated. As the Japanese saw it, possession of Australia would force the Allies to come to surrender terms favorable to Japan.

The first step in the conquest of Australia would be the invasion and conquest of New Guinea, the large island north of the Australian continent. It was a natural base from which a major invasion of Australia could be mounted. On March 8, 1942, Japanese forces seized Lae and Salamaua on the coast of New Guinea's Huon Gulf. From here, they launched the conquest of the Dutch East Indies, encompassing most of Indonesia, including Java. This gave the Japanese access to important raw materials, especially rubber, and put them in position to make an amphibious assault on Port Moresby, in southeastern New Guinea. Port Moresby was the sentinel position guarding access to Australia.

On May 4, 1942, Admiral Shigeyoshi Inouye led an invasion force from the major Japanese naval and military base at Rabaul on the New Guinea island of New Britain, and headed for Port Moresby. At the same time, another force, centered on the aircraft carriers *Shokaku* and *Zuikaku*, sailed into the Coral Sea, northeast of Australia. Recognizing these movements as an overture to a full-scale invasion of New Guinea and Australia, U.S. admiral Frank Fletcher quickly put together a task force with which to meet the approaching Japanese. Fletcher's thinking reflected that of General Douglas MacArthur, who had been evacuated to Australia from his doomed command in the Philippines to assume overall direction of Allied forces in the South Pacific theater. Before his arrival, the prevailing Allied strategy had been to prepare for an invasion of Australia and to resist it mightily when it came. Although he was aware that Allied resources in the region were woefully thin, and mindful of the juggernaut that had most recently claimed the ships of the Java Sea as victims, MacArthur nevertheless proposed not a defensive approach but a counteroffensive, an audacious strategy that would take the battle to the Japanese, in New Guinea and at sea.

On May 7, Fletcher seized the initiative, launching planes from the aircraft carriers *Yorktown* and *Lexington*, which intercepted the invasion fleet north of the Louisiade Archipelago. The Japanese were stunned by the aggression of an enemy they believed they had wholly intimidated if not beaten. The carrier *Shoho* was sunk in this initial attack. Lacking air cover, the Japanese transports—carrying the invasion force—were compelled to turn back. This was an important victory, but the Battle of the Coral Sea was hardly over.

On May 8, the main body of the American task force approached the principal portion of the Japanese fleet. In one of the most significant moments in modern military history, the two sides simultaneously commenced the attack—without sighting one another visually. They launched history's first over-the-horizon attack, in which *aircraft* were used to fight a *naval* battle at such long range that there was no direct ship-to-ship contact.

REALITY CHECK
Naval Warfare Revolution

Much as the Civil War duel between the Union's *Monitor* and the Confederacy's *Virginia* (ex-*Merrimack*) in Hampton Roads on March 9, 1862, marked the momentous transition from the age of wooden warships to the era of the modern battleship, the Battle of the Coral Sea spelled the end of the battleship as the principal naval combatant. From that battle forward, the aircraft carrier emerged as the supreme naval vessel and the carrier-launched airplane as the most significant *naval* weapon. The Battle of the Coral Sea changed naval warfare more fundamentally than any development since the submarine.

The aircraft carrier USS Lexington *falls under heavy attack during the Battle of the Coral Sea, May 8, 1942, and no aircraft can be launched until the fires burning in the hangar deck below are brought under control. A tactical victory for the Japanese, the battle nevertheless put them at a strategic disadvantage.*

The battle developed with unprecedented ferocity. Fletcher's planes badly damaged the *Shokaku,* but thirty-three of the eighty-two attacking aircraft were blown out of the sky. Japanese pilots sank the carrier *Lexington* (CV-2) as well as a destroyer and a tanker, losing in the process forty-three of the sixty-nine committed to the battle. On balance, the Battle of the Coral Sea was a tactical victory for the Japanese, especially since the Americans had suffered the loss of a precious aircraft carrier. Viewed strategically, however, Coral Sea was a Japanese defeat. For the very first time in the Pacific war, an Allied force had stopped a Japanese advance. Port Moresby was saved, and, with it, Australia. Perhaps even more significantly, the Japanese had not merely been foiled, but forced into retreat, clear out of the Coral Sea. The battle also created the circumstances under which the Battle of Midway—the single most decisive sea battle in the Pacific theater—would be fought.

Turning Point at Midway

The Japanese thought they knew enough about American aircraft to be quite convinced that the twin-engine B-25 medium bombers that had raided Tokyo and other industrial cities on April 18, 1942 (see Chapter 10, "Revenge") could not possibly have been launched from any aircraft carrier. They had to have been land based, and that meant that they were certainly launched from the Midway Islands. This mistaken "fact" made those islands a high-priority target for the Japanese.

Located in the central Pacific, thirteen hundred miles northwest of Honolulu, Midway was a coral atoll enclosing just two islands, called Eastern (or Green) and Sand. The total land area was a mere two square miles. These specks in the vast Pacific had been claimed for the United States back in 1859 by Captain N. C. Brooks and were formally annexed in 1867. In 1903, Theodore Roosevelt handed administration of the islands to the navy, and two years later Sand Island became a station of the underwater telegraph cable that ran from Hawaii to Luzon in the Philippines. Midway assumed far greater importance in 1936, with the growth of trans-Pacific aviation. It served as a way station and refueling stop for the great Pan American "clippers" plying the air route between San Francisco and Manila. As war in the Pacific loomed, in 1940, the navy started building both an air and a submarine base on Midway.

The Japanese aircraft carrier Shokaku *blazes as a result of a bomb hit by U.S. aircraft, launched from the carrier* Yorktown *during the morning of May 8, 1942, during the Battle of the Coral Sea.*

Admiral Isoroku Yamamoto, the brilliant architect of the Pearl Harbor attack, had long advocated luring the U.S. fleet to the seas adjacent to Midway and then finishing what had (as it turned out) only been started at Pearl Harbor: the destruction of the American naval presence in the Pacific. Moreover, Yamamoto argued, Midway would provide whoever held the islands with a base for major offensive actions in a vast sector of the ocean. Still, Japanese high command was reluctant to risk so much of the Imperial fleet on an all-out battle at Midway—that is, until the Doolittle Raid on Japan seemed to prove the threat posed by American possession of the islands. After the raid, all objection to Yamamoto's proposal dissolved.

Yamamoto planned out the battle on the vastest possible scale. He dispatched a large fleet to the Aleutians, the chain of islands that arc southwest from Alaska and that, in 1942, formed part of the U.S. territory of Alaska. Yamamoto believed that a threat to U.S. territory would compel the U.S. Pacific Fleet to divert a significant portion of its forces far to the north, away from Midway. While the Aleutian diversion was under way, Yamamoto sent a four-carrier striking force in advance of an eighty-eight-ship invasion fleet to Midway. Its commander was Chuichi Nagumo, the very man who had led the attack on Pearl Harbor.

Cool, calm, and bold, Admiral Chester W. Nimitz, U.S. Navy, was one of the Pacific war's most brilliant strategists and tacticians.

Key to the success of Yamamoto's plan was close coordination and absolute secrecy. Like the Imperial Japanese Navy's other commanders, Yamamoto had no idea that U.S. code breakers had cracked the Japanese naval codes. Radio intercepts vaguely hinted that Midway was the objective of an invasion. It was up to U.S. Pacific Fleet commander Admiral Chester W. Nimitz to decide how to interpret

American torpedo bombers roll in for the attack during the Battle of Midway, June 4–7, 1942. Despite heavy losses, the U.S. Navy dealt the Imperial Japanese Navy a decisive defeat, which put Japan on the defensive for the rest of the war.

the hint—which was by no means unambiguous. American naval resources in the Pacific, these few months after Pearl Harbor, were already stretched thin. If Nimitz sent the bulk of the fleet to Midway, he would leave Hawaii and, ultimately, the American West Coast, virtually undefended. It was a gamble worth taking—if he interpreted the intercepted hints correctly, and the Japanese really were converging on Midway. For here was a chance to strike a decisive blow against the Imperial Navy. If, however, the intercepts were invalid or a deliberate deception, it was certain that the Japanese would strike at the exposed Hawaiian Islands and the continental United States itself. And even if the U.S. Pacific Fleet did engage the Japanese, there was every possibility of defeat, destroying the fleet, and opening the western United States to invasion.

Against the advice of high command in Washington, Nimitz decided to roll the dice. He would give Yamamoto the decisive battle he wanted—but he would engineer a very different outcome.

> **"Plane reports two carriers, two battleships, bearing 320 degrees, distant 180 miles, course 135 degrees, speed 25 knots."**
>
> *Lieutenant Howard B. Ady, U.S. Navy pilot, report of sighting Japanese task force off Midway, 6:00 A.M., June 4, 1942*

Nimitz rushed to put together a pair of task forces east of Midway. The first, designated Number 16, was put under the command of Raymond Spruance, while Number 18 was assigned to Frank Fletcher. Carrier-launched planes from the *Enterprise*, *Hornet*, and *Yorktown* would be supplemented by land-based flights from Midway. It was the Midway-based aircraft that struck the battle's first blows, attacking the Japanese fleet when it was still more than five hundred miles west of Midway on June 3. A long reach and a bold strike, it nevertheless did little damage and cost heavily in American casualties. It was followed the next morning by a large Japanese sortie of

108 planes, which bombed and strafed Midway, inflicting heavy damage, including the destruction on the ground of fifteen of the twenty-five Marine Corps fighter planes assigned to defend the island.

While the Japanese hit Midway on June 4, American torpedo bombers from the aircraft carriers made a second air attack against the Japanese fleet. The results were again profoundly disheartening. Not a single enemy ship was hit, and seven of the bombers were downed. Before the day was over, another U.S. strike was launched, this time by Marine Corps dive-bombers. Eight of the twenty-seven aircraft sortied were lost, and yet again no serious damage was inflicted. This was followed by a flight of 15 four-engine B-17 bombers, out of Midway. Even their barrage of bombs managed to do little harm. All of the Japanese carriers emerged from the attack unscathed.

With the grimmest of determination on this bloody day, another flight of torpedo bombers was launched from all three U.S. carriers. Not only did they inflict little damage, their losses were catastrophic: thirty-five of forty-one shot out of the sky.

It was a dark hour. Had Nimitz blundered into a Japanese trap?

Then, at the height of apparent triumph, the Japanese were about to suffer an irrecoverable blow. The final torpedo bomber attack had forced the Japanese carriers to launch all of their aircraft in defense. This left the carriers exposed. Deck crews were just beginning to service the returning aircraft when fifty-four dive-bombers from the *Enterprise* and *Yorktown* (none of the planes launched from the *Hornet* found their targets) suddenly fell upon three of the Japanese carriers—*Akagi, Kaga*, and *Soryu*. On these ships, none of the aircraft was ready to fly. In the space of five minutes, all three carriers were devastated, sent to the bottom of the Pacific, together with ships' crews, aircraft, and pilots. The fourth carrier, *Hiryu*, met an identical fate a few hours later, by which time, however, *Hiryu*'s aircraft had managed to sink the carrier *Yorktown*. The reversal of Japanese fortunes in this battle was staggeringly sudden, and the battle suddenly reversed the fortunes of Japan in the war as a whole. Although Midway cost the Americans heavily in pilots, ships, and sailors, it inflicted a mortal wound on the Imperial Japanese Navy. Having lost four aircraft carriers, a great many planes, and many of its irreplaceable pilots, the survivors of the Japanese fleet withdrew on June 5. Giving chase was out of the question. The U.S. fleet was simply too

ALTERNATE TAKE

Pilot Program

The loss of aircraft was always more damaging to the Japanese than to the Americans because of a key difference between Japanese and American policy with regard to pilots. Japanese combat pilots flew until they were killed. American combat pilots flew a set number of missions and then were rotated out of combat to serve as flight instructors. In this way, the American navy and air force were ensured of a steady supply of new combat pilots trained by experienced combat pilots. In contrast, new Japanese pilots came into battle with nothing beyond basic flight training. The Japanese policy simply consumed Japan's best, most experienced fliers, who, once lost, could not be replaced. Had the Japanese adopted a policy similar to that of the Americans, they might well have prevailed in key naval air engagements, which, at the very least, would have prolonged the Pacific war.

NUMBERS

U.S. and Japanese Losses

At Midway, the United States lost 150 planes, 307 sailors and airmen, a destroyer, and the carrier *Yorktown*. Japanese losses included 275 planes, 4 carriers, a heavy cruiser, and some 5,000 sailors and airmen, including some of the Imperial Japanese Navy's best pilots.

spent—although, on June 6, U.S. ships did sink the *Mikuma*, a heavy cruiser. After Midway, the Japanese were compelled to fight a defensive war. Their epoch of conquest was at an end.

Aleutian Interlude

Another part of Yamamoto's plan was to attack the Aleutians, a chain of fourteen small islands and some fifty-five even smaller islets separating the Bering Sea from the rest of the northern Pacific. The attack was meant as a diversion to draw a significant portion of the U.S. fleet away from Midway. Instead, Admiral Nimitz dispatched only a modest force to deal with the attack on the Aleutians. Against elements of the Japanese Fifth Fleet, under Vice-Admiral Hosogaya Boshiro, Nimitz sent Task Force 8, also known as the "North Pacific Force," under Rear Admiral Robert Theobald. The task force consisted of old, even obsolescent ships, including five cruisers, fourteen destroyers, and six submarines.

"Five minutes! Who would have dreamed that the tide of battle would shift completely in that brief interval of time?"

Mitsuo Fuchida, Japanese officer aboard the aircraft carrier Akagi *at the Battle of Midway*

The Japanese objective was to occupy the largest of the Aleutian islands; therefore Boshiro divided his fleet into four groups to support an invasion: Rear-Admiral Kakuta Kakuji's Mobile Force (built around two light carriers and a seaplane carrier), the Kiska Occupation Force, the Adak-Attu Occupation Force, and a unit made up of supply ships, escorted by the heavy cruiser *Nachi* and two destroyers. Both of the enemies each faced a third enemy, the weather. The Aleutians were perpetually fog shrouded and, most of the time, assailed by icy rain. These conditions made seaborne navigation difficult and flying extraordinarily hazardous.

Always seeking to force Nimitz to further divide and diminish his fleet, Kakuta's Mobile Force made two raids on an American base at Dutch Harbor, Unalaska Island, in the eastern Aleutians. He then hit U.S. destroyers anchored in Makushin Bay, but was handily repulsed. Theobald saw Japanese intentions in the Aleutians as far more than a mere diversion. He was persuaded that they intended to secure the islands as a base from which to mount an invasion of the American mainland. Despite the age and inadequacy of his task force, Theobald therefore decided that he had to do everything he could to intercept the Japanese supply transports, which he saw as crucial to the Japanese plan to occupy the islands. By focusing on the transports, however, Theobald allowed other ships to slip

DETAILS, DETAILS

After 130 Years . . .

The invasion of Attu and Kiska constituted the only U.S. continental territory to be occupied by a foreign power since the War of 1812.

through, landing Japanese troops on Attu (June 5, 1942) and Kiska (June 7) not only without American opposition, but even—until June 10—without awareness.

Once the landings were recognized, American bombers staged a raid on Kiska to little effect. As for Attu, it was well beyond the bombers' range. Theobald unleashed the big guns of his cruisers, but the bombardment was largely ineffective. On August 27, seeking to consolidate their position, the Japanese started transferring most of the Attu garrison to Kiska, but then reoccupied Attu in October. At odd hours, whenever the almost perpetually inclement weather allowed, Theobald fired on the islands, and the air force, operating from rudimentary airstrips on Adak and Amchitka, bombed them. The flying was always extremely hazardous, and although the pounding was administered over nine long months, it did astoundingly little to wear down the garrisons. Despite this, the continual assault effectively bottled up the Japanese forces on the islands. Whatever else happened, there would be no continental invasion.

In March 1943, American forces in the Aleutians mounted a major assault on the invaders. The first push, on March 26, fizzled when severe weather conditions grounded air support of the naval battle of the Komandorski Islands. Although the engagement failed to dislodge the Japanese garrison from Attu, it did prevent the 2,630-man force there from being reinforced prior to the landing of some eleven thousand troops of the U.S. 7th Infantry Division on May 11, 1943.

U.S. landing craft pour soldiers and equipment on the beach at Massacre Bay, Attu, in Alaska's Aleutian Islands on May 11, 1943.

REALITY CHECK

New Ships

Theobald was given no battleships and no fleet aircraft carriers. But his task force did have some small escort carriers, a relatively new type of combatant designed to carry perhaps thirty aircraft as opposed to the eighty carried on a standard fleet carrier. Escort carriers were cheap and fast to build—compared to the full-size ships—and President Roosevelt, who believed the war would be won by out-producing the enemy, enthusiastically supported their use. The U.S. Army Air Forces also had eighty-five land-based aircraft available.

DETAILS, DETAILS

Key Escorts

The U.S. assault on Attu was the first time that air support was launched from an escort carrier—the new type of aircraft carrier, much smaller than a fleet carrier and intended (as the name implied) to accompany convoys in order to provide air support. They would play an important role in most of the major Allied landings throughout the Pacific during the offensive.

The outnumbered Attu garrison, commanded by Colonel Yamazaki Yasuyo, fiercely resisted the American forces. By May 29, the garrison had been forced to retreat to the last high ground of the island. Cornered here, they did not surrender, but instead launched a banzai charge—something that would become all too familiar in the Pacific "island hopping" campaign (see Chapter 15). A banzai charge was rarely launched early in a military action, but was a last-ditch—even suicidal—response to overwhelming force. Wild and fierce, a banzai charge was terrifying, yet, tactically, futile.

The Americans crushed a second banzai-style attack on May 30, whereupon most of the Japanese survivors committed suicide rather than submit to capture. Of the 2,630-man garrison, just twenty-eight became prisoners. The others died. U.S. casualties were six hundred killed and twelve hundred wounded.

Vice Admiral Thomas Kinkaid replaced Theobald as commander of Task Force 8 during January 1943. After Attu was retaken, Kinkaid decided to attack Kiska and began by deploying a destroyer blockade and hammering Kiska with a naval and aerial bombardment; however, in the thick fog of the night of July 28/29, during a lull in the bombardment and a break in the blockade—as Kinkaid's destroyers refueled—5,183 Japanese were evacuated in an operation so stealthy that even repeated aerial reconnaissance failed to detect it. On August 15, 1943, thirty-four thousand U.S. and Canadian troops landed on Kiska. The landings were unopposed and, after a few days, the reason for this became abundantly clear. The island had been deserted.

In the context of Midway and the great Pacific battles that followed, the Aleutian campaign was a backwater war, yet, thankless and obscure, it was a struggle both harsh and hazardous. For both sides it represented a waste of resources—though far more so for the Japanese, who certainly could have used the men and the ships to better advantage elsewhere.

ALTERNATE TAKE

Aleutian Miscalculation

Theobald could not have known that Japanese resources were stretched too thinly for them to have used the Aleutians as a base to invade North American. Operating on the assumption that they planned to invade, he concentrated his meager forces on disrupting supply vessels essential to what he saw as the enemy's long-term intentions rather than acting quickly to interdict immediate landings. It was a serious error that kept U.S. forces tied down in the harsh Aleutian environment far longer than necessary. Even the decision to drive the Japanese out, once they had landed, was dubious. The land battle against the occupiers was costly, and pilots and sailors were lost to storms and fog. Perhaps it would have been a better strategy to allow the invaders to remain, essentially isolated, on the islands—although the American public might not have long tolerated the presence of an invader on U.S. territory, no matter how remote.

THE EPIC OF GUADALCANAL

ADMIRAL ERNEST J. KING, U.S. Navy chief of operations, saw Midway as a key turning point in the Pacific war, but he also recognized that, even after suffering this defeat, the Japanese were still capable of threatening Australia. Intercepted Japanese radio traffic indicated that they intended to occupy a steamy, godforsaken jungle island called

Guadalcanal, and to hack out of it an airstrip from which to launch attacks on U.S. convoys supplying Australia.

One of the Solomon Islands in the South Pacific, Guadalcanal, ninety miles long, twenty-five miles at its widest, was like many other dots in the ocean map—obscure, essentially valueless before the war, then, in the heat of combat, transformed into real estate so precious that it had to be purchased with blood. The assault began on August 7, 1942, with the amphibious landing of the 1st Marine Division in a stunning surprise attack that immediately seized the almost completed airstrip. The marines, however, had little time to bask in their lightning victory. On August 9, a Japanese naval task force struck an Allied screening force off Savo Island, northeast of Guadalcanal. Seven Japanese cruisers fell upon and sank one Australian cruiser and three American ones, seriously damaging a fourth U.S. cruiser. So many American ships went down that the waters off Savo were christened, with grim humor, "Ironbottom Sound."

The battle of Savo Island so unnerved Admiral Frank Fletcher, tactical commander of the Guadalcanal operation, that he pulled back his aircraft carriers, a move that forced partially unloaded troop transports to withdraw as well. Marines already landed on Guadalcanal gazed at the ocean horizon, now entirely devoid of ships. They were cut off, isolated—at least until August 20, when a unit called the "Cactus Air Force" (after the U.S. code name for Guadalcanal, "Cactus") arrived to operate from the captured airfield, now renamed Henderson Field. It was a motley assemblage of mostly U.S. Marine aircraft—nineteen fighters and twelve torpedo bombers—and it provided all the air defense the marines would get for some time. Nevertheless, until the Cactus Air Force was later augmented by other air units and until the fleet returned, the Japanese exploited their newfound air and sea superiority by reinforcing their garrison on Guadalcanal. They operated by night, using destroyers to deliver men and supplies, doing so with such stealthy regularity that the marines dubbed these nocturnal visits the Tokyo Express.

Over the next three months, the well-supplied and reinforced Japanese land forces battled the marines. For their part, thanks to a growing airlift capacity, the marines were also continually resupplied and reinforced. In contrast to most other island battles, in which the numbers engaged naturally diminished, the troop strength on both

REALITY CHECK

The Few, the Proud

Guadalcanal demonstrated the marines' trademark tactical style. They were a force used to penetrate enemy positions, often deliberately inviting encirclement. Encircled, it became the marines' desperate mission to hold on—typically supplied by tenuous airlifts—fighting from the inside out until reinforcements arrived. The marines' stock in trade, it was a most perilous form of combat.

sides multiplied on Guadalcanal, so that, by November 12, thirty thousand Japanese opposed twenty-nine thousand Americans. That proved to be the tipping point. By the next month, the marines had managed to whittle down Japanese strength to twenty-five thousand, even as U.S. strength swelled to forty thousand, representing two marine divisions and two army divisions. The two sides battered one another, but American superiority of numbers ensured that the Japanese would ultimately lose—although it was at sea, not on the island itself, that the American victory at Guadalcanal was finally won.

"Before Guadalcanal the enemy advanced at his pleasure—after Guadalcanal he retreated at ours."

U.S. admiral William "Bull" Halsey, after the Guadalcanal victory

The navy intervened to block new Japanese landings on August 24, but took severe losses in the process. Vengeance came on the night of October 11/12, at the battle of Cape Esperance, in which a navy task force, with the help of a new kind of surface radar, sank a Japanese heavy cruiser and a destroyer while also damaging a second cruiser and killing Rear Admiral Aritomo Goto. This was the U.S. Navy's first victory in a night battle against the Japanese, and the sight of navy

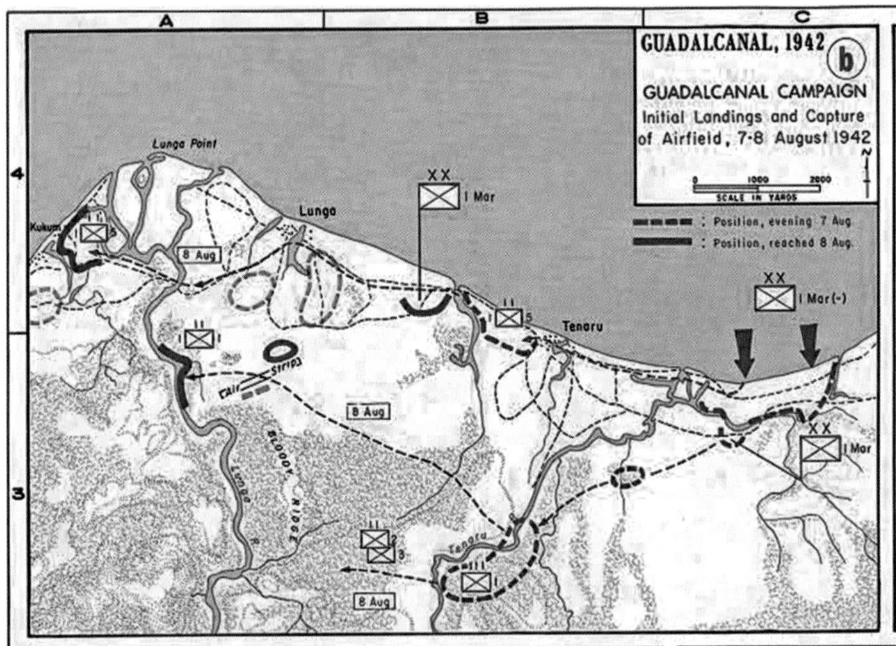

As the Battle of Midway turned the tide of the naval war in the Pacific, so Guadalcanal was the Americans' first great victory on land, which initiated the island-hopping campaign that ultimately won the war in this theater. The map shows the opening U.S. assault on the island during August 7-8, 1942.

ships defeating the Japanese vessels that were landing reinforcements on Guadalcanal gave the marines a tremendous morale boost.

Despite success at Cape Esperance, Admiral Nimitz deemed South Pacific theater commander Robert L. Ghormley too cautious. Nimitz believed that the Allies could not afford to become bogged down in a protracted battle for every Japanese-occupied island. He replaced Ghormley with a commander celebrated for his almost reckless aggressiveness, Vice Admiral William F. "Bull" Halsey.

The Guadalcanal campaign spanned August 1942 to February of the following year. For the U.S. Marines, it was a miserable and costly slog through tropical jungle, but it paid off in the first great American land victory of the Pacific war.

On October 26, Halsey struck at the battle of Santa Cruz, losing the aircraft carrier *Hornet* (with seventy-four of its aircraft), but destroying one hundred Japanese planes. During November 12–15, in the seaborne Battle of Guadalcanal, Halsey battled it out with the Japanese. During the night of November 12/13, six U.S. ships were lost versus three Japanese—including a battleship. On the morning of the thirteenth, however, a Japanese cruiser was sunk, and three others were severely damaged. With nightfall, the battle resumed, and Halsey sank another Japanese battleship, along with a destroyer. The Americans that night lost six destroyers and took damage to one battleship, but the Japanese were forced to beach their troop transports, which were bombed into junk after daybreak.

The Japanese scored a victory at sea in the battle of Tassafaronga on November 30, but they were persuaded that the losses they had sustained through months of fighting on and around the miserable island would soon wear them down to nothing. The fighting slackened until, early in January 1943, in the face of Allied air and sea superiority, the Japanese somehow managed to evacuate about thirteen thousand men from Guadalcanal, ferrying them through the dark of night to waiting destroyers.

NUMBERS

U.S. and Japanese Losses

Despite the Japanese evacuation of Guadalcanal, some 30,000 Japanese soldiers, sailors, and airmen were killed during the campaign, and 680 aircraft and 24 warships were lost. U.S. losses included about 5,000 sailors and 2,500 marines, soldiers, and airmen, in addition to 615 aircraft and 25 ships.

REALITY CHECK

Death with Honor

It is doubtful that Japanese soldiers believed a banzai charge would actually succeed in salvaging a hopeless situation. The function of the banzai charge was not to wrest victory from the jaws of defeat, but to satisfy military honor as defined by the Bushido, the ancient Japanese warrior code (see Chapter 9, "Bushido"). Bushido dictated that defeat in battle was not a disgrace, but surrender was. It was, therefore, infinitely better to die than to allow oneself to be made a prisoner of war. The banzai charge might not bring victory, but it was certain to bring death with honor.

New Guinea Campaign

Although the Battle of the Coral Sea foiled the attempt to capture Port Moresby, the Japanese had by no means given up on taking New Guinea. During July 21/22, 1942, elements of the Japanese Eighteenth Army, commanded by General Hatazo Adachi, landed at Gona and Buna, then launched a new attempt against Port Moresby. On the twenty-second, two Japanese regiments left Gona and Buna to make their way along the rugged Kokoda Trail over New Guinea's great mountain ridge, the thirteen-thousand-foot Owen Stanley Range.

The Defense

The Japanese did not reach Kokoda until August 12, then moved on to Ioribaiwa by September 17. This put the advance Japanese units just thirty-two miles from Port Moresby. But here they were observed, and the 7th Australian Division hit them, driving all of the Japanese out of the mountains and back into the swamplands surrounding Gona and Buna. The 7th Division, reinforced by American and additional Australian units, then fought a hard jungle campaign that cleared the invaders out of Gona on December 10, 1942, and out of Buna on January 3, 1943. When the remaining Japanese pocket of resistance, at Sanananda Point, was cleaned out on January 23, the southeastern end of New Guinea was liberated and no longer a threat to Australia. The Australian and American forces had achieved just what General MacArthur wanted: to fight the Japanese on New Guinea and not on the Australian mainland.

The Offensive

Having flushed the Japanese from southeastern New Guinea, MacArthur organized a general Allied counteroffensive in the Southwest Pacific. In the spring of 1943, the U.S. I Corps, commanded by Robert Eichelberger—and later expanded into the Sixth U.S. Army under Walter Krueger—coordinated with the U.S. Seventh Fleet to drive the Japanese from the still-occupied north coast of New Guinea. Starting from liberated Gona, on the coast, and the inland village of Wau, Americans and Australians made a fighting advance west and north, targeting the area of Salamaua-Lae. On the night of June 29/30, a regiment of the U.S. 41st Infantry landed at Nassau Bay, near Salamaua and, with the 5th Australian Infantry, captured the village—on September 12—after many weeks of bitter jungle fighting. While the Salamaua fight was culminating, the Australian 9th Division landed ten miles east of Lae and the U.S. 503rd Parachute Regiment and the Australian 7th Infantry Regiment were air dropped into the Markham Valley to the west of Lae, thereby surrounding this Japanese position. Lae fell on September 16 and was declared secure two days later. This was followed by the capture of the important port of Finschhafen on October 2. With that, the Huon Gulf was securely in Allied hands.

Triumph in the Bismarck Sea

During the final phase of the New Guinea campaign, the Japanese furiously sought to reinforce their positions on Lae and Salamaua by amphibiously landing more troops. American cryptanalysts intercepted Japanese radio traffic and were well aware that seven thousand reinforcements were en route at the end of February 1943. On March 2, fighters and bombers of the U.S. Fifth Army Air Force swooped down on the Japanese troop convoy, sinking one transport and damaging two others. On the next day, Australian planes and more American bombers attacked again, some of them employing a newly developed technique for bombing ships. Known as "skip bombing," it called for aircraft to drop their bombs at low altitude over the water, so that they would skip over the surface—like a hurled stone—hitting the targeted ship just below its waterline and thereby ensuring that it would rapidly sink. The technique was extraordinarily effective.

The Japanese troop transport fleet was devastated by air attack during the day of March 3. After nightfall, the Americans sent PT boats, which made hit-and-run torpedo attacks. By daybreak on March 4, just six Japanese destroyers were still afloat—and American bombers soon sank two of these.

Death of an Admiral

Admiral Isoroku Yamamoto, the bold architect of the attack on Pearl Harbor, was a changed man after the Battle of Midway Island. His confidence sorely shaken, he became a conservative, almost timid leader. Nevertheless, he remained vigorous in maintaining a

NUMBERS

Skip Bombing a Hit

Of 37 five-hundred-pound bombs dropped on March 3 using the "skip bombing" technique, 28 scored hits—an unparalleled achievement in bombing naval targets.

NUMBERS

Allied and Japanese Losses

American and Australian forces lost 8,546 men killed or wounded clearing southeastern New Guinea to prevent the invasion of Australia. Japanese losses were estimated at 12,000 killed and 350 captured. About 4,000 Japanese troops managed to withdraw.

NUMBERS

Japanese Convoy Losses

Of the 7,000 troops the Japanese were convoying to Lae and Salamaua, just 950 managed to reach Lae. Some others survived the sinking of their transports and were rescued by Japanese destroyers, but total Japanese battle deaths were 3,660.

PACIFIC NURSES

The women of the U.S. Army Nurse Corps were routinely stationed in field hospitals on the front lines in North Africa and Europe, but were generally restricted to rear areas in the Pacific campaign, or stationed on islands that had been retaken by the Allies, such as Guadalcanal.

In part, this was a by-product of island-hopping. The "front" was simply too fluid and fast moving to establish major field hospitals close to the fighting. But the policy was also due to a feeling among American politicians and army administrators that women should not be exposed to existence in "uncivilized"—by which was meant non-white—jungle areas, where they might be subject to attack, capture, and even rape by an Asian enemy.

Stationed well behind the lines, the army nurses in the Pacific nevertheless performed heroically, caring not only for men wounded in battle but for the many more suffering from the various diseases endemic to tropical and jungle environments, especially malaria, which accounted for half of all army hospital admissions. Because of the shortage of doctors and the large volume of wounded, nurses routinely assumed responsibilities ordinarily handled by physicians. They administered transfusions and performed advanced wound care just short of surgery. Nurses also trained wardmen (equivalent to hospital orderlies) to perform many nursing functions.

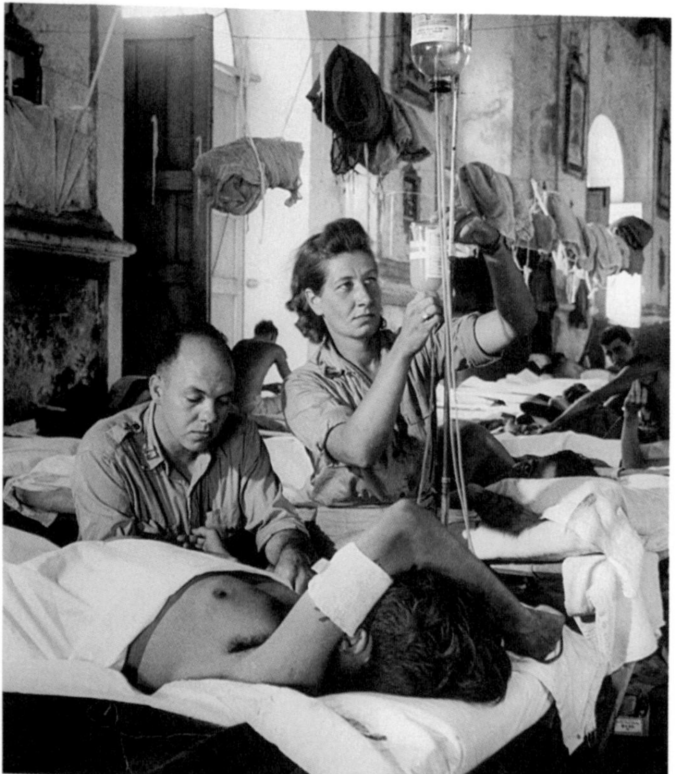

In the Pacific theater, the women of the U.S. Army Nurse Corps often stationed in evacuation hospitals improvised wherever they could be. Here, Nurse Captain Catherine Acorn assists Captain D. E. Campbell, an army surgeon, in treating wounded at Leyte Cathedral, Philippines, which was hastily converted into a hospital. The photograph was taken on December 18, 1944.

In the Pacific, airborne assaults were smaller and more surgically precise than in the European theater, but they served the same purpose: to get soldiers behind enemy lines quickly and with the utmost of stealth. These paratroopers are attacking Japanese positions near Lae, New Guinea, in 1943. A smokescreen hides them from the Japanese defenders.

strong personal presence throughout the far-flung Pacific Front, and, on April 18, 1943, embarked on a tour of Japanese bases on Shortland Islands in the bitterly contested Solomon Islands group. Once again, American code breakers intercepted and decrypted a valuable radio message. This one revealed the admiral's route and destination. Immediately, fighter planes were scrambled on an interception course. Near Bougainville Island, they shot down the bomber carrying Yamamoto. It was, for Americans in the Pacific and Americans at home, the crowning triumph in a series of heartbreakingly costly victories. The man behind the calamity of Pearl Harbor had been killed.

TAKEAWAY

Reversal in the Pacific

Three major Pacific battles turned the tide against Japan in the Pacific: The Battle of the Coral Sea, although it was a tactical victory for the Japanese, halted the Japanese advance and was therefore a major strategic reversal. The Battle of Midway broke the back of the Japanese Pacific offensive. For the remainder of the war, the Japanese fought a desperate defense. The Battle of Guadalcanal stopped the Japanese on land, putting the Allies in position for the decisive island-hopping campaign (Chapter 15).

CHAPTER 15

ISLAND HOPPING

Tightening the Pacific Noose

EVEN AS AMERICA WAS STILL ON THE RUN early in the Pacific war, U.S. admiral Chester Nimitz proposed an aggressive strategy for a counteroffensive. It was dubbed "island hopping" and consisted of planning a series of amphibious assaults on selected Japanese-held islands, progressively working closer to the Japanese home islands, skipping over some islands along the way while subjecting others to no more than air attack, without ground invasion. Nimitz saw—and General Douglas MacArthur enthusiastically seconded him—that merely isolating some Japanese forces on their islands was as effective in neutralizing them as actually attacking and destroying them. More important, cutting off selected island garrisons was far less costly than doing battle with them.

THE LEAP FROG CAMPAIGN

IT WOULD HAVE BEEN EASY TO GIVE WAY TO PANIC AND DESPAIR during the first few months of the Pacific war; after all, the Japanese made one conquest after another. What both Nimitz and MacArthur recognized was that holding captured territory—especially when that territory was spread over a vast expanse of ocean—was a costly drain on manpower. The Japanese thought of their newly acquired Pacific empire as a source of great strength. The American commanders began to look at it as Japan's greatest vulnerability.

As America's top military planners developed it, the island-hopping or "leap frogging" campaign was divided into two prongs, one aimed north of the other. The northernmost prong began from Midway and took a trajectory that led it to Iwo Jima in February 1945. The southern prong started at Guadalcanal, then moved through to the Solomon chain of islands and, from these, in early 1945, to the Philippines.

REALITY CHECK

Sitting Ducks

Landing craft had flat bottoms, which made them shallow-draft boats—vessels designed to operate close to shore. Those flat bottoms, however, were highly vulnerable to underwater obstacles, of which tough, jagged coral was among the most dangerous. Running aground on a coral reef could easily tear a hole in the bottom of a landing craft, either sinking it—and quite possibly drowning all aboard—or rendering it a sitting-duck target for enemy fire.

At Bougainville

Located in the southwestern Pacific, near the northern end of the Solomon Islands, Bougainville, seventy-five miles long and forty to sixty miles wide, is the largest island of the chain. A volcanic island, its fiery origin is dramatically reflected in its rugged landscape, which is surmounted by the nine-thousand-foot Emperor Range at its northern end and, covering the entire southern half, the somewhat lower Crown Prince Range. As the land is rough, so are the sea approaches. Bougainville is surrounded by coral reefs, which presented serious obstacles to amphibious assault.

After achieving hard-won victory in the New Guinea campaign as well as success in the New Georgia islands, the Americans closed in on the major Japanese base at Rabaul, on the island of New Britain. Bougainville figured as the last-ditch Japanese line of defense, protecting Rabaul from American forces moving up the Solomon chain. As the Japanese found themselves conducting a fighting withdrawal from their island outposts, Bougainville loomed for them with greater and greater importance, and they reinforced the garrison there by sending 37,500 men of the Japanese Seventeenth Army under Lieutenant General Hyakutake Haruyoshi.

Always on the look out for offensive opportunities, the American commanders noted that the Japanese reinforcements were all deployed at the southern end of Buin, on Bougainville, and on small islands off the main island's shore, whereas Empress Augusta Bay, to the north, was open. That is where the U.S. Marines landed on November 1, 1943, after the 3rd New Zealand Division had assaulted and captured the nearby Treasury Islands. Once in place, the marines

U.S. ARMY IN NEW GEORGIA

Typically, amphibious assaults on the Pacific islands either began with U.S. Marine operations—only later reinforced by the army—or were entirely carried out by the marines. The New Georgia campaign, however, began as an army operation, with marines playing a largely supporting role.

A soldier of Company K, 3rd Battalion, 27th Infantry, advances through dense jungle growth along the Zieta Trail in the U.S. Army's assault on New Georgia Island, August 12, 1943.

It began on June 20, 1943 when a specially trained U.S. Army Raider battalion landed at Segi Point on the main island of the Solomon Islands group, New Georgia. Over the succeeding two weeks, soldiers of the U.S. Army 43rd Division, supplemented by marines, landed on Rendova and Vangunu islands and on western New Georgia. Here they captured a Japanese airfield at Munda Point.

Throughout the ground phase of the campaign, U.S. Navy ships fought the sea battles of Kula Gulf and Kolombangara; nevertheless they were unable to prevent the landing of some four thousand Japanese reinforcements, which augmented the 10,500-man New Georgia garrison—under Major General Noboru Sasaki—taking up positions on Munda, the focus of the Japanese defense. The American attackers were introduced to a new and terrifying form of defense. Customarily, the Japanese dug into the islands, firing on invaders from extremely well-prepared defensive positions. On Munda, they combined this type of defense with night infiltration, penetrating American lines under cover of darkness. The U.S. Army troops who followed the initial Raider battalion were mostly inexperienced; the night infiltration tactics took a terrible toll on their morale, which was reflected in a very high rate of battle fatigue. That, however, resulted in the replacement of many green 43rd Division troops with veteran soldiers of the 37th Division—a move that reinvigorated the entire campaign. After an attack by an entire U.S. Army corps on July 25, the Japanese, overwhelmed, withdrew by August 1. The addition of more ships in the waters surrounding the islands prevented the arrival of new Japanese reinforcements; no fewer than three Japanese troop transports were sunk at the battle of Vella Gulf on August 6–7.

Munda was finally declared secure in August and was immediately exploited as a base from which the marines launched an amphibious assault on Vella Lavella on August 15, hopping over—and thereby cutting off—the Japanese garrison on Kolombangara. With the capture of Vella Lavella, the New Georgia campaign was ended.

set up a defensive perimeter and began scratching out airstrips so that the ground assault would be well provided with air cover. As this was progressing, the battle of Empress Augusta Bay began at sea on November 2. American ships tangled with thinly distributed Japanese defenders, sinking a Japanese cruiser and a destroyer while the U.S. Fifth Army Air Force bombed Japanese airstrips and provided close air support for the marines.

The initial success of the Bougainville campaign was most encouraging, but with Rabaul—the very objective of the campaign—so close by, the assault forces were gravely menaced by the powerful naval force of Vice Admiral Takeo Kurita based there. Instead of taking defensive measures, U.S. admiral William Halsey lived up to his universally recognized nickname—"Bull" Halsey—and boldly seized the initiative by attacking Kurita's fleet at Rabaul, before it had even gotten under way. It was the most audacious of gambles, because it put the two-carrier American task force well within range of the very large air arm based at Rabaul. Committed to supporting operations on Bougainville and eager to hit Kurita precisely where he thought he was safest, Halsey did not merely risk losing his aircraft carriers, he even expected them to be sunk. Nevertheless, he deployed land-based aircraft so skillfully that the Japanese aircraft were kept at bay, and the carriers escaped unscathed, launching wave after wave of torpedo bombers and dive-bombers against Kurita's fleet, which was so badly battered that it had to withdraw to distant Truk Island.

Five ships of U.S. Destroyer Squadron 12 smartly execute high-speed S-turns in formation as a victory salute following a successful raid against the Japanese base at Rabaul in February 1944. Ships of this squadron made this salute a custom, to honor the lost crews of three squadron ships sunk during the battle of Savo Island. That battle's namesake island rises in the background.

As the raging sea battle was just reaching its final stages, the Bougainville marines finished building enough airstrips to launch a series of intensive air raids against Rabaul. At last, the Japanese were forced to withdraw from this major base. Once Rabaul fell, U.S. forces were rapidly built up on Bougainville and repulsed repeated

NUMBERS

Australian Army

At the beginning of World War II in Europe, in September 1939, the entire Australian army consisted of 82,800 soldiers, of whom 80,000 were militiamen, with little training and less equipment. Well aware of the dangers to their homeland, the Australians built up by war's end an impressive force of 691,400 men and 35,800 women. The Bougainville fight was among the hardest the Australians faced during the war.

Japanese counterattacks. On March 27, 1944, the Japanese mounted one final ambitious counteroffensive. Major General Oscar Griswold, the army commander at the front, had assembled a force of sixty-two thousand, which overwhelmed the men of the counteroffensive. With this, Bougainville grew unaccustomedly peaceful. Methodically, Griswold enlarged his perimeter to ensure that the island would be held, then relinquished it to the care of the Australian II Corps during December 1944.

As it turned out, the Australians—and the Americans—had seriously underestimated the number of Japanese troops still holed up on Bougainville. Optimists believed twelve thousand remained, but even the most pessimistic among the Allied commanders guessed that there could be no more than twenty-five thousand. The fact was that some forty thousand Japanese soldiers were still on the island, and they sprang into action after the Americans had left, offering fierce resistance to the Australians, who nevertheless defeated them.

Terrible Tarawa

The Pacific war seared into the consciousness the names of many places that would otherwise have remained utterly unknown to the vast majority of Americans. Geographically, the names were attached to a few square miles of coral, volcanic rock, or bleached-white sand scattered across the Pacific. Emotionally, they became, for American marines and soldiers, so many synonyms for hell.

The small but determined Australian army fought a fierce fight at Bougainville. Here, on February 8, 1945, an Australian mortar crew bombards Japanese defenders in the Tsimba area. The upturned helmets on the perimeter of the mortar pit are those of dead Japanese soldiers.

Tarawa was one such name. It labeled an atoll in the Gilbert Islands of the central Pacific—a most inconsequential atoll, whose largest islet, Betio, was a mere two and a half miles long. Yet, into this speck forty-five hundred Japanese had dug. It was a garrison under the command of Keiji Shibasaki, who boasted to his men that such were the defenses scratched into this island full of caves and concrete pillboxes—low-profile, hardened gun emplacements—that Betio and all

Tarawa could not be taken by a million soldiers in a hundred years. To the marines who finally did take Tarawa, Shibasaki's boast would not have seemed empty.

The invasion was preceded by a massive naval bombardment supplemented by aerial bombardment. Intensive though the bombardment was, the Japanese were so well dug into the island that it killed very few of the defenders, who put up a fierce resistance to the U.S. Marine landings on November 20, 1943. The bombardment severely crippled Japanese communications, thereby preventing them from organizing a massive, full-scale counterattack on the first night after the landings.

"We jumped into the little tractor boat and quickly settled on the deck. 'Oh, God, I'm scared,' said the little Marine, a telephone operator, who sat next to me forward in the boat. I gritted my teeth and tried to force a smile that would not come and tried to stop quivering all over (now I was shaking from fear). I said, in an effort to be reassuring, 'I'm scared, too.' I never made a more truthful statement in all my life."

War correspondent Robert Sherrod, with marines making an amphibious assault on Tarawa

For the first time in amphibious assault, a new type of amphibious landing vehicle was used, the LVT: Landing Vehicle, Tracked. The only problem was that the new LVTs were in critically short supply. The first wave of assault troops rode in them, but the second wave were carried by landing craft and waded ashore, taking heavy casualties in the process. To compound the hazard, planners had incorrectly calculated the tides, which were lower than anticipated. Many of the landing craft ran aground on coral reefs and had to disembark their marines much farther from the shore than planned. For many yards, therefore, the troops were exposed to heavy enemy fire.

Despite unexpectedly heavy casualties incurred during the landing, Major General Julian Smith, commanding the 2nd Marine Division, pushed into positions along the southern shore of

DETAILS, DETAILS
LVTs

Conventional landings were made from landing craft—flat-bottom barge-like vessels that approached the shore as closely as possible then dropped a bow ramp, down which the marines or soldiers scrambled, typically having to wade ashore. Depending on the depth of the water and the conditions of the beach bottom—which was often rocky or sandy, making movement difficult—wading slowed troops down and made them especially vulnerable to enemy fire. The new LVTs, however, were true armored amphibians. They were launched from large landing ships into the water, driven directly up to the beach, then driven—on caterpillar tracks—directly onto the shore and even well inland before its cargo of troops disembarked. Thus the landing parties were afforded ample shelter against enemy fire.

DETAILS, DETAILS

First Step

The small reconnaissance landings on Majuro Atoll, on January 30, 1944, marked the first time in World War II that Americans had set foot on Japanese soil. This was profoundly unnerving to the Japanese, whose lands, throughout history, had never been successfully invaded.

Betio and on the western end of the island as well. This forced the Japanese garrison to divide, and it was this division that spelled the end for the garrison. Not that Shibasaki gave up easily. He ordered numerous counterattacks in the form of banzai charges, against which the marines held their positions. By November 23, Betio had fallen to the Americans.

The cost of this infinitesimal speck of coral shocked the American public: 1,009 marines killed and 2,101 wounded. The marines themselves christened the atoll "Terrible Tarawa." Yet both the American people and the U.S. Marine Corps would soon discover that Tarawa had been nothing more than a baptism of fire in the central Pacific. There would be more victories, but they would cost even more.

The Marshall Islands Campaign

The taking of Tarawa was the first step in the Marshall Islands campaign, which began the American drive across the central Pacific. The Marshalls are a cluster of thirty-six Micronesian atolls, including the world's largest atoll, Kwajalein. The peace settlement that followed World War I mandated the Marshalls to Japan, which used them to anchor its outermost defensive perimeter in the Pacific.

On January 30, 1944, a U.S. Marine and Army amphibious assault force of eighty-five thousand men, escorted and carried by some three hundred warships, approached the Marshalls. Reconnaissance patrols landed on Majuro Atoll, and these landings were followed on February 1 by the major assault as the 4th Marine Division and 7th Infantry (Army) Division hit the beaches on the inner islands of Kwajalein Atoll: Roi-Namur and Kwajalein.

"Terrible Tarawa," the marines called this atoll in the Gilbert Islands. A heavily engaged assaulting party crouches below a "hasty defense" of sandbags. One marine has just risen and is about to throw a hand grenade.

As usual, massive air and naval bombardments preceded the landings at Kwajalein Atoll. Charles Corlett led the army's 7th Infantry Division onto Kwajalein Island, while marine general Holland "Howlin' Mad" Smith commanded the 4th Marine Division in landings on the twin islands of Roi and Namur, forty-five miles to the north of Kwajalein Island. A single marine regiment captured Roi on the first day, and another took Namur by noon of the second day.

Capturing Kwajalein Island took longer, as the 7th Infantry pounded the Japanese garrison for three days before the island was declared secure on February 4.

Kwajalein Atoll was by no means an easy victory for the Americans, but it was accomplished even more rapidly than Admiral Nimitz had hoped, a fact that prompted him to begin, sixty days ahead of schedule, another Marshall Islands battle, at Eniwetok Atoll, four hundred miles northwest of Kwajalein.

Five marine and army battalions landed in the atoll on February 17. The three major islands of the atoll, Engebi, Parry, and Eniwetok, were held by about thirty-five hundred Japanese troops. The American forces attacked each island in succession while U.S. aircraft carriers and battleships launched a diversionary air attack on Truk Island, mainly to prevent the Japanese from launching air raids against the landings.

As with Kwajalein Atoll, Eniwetok fell quickly, giving the U.S. Navy a major anchorage and staging area from which to continue amphibious operations. In the bigger strategic picture, taking Eniwetok intensified the growing isolation of the Japanese island outposts that had been skipped over in the island-hopping campaign. Having deprived the Japanese of their Eniwetok foothold, the Americans prevented the reinforcement or resupply of the islands that had been passed over—among them Wake Island, which had fallen to Japan at the very start of the Pacific war.

REALITY CHECK

Inner Atoll Attack

The choice of landing points was made as a result of intercepted Japanese radio traffic, which indicated that the defense troops had been transferred to the outer atolls because, logically, that is where the invasion was expected. Pursuant to the Allied island-hopping strategy, the army and marines skipped over the outer atolls to attack the inner atolls and the innermost islands of those atolls. The outer atolls were attacked exclusively by air. Indeed, the outer atolls did not surrender until the end of the war—but, cut off, their Japanese garrisons were useless and effectively neutralized.

Taking Truk

In the vast Pacific battlefield, the Caroline Islands were fifteen hundred miles west of Tarawa and eight hundred miles north of Rabaul. Among these islands was Truk, a major Japanese naval and air base. While the Kwajalein Atoll was being taken, Admiral Raymond Spruance led his Fifth Fleet into the Carolines during February 17–18, 1944. The battleships *New Jersey* and *Iowa* and the cruisers *Minneapolis* and *New Orleans*, along with four destroyers, fell upon Japanese ships outside the Truk lagoon, while Rear Admiral Marc Mitscher launched from Task Force 58 seventy-two Hellcat fighter-bombers in a raid on the inner protected anchorage of the Truk lagoon. The results of what

NUMBERS

U.S. and Japanese Losses

Japanese casualties on Roi and Namur were 3,500 killed and only 264 captured. The marines lost 190 killed and 547 wounded. On Kwajalein Island, 3,800 Japanese were killed, with only a handful captured. The 7th Infantry lost 177 men and 1,000 wounded.

DETAILS, DETAILS

Hellcats

The Grumman F6F Hellcat began to appear in the Pacific at the start of 1943. It replaced the earlier F4F Wildcat and earned a reputation as a war-winning naval aircraft. The compact, pugnacious planes—sturdy, well armed, and able to outmaneuver their adversaries—were produced in a quantity of 12,272, enabling their deployment from aircraft carriers in swarms. By late 1944, the Hellcats had mastered the Pacific skies.

was mainly intended as a diversionary attack, to keep the Japanese from launching aircraft against the Kwajalein landings, were in themselves devastating. Two Japanese light cruisers, four destroyers, nine smaller naval vessels, and twenty-four merchant ships were sent to the lagoon bottom. Even worse, virtually all of the 365 Japanese planes on the fields of Truk were destroyed or severely damaged. Mitscher's task force suffered the loss of twenty-five aircraft and serious damage to the aircraft carrier *Intrepid.*

With a smile radiating confidence and proudly sporting his aviator's wings, Vice Admiral Marc A. Mitscher, skilled exponent of naval air power, is pictured aboard his flagship, the carrier Lexington, *during the Marianas campaign, June 1944.*

Truk was battered but not beaten, and on April 28–29, Mitscher returned with Task Force 58 to finish off what Allied planners sometimes called the Japanese "Gibraltar of the Pacific." Mitscher sent a massive air attack against Truk, sinking several ships and destroying ninety-three aircraft—although at the heavy cost of forty-six U.S. aircraft downed (though most of the pilots were rescued). With the February battle, the April assault finally knocked Truk out of the war and cleared the way for an advance beyond the Carolines and into the Marianas. The cordon the Japanese had thrown around their home islands was inexorably contracting into a noose.

The Marianas Campaign

With the successful completion of actions in the Marshalls and the Carolines, Japan's outermost defensive ring in the central Pacific had

The Grumman F6F-3 Hellcat was the greatest naval fighter plane of World War II, a war-winning aircraft that proved more than a match for the best the Japanese threw at it, the infamous Zero. These planes are landing on the deck of the USS Enterprise *after strikes against the major Japanese base on Truk Island during February 17–18, 1944. It is the job of the deck crews to get the planes landed as quickly as possible. No sooner does an aircraft pause in its post-touchdown taxi than deck crews fold its wings to make room for more planes.*

been shattered. The next objective was the Mariana group, fifteen islands that extended in a five-hundred-mile arc halfway between Japan and New Guinea. Some of the major islands of the group were U.S. possessions held by the Japanese. These included Saipan, Tinian, Rota, and Guam. The rest of the Marianas had belonged to Germany until they were captured by Japan during World War I, then mandated to that country by the League of Nations after the war. Not only did American military planners want to reclaim the U.S. possessions, but they also were well aware that, from the Marianas, the new U.S. B-29 bombers—the biggest bombers in World War II, with the longest range and greatest bomb capacity—could reach the Japanese homeland as well as well as the Philippines. Finally, the Marianas were headquarters of the Japanese Central Pacific Fleet, under the command of Admiral Chuichi Nagumo, the very man who had led the striking force that raided Pearl Harbor. Admiral Nimitz was convinced that victory in a contest for the Marianas would be decisive in the Pacific war. The Japanese probably felt the same way for they garrisoned the islands with the entire Thirty-first Army, under General Hideyoshi Obata.

The island of Saipan served as an important Japanese military and administrative base in the Marianas. It was formidably defended, the Japanese taking full advantage of the topography, which offered high ground that overlooked the western landing beaches. From these

DETAILS, DETAILS

Task Forces

U.S. warships in the Pacific typically operated in combat groups called task forces. At the time of the battle of Truk, Task Force 58 was the navy's principal striking force in the Pacific. Under the command of Rear Admiral Marc Mitscher, it consisted of a dozen aircraft carriers (with 650 aircraft), eight battleships, and an escort of cruisers and destroyers. Operationally, the task force was divided into four task groups.

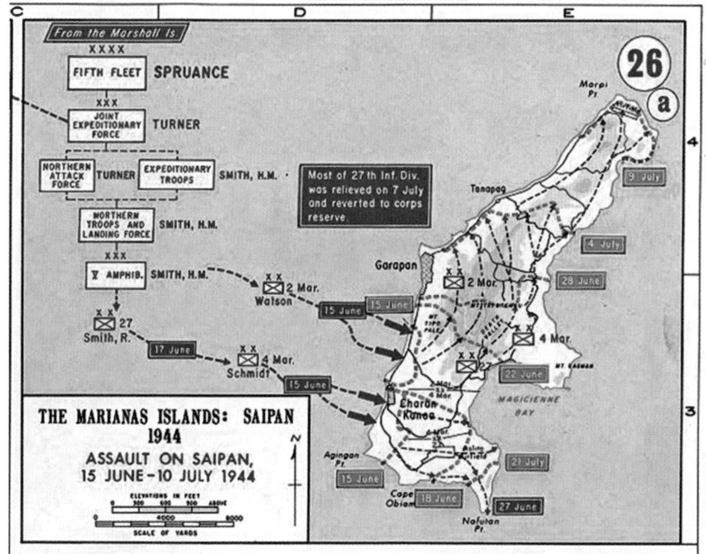

This map indicates the complexity of the assault on heavily defended Saipan, the culmination of the Marianas campaign.

Irascible and unbeatable, Lieutenant General Holland M. "Howlin' Mad" Smith (seated in the rear of the jeep, pointing) is an icon of the World War II U.S. Marine Corps field commander. Here he tours a captured Japanese airfield on Saipan, July 1944.

lofty, well-protected positions, defenders could readily transform those beaches into killing fields. Offshore, the island was surrounded by coral reefs through which U.S. Navy demolition divers had to blast passages for the landing craft that brought seventy-seven thousand men of the 2nd and 4th U.S. Marine divisions under Lieutenant General "Howlin' Mad" Smith. Together, these forces were designated the V Amphibious Corps.

The landing, on June 15, 1944, did not go well. Although the customary "preparation" by naval and aerial bombardment had been made, it proved neither sufficient nor sufficiently effective. The marines were pounded by the island's defenders, thirty-two thousand men under Lieutenant General Yoshitsugu Saito, who killed or wounded four thousand marines in the first forty-eight hours of battle.

Saito's objective was not merely to stage a defense-to-the-death, but to keep the marines pinned down on the beaches until the arrival of the Japanese Mobile Fleet, which would shell them there, killing them and destroying their landing craft. For the marines, that eventuality would have been a disaster of tragic proportions—and it would have happened, had it not been for Marc Mitscher and his Task Force 58.

What Saito saw as an opportunity for the Imperial Japanese Navy to destroy the U.S. Marine landing force, Raymond Spruance, commander of the U.S. Fifth Fleet, saw as a chance to bait the Japanese fleet into a full-out fight for the first time since the naval battles of the Guadalcanal campaign during the fall of 1942. When Admiral Soemu Toyoda dispatched nine aircraft carriers and eighteen battleships and cruisers to confront the American ships covering the Saipan landings, Spruance sent Mitscher to intercept the Japanese attack fleet about ninety miles from Saipan. What resulted was the Battle of the Philippine Sea, fought in the waters separating the Marianas from the Philippines.

The contest began on June 19, 1944, as Japanese land-based planes from Guam and Truk attacked Mitscher's task force. In response, U.S. Navy Hellcats rapidly downed thirty-five Japanese fighters and bombers. Then the air battle over the central Pacific intensified, ultimately pitting about 430 Japanese carrier-based planes against 450 U.S. aircraft in eight grueling hours of combat. When it was over, only one hundred Japanese aircraft survived. The

Wild contrails—condensation trails created by the hot exhaust of high-performance aircraft engines—mark the virtuoso maneuvers of the American pilots of Task Force 58 during the "Great Marianas Turkey Shoot" over the Philippine Sea, June 19, 1944.

Japanese ranks of experienced combat pilots had been depleted, and American fliers found the sky so rich in targets that they dubbed the aerial battle the "Great Marianas Turkey Shoot."

While the Battle of the Philippine Sea raged in the air, two U.S. submarines made their way stealthily through the destroyer escort screen protecting the Japanese carriers. Firing just one torpedo, USS *Albacore* sank the thirty-three thousand-ton *Taiho*, Japan's largest aircraft carrier, killing 1,650 Japanese sailors and airmen. The other submarine, USS *Cavalla*, hit the twenty-two thousand-ton carrier *Shokaku* with three torpedoes, sending it to the bottom as well.

When night fell on June 19, the surviving Japanese ships attempted withdrawal to the northwest. Mitscher's carriers pursued, and on the night of June 20, the Americans sent 209 aircraft against the ships, which were about three hundred miles ahead. This sortie sank the aircraft carrier *Hiyo*, also shooting down forty of the seventy-five Japanese planes launched to defend against the attack. It was an important victory, but, this time, it came at a heavier price. Twenty U.S. planes were shot down—and *eighty* more were lost when they were unable to make successful carrier landings at night. Fifty-one pilots were rescued.

For the Japanese, the consequences of the Battle of the Philippine Sea were devastating. Six of their aircraft carriers had escaped destruction, but most of their remaining veteran aviators had been killed and their aircraft lost. As for the U.S. Marines on Saipan, they were able to fight through to victory over Saito, who, in the absence of the Mobile Fleet, was now forced to pull his garrison back to the center of fourteen-mile-long Saipan.

REALITY CHECK

The Japanese Military

The American press and public often referred to the Japanese soldiers and their commanders as fanatics who fought in the war mainly for the privilege of "dying for their emperor." Yet U.S. military commanders and their men understood that the Japanese were no mere fanatics. The best of them were skilled soldiers led by dedicated officers, as proved by the effectiveness of the Japanese defense against the landings at Saipan. Saito had expected the landings to come elsewhere, yet nevertheless managed to transfer his men to the actual points of the landing swiftly and efficiently. He was, in fact, supremely confident that he could pin the marines to their beachhead—fully exposing them to fire from the Japanese Mobile Fleet. What prevented this from happening was U.S. victory in the Battle of the Philippine Sea (June 19–20, 1944), which checkmated the Mobile Fleet.

DETAILS, DETAILS

Battle Supreme

Military historians consider the air portion of the Battle of the Philippine Sea the most decisive aerial combat of World War II. Some believe it was the single most important battle in the entire history of air combat. The United States lost just thirty aircraft, and the ships of Mitscher's task force suffered little damage.

Saito now had no real hope of saving the island, but he was determined to make its conquest as costly as possible. Marine commanders had promised to take the island in three days. In the face of Saito's resistance, it took three weeks.

On June 18, the marines managed to capture Aslito airfield on the south end of Saipan—the first major inland objective to be obtained. From here, they tried to advance north, only to encounter deadly fire in the rugged terrain near Mount Tapochau. By this time, the army's 27th Infantry Division had been landed to reinforce the marines. Sent to this sector, the 27th suffered such heavy casualties that a wooded rise it struggled to take was dubbed Purple Heart Ridge. Here the soldiers were pinned down until naval support fire finally suppressed the Japanese defenders.

> "Whether we attack or whether we stay where we are is only death. But realizing that in death there is life, let us take this opportunity to exalt Japanese manhood. I shall advance upon the American to deliver still another blow and leave my bones upon Saipan as a bulwark of the Pacific."
>
> *Vice Admiral Chuichi Nagumo, regarding strategy for defending Saipan*

In their last extremity, the Japanese mounted a spectacular banzai charge during the night of July 6/7. An all-out suicidal attack screaming out of the night was calculated to terrorize and to kill. The Americans, however, held fast, and this charge, at the cost of forty-three hundred Japanese soldiers, was the defenders' last major action. Nevertheless, in small groups, Japanese diehards continued to fight for months after the island was declared secure on July 9. Most of those who did not fight on committed mass suicide on the ninth.

> "I advance to seek out the enemy. Follow me."
>
> *The supposed last words of Yoshitsugu Saito, before committing hara-kiri*

Retaking Guam

After Saipan had been declared secure, Roy Geiger, the marine general commanding the newly created III Amphibious Corps, landed his 3rd Marine Division (under Allen Turnage) north of Apra Harbor on Guam and the 1st Brigade (commanded by Lemuel Shepherd) along with the army's 77th Infantry Division (Andrew Bruce) south of the harbor on July 21. The island was defended by a Japanese garrison of nineteen thousand men led by General Takeshi Takashima.

The marines on the southern beachhead advanced swiftly inland, but the 3rd Marine Division, to the north, encountered much stiffer resistance. The southern landing force advanced inland a full mile by the first night. The 3rd Marine Division took four days to make a mile and link up with the southern force. But no sooner was the link-up completed than, on the night of July 25/26, the Japanese garrison counterattacked. Surprise was total, and the marine positions were nearly overrun before the Japanese were finally forced to fall back. With the defeat of this counterattack, all that was left in the south was for the 1st Marine Brigade to mop up the remnants of resistance between the two landing beaches.

On July 21, 1944, a scant eight minutes after hitting the beach in the reconquest of Guam—the American island held by the Japanese since the start of the war—these marines plant the Stars and Stripes.

REALITY CHECK

Saipan Tragedy

The brutality of the Pacific war was unparalleled. On Saipan, large numbers of civilians, whom the Japanese commanders had persuaded would be raped, tortured, and even cannibalized by the Americans, chose to emulate the Japanese soldiers by committing suicide rather than submitting to the American invaders. U.S. soldiers and marines, who had just come through the worst of battle, were horrified by the sight of men and women—many clasping children—leaping to their deaths from rocky Marpi Point.

NUMBERS

U.S. Captures, Losses

American soldiers and marines took just 1,000 prisoners. U.S. casualties on Saipan totaled 10,347 marines and 3,674 soldiers, including 3,426 marines and soldiers killed.

NUMBERS

U.S. and Japanese Losses

Recovering Guam cost 6,716 marine, 839 army, and 245 navy casualties. Of the total, 1,023 men were killed in action. Few of the 19,000 Japanese defending Guam survived to be taken prisoner.

The northern portion of Guam was still held by the Japanese, and, as the 1st Brigade mopped up, the 3rd Marine and the 77th Infantry divisions began to attack in a northeasterly direction on July 31. After a week of conducting a fighting advance, these two units were joined by the 1st Brigade. By August 10, the offensive had pushed through to the northern tip of the island, and all of Guam was declared secure.

Fateful Tinian

Three days after the marines and army invaded Guam, V Amphibious Corps—U.S. Marines under the command of Harry Schmidt (replacing Howlin' Mad Smith, who had been promoted to command of the General Fleet Marine Force, Pacific)—landed on Tinian. As obscure as any other piece of Pacific real estate, the island was defended by nine thousand Japanese soldiers and sailors. It had been identified as a high-priority objective, not so much because of the Japanese presence there, but because military engineers had judged it ideal for the building of the long runways required by B-29s.

The LVT2—Landing Vehicle, Tracked—was christened the "Water Buffalo" and served the U.S. Marine Corps as its standard amphibious assault craft. Eleven thousand of these remarkable vehicles were manufactured by FMC—the Food Machinery Company—which had retooled them for war production. This Water Buffalo approaches the beach at Tinian Island in July 1944. Loaded with marines, the landing craft was operated by a U.S. Coast Guard coxswain. Coast Guard personnel were often assigned the hazardous task of piloting landing craft.

The 2nd Marine Division made a diversionary landing near Tinian Town on the southwest coast of the island on July 24, just as the 4th Marine Division, commanded by Clifton Cates, assaulted the beach in the northwest. This was the principal landing. Despite resistance from the Japanese garrison, the 4th Marines had advanced inland about a mile by nightfall. On the next day, 2nd Marine Division landed, sweeping rapidly through the northern end of the island before turning sharply right to attack southward, down the east coast, in close coordination with the 4th Marines. By July 31, the island belonged to the Americans. Tinian would become the base from which the B-29s carrying the world's first two operational atomic bombs would embark for Hiroshima and Nagasaki (see Chapter 22, "Little Boy").

40 PERCENT

THERE WERE TWO WAYS TO VIEW THE AMERICAN OFFENSIVE IN THE PACIFIC. Through the eyes of the marines and the soldiers who clawed their way across the coral or hugged the sand under heavy fire, it was an agonizingly slow business of bloody murder. As the top commanders saw it, however, the islands were so many stepping-stones leading to two destinations: the Philippines and Japan. The sooner each of these stepping-stones was traversed, the sooner the war would be over and won.

To Admiral Chester Nimitz, the next stepping-stone after the end of the Mariana Islands campaign was the Palau Islands in the western Carolines. Once these were held, the United States would possess the stage from which to launch a campaign to retake the Philippines.

By September 1944, the III Amphibious Corps, marines under the temporary command of Julian Smith, was in position to launch against two of the Palau group, Peleliu and the smaller Angaur, just south of Peleliu. Although it was a mere six miles long and two miles wide, Peleliu was held by a garrison of more than ten thousand Japanese troops under General Sadae Inoue. The volcanic island was riddled with caves, and Inoue had deployed his men in some eight hundred of them, which had been interconnected to a great degree by tunnels. Assaulting Peleliu was the equivalent of attacking a fortress.

William Rupertus led the 1st Marine Division in a landing on the southwest corner of the island on the morning of September 15 after an intensive air and naval bombardment—which did very little to dislodge the defenders from their caves. Indeed, dug in, the Japanese in the southwest held out against the marines for four days.

After securing the southwest, including an important airstrip, the marines turned north and started an advance up the island. They were targeted all the way from positions dug into Umurbrogol Mountain, which the marines christened Bloody Nose Ridge. As a nickname, it was a profound understatement. From the mountain came a shower of heavy artillery fire as well as an endless fusillade of small arms, which, for a time, stopped the marines' advance.

NUMBERS

U.S. and Japanese Losses

American casualties in the battle for Tinian were relatively light at 327 marines killed and 1,771 wounded. Except for a handful of prisoners, the 9,000-man Japanese garrison either died in battle or committed suicide when it was over.

TAKEAWAY
Stepping-Stones
U.S. military planners in the Pacific saw the Japanese-held islands that formed the perimeter of the Japanese Empire as so many stepping-stones leading to the enemy's home islands; however, U.S. admiral Chester Nimitz determined that it was unnecessary to capture each of these stepping-stones. Capture certain key islands, and the others, cut off and isolated, would become useless to the Japanese. This was the island-hopping strategy, which proved decisive for victory in the Pacific.

While the marines writhed under Bloody Nose Ridge, the army's 81st Infantry Division, commanded by Paul Mueller, landed at Angaur Island on September 17. Here fourteen hundred Japanese resisted fiercely for three days before most of the tiny island was taken—though even after it was declared secure, sporadic fighting continued until October 13.

Having resumed permanent command of III Corps, Roy Geiger sent 321st Regiment to help the marines at Peleliu while the 323rd Regiment took the island of Ulithi without opposition. On September 24, the 321st reinforced a fresh marine attack against Bloody Nose Ridge, hitting it from the west, so that, within three days, the combined army and marine forces had enveloped the Japanese positions on the mountain. Despite this, they held out and had to be dislodged inch by bloody inch. October came and went, and, even after the 321st and the marines had been reinforced by the 323rd Regiment, Bloody Nose Ridge was not neutralized until November 25. As usual, it was not a case of the defenders surrendering. The objective was attained only after virtually all of the enemy had been killed.

The stepping-stone known as Peleliu exacted the highest casualty rate of any amphibious assault in American military history. Forty percent of the marines and soldiers who fought for this island either died or was wounded. And it was all a prelude to a much bigger, much costlier campaign: the struggle to redeem the pledge Douglas MacArthur had made when he left the Philippines in 1942: *I shall return.*

In a typical Pacific island assault, marines hit the beach at Palau on Peleliu Island during September 1944. They hug a narrow margin of sand separating them from the enemy-held high ground and the ocean. Their next task: fight their way up.

CHAPTER 16

C-B-I

War on a Shoestring

WITH JUST THREE LETTERS, *C-B-I*, the Allies identified a vast theater of the war encompassing China, Burma, and India. The nondescript brevity of the label betrayed the Allies' attitude toward the theater. Critically important as this intersection of East Asia, Southeast Asia, and South Asia was in the war against Japan, the C-B-I languished at the bottom of the Allied priority list for receiving troops, supplies, air cover, and weapons. The commanders and soldiers who labored here fought their war on the thinnest of shoestrings.

THE ABDA EXPERIMENT

IN DECEMBER 1941, days after the United States entered World War II, British prime minister Winston Churchill met with President Franklin D. Roosevelt in Washington for what was called the Arcadia Conference, the first of the great Allied conferences of World War II. Among other things, the two war leaders decided that the United States, Britain, the Netherlands, and the British Commonwealth nations would create a joint command for the China-Burma-India theater, which was dubbed the ABDA (American-British-Dutch-Australian) Command, under British general Archibald Wavell.

The United States installed Lieutenant General Joseph Stilwell as its senior ABDA commander. A remarkable officer, Stilwell was what was known during the era leading up to World War II as a "China hand." He had served in China between the world wars, including as

REALITY CHECK

ABDA, no C

Conspicuously missing from the ABDA Command was China, whose war leader was the Nationalist Party "Generalissimo" Chiang Kai-shek. The Allies named him separately as the supreme commander of the China theater, intending for this recognition to bolster Chiang and China with moral support. After all, by December 1941, China had already been fighting Japan for some four years in the Sino-Japanese War. The fact was that Chiang Kai-shek would never have agreed to incorporation into ABDA because he was adamant that no foreign entity ever be given authority over any region of China. Like the Free French leader in Europe, Charles de Gaulle, Chiang Kai-shek held so fiercely to his nationalism that he often proved a thorn in the side of his allies.

DETAILS, DETAILS

Vinegar Joe

Stilwell became famous for his blunt, shoot-from-the-hip comments to the press, which relished his acidic temperament and affectionately dubbed him "Vinegar Joe" Stilwell.

America's "China hand," Lieutenant General Joseph W. Stilwell, was assigned to command the chronically undermanned and underequipped China Expeditionary Forces. A tactical genius, his acidic, blunt-spoken, shoot-from-the-hip style earned him the sobriquet "Vinegar Joe" from the American press. He is shown here in April 1942 with Generalissimo Chiang Kai-shek—with whom he often came into conflict—and the politically savvy Madame Chiang Kai-shek.

U.S. military attaché, spoke the language fluently, and was very much up to speed on the ongoing struggle between China and Japan. Nevertheless, the scope of his authority was ambiguous from the very beginning. He was both "Commanding General of the United States Army Forces in the Chinese Theatre of Operations, Burma, and India" and chief of staff to Chiang Kai-shek, the supreme commander of the Chinese theater. As senior commander of the U.S. forces in ABDA, Stilwell was subordinate to Wavell—yet he was chief of staff to Chiang Kai-shek, who was not a part of ABDA and who was subordinate to no one. This command structure became especially confusing in the region of Burma—through which the critical supply route to China lay—where Wavell had *supreme* command, but where Stilwell had *direct* command over Chinese forces assigned to Burma—a total of some eighty thousand to one hundred thousand men. Adding to the difficulty of Stilwell's position was his relationship with Chiang Kai-shek, who frequently interfered with the exercise of his authority in Burma and elsewhere.

FLYING TIGERS

ADMINISTRATIVELY, TACTICALLY, AND STRATEGICALLY UNWIELDY, ABDA proved short lived. It was disbanded in February 1942, after the Japanese captured Singapore and invaded Java. From this point on, the Pacific theater was put in charge of the Americans. Britain was responsible for everything from Singapore to Suez. Chiang Kai-shek still held on to the title of supreme commander of the China theater, and General Wavell remained overall commander in India and

Burma. Stilwell was instructed to create "Headquarters, American Armed Forces: China, Burma, and India," a command that took in the tiny American Military Mission to China (AMMISCA)—which had existed even before the war—as well as the new American Volunteer Group (AVG), which was much better known to the world as the Flying Tigers.

> "If a man has enough character to be a good commander, does he ever doubt himself? He should not. In any case, I doubt myself. Therefore, I am probably not a good commander."
>
> *Joseph "Vinegar Joe" Stilwell, quoted by Anton Myrer in* Once an Eagle, *1968*

DETAILS, DETAILS

Up in the Air

Until June 1941, the air arm of the U.S. Army was called the U.S. Army Air Corps. It then officially became the U.S. Army Air Forces—but the public and USAAF personnel generally continued to refer to it as the "Air Corps" throughout the war.

During 1940, President Franklin D. Roosevelt authorized a covert—and quite unofficial—United States air force to fight on behalf of China in its struggle against Japanese invasion. As created, the AVG was to consist of two fighter groups and one medium bomber group. FDR diverted one hundred Tomahawk IIB fighters (equivalent to Curtiss P-40C pursuit craft) from a British order and turned them over to the AVG to equip the two fighter groups. At the same time, one hundred U.S. military pilots and two hundred enlisted military aircraft technicians—all men who burned to see combat—officially resigned from the military to accept employment in the AVG as civilian mercenaries. Because of U.S. neutrality laws, FDR could not legally commit American military personnel to serve against Japan.

The first group, designated the First American Volunteer Group (1st AVG), was organized and commanded by Claire Chennault. Texas-born Chennault was commissioned in the infantry as a first lieutenant in 1917 and transferred to the Signal Corps for flight training in 1919. A pioneer in fighter strategy and tactics, Chennault was a passionate advocate of the strategic importance of fighters at a time when the Army Air Corps was controlled by a "bomber mafia"—senior officers who believed in developing the bomber as the only air weapon of strategic importance. Discouraged by the Air Corps attitude toward fighters, Chennault retired from the army in

DETAILS, DETAILS

Tiger Sharks

The "Flying Tigers" name was coined by journalists who, seeing the fierce rows of shark teeth AVG crews had painted on either side of the gaping air scoop under the fuselage of the supercharged P-40, interpreted the visual effect as a tiger's mouth, rather than a shark's. The name became a great Allied morale booster.

Major General Claire Chennault was the charismatic creator and leader of the American Volunteer Group (AVG), better known as the Flying Tigers, a tiny fighter group flying obsolescent Curtiss P-40 Warhawk pursuit craft but wreaking havoc on Japanese pilots flying far more numerous and far more advanced aircraft over China. Chennault poses in front of the supercharger scoop of a Warhawk, painted with the group's trademark row of shark's teeth—which apparently looked to the world more like the jaws of a tiger.

1937 with the junior rank of captain. That very year, Madame Chiang Kai-shek, the beautiful, charismatic, and politically skilled wife of Chiang Kai-shek, recruited Chennault to organize and train what became the AVG.

Chennault's genius lay in his electrifying leadership presence as well as his skill in developing tactics. His P-40s were already obsolescent by 1940–41 and were outclassed by most Japanese fighter aircraft. Chennault did not try to deny or discount this, but he developed tactics that exploited the shortcomings of the P-40 to his advantage. He also handpicked his pilots and trained them—in what was at the time neutral Burma—to master superior tactics that more than compensated for the limitations of their aircraft.

> "1. Japan can be defeated in China.
> 2. It can be defeated by an air force so small that in other theaters it would be called ridiculous.
> 3. I am confident that, given real authority in command of such an air force, I can cause the collapse of Japan."
>
> *Claire Chennault to U.S. politician Wendell Wilkie, October 8, 1942*

As it turned out, events overtook the 1st AVG. Although trained before the entry of the United States into World War II, it did not engage in actual combat until after Pearl Harbor. U.S. entry into the war meant that plans for creating a 2nd AVG were cancelled, as was the creation of the bomber group. Since the 1st AVG was already in place, however, it continued to operate under Chennault, and during the bleak early days of the Pacific and Asian war, the unit came to be known as the "Flying Tigers" and provided the Allies—especially the American public—with some of their few precious nuggets of good news early in the war.

Chennault's Flying Tigers valiantly defended Burma until the Japanese routed the Allies there in May 1942. Transferred to China after the fall of Burma, the 1st AVG—small and outnumbered though it was—played a key role in holding western China until reinforcements reached Chiang Kai-shek's Nationalist army.

The Flying Tigers were disbanded on July 4, 1942, when the AVG was merged into the 23rd Pursuit Group of the U.S. Army Air Forces.

Initially, just five AVG pilots accepted induction into the new army air forces unit while they were in China; later, however, others rejoined the U.S. military. As for Chennault, he was welcomed back into the U.S. Army Air Forces in April 1942 with the rank of colonel, then was promoted to brigadier general and, later, major general. After the Flying Tigers were absorbed into the USAAF, he was assigned as commanding general of all army air forces in China, then, in March 1943, was named to command of the Fourteenth Air Force, a unit that specialized in close air support, providing air cover for Stilwell's C-B-I operations.

NUMBERS

On a Low Budget

Like everything else in the C-B-I, the Flying Tigers operated in isolation and on a bare-bones budget. Despite the hardships, the unit was credited with having shot down nearly three hundred Japanese aircraft for a loss of thirty-two planes and twenty-three pilots killed or captured. Some recent military historians have disputed the number of AVG victories, claiming that the figures were inflated.

Burma's Burdens

The now independent nation known since 1989 as Myanmar was, at the time of World War II, a British colony. Located on the Andaman Sea and Bay of Bengal, it is bordered by China on the north and northeast and by India to the west and northwest. It provided China with an outlet to the Indian Ocean and also a supply and communications route to India. The Japanese were anxious to capture and occupy Burma to serve as guard for the flank of its forces in Malaya as well as those, early in the war, that were advancing to the capture of Singapore. After Singapore fell,

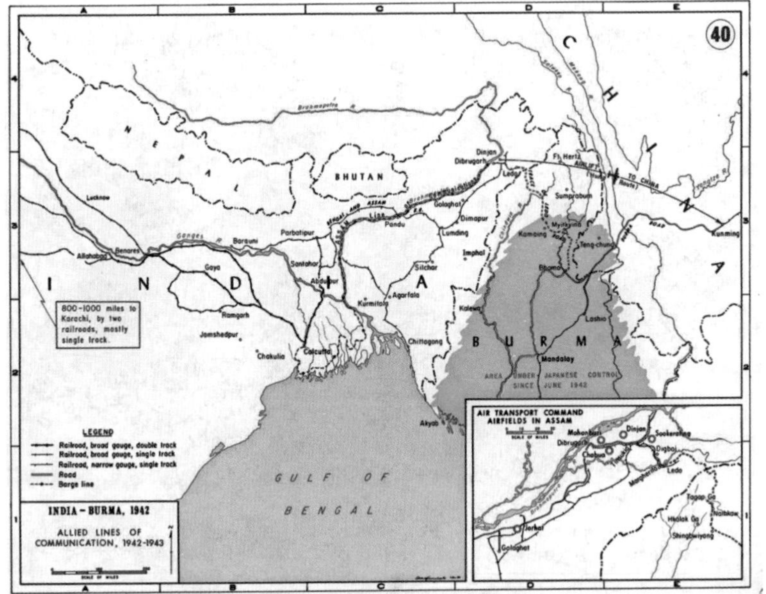

This map of the critical junction of India, Burma, and China—heart of the China-Burma-India (C-B-I) theater—shows how Burma figured as the passage between British-held India and China, struggling under Japanese occupation.

REALITY CHECK

Solo Flier

Even as a high-ranking USAAF officer, Chennault remained a military maverick. He continually frustrated his superiors by running around them to work directly with Chiang Kai-shek. His behavior was tolerated because, in this most undermanned and undersupplied of Allied theaters, Chennault consistently produced victory. His colorful personality was the perfect compliment to the romantic mercenary force he commanded, and while some recent historians have claimed that the achievements of the Flying Tigers were inflated, no one denies that the AVG was highly effective against Japanese air and ground forces during the winter of 1941–42, when the Japanese seemed unstoppable.

"I claim we got a hell of a beating. We got run out of Burma and it is humiliating as hell. I think we ought to find out what caused it, and go back and retake it."

Joseph Stilwell, New York Times, *May 26, 1942*

the Japanese continued to see Burma as strategically important because the "Burma Road" was the major supply route into China and because Burma would serve nicely as the westernmost anchor of the greatly expanded Japanese Empire. Finally, Burma was an ideal staging area for a planned massive invasion of British-held India.

In addition to its geographically based strategic importance, Burma was a political prize of great value. Since the late 1930s, a Burmese nationalist named Aung San had been leading the Dobama Asiayone ("We Burmans") Society—popularly known as the Thakin ("Master") Society—in a drive to achieve independence from the British Empire. In 1940, Aung San temporarily fled Burma for China, where he campaigned for international support for the independence movement. He was approached by Japanese agents, who helped him to create the Burma Independence Army (BIA). Promised by the Japanese that Burma would be granted independence, Aung San led the BIA in aiding Japanese invasion forces. The Burmese independence movement was important to the Japanese war effort not only as a way of undermining the British hold on the country, but as a demonstration to a properly skeptical Southeast Asia that Japan intended not to conquer the nations of the region, but to liberate them from European colonial domination and create the "Greater East Asian Co-Prosperity Sphere."

The struggle for Burma spanned the entire Pacific war, beginning in December 1941 and lasting until August 1945. U.S., British, and Commonwealth forces fought in the long campaign, but most of the fighting for the Allies was the work of Indians, Burmese, Chinese, members of Burmese ethnic groups—Chins, Gurkhas, Kachins, Karens, and Nagas—as well as native soldiers from British East Africa and British West Africa. Although the British hoped to avoid the costliest aspects of a land battle by employing naval action and an amphibious campaign aimed at capturing Rangoon, the Burmese capital, these plans came to nothing because the C-B-I was always at the bottom of the list for the distribution of resources, including ships and landing craft. Without these, British general William Slim, the principal commander in the theater, had no choice but to fight a long and debilitating overland campaign with the inadequate forces he had.

The Japanese occupied Victoria Point and its airfield at the southern tip of Burma on December 14, 1941, making it impossible for the British to fly reinforcements from India to Malaya. During January 1942, Tavoy, Kawkareik, and Moulmein—settlements north of Victoria Point—fell to the Japanese. Major General John Smyth, commanding the 17th Indian Division, mounted a campaign to retake these places by attacking from behind the Salween, Bilin, and Sittang rivers. On February 23, however, Smyth was outflanked by the 33rd Division under Lieutenant General Sakurai Shozo. With Smyth pinned down, Shozo pressed quickly toward Rangoon. Desperate to stop the Japanese, Smyth ordered the Sittang Bridge detonated. Although this did slow Shozo, it also cut off five thousand Indian soldiers, who, along with their artillery, were captured by the Japanese. Shozo went on to take Rangoon on March 8. Smyth was relieved of command and replaced by Lieutenant General Harold Alexander.

ALTERNATE TAKE

Following Orders

Shozo fought brilliantly against Smyth and Alexander. Not only did he succeed in capturing Rangoon, he very nearly captured Alexander and the entire Burma Army. This would have magnified the Burmese disaster manyfold. Fortunately for the Allies, Shozo's subordinates were not as flexible as their commander. One of Shozo's key officers insisted on adhering absolutely to Shozo's earlier orders to enter Rangoon, even though doing so made it necessary for him to withdraw from a position blocking Alexander. This withdrawal allowed Alexander and his army to escape intact.

The Long Retreat

The Chinese sent reinforcements into Burma, which advanced as far south as Toungoo before the Japanese 56th Division pushed them back. Nevertheless, the Chinese troops did rescue the 1st Burma Division, which had been cut off at Yenangyaung, and, along with this force, continued to retreat through Imphal and into India. At the same time, William Slim led all that remained of the British forces in Burma—called the Burcorps—in a retreat that spanned March to May 1942, and, as with the Chinese withdrawal, ended in India.

As the Allies withdrew, the Japanese rushed to fill the vacuum. By the end of April 1942, the Japanese 18th and 56th Divisions had reached the Chinese frontier. They took Akyab and its airfields on the Bay of Bengal on May 4 and the important Burmese town of Sumprabum on June 17. Seeking to arrest this train of disaster, Archibald Wavell, as commander in chief of India, sent the 14th Indian Division on a mission to begin retaking Burma. The 14th was defeated in December 1942, as it fought to recapture Akyab. The Indian troops made a second assault on Akyab and again failed. Turning next to the village of Donbaik, they were defeated March 1943. Wavell's campaign to retake Burma had gained nothing at all.

British general Sir William Slim was one of the unsung heroes of World War II. He fought a brilliant campaign in Burma—always on the thinnest of shoestrings and with the greatest of tactical brilliance.

DETAILS, DETAILS
Milestone

Slim's remarkable retreat from Burma—which saved Burcorps—was the longest fighting retreat in British military history.

The Hump

With the fall of Burma, there was no possibility of overland supply from India to China. In this crisis the U.S. Air Transport Command began, in July 1942, to fly the "Hump," making regular airlifts from Dinjan, India, to Kunming, China, five hundred miles over extremely treacherous mountain ridges as high as fifteen thousand feet. For most of the war, the Hump would be the only military means of keeping China supplied—and in the war.

American transports flew over the Patkai, Kumon, and Santsung mountains, operating very near the absolute maximum ceiling of fully loaded aircraft. Typically, flights were made in bad weather with much turbulence and heavy icing. For part of the year, monsoon rains were an extreme hazard.

New Starts

In August 1943, under rigid Japanese control, Burma declared its independence from Britain. Recognizing that the situation in the C-B-I was deteriorating, the Allies once again reorganized the theater in October 1943 by forming the South East Asia Command (SEAC) under General Slim, who had proven himself an extraordinary commander. He immediately planned a comprehensive counteroffensive in the Arakan region, beginning with a campaign to retake Akyab on the Bay of Bengal in southern Burma. While British XV Corps under Lieutenant General Sir (Alexander Frank) Philip Christison attacked here, American lieutenant general "Vinegar Joe" Stilwell would lead U.S. and U.S.-trained Chinese forces—collectively called the "Northern Area Combat Command"—in concert with forces under Chiang Kai-shek to capture and occupy Myitkyina, a northern Burmese Japanese stronghold. Stilwell's advance, supported by Wingate's elite Chindits, would also allow the Allies to complete

The C-47 "Gooney Bird"—military version of the civilian DC-3—was the workhorse of Allied airlift in World War II. This C-47 has been customized for cargo transport and, although this one was probably photographed somewhere in South America, it is typical of the aircraft that flew the treacherous "Hump" over the Himalayas in an effort to keep China supplied.

the Ledo Road. A replacement for the Burma Road, which the Japanese now controlled, the Ledo Road would provide a new means of supplying China from India.

A third major operation was to be coordinated with those of Christison and Stilwell, on the Assam Front in central Burma. Here the 17th and 20th Indian Divisions, under Lieutenant General Geoffrey Scoones, would make deep reconnaissance patrols into Japanese-held territory.

As these operations got under way, the Japanese replied by creating a whole new army in Arakan—the Twenty-eighth—and another in northern Burma, the Thirty-third Army. The Japanese had a plan to invade India from Burma, called the Imphal Offensive. As a supplement to the Imphal campaign, the new Japanese armies launched Operation Ha-Go, in Arakan, with the objective of encircling and cutting off the Allied forces there.

NUMBERS

Hump Hazards

Although enemy opposition was negligible, flying the Hump was among the most hazardous air missions of the war. Typical losses were those incurred in just one month, January 1945: 44,000 tons of supplies were airlifted at the cost of 36 lives in 23 major accidents. Hump operations lifted a total of 650,000 tons of supplies into China and required 22,000 military personnel and some 47,000 civilian laborers. About 300 transport aircraft were used.

Victory at Imphal

Lieutenant General Renya Mutaguchi led the Japanese Fifteenth Army in a campaign against the Allied supply bases at Imphal in Manipur, India. This Imphal Offensive would serve two purposes. It would check an offensive by Slim's Fourteenth Army, and would gain a foothold for the Japanese-controlled Indian National Army, which was poised to incite a revolution against the British in India.

The Imphal Offensive was a high-stakes gamble for Mutaguchi, who was well aware that he was outnumbered and lacked air superiority. However, Japanese success elsewhere throughout the C-B-I persuaded him that, if he achieved total tactical surprise and proceeded with great speed, he would prevail. Operation Ha-Go, under Lieutenant General Masakazu Kawabe, was launched in February to draw off and pin down some of Slim's reserves, thereby making them unavailable against Mutaguchi's main force. To deal with the remnant of Slim's army, Mutaguchi planned to attack in ways that divided and diluted the British commander's forces. On March 7, Mutaguchi sent his 33rd Division against Slim from the south. Slim's 17th Division gave way at Tiddim and made a fighting retreat. At the same time, Mutaguchi's "Yamamoto Force" attacked Slim's 20th Division near Tamu, but was checked at a place called Shenam Saddle. A week later, Mutaguchi sent his 15th and 31st

The so-called Ledo Road into Burma was more mud trail than road, but it was a vital link in the fragile supply chain of the C-B-I theater.

Divisions across the Chindwin River, planning to crush Slim's troops in the jaws of a pincers. It was a good, vigorous plan, but it failed because, by this time, Operation Ha-Go had collapsed, freeing up Slim's 5th and 7th Divisions, which he airlifted to Imphal beginning on March 19.

As timely as the arrival of Slim's reinforcements were, the main body of the Japanese advance was just thirty miles away. Slim had little time or space to block the Japanese and prevent an encirclement. He figured that Mutaguchi would attack Kohima, northwest of Imphal, but he believed that the mountainous terrain in the area would greatly impede the attack, so that the Japanese could not deploy more than a single regiment. Slim was shocked when Lieutenant General Kotuku Sato fielded not a single regiment, but the entire 31st Division, which battered the 50th Indian Parachute Brigade at Sangshak and captured Kohima on April 3. On April 12, Mutaguchi's 15th Division took control of the road between Kohima and Imphal and was positioned to strike Slim's IV Corps.

Slim could not help but admire what Sato and Mutaguchi had achieved: extraordinary mobility in hostile terrain. But the journey had cost them. Having arrived to do battle, the Japanese were simply too exhausted to exploit their advantages. Slim was able to mount a counterattack using tanks—which the Japanese largely lacked—and shoved Mutaguchi back. Despite the success of the counterattack, Slim was unable to retake the Kohima-Imphal road and so had to rely

REALITY CHECK

Winged Lions

Against the grim backdrop of one British and British-allied defeat after another, the bold operations of dashing Brigadier General Orde Wingate offered a welcome boost to morale. On February 13, 1943, he launched Operation Longcloth, the first of his celebrated Chindit Raids. The Chindits were elite "Long-Range Penetration" troops, who took their name from a corruption of the Burmese word *chinthe*, describing the winged stone lions that guard Buddhist temples; these lions became the insignia of the unit. Operation Longcloth, intended to destroy railroad lines in northern Burma, succeeded only partially, but was inherently so spectacular—three thousand Chindits (of whom 2,182 survived) traveled one thousand jungle miles on foot—that it was hailed as a triumph. After Wingate's death in a plane crash on March 24, 1944, the Chindits ceased to function as an effective force.

INDIAN NATIONAL ARMY

The Indian National Army (INA) was created in February 1942 out of the Indian Independence League (led by a Bangkok-based Sikh missionary, Giani Pritam Singh) and an Indian independence organization called F. Kikan, which had been founded by Japanese army major Fujiwara Iwaichi. The ranks of the INA were filled by Indian Army POWs captured after the fall of Malaya and Singapore. A women's auxiliary, called the Rani of Jhansi Regiment, was also created.

The field commander of the INA was Mohan Singh, one of the POWs who had formerly served in the army of colonial India. With Major Fujiwara, Singh recruited new members by selling the INA as the fastest possible means of achieving independence for India. Some twenty thousand of sixty thousand POWs from the Singapore catastrophe joined; however, by December 1942, Singh began to realize that the Japanese had little interest in allowing the creation of an independent India. When he voiced his misgivings, he was arrested, and the INA was temporarily disbanded, only to be reconstituted in June 1943 under the nationalist Indian leader Subhas Chandra Bose, who intended to use the INA as the vanguard of a Japanese invasion of India. Such an invasion, he believed, would trigger a popular rebellion against the British. Bose's Japanese handlers were not convinced that such a rebellion would take place. They wanted to use INA troops as mere adjuncts to Japanese units for purposes of sabotage and propaganda. Bose persisted, however, until the Japanese agreed to use about seven thousand INA troops in the Imphal Offensive, the abortive invasion of India.

The Imphal Offensive was a disaster for the Japanese, and the INA performed especially poorly in it, with many INA recruits deserting or surrendering en masse, especially in Burma. The five-thousand-man INA garrison at Rangoon surrendered without even offering resistance when that city was retaken by the British.

Although the INA was a total military failure, the British Indian administration made the mistake of putting many INA members on trial following the war. In the minds of independence-hungry Indians, this made them look like heroes, and thus the INA, a miserably failed military organization, became a rallying point in the postwar independence movement.

exclusively on airlift for supplies. It was a desperate situation, but Slim understood that it was even more desperate for Mutaguchi.

At length, in extreme need of supplies, the Japanese general stretched his forces thin in an attack on Dimapur. Slim easily blocked this attack, then maneuvered Mutaguchi into a battle of attrition. The onset of the monsoon season in May brought the Japanese starvation and disease, ultimately forcing Mutaguchi to withdraw across the Chindwin River on July 18. Slim gave chase, turning Mutaguchi's withdrawal into a rout that was disastrous for Japan's Burmese forces.

NUMBERS

Fatal Imphal

Of 85,000 Japanese troops committed to the Imphal Offensive, 53,000 became casualties. Of this number, 30,000 were killed in combat, while thousands succumbed to disease and privation. Had the Japanese succeeded with their Imphal Offensive, it is likely that Britain would have been defeated in India, and the China-Burma-India theater would have been controlled by the Japanese. At the very least, this would have prolonged the war by years.

The defeat of the Imphal Offensive also permanently ended the Indian National Army as a serious threat. In all, it was the worst Japanese military defeat in that nation's history.

More Japanese Defeats

North of Assam, General Stilwell led two Chinese divisions and a unit of American rangers dubbed "Merrill's Marauders" (after their commanding officer, Frank Merrill) in an attack on the Hukawng Valley during March 1944, just as the Japanese were suffering humiliation at Imphal. Stilwell cajoled Chiang Kai-shek into giving him five more Chinese divisions, and now, with an overwhelming force, he took the precious airfield at Myitkyina on May 17, 1944, depriving the Japanese of air superiority in the area. It was August 3 before Myitkyina itself was liberated.

Stilwell's triumph was followed in January of 1945 by the capture of Buthidaung by a unit of West African colonial troops. These soldiers then overran a major Japanese communications center at Myohaung. By the time the 25th Indian Division landed on the island of Akyab later in January, the Japanese had withdrawn, clearing the way for an Allied advance through Arakan. Once this area was secured early in 1945, the Allies hurriedly built airstrips to support an all-out assault on Rangoon.

A rare photograph of action in the C-B-I: Gurkhas in the British colonial service advance alongside tanks along the Imphal-Kohima road, clearing the country of Japanese.

Retaking Rangoon

William Slim's campaign to retake Rangoon became the crowning achievement of operations in the C-B-I. With consummate skill, Slim deployed his forces so stealthily that the Japanese were utterly bewildered. He sent the 19th Indian Division across the Irrawaddy River toward Mandalay in mid January, so that it approached that objective from the north. He sent the 2nd British and 20th Indian Divisions, as well as the 7th Indian Division, across the river at other points during February.

While the river crossings were in progress, the 20th Division suddenly turned to the south, cutting rail and road routes to Rangoon. Slim simultaneously sent the 2nd Division east to approach

Mandalay from the south, even as the 19th Division attacked that city, taking it from the north on March 20. The effect stunned the Japanese defenders into inaction.

Slim was greatly surprised that the Japanese did not make their customary fight-to-the-death stand to prevent the taking of Mandalay, and he correctly surmised that Lieutenant General Hyotaro Kimura had withdrawn in order to regroup for a counterattack. Slim understood that taking a city, even a key city such as Mandalay, meant nothing if the enemy army was not destroyed in the process. He therefore deployed his men south of Mandalay, fighting Kimura at Meiktila in central Burma. It was an epic four-week battle that lasted through February and March until, on March 28, Kimura withdrew, thereby opening the way to Rangoon.

After a brief but sharp battle at Pyawbwe, Slim's 17th Division reached the edge of Pegu, just fifty miles from Rangoon, on April 29. Nature intervened, in the form of heavy rains, to delay Slim's final push. When that came, the Allies entered Rangoon unopposed, the Japanese having pulled out.

DETAILS, DETAILS

Crossing the Irrawaddy

Slim's Irrawaddy crossings constituted the longest opposed river crossing of World War II. Entire divisions crossed the river at places where the width varied from 1,000 to 4,500 yards.

THE LONG RETREAT—FOR JAPAN

Through the summer of 1945, the Japanese made a long fighting retreat, which would have taken a heavy toll on Slim's pursuing forces had the British not intercepted the Japanese battle plans. Slim made good use of the captured intelligence, putting his men wherever he knew the Japanese wanted to be. In the space of ten days in July, Slim exacted some seventeen thousand casualties against the Japanese Twenty-eighth Army while losing just ninety-five of his own men.

A column of the Royal Indian Army crosses the breadth of the shallow Irrawaddy River in its advance on Japanese-held Rangoon, Burma. Led by the inimitable William Slim, the Irrawaddy crossing was the longest enemy-opposed river crossing in any theater of World War II.

NO SURRENDER

The Allied liberation of Rangoon ended the Burma campaign in the strategic sense. Militarily, Japan had lost Burma. Yet—as they did everywhere in the Pacific theater—they continued to fight, and it was August 28, 1945—a full two weeks after the Emperor Hirohito had broadcasted his surrender message to the people of Japan—that preliminary surrender documents were signed in Burma.

The exigencies of war and the common goal of repelling the Japanese invasion made wary allies of Chinese Communist leader Mao Zedong and Chinese Nationalist leader Chiang Kai-shek, seen here together back in December 1944, after a tenuous meeting with U.S. ambassador to China Patrick J. Hurley. After Japan's formal surrender in September 1945, Hurley worked in vain effort to extend the alliance into the postwar era.

CHINA

THROUGHOUT THE WAR, China remained extensively occupied by the Japanese, and even late in the war, when they were on the defensive on all other fronts, the Japanese launched the Ichi-go campaign, in which every major airfield in China was captured without significant resistance. This failure precipitated a crisis between the United States and China and prompted President Roosevelt to urge Chiang Kai-shek to make extensive reforms in the Chinese military, including putting all Chinese forces under a U.S. commander—most likely Vinegar Joe Stilwell. Chiang promised changes, but he insisted that the blunt Stilwell be recalled in favor of another American commander. Accordingly, Lieutenant General Albert C. Wedemeyer assumed the post of Chiang's chief of staff in October 1944. He worked more harmoniously with the Chinese leader than Stilwell had, but little progress was made. At this point in the war, however, China's military significance had greatly diminished. The defeat of Japan, it was now clear, would not come by means of defeating Japan in China, but by defeating Japan in the Pacific and then in its own home islands. The growing strife between the pro-American Nationalists and the pro-Soviet Chinese Communists became an even more critical issue than the ongoing Japanese presence in China. During the height of the Japanese invasion, the two factions united against the common enemy, but now, in the war's closing year, they turned increasingly against one another. Patrick J. Hurley, personal representative of Franklin D. Roosevelt, worked desperately to mediate between the Nationalists and the Communists, but to no avail. Effectively sidelined during the war's last twelve months, China was feeling the forces that would erupt into one of the postwar world's first great crises—the Communist revolution that would produce the People's Republic of China.

TAKEAWAY

Shoestring Theater

The vast China-Burma-India theater was at the very bottom of the Allies' priority list during most of World War II. Extraordinary commanders, such as British general William Slim and Americans "Vinegar Joe" Stilwell and Claire Chennault, alternately staved off outright defeat and achieved remarkable victories—all on the very thinnest of shoestrings.

CHAPTER 17

MacArthur Returns

The Philippines Are Redeemed

On March 13, 1942, after a harrowing voyage from Corregidor aboard a tiny plywood PT boat, Douglas MacArthur, his wife, and his son reached Mindanao in the southern Philippines, then were flown by B-17 bomber to Australia. Immediately on landing on March 17, the general broadcasted his famous pledge to the defenders and the people of the Philippines: "I came through and I shall return." Throughout the succeeding months, even as he oversaw the great success of the Allied "island-hopping" campaign, the redemption of that pledge was never far from MacArthur's mind. Although the Japanese discovered that occupying the Philippines was far more difficult and costly than they had imagined—resistance groups and guerrilla fighters continually took a heavy toll among Japanese troops—the Filipino population and the American and Filipino prisoners of war fared far worse. MacArthur burned to liberate his old command and the Filipino people he had come to know and respect.

Targeting the Philippines

In July 1944, as the Allies closed on the Japanese homeland, Admiral Ernest J. King, U.S. chief of naval operations, saw an opportunity to accelerate the Pacific war by hopping over the Philippines themselves in order to attack Japanese-held Formosa (present-day Taiwan) immediately. It was a reasonable plan, but MacArthur refused to even consider it. Liberating the Philippines was a personal priority—not that he argued from this premise. Instead, MacArthur pointed out the strategically critical position of the islands and went on to argue that the United States had a moral obligation to free the Filipino people from Japanese bondage. In the end, President Roosevelt agreed, and retaking the Philippines became, as of the summer of 1944, a prime objective of the Pacific war.

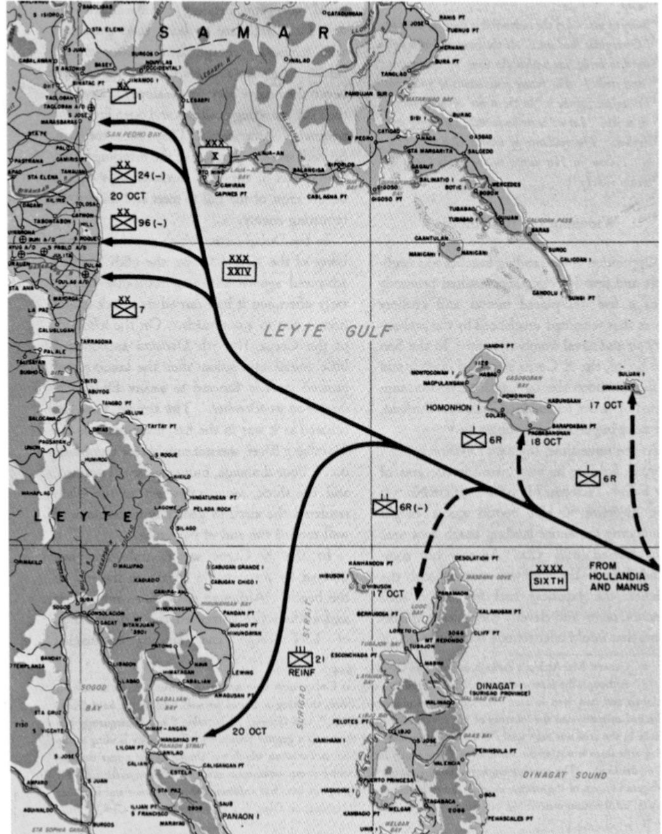

The island of Leyte, together with the small islands guarding the Surigao Strait, was the doorway to the liberation of the Philippines, which began on October 20, 1944.

ALTERNATE TAKE

Formosa vs. the Philippines

Historians have long debated King's proposal to bypass the Philippines versus MacArthur's insistence on liberating the islands. Attacking Formosa was the equivalent of pounding on Japan's back door. The Japanese would have had no choice other than to respond with massive forces, which would then have been vulnerable to destruction by Allied counterattack. While it's true that the defense of the Philippines was ultimately an Allied strategic success, the campaign was costly and time consuming for the Americans. The war might well have been shortened by a direct attack closer to Japan. On the other hand, such an attack might have heightened the Japanese will to fight to the death. It is possible that bypassing the Philippines could have put the Allies in position to invade the Japanese home islands sooner, yet the war still might not have ended until the dropping of the atomic bombs, which were not ready until July 1945.

The Assault Begins

In September, American carrier-based aircraft began bombing Japanese airfields on central Luzon, the biggest of the Philippine Islands, damaging or destroying about four hundred Japanese planes. This preparation gained the Americans air superiority—although not air supremacy.

By this time, U.S. Army forces had captured Morotai, between New Guinea and Mindanao, even as the III Marine Corps took Peleliu and Angaur in the Central Pacific. These conquests positioned American land forces to begin the liberation of the Philippines. MacArthur had planned on beginning with the southern islands, but Admiral William "Bull" Halsey, commanding the U.S. Third Fleet, had met with such thin Japanese opposition at the battle of Mindanao during September 9–10, that MacArthur decided he could afford to bypass the south and instead make a direct assault on Leyte, in the center of the Philippine archipelago.

The Leyte landings—first step in the invasion of the Philippines—was assigned to the Sixth U.S. Army under Walter Krueger. The Sixth was composed of the XXIV Corps (John Hodge commanding) and X Corps (Franklin Sibert). These commanders would be going up against Sosaku Suzuki's Japanese Thirty-fifth Army. The Americans would be transported to their landings by ships of the U.S. Seventh Fleet, commanded by Thomas Kinkaid, and air cover was supplied by carrier-based naval aviators as well as the land-based Southwest Pacific Air Forces under George Kenney.

On October 17–18, elite army Rangers landed on the small islands guarding the eastern entrance to Leyte Gulf. They quickly neutralized Japanese resistance there, and, at dawn on October 20, 1944, Kinkaid laid down an intense two-hour naval barrage, which was followed at 10:00 A.M. by the principal landings—four divisions—

NUMBERS

Pacific Armada

The amphibious invasion force MacArthur assembled was massive, consisting of more than seven hundred ships, hundreds of aircraft, and about 160,000 men.

"I told the President [that] we had been thrown out of Luzon at the point of a bayonet and we should regain our prestige by throwing the Japanese out at the point of a bayonet."

Douglas MacArthur, on his meeting with FDR in Hawaii, July 27, 1944

Giant LSTs (Landing Ships, Tank) prepare to disgorge troops and vehicles onto the shore of Leyte Island in the first phase of the liberation of the Philippines.

POP CULTURE

Photo Op

In October 1944, General MacArthur provided one of the most memorable images of the war as he waded ashore with other officers during the initial landings at Leyte. The event was covered by still photographers and U.S. Army Signal Corps cinematographers. After the war, researchers discovered that MacArthur had actually shot several "takes" of the celebrated walk. No American commander was more concerned about his public image than MacArthur. Many criticized him as vain-glorious. He believed, however, that the public and soldiers alike needed heroic commanders who looked bigger than life but with whom they could readily identify.

along seventeen miles of the east coast of Leyte between Tacloban and Dulag. The two divisions of X Corps landed on the right, and the two divisions of XXIV Corps landed on the left. Together, they fought their way inland over four days, securing airfields. By November 2, Sixth Army had gained control of the Leyte Valley, from Carigara on the north coast to Abuyog in the southeast. This accomplished, the U.S. 7th Infantry crossed Luzon to Baybay on the west coast.

The Main Phase

The invasion proceeded steadily, but was retarded by a combination of torrential rains and intensified resistance from Japanese forces that was concentrated in the mountainous interior. Tomoyuki Yamashita, the Japanese commander in charge of the islands, called in reinforcements from surrounding islands. Despite the U.S. Navy's success in the Battle of Leyte Gulf (see next section), nearly forty-five thousand Japanese reinforcements landed at Ormoc on Leyte's west coast between October 23 and December 11. General Krueger was keenly aware of the urgent necessity of bringing a halt to the Japanese buildup. He launched a double-barreled offensive into the Ormoc Valley beginning in November. On the right, X Corps, which was reinforced by the 32nd Infantry Division, attacked Limon, a village that guarded the northern entrance into the valley. The Japanese held out at Limon until December 10. In the meantime, on the left, the 11th Airborne Division joined XXIV Corps, as the 7th Infantry lunged across Leyte, at Balogo, on November 22. While these units fought their way across the island, the 77th Infantry landed at Ipil to begin the main assault on Ormoc, which, like Limon, fell to the Americans on December 10.

In one of the most famous images of World War II, Douglas MacArthur wades ashore at Leyte, on his way to announce to the people of the Philippines: "I have returned." The man at the left of the photograph, wearing a pith helmet, is Philippine president Sergio Osmeña, who returned to his country with MacArthur.

After making contact with one another, the 7th and the 77th divisions marched up both ends of the Ormoc Valley, converging at Libungao on December 20. On Christmas day, the last Japanese-held port on Leyte, Palompon, was captured, and the day after Christmas, the Eighth U.S. Army, under the command of Robert Eichelberger, took over the Leyte campaign, freeing up XXIV Corps to fight in Okinawa (see Chapter 18). For the next four months, Eighth Army conducted what was officially called a "mop-up" operation, but that was, in fact, the terrifically difficult task of extirpating large numbers of dug-in Japanese defenders.

American soldiers regroup in an abandoned Filipino village in November 1944, during the Battle of Leyte.

Leyte Gulf

While the armies fought for the island of Leyte, the Battle of Leyte Gulf erupted at sea on October 23–26, 1944. A desperate Japanese attempt to destroy the American fleet that covered the invasion, thereby isolating the landed troops, Leyte Gulf was—and still remains—the biggest naval battle in history. The battle also introduced a new and terrible Japanese weapon: the kamikaze attack.

Having discovered where the American landings on Leyte were to take place, Admiral Soemu Toyoda, commanding the Japanese Combined Fleet, launched Operation Sho-Go (Victory). His objective was to draw Admiral Halsey's U.S. Third Fleet into battle north of the Leyte Gulf, leaving exposed the landing forces and the smaller U.S. Seventh Fleet under Vice Admiral Kinkaid, the fleet covering the landings. The American commanders were hampered by a dearth of intelligence because the Japanese had changed codes just prior to the battle—so American "Ultra" decrypts were of little use—and they also maintained a remarkable degree of absolute radio silence. Thanks to the element of surprise, Toyoda's trap would very nearly succeed.

"The purity of youth will usher in the Divine Wind."

Vice Admiral Onishi, 1944, invoking the semi-official mantra of the kamikaze ("divine wind")

Tactical command of Operation Sho-Go was assigned to Vice Admiral Jisaburo Ozawa, commander in charge of the Mobile Force. Ozawa organized his ships—which included the world's two largest battleships, *Yamato* and *Masashi*, as well as five conventional battleships

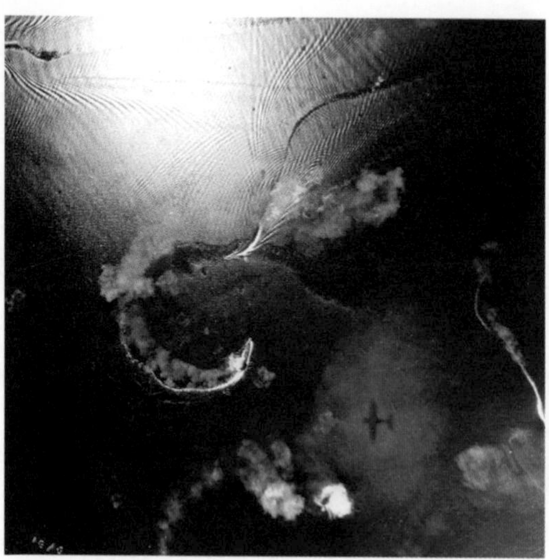

This remarkable aerial reconnaissance photograph documents the battle of the Sibuyan Sea, October 24, 1944. Japanese ships, including the giant battleship Yamato, *undertake swift, tight evasive maneuvers in an effort to avoid the bombs and torpedoes of U.S. carrier-based planes. Note the shadow of one plane at the lower right.*

and sixteen cruisers—into two striking forces, one under Vice Admiral Takeo Kurita and the other commanded by Vice Admiral Kiyohide Shima. Ozawa assumed command of the decoy force intended to bait Halsey into sailing north while Kurita and Shima closed the vise on Kinkaid's Seventh Fleet. Part of Shima's force, along with some of Kurita's ships under Vice Admiral Shoji Nishimura, was assigned to sail into the Leyte Gulf via Surigao Strait, while Kurita himself approached the gulf via the San Bernardino Strait. In the meantime, the rest of Shima's ships escorted Japanese troop reinforcements to Leyte Island.

On October 24, the aircraft carriers of Vice Admiral Marc Mitscher's Task Force 38 launched strikes against Kurita just as his fleet began crossing the Sibuyan Sea. Mitscher's planes sunk a battleship and damaged others, sending Kurita into a 180-degree turn. Kurita's besetting fault was an excess of caution—understandable, given the ferocity of Mitscher's attack, but misplaced, given the desperate situation of the Japanese war effort at the time. Halsey, however, mistook Kurita's delay for evidence of much greater damage than had been inflicted, and he accordingly discounted Kurita as a threat. This was precisely the effect Toyoda had hoped to achieve with the Sho-Go plan. Believing Kurita had been neutralized, Halsey gamely pursued Ozawa's decoy fleet, sailing north, away from the U.S. Seventh Fleet—and the Leyte invaders.

Toyoda's trap was set, but he had not counted on swift U.S. PT boats—soon backed by destroyers, followed by cruisers and battleships—intercepting Nishimura as he entered Surigao Strait on the night of October 24. Not only was the Japanese admiral killed, but every ship under his command, save one destroyer, was sent to the bottom. Seeing this, Shima, who had been following Nishimura, withdrew without a fight.

One entire jaw of Toyoda's vise had been destroyed, but Kurita's own force was still intact. As planned, he sailed into Leyte Gulf by

NUMBERS

Leyte Losses

Taking Leyte cost 15,584 American casualties, including 3,584 killed. Japanese casualties were more than 70,000 men, mostly killed. The Japanese lost 3 battleships, 4 aircraft carriers, 10 cruisers, and 9 destroyers as well as many aircraft. These were blows from which the Imperial Japanese Navy could not recover. Even more important, Toyoda failed to disrupt the Leyte landings. His defeat all but guaranteed that the Americans would retake the Philippines.

way of San Bernardino Strait on the morning of the 25th. Kurita assumed that, with Halsey chasing a decoy, he would be unobserved as he approached the U.S. Seventh Fleet; however, a U.S. escort carrier group under Rear Admiral Clifton Sprague sighted Kurita off Samar Island. Neither commander had expected the other. For Kurita's part—always cautious—he assumed that Sprague's modest force was part of something much larger. Unwilling to risk the entrapment of his entire fleet, Kurita ordered his ships to attack independently. It was a fatal error born of an abundance of caution. Had Kurita attacked in force, he would have easily rolled over Sprague's outnumbered and outclassed force. By attacking piecemeal, however, Kurita made himself vulnerable to the determined Sprague, whose aircraft sank two Japanese cruisers while a torpedo launched from one of Sprague's destroyers damaged a third cruiser. Sprague suffered severe damage, too, losing a pair of escort carriers, including one to a kamikaze attack. Two of his destroyers and a destroyer escort were also sunk, and other ships were badly damaged. Yet it was Kurita, not Sprague, who broke off the engagement. Presumably short on fuel and still believing that a much larger force was about to descend on him, he withdrew. The U.S. Seventh Fleet and the troops it protected had been saved by Sprague's courageous stand.

Flawed Victory

While Sprague desperately battled Kurita, Admiral Kinkaid radioed Halsey, hot in a fighting pursuit of Ozawa. Unwilling to disengage completely from his prey, Halsey responded to Kinkaid by sending just one of Mitscher's task groups to engage Kurita. He kept back a number of ships, under Rear Admiral Willis A. Lee, to press the fight against Ozawa—who had already lost four carriers to Mitscher. Clearly, Halsey failed to realize—or was too caught up in the chase to recognize—the full peril of the situation in Leyte Gulf. It was only after Lee was within range of what remained of Ozawa's force that Halsey at last awoke to the jeopardy in which he had allowed the Leyte landings and the Seventh Fleet to fall. He now ordered Lee to break off against Ozawa and follow Mitscher south. Even so, Halsey continued to pursue Ozawa with a smaller force and managed to sink two more ships.

ALTERNATE TAKE

Halsey and Sprague

The Battle of Leyte Gulf was an important American victory, but, by taking Toyoda's bait and pursuing Ozawa, Halsey missed an opportunity to destroy the remnant of Kurita's fleet. Forced to break off from Ozawa, he also allowed that force to escape total annihilation. Had the legendarily pugnacious Halsey been less anxious for a fight—*any* fight—he would have bagged two major Japanese forces in their entirety. On the other hand, had Admiral Sprague faltered in his stand, the Seventh Fleet might well have been destroyed, and the entire Leyte landing force greatly imperiled.

Liberating Luzon

After the Battle of Leyte had been won at the end of December 1944, MacArthur turned to the principal island of the vast Philippine archipelago, Luzon, which lay across the San Bernardino Strait from Leyte.

Preparatory to the invasion, Robert Eichelberger led elements of his Eighth U.S. Army in an amphibious assault against Mindoro, south of Luzon, on December 15, 1944. His troops secured a substantial beachhead at San José, and engineers immediately set to work carving out a pair of airstrips to accommodate planes used to support the Luzon invasion.

MacArthur's plan was to surprise Yamashita by refraining from the obvious—an attack from the south—and instead maneuvered into position to attack from the north. Yamashita's superb reconnaissance efforts detected MacArthur's dodge, however, and a Japanese fleet was sent to intercept the advance. But by this time the Japanese fleet was so depleted that it was handily outgunned by the U.S. Navy, and thus the landings on Luzon proceeded as MacArthur had planned—from the north. MacArthur sought to accomplish what the Japanese had achieved against him at the start of the war. A major difference, however, was that whereas MacArthur wanted to spare Manila the worst of the invasion by declaring it an open city, Yamashita defended it fiercely in a battle that consumed an entire month and resulted in the destruction of most of the capital. Manila would not be liberated until March 3, 1945, when much of it lay in ruin.

NUMBERS

Kamikaze Hits

Official Japanese sources claim that kamikaze attacks sank 81 ships and damaged 195, accounting for about 80 percent of U.S. naval losses in the closing months of the Pacific war. U.S. sources, however, record that approximately 2,800 kamikaze attacks sank 34 U.S. Navy ships and damaged 368 others. Navy records indicate that about 4,900 sailors were killed in the attacks and another 4,800 were wounded. Japanese losses were 2,525 naval kamikaze pilots killed, along with 1,387 army pilots. It is calculated that about 14 percent of kamikaze attacks actually scored hits and 8.5 percent of all ships attacked sank.

General Tomoyuki Yamashita, who had proven himself brilliant on the offensive, now showed great skill in preparing defenses against the invaders. He divided his Fourteenth Army into three defensive groups. The northern unit, of 140,000 men, was designated Shobu; the center, Kembu, consisted of thirty thousand troops; and the southern defense, Shimbu, had eighty thousand. The Imperial Japanese Navy made extensive use of kamikaze attacks against the U.S. Third and Seventh Fleets.

On January 9, 1945, General Walter Krueger's forces landed at Lingayen Gulf, sixty-eight thousand men pouring ashore on that first day. Without pause, they commenced their inland drive, penetrating some forty miles by January 20. I Corps, assigned to advance to the east, dueled with Yamashita's Shobu Group, against which Eichelberger poured reinforcements, including the entire 158th Regiment, the 25th Infantry Division, and the 32nd Infantry Division.

KAMIKAZE

The Japanese word *kamikaze* is commonly translated as "divine wind" and refers to a legendary typhoon that is believed to have saved Japan from a Mongol invasion fleet in 1281. During World War II, the word was borrowed into English to describe the suicide attacks made principally by Japanese pilots. The Japanese themselves reserved the word *kamikaze* to describe only the 1281 typhoon.

During the war, the Japanese called a suicide attack unit *tokubetsu kōgeki tai*, "special attack unit," which was typically shortened to *tokkōtai*. The Imperial Japanese Navy called its suicide squads *shinpū tokubetsu kōgeki tai*, and the word *shinpū* uses the same characters that form the word *kamikaze*.

As the tide of war turned against Japan, First Air Fleet commandant Vice Admiral Takijiro Onishi proposed forming a suicide attack unit, and in October 1944 Commander Asaiki Tamai organized twenty-three promising student pilots and one experienced lieutenant to join the new special force. All were volunteers.

Late in 1944, the USS *Indiana* and USS *Reno* were hit by Japanese aircraft, but most modern historians believe these were accidental collisions. On October 25, the Imperial Japanese Navy's Kamikaze Special Attack Force (as the unit was called in English) carried out its first mission, five "Zero" fighters targeting the USS *St. Lo* and other ships. The *St. Lo* was sunk. The October 25 attacks encouraged the Japanese to expand the suicide attack program, and over the next several months more than twenty-five hundred planes and pilots made kamikaze attacks. Many military historians believe that the first purposeful attack was led by Captain Masafumi Arima, commander of the 26th Air Flotilla, on October 30, 1944. On that day, no fewer than one hundred Yokosuka D4Y Suisei ("Judy") dive-bombers attacked the carrier *Franklin* near Leyte Gulf, and Arima crashed his plane into the ship. Others argue, however, that even the first indisputably deliberate kamikaze attack was against the heavy cruiser HMAS *Australia*, flagship of the Royal Australian Navy, on October 21, 1944. The pilot and aircraft involved were apparently attached to the Imperial Japanese Army Air Force, not the navy.

The peak of the kamikaze campaign came during April–June 1945 during the Battle of Okinawa (see Chapter 18), when suicide attacks by aircraft or vessels sank or put out of action some thirty American warships and three American merchant ships. Other Allied craft were also hit. The cost to the Japanese was a staggering 1,465 planes.

Kamikaze tactics were born of great desperation and, self-destructive, were doomed—yet they took a terrible toll on American ships. Here the fleet aircraft carrier USS Franklin *(right) and smaller escort carrier USS* Belleau Wood *smolder from kamikaze hits. Attacked on October 30, 1944, the ships were supporting the Leyte landings.*

The only defense against kamikaze pilots determined to die was to shoot the incoming aircraft out of the sky with antiaircraft fire. In action off Luzon, the "Zero" pictured here made it through the defensive fire and crashed near the "island" (control superstructure) of the aircraft carrier Lexington *CV-16, sending fire in all directions. Crewmen got the blaze under control in less than a half hour, and the carrier not only remained in the battle, but managed to shoot down a kamikaze heading for the carrier* Ticonderoga.

While the reinforced I Corps battled Shobu group, XIV Corps, to the right (south) of I Corps, peeled off to the south, advancing swiftly over Luzon's Central Plain until January 23, when it reached Clark Field, which had been held by the Japanese since the beginning of the war. A week-long firefight retook this major base, from which XIV Corps pushed another twenty-five miles south to Calumpit.

On January 29, XI Corps landed to the right (west) of XIV Corps, at San Antonio. This force attacked Kembu group. In concert with Filipino guerrillas, the 38th and 24th Infantry divisions of XI Corps managed to liberate Bataan and Corregidor then cut off and isolate the entire Bataan Peninsula. With the Kembu group defeated, Krueger sent XIV Corps on a rapid advance to Manila beginning on February 2. The 1st Cavalry Division reached the capital's outskirts on the night of February 3/4 and quickly freed thirty-five hundred Allied prisoners held at the University of Santo Tomas. On the night of February 5/6, the 37th Infantry marched into northwestern Manila, where they located and liberated another thirteen hundred POWs from Bilibid Prison.

NUMBERS

U.S., Japanese, and Civilian Losses

About 1,000 Americans and 16,000 Japanese were killed in the battle of Manila. Filipino casualties—overwhelmingly civilian—were catastrophic, totaling at least 100,000 killed.

Free at last—Americans held prisoner since the fall of Bataan and Corregidor in 1942 are liberated by the 6th Battalion in January 1945.

In the face of the American advance, the Japanese fell back behind the Pasig River and here mounted a savage resistance, which tied down the U.S. advance for about a month. It was during this time that most of Manila was reduced to ashes before the Japanese yielded the city on March 3.

While the fight for Manila raged, I Corps, operating to the north, battered against the stout Shobu defenses, which took full advantage of the mountainous terrain. At last, I Corps' 6th Infantry broke through at Bongabon, and advanced to the east coast on February 14, 1945. From here, it took its place on the Manila Front. The Philippine summer capital, Baguio, was liberated on April 27, followed by Santa Fe—which had been a major Japanese communications center—exactly a month later.

Before he withdrew from the Philippines in 1942, General MacArthur declared Manila an open city, hoping to spare it wholesale destruction. The devastation came, however, during the liberation in March 1945, when the Japanese occupiers, surrounded, razed most of the Filipino capital.

Once Baguio and Santa Fe had been secured, the 37th Division moved down Cagayan Valley, driving a wedge into the Shobu group, splitting it in two by June 26. Thus divided, the Shobu troops were unable to mount an effective counterattack.

While the northern fight was ongoing, XI Corps, fighting in the south (east of Manila), hacked away at the Shimbu line. Mountainous terrain impeded the attack, making it slow and costly going. The 6th and 43rd Infantry, together with the 1st Cavalry, were reduced to advancing by mere inches, so that elements of XIV Corps had to be called in to push southeast as well. These troops fought down the Bicol Peninsula, where resistance persisted until June 1.

The Eighth Army arrived in Luzon in July 1 and assumed responsibility for bringing the campaign to a conclusion, so that the Sixth Army could begin to prepare for the planned invasion of Japan, which was scheduled to step off in the fall of 1945. Within just four days—on the Fourth of July, no less—General MacArthur declared Luzon secure.

Ragged Ending

Victory on Luzon—including the liberation of Manila—marked the end of the major phases of the Philippines campaign. Yet few of the island battles in the Pacific ever ended cleanly, and the struggle in the Philippines was no exception. Throughout the islands, sporadic fighting continued until the very end of the war. In some of the most remote corners of the archipelago, isolated pockets of Japanese defenders continued to fight sometimes for years after the war had ended. It was the grim way of the warrior.

TAKEAWAY

Winning Back the Philippines

The campaign to liberate the Philippines was the single biggest American campaign of the Pacific war and the most controversial, favored principally by Douglas MacArthur, who was determined to redeem his pledge to reclaim the territory he had surrendered at the beginning of the war.

CHAPTER 18

Iwo Jima and Okinawa

The Japanese Defend Their Homeland

By means of war, Japan had sought to conquer an empire that would not only give it control of vast reserves of raw materials and labor but would also create a great defensive cordon, rendering impregnable the Japanese home islands. The Allied island-hopping strategy (see Chapter 15) steadily penetrated this cordon, and the fall of Saipan to American forces in July 1944 made so gaping a breach that the administration of Japan's militarist dictator-generalissimo, Hideki Tojo, collapsed. Moreover, possession of Saipan put the Japanese home islands within range of the U.S. Army Air Forces' new long-range, heavy-capacity bomber, the B-29. By November 24, with the United States in possession of the Mariana Islands, B-29s began routinely raiding Japan, including massive raids on Tokyo. Thus, by the end of 1944, Japan was under heavy attack from the air—yet the home islands had yet to be invaded, and the Japanese militarists showed no inclination to surrender.

Sulfur Island

Of all the insignificant and inhospitable island specks for possession of which Americans and Japanese spilled so much blood, none was inherently less significant nor more inhospitable than Iwo Jima. Its Japanese name, meaning Sulfur Island, was all the description this volcanic outcropping needed. Iwo Jima was just four and a half miles long by two and a half miles wide at its widest, but to the Japanese it was of value far beyond its sterile sulfurous magma and its diminutive size. They had built three airstrips on the island and had taken full and elaborate advantage of its network of hardened caves and ravines, reinforcing these further with concrete and steel. Indeed, few places on the planet have ever been so thoroughly and formidably fortified. For Iwo Jima was a vital sentinel guarding the Japanese homeland, and, as Japanese territory, it was also part of that homeland.

The fortification of Iwo Jima was sound military strategy, but its importance to the Japanese reached beyond strategy. Inconsiderable though it was, Iwo Jima was one of the Volcano Islands, an archipelago that was actually a part of Japan, just 760 miles south-southeast of Tokyo. In the American view, it was both necessary to get Iwo Jima out of Japanese hands and to convert it for use as an advance base for the emergency landing of B-29s raiding Japan and for fighters that escorted the bombers to and from their targets. In both of these capacities, the island could save many lives and many planes.

Bombardment

American military planners had learned through bitter experience that taking an island from Japan was always much bloodier than anticipated, and they estimated that, even after extensive naval and aerial bombardment, a two-week ground battle would be required. The island was subjected to the most intensive tactical aerial and naval bombardment of the Pacific war. For seventy-two consecutive days before the first assault landings, aircraft flew 2,700 sorties in which they dropped 5,800 tons of bombs. Then, during the three days immediately preceding the assault, the bombing was intensified. During this concentrated period, an additional 6,800 tons of bombs were dropped, and 21,926 naval artillery shells were lobbed against the island.

NUMBERS

Little Fortress

In all, tiny Iwo Jima was deeply pitted by about fifteen hundred fortified and reinforced caves, which were interconnected by some sixteen miles of tunnels.

NUMBERS

Massive Buildup

Before Iwo Jima fell, after thirty-six days of continuous ground battle, 110,000 men would be landed on this volcanic speck, while 220,000 sailors, marines, and soldiers remained offshore, on approximately 800 warships.

REALITY CHECK

Digging Deeper

Not only did the intensive bombardment of Iwo Jima fail to reduce the Japanese garrison on the island, it actually hardened resistance from augmented fortifications.

Iwo Jima landing on February 19, 1945: Marines of the 4th Division hit the beach in the initial assault on "Sulfur Island."

On February 19, 1945, thirty thousand marines of the 4th and 5th Marine divisions landed on Iwo Jima. The 3rd Marine Division was held in reserve, but within days a total of 75,144 marines were committed to the invasion.

The Defenders

Iwo Jima was defended by a garrison of twenty-two thousand soldiers of the Imperial Japanese Army and naval troops (the equivalent of marines) of the Imperial Japanese Navy. The entire garrison was commanded by Lieutenant General Tadamichi Kuribayashi, who used the terrifying and tedious two-and-a-half months of preparatory bombardment to set his men to digging deeper and deeper bunkers. The continual detonation of bombs and naval artillery was a most effective spur to their labor. Kuribayashi and his men were keenly aware that they were defending Japanese soil. They were prepared to hold out in their caves and tunnels until they all were killed.

Lieutenant General Tadamichi Kuribayashi, Imperial Japanese Army, commanded the Iwo Jima garrison, which defended the island to the death—including that of the commander himself.

The Battle Begins

The first waves of the landing met with little resistance. Marines new to combat were elated, but the veterans among them knew better. They knew the enemy would not simply give up this island.

After advancing inland some 350 yards, the first wave at last met the enemy's fire. Kuribayashi had planned his defenses skillfully, so that the marines were pinned down not only by fire from the front, but by intense flanking fire from the caves and other covered positions. Despite the volume and intensity of raking fire, the marines succeeded in capturing the first of the island's three airstrips by day two of the invasion.

FLAG RAISING

On the fifth day, the second airstrip fell to the marines. They were also in position to take the highest point on Iwo Jima, Mount Suribachi, a dormant volcano rising 546 feet above the island surface. In any assault, the high ground is always a great prize, since the possessor commands the field below. In the case of Iwo Jima, the marines also considered Mount Suribachi of tremendous symbolic importance. Progress had been by inches. Each defensive position had to be destroyed, typically by explosives or flamethrower. Marine casualties mounted. The sight of the Stars and Stripes flying above Suribachi would provide an incalculable boost to morale.

On February 23, a small party was sent to scale Suribachi. While the rest of the island was furiously engaged in battle, they met with little resistance and raised a small flag. Its effect on the marines was electric—so much so that the first flag was judged too small to be seen by all of the marines scattered across the island, let alone by those still at sea. About two hours after the first flag was raised, another party was sent up with a much larger flag. Veterans of Iwo Jima remembered the sight for the rest of their lives. An American flag was waving over Japan.

An American flag was waving over Japan. That fact was not lost on the Japanese. Even as it lofted U.S. Marine morale—and conveyed to the people on the American home front the inevitability of victory in the Pacific—the capture of Mount Suribachi was a devastating blow to the Japanese garrison.

"The raising of that flag on Mount Suribachi means a Marine Corps for the next five hundred years."

Secretary of the Navy James Forrestal, 1945

DETAILS, DETAILS

On June 19, 2007, the Japansese Geographical Survey Institute announced that Iwo Jima would be renamed Iwo To as of September 1. The "new" name was actually the name given to the island by its original inhabitants. Both *iwo* and *to* mean "island" in Japanese.

Meat Grinder and Bloody Gorge

The taking of Mount Suribachi looked and felt like victory. Yet the costliest fighting was yet to come on Iwo Jima. Shaken though they doubtless were, the Japanese garrison remained determined to defend the island. They were reduced by this point to a pair of defensive lines and to a fortified position on a rise designated on Marine Corps maps as Hill 382. This position was so well defended that the marines dubbed it the "Meat Grinder." Taking it was essential to neutralizing the remaining Japanese defenses, and the only way to take it was to assault it—repeatedly—until it fell. Casualties were extremely heavy, and in the single day devoted to the assault on Hill 382, five Medals of Honor were earned.

A rare photograph of a rarer event: the surrender of Japanese soldiers on Iwo Jima. Almost all of the defenders perished, killed either by American bullets or their own hand.

Day after day, the fighting continued. Americans had become accustomed to struggling against what they deemed fanatical and

POP CULTURE

Iconic Picture

Both the first and second flag raisings were recorded by military photographers, but it was Associated Press photographer Joe Rosenthal whose photograph of the second raising created a sensation in America and throughout the Allied countries. The photo shows five marines and a U.S. Navy hospital corpsman—Sergeant Michael Strank, Corporal Harlon H. Block, Private First Class Franklin R. Sousley, Private First Class Rene A. Gagnon, Private First Class Ira Hayes, and Pharmacist's Mate Second Class John H. Bradley—as they struggled together to plant the flag (it flew from a pipe found at the scene) in the unyielding volcanic soil. The spontaneous scene had the look of a classical heroic sculpture group and instantly became the single most pervasive image of the war, reprinted endlessly in the media, on a postage stamp, in posters, and even on product packaging. The photograph earned Rosenthal a Pulitzer Prize and was immortalized in bronze at a memorial near Arlington National Cemetery.

AP photographer Joe Rosenthal's Pulitzer Prize-winning photograph of five marines and one U.S. Navy hospital corpsman raising the flag on Mount Suribachi, Iwo Jima, became the most famous American image of World War II.

suicidal resistance. Iwo Jima presented this, but with a redoubled intensity. The defenders contracted their line by inches under fire until, finally, they took up positions in a seven hundred-yard-long canyon the marines learned to call "Bloody Gorge." Against a vastly larger force of marines, the garrison held out for ten awful days. On March 16, 1945, Iwo Jima was at last declared secure.

Japanese Bastion

If Iwo Jima was sentinel to the Japanese home islands, Okinawa was their last bastion. Located just four hundred miles below southern Kyūshū—the most southerly of the home islands—Okinawa was 794 square miles in area, perfectly suited to serve as the main staging area for an invasion of Japan itself, starting with Kyūshū, an operation scheduled to begin in November 1945. For its part, Japanese high command garrisoned Okinawa with more than one hundred thousand troops of the Thirty-second Army under the command of General Mitsuru Ushijima, former commandant of the Imperial Japanese Military Academy.

Ushijima deployed most of his forces behind a fortified entrenchment called the Naha-Shuri-Yonabaru Line, which stretched completely across Okinawa's southern end, cutting off the lower fifth of the island. Ushijima's plan was to make a death stand, holding the invaders to the northern four-fifths of the island while kamikaze pilots destroyed Raymond Spruance's Fifth Fleet, which was covering the invasion. Once the fleet had been sunk, the invaders would be cut off, marooned, doomed.

The Invasion Begins

The overall commander of the invasion was Admiral Chester Nimitz. Spruance was assigned to cover the invasion, and the assault troops were the Tenth U.S. Army under General Simon Buckner, Jr. Admiral Richmond Turner took charge of transportation.

The assault began on March 26, 1945, as the 77th Infantry Division, commanded by Andrew Bruce, captured two smaller islands, Kerama and Keise, off the southwestern coast of Okinawa. Six days later, on April 1, Roy Geiger led the III Amphibious Corps of the U.S. Marines in landings on the western shore of Okinawa itself. Lemuel Shepherd's 6th Marine Division held the left flank of the assault, and the 1st Marine Division, under Pedro del Valle, took the right. Simultaneously, the 2nd Marine Division, commanded by Thomas Watson, landed on the southern tip of Okinawa as a decoy to draw off Japanese defenders. As these complex operations proceeded, the Tenth Army made up the entire right (south) wing of the first assault, consisting of XXIV Corps (under John Hodge), 7th Infantry Division (Archibald Arnold), and 96th Infantry Division (James Bradley), deployed left to right.

By sunset on April 1, fifty thousand American troops were in place along eight miles of beachhead, to a depth of three to four miles. It was a most auspicious beginning.

NUMBERS

Troop Losses

The taking of Iwo Jima cost the lives of 5,931 U.S. Marines. Another 17,372 were wounded. In sum, one-third of the Americans committed to battle became casualties. Out of 22,000 Japanese defenders, 20,703 were killed, including Lieutenant General Tadamichi Kuribayashi, who probably committed suicide rather than surrender. Before the end of the war, 2,251 B-29s made emergency landings on Iwo Jima airstrips. The lives of some 24,761 U.S. Army Air Forces aircrew members were thereby saved.

Fighting Inland

On April 3, the 1st Marine Division cleared a corridor all the way through to the east coast of Okinawa, a distance of two and a half miles. To the left of the 1st Marines, the 6th Marines advanced north in a long, gentle arc that swept up both coasts. The 6th arrived at the Motobu Peninsula on April 8.

Motobu was rugged country, and the defenders were deeply dug into it. They held out against the 6th Marines for nearly two weeks, but by April 20 the northern four-fifths of Okinawa was declared secure.

"To many a man in the line today fear is not so much of death itself . . . [as] of the terror and anguish and utter horror that precedes death in battle."

Ernie Pyle, from the last column the legendary correspondent wrote before he was killed at the Battle of Okinawa

Last Stand

With four-fifths of the island having rapidly fallen into American hands, the invasion forces responsible for the southern tip of Okinawa were left to face the last-ditch defenders at the Naha-Shuri-Yonabaru Line. After advancing east for two days, XXIV Corps turned ninety degrees to the south, the 7th Infantry Division on the left flank, the 96th on the right. On April 8, resistance

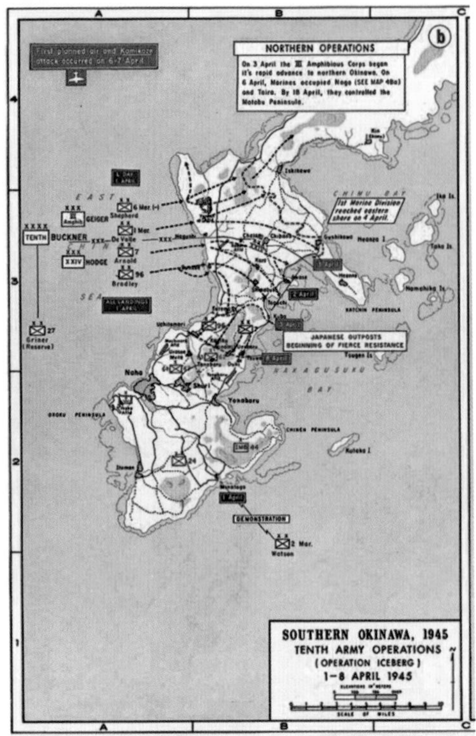

The invasion of Okinawa was intended as the prelude to the invasion of the Japanese home islands themselves.

suddenly spiked, pinning XXIV Corps just outside the Naha-Shuri-Yonabaru Line. General Hodge sought to break the deadlock by sending the 27th Infantry Division (commanded by George Griner) along the west coast to the right of the 96th. Once this advance had been completed, XXIV Corps launched a breakthrough assault on April 19 across a broad five-mile front.

Through a dozen days of fighting, XXIV Corps managed to advance just under two miles. Additional manpower was called up in the form of the Marine III Amphibious Corps on the right—the 6th Marine Division on the west coast, the 1st inland. At the same time, on the left, the 7th Infantry held the east coast, while the 77th slipped by on its right to relieve the 27th and 96th divisions, which had fought beyond exhaustion.

As the augmented southern invasion force continued to batter at the Japanese positions, Ushijima suddenly launched a massive counterattack on May 4–5, hitting the Tenth Army, hard, on its left flank.

It was a bold stroke, but proved to be a fatal mistake. Once the Japanese ventured out of their fortified entrenchments, they were exposed to the full fury of the reinforced and re-formed Americans. The counterattack was repulsed in a lopsided fight in which 6,227 Japanese troops were killed at the cost of 714 killed in the U.S. XXIV Corps.

NUMBERS

Troop Losses

Almost all of the Japanese Thirty-second Army was killed in battle—100,000 Japanese dead. Some 10,000 were captured. American casualties included 2,938 marines killed or missing and 13,708 wounded. Army dead or missing numbered 4,675, with 18,099 wounded.

Monsoon

Monsoon rains dogged the next phase of the American offensive, but Buckner refused to yield to the weather and, on May 11, resumed pounding the Naha-Shuri-Yonabaru Line until, on May 23, the 6th Marine Division finally smashed through the line into Naha. This put them into position to turn the Japanese west flank. Six days after this, on May 29, the 1st Marine Division, which had been in the center position of the attack, captured Shuri Castle. As the last-ditch Japanese line dissolved, XXIV Corps, to the right of the marines, pushed south, outflanking the Japanese on the east.

The 6th Marine Division embarked on June 4 to make a shore-to-shore amphibious assault on Okinawa's Oroku Peninsula. After ten days of nonstop combat, the marines cleared the peninsula even as the 8th Regiment of the 2nd Marine Division reinforced the main attack to advance to the southern tip of Okinawa. An amphibious assault from shore to shore was extremely rare. Marines were trained to storm the beaches from landing ships and landing craft, not to venture from one island directly to another. With victory in sight, army general Buckner was suddenly killed in an artillery barrage on June 18. Marine general Roy Geiger stepped in to command both the marine and army forces on Okinawa. On June 21, the Tenth Army reached the southern coast of Okinawa. This achieved, elements of the army sharply wheeled about and turned back to mop up isolated pockets of resistance. On June 22, 1945, Okinawa was declared secure. Mop-up operations ended there on July 2.

The terrible waste of war: Yamato, *the world's largest battleship and the pride of the Imperial Japanese Navy, explodes under attack by U.S. Navy aircraft on April 7, 1945. The ship was bound for the ultimate suicide mission, a kamikaze-style attack on the U.S. fleet supporting the Okinawa landings, when it was fatally attacked.*

The Battle at Sea

While the armies clashed on the island, a sea and air battle was also fought. A measure of Japanese desperation at this point was the Japanese plan to use *Yamato*, the world's biggest battleship, in a seagoing kamikaze attack against the Fifth Fleet. The *Yamato* was sighted by an American aircraft patrol on April 7, however, and attacked from the air. The pride of the Imperial fleet, it was sunk in the East China Sea. U.S. Navy planes also attacked and sank a Japanese light cruiser, four destroyers, and nine other Japanese ships. Naval combat associated with the Okinawa invasion effectively finished off the Imperial Japanese Navy. In its death throes, that navy fought back with intensive kamikaze attacks. About 1,900 suicide sorties were launched, the aircraft sinking 36 American ships and damaging 368. A total of 4,907 U.S. Navy sailors were killed in kamikaze attacks and another 4,824 were wounded. But the cost to the Japanese was very much higher. Over the three months of the Okinawa campaign and the sea and air battles associated with it, some 7,800 Japanese aircraft were destroyed, more than ten times the number of U.S. planes downed. Japanese air and navel power were at an end, and territory of Japan itself was now in American hands, about to be converted into a base from which the rest of the country would be attacked.

TAKEAWAY

Lead-up to Invasion

The battles of Iwo Jima and Okinawa were immediate preludes to the planned invasion of Japan itself. Iwo Jima was a highly fortified sentinel island guarding the approach to Japan, and Okinawa was Japanese territory, just four hundred miles from the southernmost of the Japanese home islands.

Part Six

CRUSADE IN EUROPE

On preceding pages: The multiple miseries of war were made more miserable by the winter of 1944–45, the worst to hit Europe in decades. These American soldiers of the 1st Infantry Division—the celebrated "Big Red One"—march through Murringen, Belgium, January 31, 1945.

CHAPTER 19

SOVIETS TRIUMPHANT

The Germans Pay the Price

OPERATION BARBAROSSA, THE GERMAN INVASION of the Soviet Union in treacherous violation of the German-Soviet Non-Aggression Pact, rolled over Russia until Hitler's armies were stopped by a combination of fierce Red Army resistance—despite catastrophic losses—the Russian winter, and tactical blunders born of Hitler's delusions of military genius. Halted before Moscow and disastrously defeated at the Battle of Stalingrad (see Chapter 7), the German invaders were in full retreat by January 1943, pursued by a resurgent Red Army.

THE FURY OF THE BEAR

BY LONG TRADITION, the symbol of Russia has been the bear, pictured as a lumbering animal, slow to anger, but when finally aroused, overwhelming in its strength and fury. And so the Soviets had responded to the invasion of their land. German victory seemed certain until the Red Army stood fast at Stalingrad, the city named for the demigod dictator of the nation. The Red Army was divided tactically into "fronts," what the Western allies called "army groups," very large units consisting of two or more armies. On January 10, 1943, the Don front—one of the Soviet army groups operating in the vicinity of Stalingrad and along the River Don—began decimating the remnants of Friedrich Paulus's German Sixth Army in and around Stalingrad. Seeking to lift Sixth Army morale by suggesting triumph, Adolf Hitler told one of his infamous "big lies" by promoting Paulus from general to field marshal on January 30. Just one day later, the new field marshal surrendered to the Red Army, and some ninety thousand German soldiers became prisoners of war. While the Don front mopped up Stalingrad, the three-army Stalingrad front—which, after victory, was renamed the South front—turned southwest, to push the remaining Germans out of the country.

"The mortuary itself is full. Not only are there too few trucks to go to the cemetery, but, more important, not enough gasoline to put in the trucks, and the main thing is—there is not enough strength left in the living to bury the dead."

Vera Inber, resident of Leningrad, diary entry for December 26, 1941

Far to the north of Stalingrad, the Red Army's Leningrad and Volkhov fronts attacked the German forces that had been laying siege to Leningrad since September 8, 1941. By January 12, 1943, the Soviets had succeeded in opening a passage between Leningrad and the shore of Lake Ladoga, which opened to the sea. By the twentieth, the corridor was more than six miles wide along the lakeshore, giving the besieged city much relief.

Between Leningrad in the north and Stalingrad in the south, on January 13, the Voronezh front commenced an offensive against the Second German Army and the German-allied Second Hungarian Army, which held the city of Voronezh just east of the Don. After a dozen days of hard fighting, the Hungarian Army was dead or captured, and the Second German Army was in retreat. Voronezh was liberated.

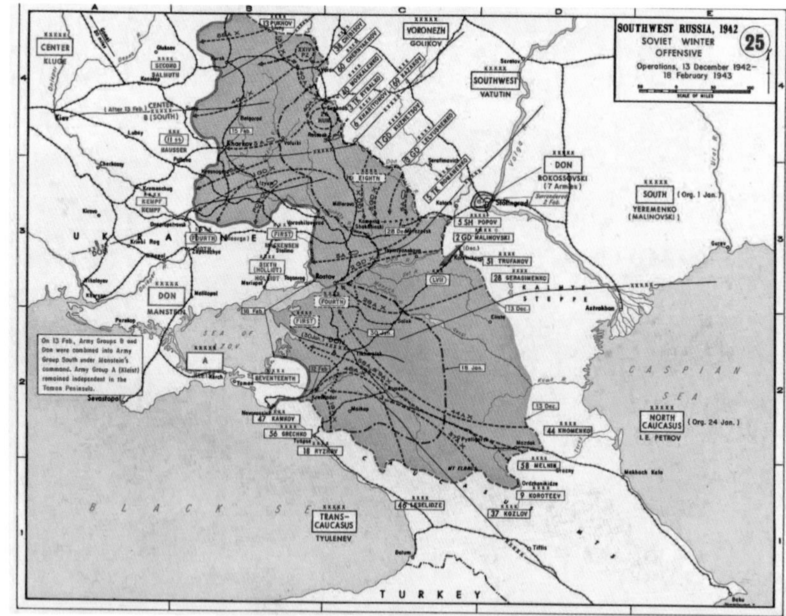

Stalingrad, the epic turning-point battle of the vast Russian Front, was the centerpiece of the great Red Army winter offensive of 1943. Nowhere was war more terrible than across the vast expanses of Soviet Russia and the Ukraine.

The Two Dictators

On January 15, 1943, when Paul Ludwig von Kleist, commander of German Army Group A, asked Adolf Hitler for permission to withdraw from the Caucasus—the vast mountainous region south of Stalingrad—the Führer withheld his answer until January 27, insisting in the meantime that Kleist hold his ground. By this time, however, the Red Army's South front had advanced closer to the Don, forcing Kleist to retreat, with or without Hitler's leave.

Leningrad (modern St. Petersburg), second city of the Soviet Union, writhed under a German siege of nearly nine hundred days—from September 1941 to January 1944. Hundreds of thousands died of starvation, privation, disease, and exposure; yet the city, meagerly and tenuously supplied by truck convoys rumbling across a frozen Lake Ladoga, never surrendered.

At the very beginning of Operation Barbarossa, Joseph Stalin had acted as if in a daze, but soon pulled himself together and began functioning as a truly inspiring war leader. Now, in defeat, it was Hitler who behaved as if to deny reality. He not only ordered all of his commanders to yield not a single yard, but also suddenly proclaimed what he called "total war" against the Soviets—not for the purpose of conquest (he said), but to defend all Europe against an invasion "out of the steppe," an invasion by a horde of Slav barbarians. Hitler's declaration was not entirely the product of denial and delusion. It was a belated recognition that the conquest of the Soviet Union required a far greater commitment of German resources than had been originally devoted to Operation Barbarossa. Hitler had believed that blitzkrieg tactics would work in the Soviet Union as they had in Poland and in Western Europe. He planned and provided for a short campaign, not a war of attrition. Indeed, only a short campaign had a realistic chance of success. Had Hitler originally acknowledged that invasion would entail "total war," he probably would not have invaded the Soviet Union in the first place. As it was, by the beginning of 1943, Germany was no longer in a position to mount a "total war"—anywhere.

NUMBERS

Siege of Leningrad

The siege of Leningrad was not lifted until January 18, 1944, after having lasted nearly nine hundred days. No one knows how many citizens of the city succumbed to disease, privation, and starvation during this time. The official Soviet report was 670,000 deaths. Others estimate between 700,000 to 1.5 million, with the most widely accepted estimate being 1.1 million.

Balance of Power

The German army did not fight like a defeated force. Even after Stalingrad and reversals elsewhere, German troops and commanders consistently outperformed the Red Army. The contest, however, had become above all a matter of numbers. At this point, Stalin had

REALITY CHECK

Brawn vs. Brains

Even at Stalingrad, a Soviet victory, the Red Army suffered greater casualties than the Germans. The Red Army was vastly improved by the elevation of Georgi Zhukov to field marshal after Stalingrad, but Zhukov, a brilliant commander, was in the minority. Most Red Army senior officers were mediocre at best. The Soviets turned the tide with overwhelming manpower and war production, not brilliance of leadership.

Georgi Zhukov, Marshal of the Soviet Union, was the senior commander of the Red Army, the principal architect of the great offensives that ended the war in the east and the conqueror of Berlin.

mobilized more than six million troops along the vast Soviet Front. By early 1943, German numbers amounted to about half of that. Equally important, the Soviets were out-producing Germany. During 1942, German factories had turned out nearly 5,000 armored vehicles, including tanks, and some 14,700 aircraft. Soviet production was 24,000 armored vehicles and 14,700 warplanes.

Following Stalingrad, Soviet morale leaped. More and more Soviet operations became offensive rather than defensive in nature. Lieutenant General Nikolai Vatutin, commanding the Southwest front, launched Operation Leap to neutralize German Army Group Don, pinning it down in the Donets River basin. Shortly after the commencement of Operation Leap, Zhukov and Aleksandr Vasilevsky launched Operation Star, which was designed to eliminate German Army Group Center.

Operation Leap came to an abrupt end on February 18 when the First Panzer Army struck back, destroying Vatutin's mobile force. Despite this reversal, the Southwest and Voronezh fronts crossed the River Donets, pushing the Germans west before it. On February 11, Hitler put Army Group South under the extremely capable Erich von Manstein, whose subordinate, Hermann Hoth, commanding the Fourth Panzer Army, counterattacked and reached the Donets River city of Kharkov on March 11. Blinded by the desire to take up a position behind the Donets, the Soviets left Belgorod, just north of Kharkov, undefended. It fell to panzers on March 18.

By the onset of spring 1943, German Army Group Center was concentrated south of Kirov, projecting a salient—or bulge—surrounding Orel, on the Oka River, north of Kursk. German Army Group South held a line running around Belgorod and Kharkov. Between Army Group Center and Army Group South was a hundred-mile gap that was filled by the Red Army's Central and Voronezh fronts, just east of Kursk.

Duel of the Tanks

Hitler planned to use the summer to regroup his forces in the Soviet Union so that he could mount a new offensive, albeit on a reduced scale. But, looking around him, he believed that the British and Americans would soon open up a second front in Europe,

The Battle of Kursk, July 1943, was the greatest tank duel in history and revealed the superiority of the remarkable Soviet T-34 tank.

either from the west or the south. (Actually, the Allied plan was to do both.) Moreover, Hitler had about half the number of troops—3.07 million—in place on the Soviet Front just now than the Soviets had (6.6 million). Both of these facts, as Hitler saw it, argued for action before it was too late. But where?

The two Red Army fronts—a total of five armies—lodged between German Army Group Center and German Army Group South around Kursk made an appealing objective.

Kursk was the principal rail and highway junction about five hundred miles south of Moscow. Possession of Kursk would mean control of a major intersection within Soviet territory—and it would also mean that five Soviet armies would suffer, perhaps even fall. Therefore, on April, 15, 1943, Hitler ordered Günther von Kluge, commanding Army Group Center, and Erich von Manstein, commanding Army Group South, to prepare for the launch of Operation Citadel, aimed at bagging those Soviet armies around Kursk.

Yet, even as he gave the order, Hitler lacked confidence. Perhaps it was better, after all, to use the summer as he had originally planned—for maneuver and consolidation of forces. The Führer temporized, and the resulting delay proved fatal.

Stalin, after consulting his top commanders, decided to use his five armies to expand the salient they held around Kursk. This, they reasoned, would drive an impenetrable wedge between the two great German forces, Army Groups Center and South. With such a wedge, the Soviets could truly seize the initiative in the war.

But now it was Stalin's turn to doubt. Finding it difficult to believe that Hitler was lost in thought, Stalin and his military planners assumed that he was actually planning a surprise attack against the two Red Army fronts. For this reason, Stalin ordered massive reinforcements to be sent to the Kursk area. That was prudent, but it also alerted the Germans to Soviet intentions, and

NUMBERS

Kursk Stats

The Germans committed 750,000 troops to the Battle of Kursk, together with 2,400 tanks and assault guns, plus 1,800 aircraft. Opposing them, the Red Army fielded 1.3 million troops, 3,400 tanks and assault guns, and 2,100 aircraft. In addition, the Soviets had prepared extensive fortifications around their position: six trench lines of three to five trenches each. Finally, six full Soviet armies were waiting, in reserve.

Hitler, alarmed, now precipitously gave the order to launch Citadel. On July 5, the German Ninth Army under Walther Model, in the north, and the Fourth Panzer Army commanded by Hermann Hoth in the south (along with Army Detachment Kempf commanded by Lieutenant General Werner Kempf) made their move.

Model sent three panzer corps against the village of Olkhovatka, just outside Kursk. Konstantin Rokossovsky deployed his Red Army troops to block Model's advance, forcing the three German corps into a knock-down fight, which so wore down Model that, on July 9, he reported to Kluge he doubted the feasibility of a breakthrough to Kursk by way of Olkhovatka. Kluge responded by ordering Hoth northward, west of the Donets River, with two of his panzer corps, while Kempf attacked east of the river. Hoth's objective was Oboyan, about halfway to Kursk and well within the Russians' final trench line.

Hoth advanced steadily, crossing the last trench line on July 12. But, at Prokhorovka, twenty-two miles southeast of Oboyan, he came up against the Fifth Guards Tank Army, one of the units the Soviets had held in reserve. The centerpiece of the Battle of Kursk now exploded: a tank battle the likes of which had never before been seen. Twelve hundred tanks—eight hundred Soviet and four hundred German—dueled across the vast steppe.

The II SS Panzer Corps performed with tactical brilliance, delivering, though outnumbered, significantly more devastation than it absorbed. Yet, strategically, the Battle of Kursk was a Soviet victory because Kluge was forced to appropriate two panzer divisions from Model in order to stop a Soviet attack against the rear of the Ninth German Army. This reduced the forces available for Operation Citadel. As fortune would have it, it was precisely at this point that the Anglo-American allies commenced Operation Husky, the invasion of Sicily (see "Operation Husky" in Chapter 13). In a panic, Hitler aborted Operation Citadel on July 13, and the Battle of Kursk ground on until July 20. He needed troops to send to Italy.

As in a titanic tug of war, when the other side looses its grip, even for a moment, it is time to pull all the harder. The Red Army did just that, and, after the Battle of Kursk, the German invaders were compelled to assume the defensive on its Eastern Front.

SLIPPING AWAY

The loss of Orel, August 5, 1943, initiated General Model's long retreat from the Soviet Front. Here, German tankers leap from their vehicle to return fire against Soviet infantry south of Orel.

Even in panic, Hitler wanted to achieve at least the appearance of a victory against the Red Army. As the Germans shifted from the offensive of the short-lived Operation Citadel to a fighting withdrawal, Hitler ordered Manstein to maintain an offensive posture so that he might be able to claim some positive progress. But the Führer soon abandoned this charade, which was eating away at his army, and ordered all SS panzer divisions out of the front.

In the meantime, Model fought a very effective defense with Army Group Center, taking a heavy toll on the Red Army. Then, on July 25, panic seized Hitler yet again. He learned that Benito Mussolini had been deposed, and he immediately sent a message to Model: Twenty-four of his divisions would have to be sent to Italy. There was nothing left for Army Group Center now but to withdraw in as orderly a fashion as possible. As Model relinquished one town after another, beginning with Orel on August 5, the German myth of absolute invincibility crumbled.

Soviet Strategy

The Soviets had now to decide just how to exploit the German withdrawal. A retreating army is like a wounded animal, simultaneously vulnerable and dangerous. It is far harder to fight a rearguard action than it is to fight while advancing; therefore, it behooves the enemy of the retreating force to pursue and attack mercilessly. On the other hand, if the pursuing force yields to temptation and overextends itself, the retreating force might suddenly wheel about and strike—with deadly consequences.

Zhukhov and Vasilevsky wanted to encircle the Germans at various points. Stalin, however, observed that, after Stalingrad, not a single Soviet attempt at encirclement had succeeded. He therefore ordered his marshal to make a broad frontal attack rather than attempt a series of encirclements. Stalin knew he had more men and more machines than Hitler. He intended to use them as the stuff of main force, delivering what he called "cleaving blows" to both drive

POP CULTURE

The Devil You Know

In Britain and the United States, public figures and government officials did their best to portray the Soviets—implacable enemies of democratic capitalism—as gallant allies. Rehabilitating the Soviet popular image was a major propaganda challenge, but Winston Churchill underscored the importance of generating positive public opinion of Stalin by remarking in Parliament, on June 21, 1941, "If Hitler invaded Hell, I would at least make a favourable reference to the Devil in the House of Commons."

the invader back even as he chopped its armies down to size. This would be a costly strategy, but Stalin believed that a soldier's function was to fight and to die. In accordance with the new strategy, by the end of August, eight Soviet fronts were deployed along a line nearly seven hundred miles long to make parallel, coordinated thrusts toward the Dnieper River in the Ukraine. Hitler, who had repeatedly denied permission to his commanders for withdrawal, approved on September 8 what he thought of as a tactical retreat behind the Dnieper. However, the Red Army outmaneuvered German Army Group South and, by December 1943, its First Ukrainian front acquired and held a massive bridgehead at the Dnieper around Kiev while the Second Ukrainian front held a bridgehead on that river taking in the towns of Cherkassy, Kremenchug, and Dnepropetrovsk. The Germans were stalled, and one entire German army, the Seventeenth, was entirely cut off in the Crimea.

January 1944

By the start of 1944, the Red Army had regained more than half the territory yielded to the Germans during the opening months of Operation Barbarossa. Hitler had already decided that, with Anglo-American landings now imminent in the West, the East would have to be sacrificed—at least to a degree. Looking at a map, Hitler could see that he could afford to lose much more of the Eastern Front than he could of the Western Front before Berlin and other centers of powers became threatened. The Eastern Front, therefore, would have to fend for itself. No more reinforcements would be sent—at least not until the Anglo-American threat had been disposed of.

For their part, Stalin and Soviet high command drew up plans to sweep their nation free of invaders with simultaneous operations in the north, the center, and the south. At the very least, the objective was to reclaim the Soviet Union as far as the boundaries as they had existed before 1939. Although the offensive would be general, the principal effort would be focused on the south, where four Ukrainian fronts vastly outnumbered the German forces in the region. But it was up north that the offensive began, when, on January 14, 1944, the Leningrad, Volkhov, and Second Baltic fronts attacked the besieging forces surrounding and to the south of Leningrad. By this stage of the war, there was little point in Germany's trying to hold on to the Soviet Union's great second city. Field Marshal Georg von Kuchler, now commanding German Army Group North, which had been reduced to two greatly depleted armies, decided that he would withdraw from Leningrad. Distracted by threats from the West, Hitler at first agreed, only to change his mind and refuse Kuchler permission to pull back. It hardly mattered. Leningrad was no longer effectively blockaded, and on January 27, 1944, when the Volkhov front crossed the Moscow-Leningrad railway, Stalin proclaimed that Leningrad had been liberated. On January 31, what remained of Kuchler's line broke in four places. Outraged, Hitler relieved Kuchler and replaced him with Model, who, within a month, retreated to precisely the position Kuchler had wanted to assume.

A siege can be terrible for those who lay the siege as well as for those who are besieged. After the collapse of the German siege of Leningrad, the Red Army rounded up thousands of prisoners, many of whom were marched through the newly liberated city.

Disappointment

Despite the dire straits in which the invaders now found themselves, the Red Army had difficulty exploiting its advantages. The offensive planned in the center never got off the ground, and bad weather impeded the southern—Ukrainian—offensives as well. In view of these nonstarters, Zhukov persuaded Stalin to allow what he had previously outlawed: an encirclement. This would require far less movement than a frontal attack across a broad front, and there were six German divisions—about fifty-six thousand troops—stalled in the February mud and snow along thirty-seven miles of the Dnieper River, precisely between Soviet bridgeheads. The prey was in the trap. All that was required was for the jaws to clamp shut.

Generals Ivan Konev and Nikolai Vatutin labored through snow, rain, and gelatinous mud to shut those jaws. By February 3, they had surrounded the German divisions with two concentric rings, but thirty thousand German troops suddenly burst through both lines on February 17. Yet another Red Army encirclement had failed—although this did not prevent Stalin from simply declaring the operation a Soviet victory. That was not so much a lie as it was a half truth—or half lie—for it certainly had been no German victory.

NUMBERS

Reduction in Force

As of May 1944, German forces in the East had been reduced through battle deaths and transfers to Italy from 3.07 to 2.2 million men.

"We must not replace crushing strikes against the enemy with pinpricks. . . . It is necessary to prepare an operation which will be like an earthquake."

Marshal Georgi Zhukov, May 12, 1944

Spring and Summer Offensives

Beginning in March, the Fourth Ukrainian front began organizing a thrust into the Crimea, and the First and Second Ukrainian fronts commenced a major spring offensive on March 5. Marshal Zhukov took the place of Vatutin, who had been severely wounded at the end of February. Zhukov now advanced in parallel formation with Konev's forces, the infantry spearheaded by tanks. In the face of the Soviet advance, Kleist withdrew the German Sixth Army, lest it be cut off between the Bug and Dniester rivers. Shortly after this, Manstein ordered the First Panzer Army to break through Zhukov's encircling line in order to withdraw. Hitler responded by decorating both Kleist and Manstein, then promptly replaced them. Field Marshal Ferdinand Schörner took over Army Group A from Kleist, and Field Marshal Walther Model Army Group South from Manstein. Hitler acknowledged that Kleist and Manstein were superior tacticians, but he believed that Model and Schörner would be more ruthless, willing to stand against the Soviets to the very last man. In the end, the replacements did a creditable job of slowing the Soviet offensives, which, by the end of spring, stopped—at least for the moment—560 miles east of Berlin.

By the end of spring 1944, the German high command came to believe that Stalin planned to make his next main thrust through southern Ukraine, with an eye toward acquiring territory in southeastern Europe. In fact, Zhukov formulated and Stalin approved Operation Bagration, a major offensive against German Army Group Center, in which 2.4 million troops, fifty-two hundred tanks, and fifty-three hundred aircraft would advance west along a line between the Dvina River and the Carpathian Mountains. Opposing them were the seven hundred thousand troops of Army Group Center, now under the command of Field Marshal Ernst Busch.

The Stalingrad Sixty-second Army marches through the streets of Odessa, from which the German invaders have withdrawn.

A commander slavishly devoted to Adolf Hitler and his doctrine of standing to the last man, Busch heavily garrisoned the towns of Vitebsk, Orsha, Mogilev, and Bobruysk, grandiosely dubbing them "fortresses" and ordering resistance "to the last man." Yet when Operation Bagration commenced on June

23, Busch rapidly lost ground. Outside of the so-called fortresses, his defenses crumbled, leaving those garrisoned towns totally cut off. It was an unmitigated disaster. The Third Panzer Army simply abandoned five of its divisions in Vitebsk. The German Fourth and Ninth Armies floundered in the marsh country along the Berezina River. Busch sent a message to Hitler, proposing to set up a new defensive line north and south of Minsk, but even Hitler recognized that good intentions born of Busch's loyalty were insufficient to stop the summer offensive. Hitler needed a leader of greater skill and, on June 28, sent Model to replace Busch as commander of Army Group Center. But there was little Model could do as Operation Bagration ended, just east of Minsk, on July 5.

Now the Red Army forces commenced the next phase of the summer offensive. The First Belorussian front turned toward Warsaw, Poland, and the Second and Third Belorussian fronts targeted East Prussia and Lithuania. Simultaneously, the First Ukrainian front attacked Lvov, Ukraine, on July 13, driving toward the Vistula River. Hoping to save as much of the remainder of Army Group Center as possible, Model withdrew, consolidating his forces as he went. By the middle of August, Model had managed to reform a front line on the Vistula River just east of the East Prussian border—the German homeland.

NUMBERS

German Losses

Overwhelmed by the Red Army's Operation Bagration, German Army Group Center's Fourth Army lost a staggering 130,000 out of 165,000 troops. First Panzer losses were comparable, whereas the Ninth Army had simply dissolved. Red Army losses were 60,000 killed or missing in action, and 110,000 wounded or sick.

A Land Cleansed

At the height of summer 1944, the First Belorussian and First Ukrainian fronts of the Red Army held bridgeheads on the Vistula, facing the remnants of German Army Group Center. In the meantime, to the north, on July 18, the Red Army's three Baltic fronts attacked Army Group North, pushing the Germans out of Soviet territory and through Estonia and eastern Latvia. The army group took refuge on Latvia's Courland Peninsula. As for Finland—which had been allied with Nazi Germany in the hope of wrenching forever free from Soviet domination—it signed an armistice with the Soviet Union on September 2, 1944, taking itself out of the war.

"Strategy is the determination of the direction of the main blow—the plan of strategy is the plan of the organization of the decisive blow in the direction in which the blow can most quickly give the maximum results."

Joseph Stalin, date unknown

In the south, on August 10, 1944, the Second and Third Ukrainian fronts massed along the Romanian border to launch what Stalin called operations to "liberate" southeastern Europe. The offensive here was not strictly necessary to achieve victory over the German invaders,

Nazi-allied Bulgaria made a separate peace with the Soviets on September 9, 1944. The man in the photograph cheers the Soviet victory during a celebration in Lovech. The signs read "Death to Fascism" and "Long Live the Leader."

but, Stalin knew, it would give Soviet forces a foothold in this part of Europe that would endure long after the war was over.

Romania offered no resistance, but surrendered to the Soviets on August 23. Bulgaria, allied with Germany but having never declared war on the Soviet Union, attempted to make an outright military alliance with the Soviets and conclude an armistice with the British and Americans, against which it had earlier declared war. Unwilling to break solidarity with his Western allies, Stalin shocked the Bulgarians by declaring war on them on September 5, diverting his Third Ukrainian front into that country on September 8. The Bulgarian government asked for an armistice on September 9, and a Communist government was immediately installed.

The detour into Bulgaria, combined with delays in getting the Fourth Ukrainian front across the Carpathians into Slovakia and a Nazi-instigated coup d'etat in Hungary (which prevented Hungary from surrendering), bought time for German Army Group South to withdraw into Hungary. These troops linked up with other German forces in the Balkans and Greece. Stalin, however, did not focus on these forces, but instead, during November 1944, concentrated on taking Budapest, the Hungarian capital. For the Red Army, this was less a strategic than a political objective, the taking of which would provide tremendous international prestige.

STALIN TRIUMPHANT

BY THE END OF 1944, the German invaders had been swept from Soviet territory, and the Red Army was driving deep into Eastern Europe, even as the Western Allies were continuing to close in from the south, through Italy, and—far more important—from the west, through France (see Chapter 21). At this point, Stalin moved to focus the final Soviet triumph on himself. Having used his best marshals—especially Zhukov—to achieve victory, he informed his top commanders in November 1944 that he, as supreme commander in chief, would from now on work directly with the general staff in creating and coordinating all plans. Henceforth, it would be his war—and his victory.

REALITY CHECK
Liberating Lie

Stalin was an even greater master of the "big lie" than Hitler was. To "liberate" southeastern Europe was actually to conquer it. Stalin sought to acquire a broad buffer zone in Eastern Europe, making political satellites out of the nations to Russia's west so that no enemy would ever be able to invade his nation again.

Stalin's plan for achieving final victory in World War II was starkly simple. Within forty-five days from the beginning of 1945, he would end the war by advancing from the Vistula—which runs from Danzig, Poland, in the north, through Warsaw and Kraców in the south—to the Oder River, which runs through Germany itself. This was projected as a fifteen-day operation. From the Oder, in the course of thirty days, he would advance to the Elbe, which runs from Hamburg in the north, through Dessau, Dresden, and Prague. This would be the farthest extent of the Soviet advance into Europe. The Western allies would link up with the Soviets here. The plan called for the First Belorussian and First Ukrainian fronts—2.2 million troops—to crush German Army Group A, which had about four hundred thousand men left. The Second and Third Belorussian fronts, representing a total of 1.6 million troops, would roll over Army Group Center to capture East Prussia and clear the Baltic shoreline.

The "Big Three"—Winston Churchill, Franklin D. Roosevelt, and Joseph Stalin—at the Soviet Black Sea resort of Yalta, February 1945.

On January 12, 1945, the Red Army launched the greatest single offensive of the war. No fewer than twenty-four parallel advances were begun against German forces. By February 3, the armies of Zhukov and Konev had reached the Oder along a line that stretched from Küstrin, just thirty-five miles east of Berlin, to the border of Czechoslovakia. The advance had taken about a week longer than planned—not because of German resistance, but because an unexpected January thaw had churned roads and fields to mud, slowing tanks and other vehicles.

REALITY CHECK

Ruthless Tactic

Stalin's apparent strategy after the Yalta Conference reveals just how ruthless he was. Although the reason for the sudden slowdown in the Soviet offensive has never been understood definitively, it is likely that Stalin saw a delay in victory as advantageous. First, he probably wanted to delay Soviet entry into the war with Japan—promised at Yalta sometime *after* victory in Europe. Second, he likely felt that the more devastation Eastern Europe suffered, the better, because a truly desolate Eastern Europe would make more fertile ground for Communist conquest.

Yalta

In February, the "Big Three"—British prime minister Winston Churchill, U.S. president Franklin D. Roosevelt, and Soviet premier Joseph Stalin—met at the Soviet Black Sea resort of Yalta to plan the conclusion of the war. For Roosevelt and Churchill, the main objective was to bring the Soviet Union into the war against Japan—something Stalin had resisted. For Stalin, the main objective was to secure Anglo-American agreement that Berlin was to be a Soviet objective. In the end, Stalin agreed to declare war against Japan "two or three months" after the surrender of Germany, and Churchill and Roosevelt agreed

The Red Army enters Vienna, early in April 1945.

that the conquest of Berlin would be left to the Red Army.

Stalin was an inscrutable leader, and for reasons that are not entirely clear, he seems deliberately to have slowed his offensive after the Yalta Conference, allowing it to become a more-or-less diffuse series of skirmishes rather than decisive battles as his forces inexorably continued their advance.

TOWARD BERLIN

BY LETTING UP ON HIS ADVANCE, Stalin gave Hitler an opportunity to stage a counteroffensive. Called Operation Awakening of Spring, it was staged in Hungary chiefly by the Sixth SS Panzer Army. For ten days, the Germans and Soviets clashed, until the Germans withdrew to take a stand—again, on orders of Hitler—at Vienna. From April 7 to April 13, the Germans and the Red Army forces fought on the outskirts of the Austrian capital. It was a pointless show of resistance on Hitler's part, and on April 13, the Germans withdrew.

In the end, it was developments on the Western Front—the speed with which Anglo-American forces advanced through Germany—and not anything Hitler did, that spurred Stalin to recommence his offensive in full earnest. Delaying victory may have had a political advantage for Stalin, but not if that meant that the Western democracies would occupy and control more Eastern territory.

With one British and five American armies already east of the Rhine by the end of March, Stalin suddenly rushed the First and Second Belorussian fronts into a position from which Zhukov could launch a frontal attack to Berlin—and beyond—while Konstantin Rokossovsky and Ivan Konev advanced to the Elbe River on Zhukov's flanks. Stalin made the mistake of thinking that Hitler's defeated army was a beaten army. In fact, the resistance the German forces were able to muster as the Red Army closed on Berlin was fierce beyond all expectation, as will be seen in Chapter 21. Anywhere from 78,000 to 305,000—estimates vary wildly—Red Army soldiers would fall in the contest for the capital of the Third Reich. By that time, however, such numbers hardly mattered to Joseph Stalin. For he already held in his fist the very heart of his enemy.

TAKEAWAY

Rise of the Red Army

The Battle of Stalingrad arrested the German advance through the Soviet Union, and the Battle of Kursk put the Germans on the run, transforming what had been a desperate Red Army defense into a massive Red Army counteroffensive that drove the invaders out of the Soviet Union, through Eastern Europe, and back into Germany—with the Red Army in pursuit.

CHAPTER 20

D-Day

The Liberation of Europe Begins

By the spring of 1944, the Western allies, chiefly the United States and Britain, had been fighting a ground war against the Axis in North Africa, Sicily, Italy, and elsewhere in the Mediterranean region. It was a full-scale war and had already resulted in the liberation of North Africa and the surrender of Fascist Italy, although the fighting on the Italian mainland continued at high cost. Yet there was a feeling, especially among the American commanders, that all of this was a mere prelude to what was planned as the principal Allied offensive of the European war: a massive invasion, from England, across the English Channel, to France—the storming of what Adolf Hitler called "Festung Europa"—Fortress Europe.

The Strategic Air War

Although major ground operations against Fortress Europe, through France, would not begin until D-Day, June 6, 1944, British and then British and American air forces began bombing France and Germany—as well as Italy and other Axis-held nations—much earlier in the war. Indeed, among Allied proponents of air power, there was much talk that the war in Europe could be won chiefly in the air, with less reliance on a ground invasion. This was a controversial position, but in the days before an Anglo-American ground

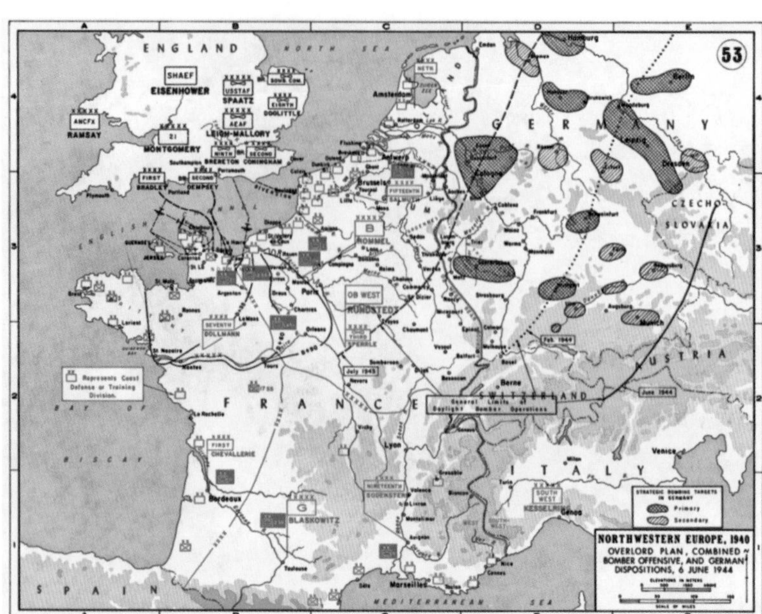

On June 6, 1944, the Western Allies staged the greatest amphibious assault in military history: the cross-Channel invasion of Nazi-held France from England, popularly known as D-Day. After establishing lodgments in Normandy, the invading forces broke out to liberate France and then the rest of Europe.

invasion was feasible, the only way the Allies could bring the war to Germany and its captive European territories was from the air.

The doctrine air-power proponents pushed was called strategic bombing. In contrast to tactical bombing, which the Germans had employed as part of blitzkrieg—bombing of military objectives in direct support of troops on the ground—strategic bombing focused on more than military targets. It was an aspect of "total war," war directed not just against soldiers, but against civilians, including cities, factories, and large military installations. In essence, strategic bombing was economic warfare, directed primarily against war production and other industrial and transportation enterprises. Strategic bombing was intended to disrupt the enemy's very civilization, thereby making it impossible for him to continue to conduct war.

Strategic bombing was not an entirely new concept. During World War I, there had been some experiments in the long-range bombing of strategic targets, including London and Paris, but it was not until World War II that the aircraft and explosives technologies existed to make strategic bombing possible on a large scale.

The pacifism that prevailed in Britain and the United States after World War I created much resistance to the building of large air

REALITY CHECK

Strategic Bombing and the Blitz

During the Battle of Britain and the Blitz (see Chapter 5), Adolf Hitler routinely bombed civilian targets, but his Luftwaffe lacked the long-range, heavy bombers to conduct a full-scale program of strategic bombing. Hitler targeted civilian objectives mainly as a means of inflicting terror, which he hoped would break the will of his enemies to continue fighting.

forces. Nevertheless, during the 1930s, advocates of strategic bombing persuaded the British and the U.S. governments to fund the design and construction of heavy four-engine bombers (such as the British Wellington, Whitley, and Hampden bombers and the American B-17, B-24, and B-29), which were necessary for carrying out long-range strategic bombing missions with heavy bomb loads. In Germany, which was anything but pacifist between the wars, advocates of strategic bombing failed to persuade Hitler, who believed that fighters, fighter-bombers, and medium bombers—all tactical rather than strategic aircraft—would be the war-winning planes. This focus left Germany largely unequipped for strategic bombing, a fact that certainly contributed to Germany's ultimate defeat.

Although equipped for strategic bombing, the British Royal Air Force (RAF), fearful of provoking Germany, avoided it early in the war. The fall of France and the Battle of Britain that followed, however, made strategic bombing Britain's only option for striking back at Germany. The RAF conducted strategic bombing raids at night, which provided a measure of cover for the large, lumbering aircraft. Few German fighter planes were equipped to intercept bombers at night, and ground-based antiaircraft fire was certainly less effective in the dark. The disadvantage of night bombing, of course, was that targets were rendered more or less invisible, especially if the enemy implemented blackouts of its cities and factories. This made precision bombing—the targeting of very specific objectives—all but impossible. The British therefore resorted to what they called carpet-bombing, Instead of targeting particular industrial plants or transportation hubs, an entire urban area was selected for attack in the hope that important industrial and war-production facilities would be hit. Carpet-bombing created many civilian casualties and did not guarantee the destruction of targets with high strategic value.

When the U.S. Eighth Army Air Force arrived in England at the end of 1942, American air planners decided to risk precision bombing in daylight and staged the first American raid against Germany on January 27, 1943. From this point on, the Allied strategic bombing campaign was a twenty-four-hour program, the Americans bombing carefully chosen targets by day, the British carpet bombing cities by night.

DETAILS, DETAILS

The Term D-Day

The momentous Normandy invasion was called by the press and the public "D-Day" and is remembered by this name today. Officially, however, it was Operation Overlord, and, in military historical terms it is best described as the "Normandy invasion." There is nothing unique about the term *D-day*, which is a generic military operational label to designate the day on which a particular operation—any major operation—is launched. (*D* is derived from the word *day*). The day before D-day is D-day minus one (or D – 1), two days before is D-day minus two, the day after is D-day plus one, and so on. The precise hour of the launch of an operation is designated *H-hour*.

"Victory, speedy and complete, awaits the side that employs air power as it should be employed."

Sir Arthur "Bomber" Harris, marshal of the Royal Air Force and a chief Allied advocate of strategic bombing

Long before a single American soldier set foot in Europe, the U.S. Army Air Forces conducted massive strategic air raids against occupied Europe and Germany proper. At first, the objectives were largely industrial—this B-17 has just dropped its ordnance on a Focke-Wulf aircraft factory at Marienburg—but soon every major German city became a target.

British and American bombers staged raids whenever weather permitted, both before and after D-Day. The major raids included a British attack on Cologne, which destroyed most of the center of this historic German city during the night of May 30/31, 1942. Forty-one bombers were lost. On July 24, 1943, a combined Anglo-American raid using incendiary bombs set off a firestorm that devastated Hamburg, killing about fifty thousand civilians. On August 1 of the same year, the U.S. Eighth and Ninth Army Air Forces staged a major raid against the oil refineries of Ploesti, Romania. The Ploesti Raid was extremely costly—fifty American bombers were lost—and although it badly damaged the refineries, they were quickly repaired. Less than three weeks later, on August 17, American bombers targeted Schweinfurt, Germany, and its ball-bearing plants. American planners reasoned that since everything that moves uses ball bearings, destroying these production facilities would cripple all aspects of German war production. At the same time, the aircraft factories at Regensburg were also targeted. Both the Schweinfurt and Regensburg plants were badly damaged, but they soon recovered. Sixty bombers were downed, and 122 badly damaged. On the same day that the Americans attacked Schweinfurt and Regensburg, the British raided Peenemünde, the principal site of German V-2 rocket production and development. The raid temporarily disrupted V-2 operations, but cost the RAF sixty-nine heavy bombers.

On October 14, 1943, the U.S. Eighth Army Air Force made a second raid on Schweinfurt, losing sixty bombers and incurring damage to 138 others. The mission was highly successful in that the ball-bearing plants were destroyed. Yet they were soon rebuilt, from the ground up.

Between November 18, 1943, and March 31, 1944, the RAF raided Berlin thirty-five times, each time using more than five hundred aircraft. Although the city was extensively damaged, the British lost 1,047 bombers during the campaign. The U.S. Army Air Forces conducted their own major offensive during February 20–26, 1944, dubbed "Big Week." By targeting a number of German aircraft

REALITY CHECK

A Necessary Evil

Doubtless, most Britons felt few pangs of conscience about the carpet-bombing of German cities and were even anxious to avenge the Blitz. Prime Minister Winston Churchill was an exception. Aggressive though he was, he found carpet-bombing highly distasteful, even immoral, yet even he resigned himself to its necessity.

Except for the dropping of the atomic bombs on Hiroshima and Nagasaki, the Allied incendiary bombing of Dresden, Germany, February 13–15, 1945, was the most controversial exercise of strategic air power in World War II. The devastation of this medieval German city, caught up in a firestorm created by the intense bombing, was total. The Dresden Raid was widely criticized as a needless waste of life motivated by naked vengeance.

factories, the Eighth, Ninth, and Fifteenth Army Air Forces wiped out nearly half of Germany's fighter production capacity. U.S. losses were 226 bombers. On March 11, 1944, the RAF hit oil and railroad facilities at Essen, Germany, causing a great deal of damage without incurring heavy losses.

On the night of February 13/14, 1945, American and British bombers attacked the medieval city of Dresden using incendiaries. These created a catastrophic three-day firestorm with temperatures reaching over 2,730°F, which killed an estimated 135,000 German civilians. Allied losses were just six bombers.

REALITY CHECK

Firestorm

Both in Europe and in Japan, the Allies implemented highly destructive incendiary bombing techniques. Typically, an incendiary raid began with the use of conventional high-explosive bombs, which created rubble that was far more combustible than intact buildings. After the high explosives were dropped, a second wave of bombers dropped incendiaries, bombs specifically designed to start fires. If they were used in sufficient numbers, the incendiaries set off overwhelming blazes so massive that their intense heat created its own local weather system in the form of very high winds. The winds, in turn, superheated the fires, creating firestorms of unparalleled destructiveness.

Overlord

At the Casablanca Conference, which took place between President Roosevelt and Prime Minister Churchill in that Moroccan city from January 14–24, 1943, a staff was authorized to plan an invasion of France from England, across the English Channel. The planning staff was called COSSAC, an acronym for "Chief of Staff to the Supreme Allied Commander." In addition, the Casablanca Conference called for a build-up of American troops in Great Britain for use in the invasion. The transportation, organization, and training of this force in England was code-named Operation Bolero.

COSSAC's first task was to decide on the best landing area for the invasion, in the Low Countries or in France. The area chosen had to be within the range of Allied fighters, had to be reasonably vulnerable (that is, offering defenses that could feasibly be overcome), and had to be accessible to a logistical arrangement that would allow for the build-up of landing troops at such a rapid rate that the build-up would overwhelm the Germans' ability to

In a conference at Casablanca, Morocco, January 14–24, 1943, Franklin D. Roosevelt and Winston Churchill, with their top military advisers, laid out strategy and policy for the joint conduct of the war, resolving, among other things, to accept no outcome other than the unconditional surrender of Germany, Italy, Japan, and the nations allied with them.

move in defenders. Of these three requirements, COSSAC determined that the most important considerations were proximity to a major port and the ability to supply troops for at least ninety days while the port was being captured and then repaired. Next came proximity to an inland road network. The worst thing that can happen to a large landing force is to be caught between the sea and a roadless interior. After careful analysis, COSSAC decided that the Baie de la Seine, off the coast of Normandy between Le Havre and the Cherbourg Peninsula, was the most promising landing place. Cherbourg was a major port, and, until that port was captured, supplies could be landed by means of artificial harbors called "Mulberries" while fuel would be pumped all the way across the English Channel through a rapidly laid pipeline system called "Pluto," for "Pipe Line Under the Ocean." It was true that landing here, in Normandy, required a longer trip across the treacherous English Channel than crossing to the north, at the narrow Pas de Calais. It was also the case that the Pas de Calais offered a more direct route from the Channel into Germany itself. Indeed, in many ways, the Pas de Calais, and not Normandy, was the obvious place for a landing. Yet because it was so obvious, COSSAC rejected it. Of all places, the Germans would expect a landing here—and they would therefore defend most heavily against it, leaving other places, including the Norman coast, less well provided for.

"Remember that this is an invasion, not the creation of a fortified beach head."

Sir Winston Churchill, April 7, 1944, addressing a planning session for Operation Overlord

COSSAC presented its initial plan at the Allies' Quebec Conference in August 1943. Winston Churchill, keenly mindful of the disastrous raid on Dieppe, insisted on a larger assault force than COSSAC originally recommended. After much consideration, the initial force was expanded from three to eight divisions, including three airborne (paratroop and glider) assault divisions.

Early in 1944, SHAEF—Supreme Headquarters Allied Expeditionary Force—was created under General Dwight D. Eisenhower, who was named supreme Allied commander, Europe. Eisenhower appointed British general Bernard Law Montgomery commander in chief of the invasion's ground troops, British air marshal Trafford Leigh-Mallory to serve as commander in chief of the Allied air forces, and another Briton, Sir Bertram Ramsay, to command the naval component of the invasion.

Operation Neptune, the landing phase of Operation Overlord (code name for the entire invasion plan), originally called for the landings at Normandy to be simultaneously coordinated with Operation Anvil, landings to the south, along the French Riviera. A chronic shortage of landing craft prevented this, however, and Anvil (later renamed Operation Dragoon) had to be delayed more than a month, until after Neptune had been completed and Overlord was well on its way.

Operation Neptune required extremely careful timing. Operating under cover of darkness would offer the obvious advantage of reducing the enemy's ability to see and defend against the landing force, but so many ships and aircraft would be operating so close to one another that, to prevent catastrophic accidents, it was decided to make the landings after sunup. Another key timing consideration was the state of the tides. It was determined that the landings would have to be accomplished no more than about one hour after low tide, which would expose the many obstacles—including explosive mines—with which the Germans had sown the Norman coast. Once visible, these obstacles and mines would be accessible to Allied engineers. Finally, the plan called for paratroop and glider units to be dropped just before the landings. These advance troops would mark landing areas and, most important, knock out various German artillery batteries. The U.S. 101st and 82nd Airborne divisions were also tasked with capturing exits into the Cotentin Peninsula, to prevent German maneuvering there. The British 6th Airborne was assigned to capture bridges over the Orne River and the Caen Canal, which would be vital to the protection of the invasion's left flank. The light of a full moon was required to make the jumps. Taken together, along with considerations of when the force would be

NUMBERS

Hazardous Mission

During the early months of the U.S. strategic bombing campaign, Allied fighter aircraft lacked the fuel capacity—and, therefore, the range—to escort bombers all the way to their targets and back. This left the bombers especially vulnerable to German fighters. Later, the development of such long-range aircraft as the P-51 Mustang—perhaps the finest fighter of World War II—and the acquisition of forward air bases in Europe, meant that bombers could be escorted to and from targets even deep inside Germany. Nevertheless, casualties among Allied airmen were terrifically high. Each U.S. airman was committed to fly no more than twenty-five bombing missions, after which he was to be sent home. Statistically, however, an airman could not expect to survive more than fifteen missions. Of 3.4 million USAAF personnel in all theaters, 54,700 were killed in action and 17,900 wounded. The overwhelming proportion of these casualties were among air crews.

MULBERRIES

The "Mulberries," code name for two innovative artificial harbors constructed specifically for use in the Normandy landings, were remarkable technological achievements. They were intended as a means of continuously supplying troops during a massive invasion before permanent harbor facilities became available.

As early as May 1942, Prime Minister Winston Churchill had ordered Louis Mountbatten, chief of Combined Operations Headquarters, to conduct research into floating piers (called "whales") with adjustable legs (code-named "spuds"). The spuds were protected by hollow concrete caissons (called "phoenixes"). This entire bizarrely named assembly was christened the "Mulberry."

Two Mulberry assemblies were entirely prefabricated in England for transportation and emplacement at Normandy. Each had 213 spuds, and some of their phoenixes were two hundred feet long and sixty feet high. To ensure against damage in severe weather, 200-foot-long floating tanks (called "bombardons") were built to provide secure anchorages along the piers, or whales.

The prefabricated components of the Mulberries consisted of four hundred separate units weighing, in total, 1.5 million tons. These pieces were towed to England's south coast, where they were temporarily submerged to prevent their being spotted by German aerial reconnaissance. Before the Mulberries could be placed, five smaller floating harbors—dubbed "gooseberries"—were formed from seventy-four blockships ("corncobs") to shelter the multitude of small craft used in the early phases of the landing operations while the phoenixes were being readied. As soon as the landings had been accomplished, the Mulberry components were towed across the English Channel and, in a spectacular marine engineering operation that employed ten thousand men and 132 tugboats, they were assembled. Once the Mulberries were in place, two of the gooseberries were integrated into them, and the rest provided boat shelters closer to shore.

U.S. Army vehicles drive ashore along the floating causeway of "Mulberry A," one of the remarkable artificial harbor facilities instantly built to feed the liberation of Europe. This scene was photographed on June 16, 1944, a mere ten days after D-Day.

The Mulberries, one at St. Laurent (to accommodate the Americans) and the other at Arromanches (for the British and Canadians), were nearly ready when, on June 19, a storm damaged the St. Laurent Mulberry so badly that it had to be abandoned. From that point on, the single Arromanches Mulberry accommodated all supplies: eleven thousand tons per day.

trained and assembled, a very narrow window of June 5–7, 1944, was open. During this brief period, the proper combination of tides and lunar phase would be available.

REALITY CHECK

Lack of Landing Craft

The Allies had no shortage of manpower, but the stumbling block to the expansion of the cross-Channel invasion was a shortage of landing craft. Although these were produced in vast quantities during the war, there were never enough.

A Vast Deception

By May 1944, the Allies had assembled forty-seven divisions—some eight hundred thousand combat troops—at various embarkation points in Britain. Preparatory to the landings, between April 1 and June 5, 1944, more than eleven thousand Allied aircraft flew some two hundred thousand sorties to drop 195,000 tons of bombs on French rail and road networks, airfields, and other military facilities, including factories and coastal batteries and radar outposts. The purpose was to weaken what Hitler called the Atlantic Wall, the perimeter of Fortress Europe. These missions were very costly—nearly two thousand Allied aircraft were downed—but they were necessary to reduce the mobility of the German defenders and to knock as many German aircraft out of the skies as possible. Operation Overlord made extensive use of intelligence supplied by the French Resistance, which also committed many acts of sabotage, especially against railroad lines. As important as gathering intelligence was the creation of disinformation to deceive the Germans into believing that the invasion would land at the Pas de Calais. The Allies employed a network of double agents who sent false reports to Germany. They also fabricated radio traffic as if among a vast invasion army gathered just opposite the Pas de Calais. Newspapers carried stories of a large army being organized under General George S. Patton Jr., whom the Germans believed was America's best general and, therefore, the man most likely to lead the invasion. Finally, all along the English coast across from the Pas de Calais, dummy camps and decoy equipment—including inflatable rubber tanks and plywood aircraft—were deployed to fool German aerial reconnaissance.

REALITY CHECK

Deadly Decoys

As part of the campaign of deception carried out in the months and weeks prior to D-Day, many Allied sorties were flown near the Pas de Calais in order to reinforce the German preconception that the invasion would land here. Because this area was already heavily defended, air attacks here were especially costly.

Airpower played a major role in D-Day operations. These A-20 ground-attack craft flew a mission against the German's coastal artillery battery at Pointe du Hoc on May 22, 1944. Tactical as well as strategic aircraft were used to disrupt German supply lines, destroy major artillery emplacements, and disrupt rail transportation—all in preparation for the invasion.

"We Must Give the Order"

In the days leading up to the date chosen for the landings, D-Day, set for June 5, all eyes were on the notoriously fickle Channel weather. On the night before the landings were to be launched, a storm blew up, forcing Eisenhower to delay the invasion. He knew that if he did not launch on the next day, June 6, the proper coincidence of tides and full moon would not come for another three weeks—three weeks in which the Germans might easily discover the hundreds of thousands of men gathered on the English shore, three weeks in which the invading force could lose both the element of surprise and its warrior edge. Eisenhower's weather officer, RAF captain J. M. Stagg, predicted a narrow window of marginally stable weather between two storm fronts on June 6. It would be a terrible gamble, sending an initial landing force of 156,000 men across the Channel during such a slim interval. But, as Ike's chief of staff, General Walter Bedell Smith, later recalled, Eisenhower "looked up, and the tension was gone from his face." The supreme Allied commander cast his eyes over his subordinate commanders.

"The question is," he said to them, "just how long can you hang this operation on the end of a limb and let it hang there?"

When no one replied, Ike continued: "I am quite positive we must give the order. I don't like it but there it is. . . . I don't see how we can do anything else."

This decision—one of the most momentous in the history of warfare—was made at quarter to ten on Sunday night, June 4, 1944.

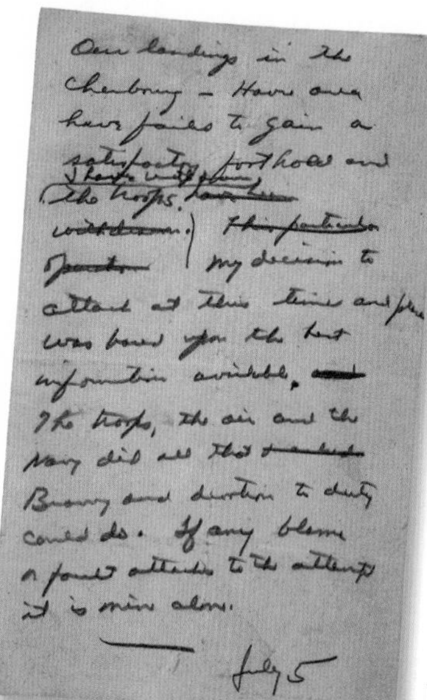

Our landings in the Cherbourg – Havre area have failed to gain a satisfactory foothold and the troops. My decision to attack at this time and place was based upon the best information available. The troops, the air and the Navy did all that Bravery and devotion to duty could do. If any blame or fault attaches to the attempt it is mine alone.

July 5

On June 5, 1944, the eve of D-Day, Dwight D. Eisenhower scrawled a speech he intended to broadcast if the landings failed: "If any blame or fault attaches to the attempt it is mine alone."

The Landings

The Allies had mapped out fifty miles of the Normandy coast, from Caen west to the base of the Cotentin Peninsula. They divided this landing area into five beaches, code-named, from east to west, Sword (to be assaulted by the British 3rd Division), Juno (Canadian 3rd Division), Gold (British 50th Division), Omaha (U.S. 1st Division and part of the 29th), and Utah (U.S. 4th Division). The first wave of troops—about 156,000 men—would face an "Atlantic Wall" made up of hardened fortresses and gun emplacements, plus an array of beach and sea obstacles and mines, defenses carefully planned by none other than Field Marshal Erwin Rommel. Behind this perimeter was the entire German Seventh Army, under Friedrich Dollmann, and part of Army Group B, under Rommel. Another German army, the Fifteenth, was commanded by Hans von Salmuth, but was held north of the Seine River—to defend against the anticipated invasion via the Pas de Calais. While Rommel was in command of the Atlantic Wall defenses, overall German command in the West was under the highly capable Field Marshal Karl von Rundstedt. He controlled thirty-six infantry and six panzer divisions in the coastal area.

ORDER OF THE DAY

On June 6, 1944, Eisenhower addressed a message to the "Soldiers, Sailors and Airmen of the Allied Expeditionary Force":

> You are about to embark upon the Great Crusade, toward which we have striven these many months. The eyes of the world are upon you. The hopes and prayers of liberty-loving people everywhere march with you. In company with our brave Allies and brothers-in-arms on other Fronts, you will bring about the destruction of the German war machine, the elimination of Nazi tyranny over the oppressed peoples of Europe, and security for ourselves in a free world. Your task will not be an easy one. Your enemy is well trained, well equipped and battle hardened. He will fight savagely.
>
> But this is the year 1944! Much has happened since the Nazi triumphs of 1940–41. The United Nations have inflicted upon the Germans great defeats, in open battle, man-to-man. Our air offensive has seriously reduced their strength in the air and their capacity to wage war on the ground. Our Home Fronts have given us an overwhelming superiority in weapons and munitions of war, and placed at our disposal great reserves of trained fighting men. The tide has turned! The free men of the world are marching together to Victory! I have full confidence in your courage and devotion to duty and skill in battle. We will accept nothing less than full Victory!
>
> Good luck! And let us beseech the blessing of Almighty God upon this great and noble undertaking.
>
> SIGNED: Dwight D. Eisenhower

REALITY CHECK

In Case of Failure

Dwight D. Eisenhower was celebrated for his magnetic smile, which radiated cool optimism. That optimism, however, belied his keen awareness of grim reality. On June 5, one day between announcing the go decision and the launch of the operation, Eisenhower scribbled a note for a press release to be issued in the event that the mission failed: "Our landings in the Cherbourg-Havre area have failed to gain a satisfactory foothold and I have withdrawn the troops. My decision to attack at this time and place was based upon the best information available. The troops, the air and the Navy did all that bravery and devotion to duty could do. If any blame or fault attaches to the attempt it is mine alone." He folded the note and tucked it into his wallet, discovering it again on July 11, five days after the success of the June 6 landings.

THE OFFICE OF STRATEGIC SERVICE

On the eve of U.S. entry into the war, America had no central intelligence agency. The Office of Strategic Service—the OSS—was largely the brainchild of General William "Wild Bill" Donovan, acting on FDR's request in July 1940 to appraise the state of U.S. intelligence and make recommendations for creating an efficient, centralized intelligence-gathering apparatus. During the war, the OSS mission was to collect and analyze such strategic information.

The organization had four intelligence branches: Secret Intelligence (SI), which obtained—by whatever means necessary—information about Axis and Axis-occupied countries; Counter-Intelligence (X-2), which monitored the intelligence and espionage operations of other nations, fielded double agents, and vetted the reliability of foreign nationals who offered their services to the United States; the Foreign Nationalities Branch (FN), which interviewed refugees and foreign citizens living in the United States; and Research and Analysis (R&A), the largest branch. Directed by Harvard University historian William L. Langer, R&A employed academic scholars (including many recent European refugees) to create analytical reports on economic, political, geographical, and cultural topics relevant to all theaters, as well as the Soviet Union and Latin America.

In addition to the four intelligence branches, OSS had operational branches, including Special Operations Branch (SO), which conducted subversion, including sabotage, support of resistance movements, raiding, and other guerrilla-style combat missions, and Morale Operations (MO), which waged psychological warfare, including the dissemination of rumor, disinformation, leaflets, and covert radio broadcasts to the people of the Axis.

Finally, the OSS technical service developed and fabricated advanced communications equipment and weapons and performed other services.

William J. "Wild Bill" Donovan (1883–1959) created the Office of Strategic Services (OSS), principal American intelligence and covert operations service of World War II and a precursor of the postwar CIA.

In one of the most dramatic photographs of World War II, Chief Photographer's Mate Robert F. Sargent, USN, captured the moment of landing at Omaha Beach on the Norman Coast, June 6, 1944. Each landing craft was equipped with a front-mounted drop-down ramp, which deposited men and vehicles in the surf. Note the churning chest-high water and the many obstacles that litter the beach ahead. All of this slowed men down, exposing them to withering machine-gun, rifle, and artillery fire for a span of minutes that must have seemed to all an eternity.

The Normandy landings began at dawn on June 6 and were closely covered by heavy naval bombardment and close air support. On four of the five beaches, the landings proceeded more quickly and with far fewer losses than anticipated—largely because the Germans had been effectively deceived into expecting the landings up the coast. At Omaha Beach, however, the U.S. 1st Division was met with very heavy German resistance and took severe casualties. By the evening of June 6, its hold on the beach-head was tenuous.

From June 6 through June 12, the Allied invaders linked up their five beachheads into an eighty-mile lodgment—a continuous presence of troops—with an average depth of ten miles. This was a solid presence on French soil. During this time, eight more combat divisions landed. The Allies as well as the Germans both knew that, whatever else happened, the invasion would not be cast back into the sea.

NUMBERS

Allied Losses

Allied casualties during the first twenty-four hours of Operation Overlord were 11,000, including 2,500 killed in action. As costly as this was, the number of casualties was far less than anticipated.

"Two kinds of people are staying on this beach, the dead and those who are going to die. Now let's get the hell out of here!"

Brigadier General Norman D. Cotta, leading his 29th Infantry in the breakout from heavily defended Omaha Beach, June 6, 1944

Preparing the Breakout

Yet breaking out of the coastal area and into the French interior was still a most formidable challenge. Every day, every hour that the breakout was delayed gave the Germans time to reinforce their defenses. On the left flank of the invasion forces, German panzers prevented for weeks the British Second Army from taking strategically vital Caen. On the right of the invasion, three corps of the First U.S. Army fiercely defended the perimeter from Caumont to Carentan. North of Carentan, the U.S. VII Corps attacked to the west across the base of the Cotentin Peninsula.

Only in an army dedicated to defense of democracy would the supreme Allied commander talk one-on-one with enlisted troops. Here, Dwight D. "Ike" Eisenhower visits with paratroops of the 101st Airborne Division in England just before they board the C-47s that will drop them behind enemy lines in occupied France.

The progress of the advance inland was resisted not only by German defenses but also by the countryside itself, which was comprised of bocage—woody pastureland networked with hedgerows made up of ancient low stone or earthen walls overgrown with thick, tangled hedges. They divided up the farmland, making for a charming landscape, but posing difficult obstacles for troops and, especially, tanks. Bogged down in hedgerow country, Allied armor and soldiers were easy targets.

It was June 18 before the Americans were able to turn north, and, on June 20, the 9th, 79th, and 4th Infantry divisions reached the outer defenses of Cherbourg. From June 22 to June 27, these units hammered at Cherbourg's defenses before the Germans finally yielded this major port.

While the battle for Cherbourg raged, Normandy erupted elsewhere as the Allies continually built up their lodgment in preparation for a breakout. During this period, German general Dollman brought up reinforcements. Dollman's death on June 28 threw Hitler into a panic. He replaced the slain general with SS general Paul Hausser, who took over the German Seventh Army, but then Hitler also decided to replace the brilliant Rundstedt as overall commander of the Western Front with Field Marshal Günther von Kluge, just returned from the Eastern Front.

At about this time, early in July, the First U.S. Army struck the Germans at the southern end of the landing area, finally taking the village of Lessay, which served to anchor the invasion's right flank. Saint-Lô, near the center of the American sector, fell to the First Army on July 18, though at heavy cost. While the Americans labored on the right, the British, on the left, finally took at least part of Caen (west of the Orne River) on July 8, but it was July 20 before the rest of the town fell.

Operation Neptune, the landing portion of Operation Overlord, had gone remarkably well. But the follow-up bogged down in hedgerow country, so that, by July 20, the invading forces

NUMBERS

Allied and German Losses

As of July 24, 1944 just before the launch of Operation Cobra, 122,000 Allies had been killed or wounded. German casualties, killed or wounded, were 117,000.

held slightly more than 20 percent of the area they had planned to take. General Omar N. Bradley, in command of First Army, put together Operation Cobra, designed to break the Allies out into the Norman interior.

The Allied planners of the invasion of Normandy thought of everything—except how to break through the infamous bocage, *the hedgerow country that crisscrosses this part of France. U.S. sergeant Curtis Culin of the 102nd Cavalry Reconnaissance Squadron, came up with the most effective solution: a cutter or plow improvised from salvaged German antitank beach obstacles and welded to the front of U.S. Sherman tanks.*

THE COBRA STRIKES

AS BRADLEY REFORMULATED IT, Operation Cobra was intended as nothing more than a limited attack to punch through the German defenses just west of Saint-Lô. If this succeeded, Bradley planned to make a deeper penetration using a large armored force as a follow-up on the initial advance. It would be Bradley's third attempt in a month to move out of the Contentin Peninsula.

Operation Cobra was to begin on July 24, 1944, but inclement weather forced delay by a day. Tragically, some of the bomber units scheduled to provide air support did not get word of the postponement and, launched on the 24th, rained down bombs on American infantry positions. This catastrophic instance of friendly fire was compounded the following day when even more bombs were dropped on U.S. positions because targets had been inadequately

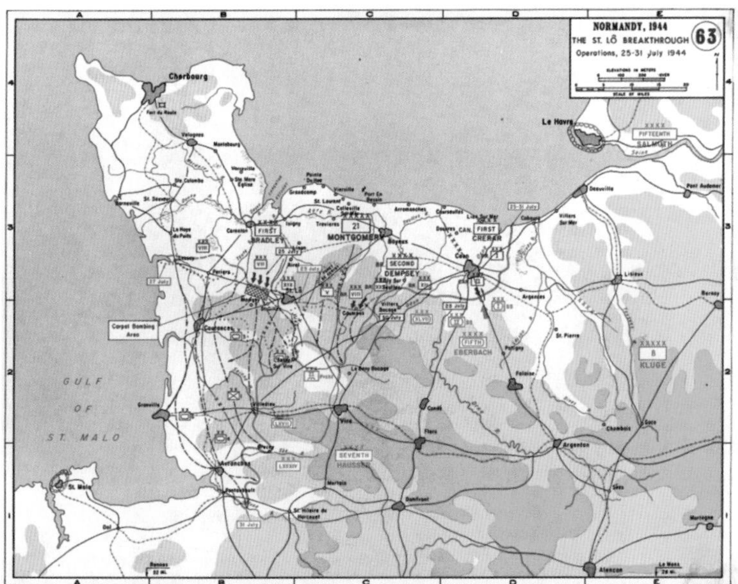

As bloody as the D-Day landings were, they proceeded faster and with fewer casualties than even the most optimistic forecasts had predicted. The breakout from the initial lodgments along the Channel coast, took much longer than anticipated, but the breakout, centered on Saint-Lô during the last week of July 1944, Operation Cobra, unleashed an eastward surge so overwhelming that Allied commanders believed the war would be won by Christmas. It was not.

REALITY CHECK

A Tamer Cobra

Operation Cobra had originated in a bold plan proposed by General George S. Patton Jr. for a major breakout. The more conservative Bradley considered it too ambitious and reformulated Operation Cobra into something much more modest—a concentrated thrust through a single point west of Saint-Lô. In Patton's hands, Bradley's modest plan exploded into a spectacular push that greatly accelerated the Allied offensive. Patton's audacity often got him into trouble and caused great controversy, yet audacity—which Bradley did not possess—is sometimes necessary to drive victory.

TAKEAWAY

Dependence Day

Although the British and the Americans had been bombing occupied France and Germany since very early in the war, the Normandy invasion—D-Day—was the major cross-Channel ground invasion on which Allied victory in Europe would absolutely depend.

marked. Bradley and Patton refused to be shaken by these tragic missteps, which had not only killed Americans but had also sacrificed the element of surprise. The Army Air Forces made up for their mistake by performing brilliantly in massive carpet-bombing raids, which were followed by an attack against German troops outside of Saint-Lô carried out by no fewer than two thousand Allied aircraft. This so weakened the German Front here that the enemy was utterly disabled from counterattacking Bradley's breakthrough. The American commander massed fifteen divisions and 750 tanks against nine German divisions, which had no more than 150 tanks. Before dawn on July 26, U.S. bombers attacked German lines, after which the 1st Armored Division advanced through the German defenders.

The Allied push through Saint-Lô was a rout. The Germans retreated in such disarray that First Army (Bradley) and Third Army (Patton) were able to drive out into opposite directions, Patton moving toward the southeast, Bradley toward the northeast.

By the end of the day on July 27, the Germans had been pushed back fifteen miles, entirely satisfying Bradley, but only whetting the appetite of Patton. He exploited the breach created by advancing at high speed, so that by July 30, the 6th Armored Division (of Patton's Third Army) crossed Bréhal and drove past Granville. At the same time, Third Army infantry took the town of Avranches. From here, the infantry secured on July 31 a bridgehead over the Sélune River at Pontaubault. The U.S. Army had now pushed beyond Normandy and was in Brittany.

Bradley had labored for a bloody month in the hedgerow country. Patton—in a single week—had advanced forty miles and had captured eighteen thousand prisoners. Operation Cobra had been transformed into a general breakout. This ensured that the liberation of Europe would not be a slow and grinding war of attrition, but—at least for a time—a great offensive that moved even more rapidly than the German blitzkrieg with which World War II had begun.

CHAPTER 21

LIBERATION

Salvation of a Continent

IN OPERATION COBRA, the breakout from the beaches of Normandy, General Omar Bradley (and subsequently Courtney L. Hodges) led the First U.S. Army against the German defenses west of the village of Saint-Lô while, on August 1, 1944, George S. Patton Jr. led his Third Army to the right of the First, breaking out of Normandy and into Brittany by way of Avranches. Thus began an astounding drive through France and into Germany itself, with Patton and his Third forming the point of the spear.

LIBERATING FRANCE

FOR THE SECOND TIME IN THE TWENTIETH CENTURY, France was a principal battlefield of war in Western Europe. After Patton's armor swept away all resistance in Brittany, it turned sharply south into the Loire Valley. Simultaneously, Patton's infantry marched to the left, bearing down on Le Mans. Now behind the Third Army, the First U.S. Army pivoted to the left.

At Avranches, the Germans made a powerful counterthrust in a tactically sound effort to cut off the Third Army from the First, but superb coordination with British ground forces resulted in a counterattack against the counterattack. Supported by close air cover, the Britons overcame resistance at Avranches.

Free Paris

Dwight D. Eisenhower, the supreme Allied commander, was not a great believer in liberating cities for the mere sake of liberating them. In the tradition of American Civil War general Ulysses S. Grant, Ike believed that the quickest way to win a war was to kill the enemy army. If that meant delaying the liberation of a civilian objective, so be it. Liberate Paris, and the war would continue. Kill the enemy army, and it would end.

> "Paris must either not fall into the hands of the enemy or the enemy must find it only a wasteland."
>
> *Adolf Hitler to General Dietrich von Choltitz, commandant of Paris, August 23, 1944*

Yet Eisenhower was an abundantly humane military leader, who understood that war was not solely about armies. The war's political leaders, Franklin D. Roosevelt, Winston Churchill, and the Free French leader Charles de Gaulle, all clamored for the immediate liberation of this most iconic of Western European capitals. Moreover, as the Anglo-American armies pushed eastward, the French Resistance, acting on its own, began the liberation of Paris

Four years earlier, it was the Nazi army marching past the Arc du Triomphe along the Champs Elysees. With the liberation of Paris on August 25, 1944, it was the forces of Free France and the United States.

ALTERNATE TAKE

Risk or Rout?

Always audacious, Patton wanted to move farther east even faster than he did, hoping to cut off the retreat of the Germans from Avranches. His more conservative British and American fellow commanders, fearful that the Third Army would find itself cut off and engulfed, restrained Patton. As a result, an opportunity to destroy much of the German 7th and 5th Panzer divisions was lost as these units were permitted to withdraw through a gap in the Allied line known as the "Falaise-Argentan Pocket." The Allies pursued the retreating German divisions during August 20–30, 1944, but Patton always regretted being stopped from taking a bigger bite out of the German defenders. Military historians disagree as to whether giving Patton free rein would have shortened the war or unnecessarily risked the Third Army, but, considering Patton's remarkable combat record, the weight of opinion is on the side of the Third Army's commander.

with a guerrilla battle against the German occupiers of that city. Eisenhower knew that he would have to slow the eastward advance of his forces just long enough to take the City of Light. The Allied nations demanded it—and, besides, he was unwilling to leave so many courageous French freedom fighters in the lurch. Thus, on August 25, with Free French forces under General Jacques-Philippe Leclerc in the vanguard, the Allies marched into Paris. Within a few days, Paris was completely liberated.

REALITY CHECK

Morale Boost

Although the liberation of Paris was a distraction from the business of destroying the German armies, its value to Allied morale was incalculable. Redeeming this beloved city—which, unlike much of the rest of Europe, was intact and largely undamaged—was a promise of imminent victory throughout the rest of Europe. It underscored what the sacrifice and heartbreak was all about.

Second Landing

On August 15, Operation Anvil—now renamed Operation Dragoon—got under way. These landings on the Côte d'Azur by the Seventh U.S. Army (including elements of Free French forces) under Lieutenant General Alexander Patch had been originally planned to coincide with the Normandy landings, but had to be delayed more than a month because of the chronic shortage of landing craft.

Operating in conjunction with Bernard Law Montgomery's and Bradley's armies in the north and with Patton's Third Army in the central sector, the Seventh Army's campaign in southern France and into the Rhône Valley had a devastating impact on German forces in these areas, so that, by the end of August, the German presence in southern France had simply crumbled. With the south of France entirely reclaimed, Patch led the Seventh U.S. Army north, into Vosges, where it tied in with Patton's Third Army and other elements as part of the general drive eastward.

DETAILS, DETAILS

Alias Leclerc

Second only to Charles de Gaulle, Jacques-Philippe Leclerc was the most celebrated general of the Free French forces. He was born Philippe François Marie, comte de Hauteclocque, but assumed a pseudonym when he joined the French Resistance to protect his prominent family from German reprisals. After the war, he legally adopted his Resistance *nom de guerre*.

AN INTERMISSION

Napoleon's celebrated observation that an army travels on its stomach is a dramatic statement of the role of logistics in any major offensive. Food, fuel, and all manner of other supplies must flow in vast and uninterrupted quantities to an advancing army, lest conquest suddenly turn into defeat. The lines of supply constitute the umbilical cord of any force, an attachment as necessary as it is burdensome and limiting. Even though Operation Overlord had carefully planned for the acquisition of key ports to keep the invasion supplied, there never seemed to be enough trucks to transport truly adequate amounts of supplies—chiefly gasoline—inland to the rapidly advancing Anglo-American forces.

AFRICAN AMERICANS IN UNIFORM

Thanks largely to, a 1952 movie starring Jeff Chandler and featuring a twenty-five-year-old Sidney Poitier, the ambitious truck convoy system of the same name was saved from postwar obscurity. As the film dramatized, the "Red Ball Express" operated for three months, from August 25 to November 16, 1944, when the Allies captured port facilities at Antwerp. During this period, trucks ran continuously, twenty-four hours a day, every day, in a gallant effort to keep Allied forces supplied during Operation Cobra.

In railroading parlance, a "Red Ball" freight is a high-priority express. Each Allied division required some 750 tons of supplies a day, making a total of about 20,000 tons for the entire invasion force. In nearly six thousand vehicles, the Red Ball Express moved 12,500 tons of supplies a day. The work was grueling and dangerous, not only because the trucks were frequently targeted by Luftwaffe aircraft but also because of bad roads, bad weather, and driver fatigue.

Sidney Poitier's presence in the 1952 film *Red Ball Express* is a rare acknowledgment of the role African Americans played in World War II. During the entire war, the U.S. armed forces were (with minor exceptions in the U.S. Navy) totally segregated. African American soldiers, sailors, airmen, and marines (the USMC did not even enlist African Americans before World War II) were trained separately. They served in segregated units, usually commanded by white officers—although a small number of African Americans were commissioned during the war. At sea, black sailors were given segregated quarters, although very modest experiments in integration were made before the end of the war. Like the Poitier character in *Red Ball Express,* the overwhelming majority of African Americans were posted to support and labor units rather than in frontline combat units. Of the four services, the army had the greatest number of African American troops, some nine hundred thousand. Of this number, nearly 90 percent were assigned to labor rather than combat units.

Most of the men of the Red Ball Express were black, but an even more famous all-African American unit was

Fighting in defense of democracy, social justice, and human rights, the United States military in World War II was nevertheless racially segregated, with most African Americans assigned to support roles, including labor details, cargo handling, and (as pictured) the manning of antiaircraft defenses. This mobile AA gun accompanies a convoy, November 9, 1944.

First Lieutenant Andrew Lane (bareheaded, in the flight jacket) was one of the celebrated Tuskegee Airmen, a member of the segregated 99th Fighter Squadron, a fighter unit staffed and flown exclusively by African-Americans.

the so-called Tuskegee Airmen—officially the 99th Fighter Squadron and subsequently the 332d Fighter Group (which included the 99th, 100th, 301st, and 302d Fighter Squadrons, all black, all segregated).

The origin of the Tuskegee Airmen came in May 1939, when two pilots of the National Airman's Association, an organization of African American aviators, met with Harry S. Truman, then a senator from Missouri. Truman agreed to sponsor a bill to allow black pilots to serve in the Civilian Pilot Training Program of the U.S. Army Air Corps, at the time an all-white force. In December 1940, President Franklin D. Roosevelt pressed the air corps to submit a plan for the creation of an "experimental" all-black fighter squadron consisting of just thirty-three pilots. The 99th Pursuit Squadron was created on January 16, 1941, to be trained at Tuskegee Army Air Field in Tuskegee, Alabama. A few months later, on July 19, 1941, the air corps (now officially renamed the U.S. Army Air Forces) began a larger program to train African Americans as military pilots, with primary flight training to be conducted by the Division of Aeronautics of Tuskegee Institute, the famed black institution of higher education first led by Booker T. Washington in 1881.

The inaugural class of "Tuskegee Airmen" graduated on March 7, 1942, and was assigned to what was now called the 99th Fighter Squadron, under the command of Lieutenant Colonel Benjamin Davis Jr., a West Point graduate and son of the army's only African American general officer, Brigadier General Benjamin Davis Sr. On April 15, 1943, the 99th shipped out to North Africa to fly fighter escort for bombers. Later in 1943, the 322d Fighter Group was organized and relocated to bases in Italy as part of the Twelfth Army Air Force. Although the Tuskegee Airmen met with prejudice from white southern politicians and from many white pilots, they quickly amassed a superb record, proving so skilled at bomber escort that bomber crews explicitly requested fighter escorts to be drawn from the black units. Four 332d pilots were decorated with the Distinguished Flying Cross, the most coveted aviator decoration in the Army Air Forces.

DETAILS, DETAILS

Operation Pressure

Operation Anvil was renamed Operation Dragoon because Winston Churchill only grudgingly agreed to its launching, claiming that he had been "dragooned" into that agreement by unremitting pressure from the Americans. Churchill believed that the landings in southern France diverted too many resources from the Italian campaign. The American commanders saw matters precisely the other way around, complaining that the Italian campaign was a diversion from the Western Front.

DETAILS, DETAILS

Million Man General

When Omar Bradley assumed command of the 12th Army Group, First Army command was transferred to General Courtney L. Hodges. With 1.3 million men, 12th Army Group was the largest force ever put under a single American operational commander.

In and of itself, the demand for fuel and other supplies was staggering, but, increasingly, the Allied commanders also began to pursue diverse objectives in the advance. As the ground war developed, the Allied armies were divided into two large army groups, the 21st Army Group under Montgomery (which included the British Second Army and the Canadian First Army) and the 12th Army Group (First, Third, Ninth, and Fifteenth armies), which was put under Bradley's command in August. The 12th, which included Patton's fast-moving Third Army, advanced through central and southern France, while Montgomery's concentrated on the north, pursuing the retreating Germans into the Low Countries. The advance could not be sustained equally across so broad a front, and, on August 30, after it had swept through France and crossed the Meuse River, at the country's eastern frontier, Patton's Third Army was ordered to halt because of a shortage of gasoline.

That gasoline, Patton angrily fumed, was being diverted to the north, to Montgomery, under whom the Canadian First Army and the British Second Army were battering away at German positions blocking Antwerp, Holland. At the same time, elements of Montgomery's army group were laying siege against Le Havre and beginning to take the Channel ports. Only grudgingly did Patton admit that possession of these ports was critical to the continuation of the invasion, but he also broadly hinted that Montgomery was (as usual) moving too slowly. Winston Churchill, who was no fan of the notoriously egocentric Montgomery, wholeheartedly supported another aspect of the general's campaign, however. Montgomery had targeted and captured the V-1 missile bases near the Pas de Calais, giving much relief to London and other cities against which the "buzz bombs" were being launched.

Knocking on Germany's Door

Every Allied commander wanted to be the first to cross into Germany. Patton was in the best position to do it, but Montgomery, getting the lion's share of fuel and supplies at the moment, decided on a bold stroke that would take the Allies into the enemy's country by way of Holland. Montgomery put together Operation Market-Garden, a plan to seize intact the Rhine River bridges at Arnhem and to secure other Rhine bridges, thereby claiming a highway into the German heartland.

Operation Market-Garden was a most seductive plan, promising a shortcut into Germany. It hinged on a large airborne assault, with paratroops dropped well behind German lines to prepare the way for the overland advance of the British Second Army. The operation was launched on September 17, 1944, when the U.S. 101st Airborne Division landed between Eindhoven and Veghel, the U.S. 82nd Airborne Division landed around Grave and Groesbeek, and the British 1st Airborne Division was dropped near Arnhem. The first drops, consisting of 16,500 paratroops and 3,500 glider troops, were remarkably accurate—the most flawless Allied airborne assault of the war—and put the two American divisions very close to their bridgehead objectives. Tragically, however, the British airborne troops were dropped inaccurately, much too far from Arnhem to efficiently penetrate German defenses and take the bridges there. This heartbreaking failure cost the success of the entire operation. As luck would have it, two SS panzer divisions, the 9th and 10th, were being refitted near Arnhem. It took four long hours for the British paratroops to march to the Arnhem bridges, by which time the German divisions were more than ready for them. The panzer troops blew up the railway bridge at Zon (Son) and then pinned down the paratroops. British commanders sought to rush reinforcements in the form of the Polish Parachute Brigade, but bad weather set in, greatly delaying their arrival. When they finally were dropped, continued bad weather forced them to divert to Driel, far from Arnhem, and the Germans simply bottled them up there.

British field marshal Bernard Law Montgomery conceived Operation Market-Garden as a "dagger thrust" into Germany across the lower Rhine by way of the Dutch city of Arnhem. British and American paratroops were combined to create the First Allied Airborne Army for a massive airborne assault—but Montgomery overreached, the British paratroops landed too far from Arnhem, the position was massively reinforced by the Germans, and Market-Garden ended in Allied retreat and bloodshed.

The consolidation of German resistance also slowed the elements of the British Second Army that were advancing overland. That army's XXX Corps was late in linking up with 101st Airborne Division near Eindhoven. To make matters worse, the British had to erect a temporary bridge—called a Bailey bridge—at Zon to replace the permanent bridge the Germans had destroyed. This increased the delay, exposing the 101st Airborne to attack along its

November, 1944: "dragon's teeth," concrete tank traps, mark the so-called Siegfried Line or "West Wall" defenses of Germany.

flanks. The Germans were able to hit the Eindhoven-Nijmegen road—along which XXX Corps and the 101st were supposed to link up—so often that paratroops called it "Hell's Highway."

For a time, the 82nd Airborne Division managed to do better. It took the Groesbeek Bridge, blocking German counterattacks via that crossing, and, on September 20, when elements of the British XXX Corps finally began arriving, a battalion of the 82nd crossed the Waal River in assault boats and captured both Nijmegen bridges. After this, however, the 82nd found itself in the same predicament as the 101st, forced to wait for the arrival of the main body of XXX Corps. It was this final delay that put the nail in Operation Market-Garden's coffin. By the time most of XXX Corps was on the move, the Germans had already driven the British airborne troops from the Arnhem bridgehead. This made way for German artillery to cross the bridge and easily stop the advance of XXX Corps at Ressen.

On September 25, nearly twenty-three hundred British and Polish paratroops began to withdraw from Arnhem, but they left behind more than six thousand of their comrades—about half of them wounded—who became prisoners of war. For their part, the U.S. 101st and 82nd Airborne divisions did not want to yield the ground they had gained. These troops continued to engage the Germans in the north for two more months, carving out a salient into German-held territory, from which, in February 1945, an advance into Germany (called Operation Veritable) would be launched. This salient was the only benefit derived from Operation Market-Garden, which, in all other respects, was a costly failure.

"I think we might be going a bridge too far."

Attributed to British general Sir Frederick Browning, September 10, 1944, in response to Montgomery's plan for Operation Market-Garden

The Advance Resumes

The failure of Market-Garden was a great blow to Montgomery's prestige. A seasoned commander, he nevertheless continued his efforts to capture Antwerp, a port that was essential to the ongoing invasion. During October-November 1944, he led a hard fight to take the South Beveland Peninsula and Walchern Island, two great Scheldt Estuary fortresses that stood as sentinels guarding Antwerp. The fortresses fell by November 8, after which Allied minesweepers laboriously cleared the Scheldt of German mines so that Allied convoys could safely pass. By the end of November 1944, the convoys began arriving, and a much-needed new Allied supply line was up and running.

While Montgomery fought in the Low Countries, Bradley's army group hammered away at the so-called Siegfried Line, an elaborate system of fortifications, including pillboxes (concrete machine-gun emplacements) and other strong points erected all along Germany's western frontier. This was the last-ditch German defense on the Western Front, and it was defended tenaciously. Nevertheless, Patton's Third Army took the fortress town of Metz (in the Alsace region of France) on October 3, and, on October 21, the First U.S. Army captured Aachen, the first German city to fall to the Allies.

All through November, the Anglo-American armies fought German forces deployed west of the Rhine—the river running through Germany's industrial heart and a waterway that symbolized the German homeland. Fighting was especially bitter in the tangled Roer River–Hürtgen Forest region from November 16 to December 15. South of this area, Patton's Third Army resumed its advance, sweeping through the Lorraine, while the Free French liberated the important Alsatian towns of Mulhouse and Strasbourg.

DETAILS, DETAILS

American's First

In his diary, Patton recorded his disappointment that the First Army had beaten the Third into Germany; however, his chagrin was greatly tempered by the fact that an American army, not Montgomery, had been the first to enter the land of the enemy.

The Bulge

After the heartbreak of Market-Garden and the bloody fighting in and around Hürtgen Forest, the Allied advance gained solid momentum. As December approached its close, there was a general feeling that the advance was a juggernaut, unstoppable. Eisenhower feared that his commanders were falling victim to what he called "victory fever." Perhaps they were taking too much for granted. Nevertheless, the evidence of Allied triumph did seem undeniable: Hitler's armies were in complete collapse or falling back. Yet, somehow, Hitler managed to motivate his forces to make one final counteroffensive. Wholly unanticipated, its effect was devastating.

The purpose of the German offensive through the Ardennes, the thick forest between Belgium and Luxembourg, the very portal through which blitzkrieg had been brought to France in 1940, was to drive a wedge between the Allied forces, defeating them in detail north of the line formed by Antwerp, Brussels, and Bastogne. This

POP CULTURE

Nuts

The German commander of forces surrounding Bastogne was well aware of the desperate situation in which he had placed the 101st Airborne and the 10th Armored. He sent an officer under a flag of truce to demand surrender. Major General Anthony McAuliffe, acting commander of the 101st Airborne Division, examined the surrender demand. Asked by his aide how he wanted to reply to the demand, McAuliffe uttered a single word: "Nuts!" At once defiant, casually contemptuous, and quintessentially American, this reply became a byword of the American spirit during World War II. Curiously lighthearted, it instantly entered into the folklore of this terrible war.

accomplished, the Germans would drive through to Antwerp, taking the port that Montgomery had sacrificed so much to capture.

The Ardennes Offensive began on December 16, 1944. Because it overwhelmed the thin First U.S. Army line in this sector, creating a major German salient, or bulge, in the Allied line, it was popularly known as the Battle of the Bulge.

Twenty German divisions stormed out of fog and snow, forcing the First Army to fall back. At first Bradley thought it was a local action, but he, Eisenhower, and Patton soon realized that it was a massive—shockingly massive—offensive, in which some two hundred thousand Germans bore down on eighty-three thousand Americans. Aware that the town of Bastogne in Luxembourg was key to the entire Ardennes—for its crossroads was the nexus of communication and transport in the region—Bradley was determined not to yield it. He accordingly ordered the U.S. 101st Airborne to join the 10th Armored Division in Bastogne to hold the town until the arrival of major reinforcements.

Bastogne was quickly surrounded by the Germans. Entirely cut off, the 10th and the 101st fought from behind a hastily arranged defensive perimeter. Compounding the desperate situation of these two units was the winter weather, which not only made life miserable for defenders and attackers alike, but also kept the Allies from launching badly needed air support. This critical component was missing for the full first week of the battle.

In the proverbial nick of time, the weather lifted, permitting the launch of extensive air support. In addition, Patton—in a spectacular maneuver—arrested the eastward thrust of his Third Army and turned the entire force 90 degrees to the north, advancing on the double nearly one hundred miles to relieve Bastogne. It is a testament to his men that, after three solid months of combat and rapid movement, they mustered the strength and will to move one

Looking far from beaten, German troops advance across a road somewhere in Belgium or Luxembourg during the opening phases of the Ardennes Offensive, popularly called the Battle of the Bulge.

hundred miles over three days into a new battle, without rest, and without complaint. Patton's quick action turned what could have been a disastrous defeat into a major counterattack that not only stopped the Ardennes Offensive but also broke the back of the German army. After the Bulge, it was never able to mount another major offensive.

Closing the Vise

By the start of 1945, Germany was about to suffer a general invasion. Anglo-American armies were closing in from the west and also, via Italy, from the south (although final victory would not come in Italy until the very end of the European war). From the east, the Soviet Red Army was bearing down on the German homeland.

Crossing the Rhine

On the Western Front, after crushing a short-lived resurgence of German activity in Alsace and Lorraine during January 1–21, the Allies began to cross the Rhine into the heart of Germany. By early February, the so-called "Colmar Pocket"—a stronghold the Germans held in the Vosges—was cleared, and Anglo-American forces proceed to the Rhine. On March 7, a task force of the U.S. 9th Armored Division, heading up the First Army's advance, stumbled on a railroad bridge that crossed the Rhine at Remagen. Somehow, the Germans had neglected to destroy it. Aware that they would soon correct that oversight, the task force rushed to take and hold the bridge, possession of which greatly—and unexpectedly—accelerated the Allied advance across the Rhine.

After a short time of use, the railroad bridge collapsed under the weight of endless Allied convoys. By this time, however, more bridges had been erected, and, on March 22, Patton led the 5th Division across the Rhine at Oppenheim. As American engineers threw more bridges across the river, the main units of the Third Army began rolling into Germany. Just behind Patton was Montgomery, who crossed his forces above the Ruhr, north of Patton's crossing. On March 24, the Ninth U.S. Army crossed at Dinslaken, and the First U.S. Army broke out of its Remagen bridgehead on March 25, crossing en masse there. Before March ended, even more units rumbled across hastily erected bridges.

NUMBERS

U.S. and German Losses

The tide of battle turned on December 26, 1944, and by January 16, 1945, Patton had pushed the "bulge" back. For the Americans, the cost of the Ardennes Offensive was 7,000 killed, 33,400 wounded, and 21,000 captured or missing. German losses were ultimately much heavier: about 120,000 killed, wounded, or captured. Perhaps even more significant was the equipment loss: 600 tanks and assault guns destroyed, along with 6,000 other vehicles. About 1,600 German aircraft of the already badly depleted Luftwaffe were damaged or destroyed. The Battle of the Bulge was, for the American forces, the most desperate engagement of the war in Europe.

NUMBERS

Russian War Machine

The three army groups that Stalin aimed toward Berlin comprised 2.5 million men, 6,250 tanks and other armored vehicles, and 7,500 aircraft.

ALTERNATE TAKE

Leaving Berlin

None of Eisenhower's wartime decisions was more controversial than that of leaving Berlin to the Soviets. Certainly, taking Berlin would have cost many American lives, but, as Ike's critics have pointed out, complete Anglo-American control of Berlin would very likely have changed the balance of power in the postwar world by reducing the Communist footprint in Germany. As for the feared and anticipated concentration of diehard Nazi guerrilla resistance in Bavaria, it failed to materialize.

Endgame

When the advance across France had begun in earnest, Eisenhower assumed that Anglo-American troops would take the German capital, Berlin. So rapid was the progress of Third and First armies, however, that Eisenhower decided to target Leipzig instead. He also believed that diehard Nazis would gather in southern Germany, in Bavaria—the birthplace of the Nazi Party—and mount a guerrilla resistance there, perhaps even after the German government officially surrendered. Therefore, in addition to taking Leipzig, he thought it best also to focus chiefly American efforts toward the south and leave Berlin to the Red Army.

Having left Berlin to the Soviets, Eisenhower sent his forces into the industrial Ruhr Valley, where they encircled about three hundred thousand survivors of German Army Group B. Army Group G, positioned to the east and the south of the now wholly enveloped Army Group B, continued a surprisingly fierce resistance, but did so with little organization or coordination. In the north, Montgomery finished off German Army Group H.

The U.S. 12th Army Group advanced in an arc far to the east, well into Czechoslovakia, making contact on April 25 with Red Army forces at Torgau. The more recently formed U.S. 6th Army Group marched through southern Germany and into Austria, taking, among many other key objectives, Berchtesgaden and, above it, Hitler's mountain retreat. At the Brenner Pass, Austria's frontier with Italy, the Seventh U.S. Army finally tied in with the Fifth U.S. Army, which had just completed its long northerly advance up the Italian Peninsula.

EYEWITNESS

On March 24, 1945, General Patton recorded in his diary, "I drove to the Rhine River and went across on the pontoon bridge. I stopped in the middle to take a piss and then picked up some dirt on the far side in emulation of William the Conqueror." This ancient if uncouth rite of conquest was also performed by Prime Minister Winston Churchill (in the Rhine on March 26), and, on March 3, British general Sir Alan Brooke recorded that Churchill and his entire entourage urinated on the Siegfried Line: "As the photographers rushed up to secure good vantage points," Brooke noted, the prime minister "turned to them and said, 'This is one of the operations connected with this great war which must not be reproduced graphically.'" It never was printed, but Brooke observed: "I shall never forget the childish grin of intense satisfaction that spread all over [Churchill's] face as he looked down at the critical moment."

The Führer's Last Stand

Early in February 1945, the Red Army's First Belorussian Front, commanded by Marshal Georgi Zhukov, and the First Ukrainian Front, under Marshal Ivan Konev, reached the Oder River, thirty-five miles east of Berlin. Holding his forces at Küstrin, on the Oder, Zhukov requested Stalin's permission to make an immediate advance on Berlin. Stalin, however, wanted to attack with overwhelming numbers and ordered Zhukov to await the arrival of Konev. Zhukov's instinct to move quickly had been correct, because, at the time, Berlin was defended by nothing more than the remains of the Third Panzer Army and those of the German Ninth Army, which were collectively designated Army Group Vistula. The delay gave the Germans time to assemble a stronger defense, which would make the Battle of Berlin that much more costly. Nevertheless, Konev and Zhukov attacked from two different directions—Konev from the south, Zhukov from the east—which forced the Germans to divide their defenses.

The situation for Germany was quite hopeless. Hitler, however, was not tempted to surrender. Instead, he ordered his soldiers to defend the capital "to the last man and the last shot," and he mustered a home guard called the Volkssturm, made up of ill-equipped overage men and underage boys. These forces were arrayed in four concentric rings around Berlin, the outermost ring twenty miles out from the center city, the second ten miles, the third deployed along the S-Bahn, the city's suburban rail system, and the innermost ring, called the Z-ring—Z for Zitadelle ("citadel")—arranged within the center of the city itself. The Citadel ring was intended to protect the government buildings and the Füherbunker, the underground shelter that housed Hitler and his immediate staff below the ruins of the Reich Chancellery, administrative center of the govvernment.

On March 31, Stalin informed Zhukov that he would, after all, be accorded the honor of taking Berlin. Konev's advance would serve mainly to screen and support Zhukov's left flank. Konev would also advance against Dresden. In coordination with Zhukov's move directly against Berlin, a third Red Army group, the Second Belorussian front, under Marshal Konstantin Rokossovsky, was deployed to the lower Oder River to cover Zhukov's right flank.

REALITY CHECK

High Cost

The fact that Stalin had been promised Berlin at the Yalta Conference was of secondary concern to Eisenhower. His principal reason for leaving Berlin to the Soviets was so that he could concentrate on destroying every last vestige of military resistance in Germany. He felt about Berlin as he had felt about Paris. Both cities were certainly of great symbolic importance, but their strategic significance was not high. Moreover, General Bradley had predicted that taking Berlin would cost upward of 100,000 Allied lives. It seemed too high a price to pay. As it turned out, some 300,000 (estimates vary from less than 100,000 to substantially more than 300,000) Red Army troops may have been killed in the Battle of Berlin.

What the Arc du Triomphe was to Paris, the Brandenburg Gate was to Berlin: a symbol of national might and national pride. In this photograph, soldiers of the Red Army assemble before the battered gate.

"We shall go down in history as the greatest statesmen of all time, or as the greatest criminals."

Joseph Goebbels, just before committing suicide, May 1, 1945

Overwhelmingly outnumbered and thoroughly exhausted, the regular German army, together with the Volkssturm, resisted the assault on Berlin with suicidal determination. Zhukov started his attack at dawn on April 16, focusing on Seelow Heights, west of the Oder. Seeking to confuse and blind the defenders, he shined huge antiaircraft searchlights directly on the German positions. This trick backfired, reducing visibility for the Russians at least as much as for the Germans. The first Soviet thrust dissolved in chaos, forcing Zhukov to withdraw and regroup. His new assault on April 17 consisted of six armies, including two tank armies. This force also made a fierce thrust, only to withdraw again. On April 18, a third attack finally pushed back the German lines, but failed to break through.

Yevgeni Khaldei's image of a Red Army soldier raising the Hammer and Sickle over the ruined German Reichstag symbolizes Soviet victory in what Stalin called the "Great Patriotic War."

Appalled by the lack of progress against Berlin, Stalin personally ordered Zhukov to break off his attack from the east and march to the north to resume the attack from that direction. At the same time, Stalin ordered Konev to begin the advance of two tank armies from the south. Rokossovsky, positioned to the northeast with his Second Belorussian front, was ordered to support Zhukov as he bore down from the north. Stalin had placed the German capital in the gaping jaws of a Soviet pincer. Under relentless attack, Hitler retreated into delusion. He ordered the German Ninth Army to "stand fast" on the Oder—an impossibility. On April 20, Adolf Hitler's birthday, Konev's tanks reached Jüterbog, the German army's major ammunition depot. Konev captured this objective, then marched against the communications center at Zossen. In the meantime, holed up under the streets of Berlin, Hitler gave members of his inner circle permission to leave Berlin and save themselves, if possible. He announced that he would remain in the city to the end. Hitler's few remaining loyalists believed that this decision was a courageous act. It was, in fact, both selfish and foolish, since Hitler's presence in the capital made the Soviets that much more determined to take the city.

NUMBERS

Rhineland Toll

The Rhineland campaign had cost 20,000 Allied casualties and had inflicted heavy casualties on the German defenders of the region. German losses included 60,000 killed or wounded and 250,000 taken prisoner.

Inexorably, the noose closed around Berlin and the Third Reich. Zhukov reached the outermost defensive ring on April 21, and by the 25th had tied in with Konev, so that Berlin was completely encircled. Hitler continued to issue orders to mostly nonexistent armies. The

Evidence of German desperation: These Wehrmacht troops have been forced to use an 88-milimeter antiaircraft gun as ground artillery in a last-ditch defense of an Oder River bridge in March 1945. The Oder was the last natural barrier separating Berlin from the westward advance of the Red Army.

Ninth German Army, reeling, was wholly encircled. The Twelfth German Army was marching toward Berlin from the west, but had too few men to make any impact on the outcome. In the very center of the city were veterans (who had retreated from the outer defense) and a collection of Hitler Youth—teenagers and even younger boys. Mixed in among these was the Volkssturm—more boys and old men, many unarmed. Remarkably, however, the Germans continued to fight for possession of each and every street until, on April 29, Lieutenant General Karl Weidling, commander in charge of the capital's defenses, reported to Hitler that all of his ammunition would be exhausted by the next day. When that day came—April 30, 1945—the Red Army stormed the Reichstag, seat of the German government. They did not know that, nearby, under the Reich Chancellery, Adolf Hitler had shot himself in the head while simultaneously biting down on a capsule of cyanide. His former mistress—and bride of a single day—Eva Braun, had poisoned herself as well.

Surrender

The death of the Führer did not bring an immediate end to the fighting in the streets. On May 1, Lieutenant General Hans Krebs, chief of the German general staff, attempted to negotiate surrender terms. The Soviet reply was curt. The only acceptable terms were unconditional surrender. On May 2, Weidling tendered precisely that.

Before taking his life, Hitler had appointed Admiral Karl Dönitz as president of Germany and Joseph Goebbels as chancellor (Goebbels, however, committed suicide on May 1 along with his wife, after poisoning their six children with cyanide). It now fell to Dönitz to authorize the unconditional surrender of all German military forces. General Alfred Jodl, Hitler's chief military adviser, reported to Eisenhower's headquarters in Rheims, France, to sign an unconditional surrender. Contemptuous of the Nazi high command, Eisenhower declined to attend the signing personally, sending his chief of staff, Walter Bedell Smith, in his place. Jodl signed the surrender at 2:41 on the morning of May 7. Stalin refused to accept the Reims surrender and demanded another, at Berlin. This document was signed one-half hour before midnight on May 8. The war in Europe was ended.

TAKEAWAY

Victory in Germany

Despite colossal problems of supply, the Allied armies, having broken out of Normandy, advanced with startling speed through occupied Europe to invade and defeat Hitler's Germany.

Part Seven

DEVASTATION AND RECOVERY

Previous pages: Hiroshima, Japan, sometime after the morning of August 6, 1945.

CHAPTER 22

"A CRUEL NEW BOMB"

Japan Surrenders

WHEN HARRY S. TRUMAN TOOK THE OATH OF OFFICE AT 7:09 P.M. ON APRIL 12, 1945, two hours and twenty-four minutes after Franklin Roosevelt died suddenly of a cerebral hemorrhage, he knew nothing of an "atomic bomb." As a senator from Missouri, Truman had made a national reputation when he organized and chaired a wartime watchdog committee that identified—and remedied—cases of inefficiency, corruption, and fraud among defense contractors. The Truman Committee, as it was called, made its chairman sufficiently popular with the public that, when FDR ran for his fourth term in 1944, he tapped the senator as a running mate preferable to the sitting vice president, Henry Wallace, whose politics had become unpalatably socialist.

The president did not know Truman personally or professionally, and he really did not care to. He met with him, briefly, just twice during the eighty-two days in which Truman served as his vice president, and he never briefed him on what was called the Manhattan Project, the massive top-secret effort to create an atomic weapon. The first he heard of it was just after his swearing-in and a brief meeting with the Cabinet, when Secretary of War Henry L. Stimson quietly took Truman aside, telling him nothing more than that they needed to talk soon about a "new explosive of incredible power."

Defeated but Deadly

"Stimson, what was gunpowder? Trivial. What was electricity? Meaningless. This Atomic Bomb is the Second Coming in Wrath."

Winston Churchill to U.S. secretary of war Henry Stimson, July 1945

As early as 1944, a secret study by the Japanese military determined that Japan had suffered military defeat. Yet no one in the military suggested surrender. During its entire existence, Japan had never been successfully invaded and had never surrendered. Joseph Grew, the prewar American ambassador to Japan, believed that surrender did not even exist as a concept in Japanese culture. In effect, he believed, even if they wanted to surrender, the Japanese simply did not know how to do so. Certainly, the record of the Pacific war supported this view. Each Japanese island outpost the Allies conquered had been defended virtually to the last man. The few prisoners taken typically fell captive by accident, often before they had time to take their own lives. For the Japanese warrior, the only honorable alternative to victory was death.

The militarist government of Japan had done its utmost to inculcate in the ordinary Japanese civilian this same ethic of death before the dishonor of surrender. Anticipating an invasion, Japanese authorities instituted citizen-training programs in which women, old men, and children were armed with sharpened bamboo poles and taught to kill as many invaders as possible before they themselves were killed. Already, of course, the Japanese people had learned to endure terrible hardships. Defeat throughout the Pacific had strangled the home islands, so that citizens lived on the barest of subsistence rations. They were subjected to massive aerial bombardment. U.S. air planners made an effort to identify industrial and military targets, but these were typically located adjacent to ordinary civilian communities, so that raids on the densely populated cities became routine. Domestic architecture, even in modern Japan, was largely fashioned of wood and paper, making the cities ideal targets for incendiary raids.

The B-29 Superfortress, the most advanced strategic bomber of World War II, was used exclusively in the Pacific, visiting greatest devastation on Tokyo, which was bombed and fire-bombed repeatedly, as shown above.

During the last year of the war, B-29 heavy bombers attacked Japan with near impunity. The Japanese army and naval air forces had been largely destroyed, and, in any case, the ultramodern B-29s were capable of flying well above the service ceiling of the few surviving Japanese fighters. Japanese cities were protected by few antiaircraft guns, and few resources had been devoted to the development of antiaircraft radar. Civil defense was also grossly inadequate. Shelters were few. When cities were bombed, people died. That was Japan's reality.

Rational policy dictated surrender. But it became increasingly clear to the Allies that Japanese policy was in the hands of militarists who operated by a warrior code that lay outside of the realm of rationality. The most extreme of the militarists were quite willing to fight the war until Japan was utterly destroyed. During the three months between April 12, when Truman took office, and July 16, the date on which the atomic bomb was successfully tested in the New Mexico desert, Japan—a militarily defeated power—inflicted American battle casualties amounting to nearly half the total from three full years of the Pacific war. In its death throes, Japan was deadlier than ever.

When Truman assumed office, the war in Europe was nearly over and won, and although the Manhattan Project was drawing to a successful conclusion, the atomic bomb was not yet a reality. On the president's desk were two proposals for ending the war in the Pacific.

One option was to continue the conventional bombing of Japan, coupled with the intensification of the ongoing naval blockade. The combination would simultaneously pummel and strangle Japan, presumably leaving no choice but surrender. The civilian death toll would be astronomical, and the war would drag on for well over another year, perhaps more, during which U.S. and other Allied forces would have to continue to fight and die. At that, a significant number of American strategists doubted that the combination of bombing and blockade would produce unconditional surrender. The

NUMBERS

The Burning of Tokyo

The most destructive incendiary attack was the fire-bombing of Tokyo on March 9, 1945, in which a fleet of B-29 bombers dropped over 1,600 tons of napalm-filled bombs on the city. More than fifteen square miles of the capital were completely obliterated and 100,000 to 150,000 persons killed—incinerated in a horrific firestorm. This single raid was more destructive than the atomic bombing of either Hiroshima or Nagasaki and nearly as devastating as the bombing of those two cities combined. Indeed, by August 6, 1945, when Hiroshima was bombed, more than 10 million Japanese urban dwellers (mostly women and children) had already fled into the countryside.

Major General Curtis LeMay, commanding the U.S. XXI Bomber Command, led a strategic bombing campaign against Japan that was unprecedented in its destructiveness.

REALITY CHECK

Stripped-down Bombers

In January 1945, Curtis LeMay, a tough, taciturn, cigar-chomping U.S. Army Air Forces general, assumed command of the XXI Bomber Group, on Guam. Early results of B-29 raids had been disappointing, and LeMay was assigned to get results. He shocked his aircrews by stripping the Superfortress bombers of their defensive guns—as well as gun crews and ammunition—so that each ship could be packed with more bombs. Then he ordered these aircraft, bombers specifically designed to fly at very high altitudes, to make their bomb runs from low altitudes in order to achieve greater accuracy. LeMay's crews anticipated that they would be slaughtered, but, remarkably, survival rates actually increased—and bombing accuracy and effectiveness dramatically improved.

When Harry S. Truman, seen here addressing a joint session of Congress on April 16, 1945, became president on the sudden death of Franklin D. Roosevelt, he turned to the White House press corps: "Boys," he said, "if you ever pray, pray for me now. I don't know whether you fellows ever had a load of hay fall on you, but when they told me yesterday what had happened, I felt like the moon, the stars, and all the planets had fallen on me." Frank, gifted with blunt eloquence, and animated by an abundance of straightforward compassion, Truman led the nation to final victory in World War II.

Japanese, they believed, would rather watch their cities fall and their people starve than surrender, especially if any part of the military was still capable of taking a toll on the Allies. This was not mere fanaticism. The Japanese knew that the longer the war took, grinding on without decision, the less inclined the Allies would be to hold out for unconditional surrender. The Japanese willingness to die could well purchase a negotiated end to the conflict.

The second option was to continue and intensify the blockade, but follow up the bombing with a massive invasion. General MacArthur and most other senior American military commanders favored this approach, admitting, however, that Allied casualties would be extremely heavy and that the war would still continue until roughly June 1946. President Truman ordered MacArthur and others to plan for the invasion of Japan.

Operation Downfall

With Hitler's Operation Sealion (see "Operation Sealion" in Chapter 5), the plan to invade Britain, Operation Downfall, the plan to invade Japan, was one of the most momentous World War II operations destined never to be launched. As planned, Operation Downfall consisted of two parts: Operations Olympic and Coronet. Operation Olympic was to step off in November 1945 and was aimed at capturing the southern third of Kyūshū, the most southerly of the main Japanese islands. The recently captured Okinawa would be the staging area for Olympic. In the spring of 1946, Operation Coronet would be launched. It was the invasion of the Kantō plain adjacent to Tokyo on the island of Honshū. Airfields in Kyūshū would support this invasion. The Allies believed that the successful culmination of these two operations would bring about the final surrender of Japan. Optimists predicted that Operation Downfall would cost five hundred thousand Allied casualties, half of them fatal. MacArthur, although he was an ardent supporter of the operation, predicted twice that number: the death or wounding of a million young Allied men, mostly Americans.

The Manhattan Engineer District

It was April 25 before Secretary of War Stimson presented Truman with the details of the atomic bomb project. As the man in charge of the War Department, Stimson could have been forgiven if he had boasted proudly to the president of the new weapon. Instead, he made no secret of his moral reservations about it. The new bomb would be so powerful that it could shape the future of humankind itself. Using it would change the world. James F. Byrnes, the blunt and ambitious South Carolinian who had served FDR as a key adviser and whom Truman was about to appoint as secretary of state, shared none of Stimson's moral qualms. He advised the president that a single atomic bomb could probably wipe out an entire city, "killing people on an unprecedented scale." And that, Byrnes said, would probably not only end the war, but would put the United States in position to dictate whatever terms it wished for the postwar world.

The project to create the atomic bomb had its origin even before World War II began in Europe. In 1939, a band of American scientists, which included recent refugees from European Fascist and Nazi regimes, became increasingly alarmed by progress in work they knew to be under way in Germany. Led chiefly by the brilliant German physicist Werner Heisenberg, this research explored nuclear fission, the process by which the energy of the binding force within the nucleus of the uranium or plutonium atom—the powerful force that holds the constituents of the nucleus together—might suddenly be liberated to yield a release of energy in an explosion of unprecedented magnitude: in other words, an atomic bomb. The American group decided to approach U.S. government officials at the highest levels to commence a project to

ALTERNATE TAKE

Terms of Surrender?

During the final months of the war, there was a belief in some Allied circles that a growing faction of the Japanese government was becoming increasingly opposed to the extreme militarists. (This, in fact, proved to be the case.) Some of President Truman's advisers believed that the Japanese would be willing to negotiate an end to the war. Truman, however, held to the pledge the Allied leaders had made as early as the Casablanca Conference, to accept nothing less than unconditional surrender. Some later historians believe that had Truman (and the other Allies) yielded on the demand for unconditional surrender, the war would have ended sooner—and without the use of the atomic bomb.

"The atom bomb will never go off, and I speak as an expert in explosives."

Admiral William Leahy to President Harry S. Truman, shortly before August 6, 1945

beat Germany to the punch by developing, as rapidly as possible, nuclear fission for military purposes. Accordingly, Columbia University physicist G. B. Pegram arranged a meeting between the eminent Italian expatriate physicist Enrico Fermi and the U.S. Department of the Navy in March 1939. Some months later, Leó Szilárd, an expatriate physicist from Fascist-dominated Hungary, called on America's most famous refugee scientist, Albert Einstein, to write a personal letter directly to President Roosevelt, which he did on August 2, 1939. Einstein's letter advised FDR of the urgent necessity of beginning work on a military fission project because of the dangers posed by the German research:

> Sir:
>
> Some recent work by E. Fermi and L. Szilard, which has been communicated to me in manuscript, leads me to expect that the element uranium may be turned into a new and important source of energy in the immediate future. Certain aspects of the situation which has arisen seem to call for watchfulness and if necessary, quick action on the part of the Administration. I believe therefore that it is my duty to bring to your attention the following facts and recommendations.
>
> In the course of the last four months it has been made probable through the work of Joliot in France as well as Fermi and Szilard in America—that it may be possible to set up a nuclear chain reaction in a large mass of uranium, by which vast amounts of power and large quantities of new radium-like elements would be generated. Now it appears almost certain that this could be achieved in the immediate future.
>
> This new phenomenon would also lead to the construction of bombs, and it is conceivable—though much less certain—that extremely powerful bombs of this type may thus be constructed. A single bomb of this type, carried by boat and exploded in a port, might very well destroy the whole port together with some of the surrounding territory. However, such bombs might very well prove too heavy for transportation by air.

The United States has only very poor ores of uranium in moderate quantities. There is some good ore in Canada and former Czechoslovakia, while the most important source of uranium is in the Belgian Congo.

In view of this situation you may think it desirable to have some permanent contact maintained between the Administration and the group of physicists working on chain reactions in America. One possible way of achieving this might be for you to entrust the task with a person who has your confidence and who could perhaps serve in an unofficial capacity. His task might comprise the following:

a) to approach Government Departments, keep them informed of the further development, and put forward recommendations for Government action, giving particular attention to the problem of securing a supply of uranium ore for the United States.

b) to speed up the experimental work, which is at present being carried on within the limits of the budgets of University laboratories, by providing funds, if such funds be required, through his contacts with private persons who are willing to make contributions for this cause, and perhaps also by obtaining co-operation of industrial laboratories which have necessary equipment.

I understand that Germany has actually stopped the sale of uranium from the Czechoslovakian mines which she has taken over. That she should have taken such early action might perhaps be understood on the ground that the son of the German Under-Secretary of State, von Weizsacker, is attached to the Kaiser-Wilhelm Institute in Berlin, where some of the American work on uranium is now being repeated.

Yours very truly,
Albert Einstein

The president responded to Einstein's letter by authorizing, in February 1940, six thousand dollars to begin preliminary research into the feasibility of a fission project. L. J. Briggs, head of the National Bureau of Standards, chaired a research committee, whose work proved sufficiently promising to warrant transfer of the research project to a much higher level, the Office of Scientific Research and Development, which was headed by Vannevar Bush, a scientist especially prominent in government circles.

With America's entry into the war, the War Department was given joint responsibility for the project, and by mid 1942, the researchers had definitively concluded that the military application of fission was feasible, but they also observed that extensive—indeed, unprecedented—research and manufacturing facilities would be required, including laboratories and industrial plants. Management of a vast construction and engineering project, the War Department concluded, should be handled by the U.S. Army Corps of Engineers. Because most of the early-phase research was being conducted at Columbia University, in Manhattan, responsibility for the project was assigned to the Corps' Manhattan Engineer District in June 1942. From then on, the project, assigned the most rarified top-secret status, was referred to—when it was referred to at all—as the Manhattan Project.

Building the Bomb

The Manhattan Project rapidly developed into the largest scientific and industrial enterprise ever undertaken by the United States. Hundreds of scientists would be involved, together with thousands of civilian workers and military personnel. Vast production plants and major research facilities would be built. Yet all of this was kept under such tight security that not even the vice president of the United States knew about it.

At first, the role of the Corps of Engineers was to oversee construction of the various facilities the project required. Almost immediately, however, the role of the Corps was expanded to direct every aspect of the undertaking. In September 1942, Brigadier General Leslie R. Groves, the army engineer officer who had just finished managing the design and construction of the Pentagon outside of Washington—at the time, the biggest office building in the world—was put in charge of all military and engineering aspects of the Manhattan Project. Groves received a second star, but his authority extended far beyond that usually accorded major generals. Groves was absolute ruler of a scientific and industrial empire.

In the meantime, beginning in the autumn of 1941, Professor Pegram and fellow physicist Harold C. Urey were sent by the U.S. government to Britain, which had a fission research project under way. Pegram and Urey set up a fully cooperative program between scientists in America and England, and by 1943, the United States had created a joint policy committee with Great Britain and Canada. A number of leading British and Canadian nuclear researchers came to the United States to work on the Manhattan Project, which was now an international effort among the Allies.

Rarely remembered today, Vannevar Bush was one of the most famous scientists of the World War II era. As the U.S. government's chief of scientific research and development in the Office of Production Management (OPM), he had ultimate control of science and technology as applied to the war effort and was an early champion of the Manhattan Project, which produced the atomic bomb.

The task was as daunting as any mission in World War II. The Manhattan Project not only had to research an entirely new theoretical field, it had to transform each aspect of theory into a practical demonstration, and then create from the demonstrations a workable prototype, which, finally, had to be fashioned into a practical combat weapon. At the outset, the unknowns far outnumbered the knowns, but one known outweighed everything else. Nazi Germany was working toward the same end.

General Groves boldly decided to save time by authorizing a number of research programs simultaneously, knowing that some would prove costly dead ends. Long before research was completed, Groves also authorized the design and construction of the production plants that would be required to prepare the fissionable material at the heart of the bomb. Huge amounts of money and a massive effort were expended even before some of the most basic theoretical work had been done.

The first practical problem that had to be addressed was the separation of Uranium-235, the fissionable material—material whose atomic nuclei would undergo fission, or splitting apart—from its companion isotope, Uranium-238. A staggering quantity of U-238 was required to obtain a minute quantity of U-235. That was a difficulty formidable enough, but the fact was that no chemical means was even known capable of separating U-235 from U-238.

DETAILS, DETAILS

Fateful Dates

Vannevar Bush took over the fission research project at a most fateful moment: December 6, 1941. Pearl Harbor was bombed the next day. The United States entered World War II on December 8. The atomic weapons project was suddenly assigned a very high priority—a remarkably far-seeing step, given the purely theoretical nature of the science involved at the time.

REALITY CHECK

Friendly Spy

Despite the extraordinary security surrounding the Manhattan Project, theoretical physicist Klaus Fuchs, who had fled Nazi Germany for Britain before the war and who worked in the United States at the Los Alamos Laboratory, was moved by his Communist sympathies to secretly supply information on the atomic bomb (and, later, on the hydrogen bomb) to the Soviet Union. (He was later convicted in Britain and sentenced to fourteen years in prison.) Scientists are divided on whether or not Fuchs's espionage truly benefited successful Soviet efforts to create both atomic and hydrogen weapons after the war.

Manhattan Project scientists had to invent a new process, physical rather than chemical. Two candidates rapidly emerged. Ernest Lawrence, of the University of California, developed the electromagnetic process, and Columbia's Harold Urey developed the gaseous diffusion process. The electromagnetic process worked on the principle that charged particles of the lighter isotope, U-235, would be deflected away from their companion U-238 particles when the combined U-238 and U-235 was passed through a magnetic field. Deflected, the U-235 particles could be captured and thereby isolated from the U-235. Radically different from this was gaseous diffusion, which was based on the principle that molecules of the lighter isotope, U-235, would pass more readily through a porous barrier than the heavier U-238 particles. As different as they were, both processes demanded equally large and complex industrial plants with access to massive amounts of electric power.

Normally, the engineer in charge would order small pilot plants to be built in order to determine which process was superior before a major investment was made in a full production plant. Groves had no time for this. Instead, he ordered the construction of two full-scale plants, one for the electromagnetic process, the other for diffusion. Construction of both facilities was immediately started at Oak Ridge, a seventy-square-mile tract near Knoxville, Tennessee.

Initially, uranium was seen as the necessary basis of an atomic bomb. But when Arthur Compton of the University of Chicago isolated plutonium 239, this isotope offered itself as yet another candidate for fission. Seeking to hedge his bets, Groves authorized full-scale production of this material in addition to the enriched uranium. Pu-239 could be produced only by transmuting U-238 by means of a fission chain reaction. Such a reaction had been made possible only very recently, when, in December 1942, Enrico Fermi created the world's first nuclear reactor, producing a controlled U-238 fission chain reaction in a "reactor pile" constructed under the stands of the University of Chicago's Stagg Field. This—more than the

Portly, irascible, egotistical, Major General Leslie R. Groves was the brilliant army engineer and organizational genius who, having completed construction of the massive Pentagon—in just eighteen months—took up the mission of creating an atomic bomb.

atomic bomb that followed little more than two years later—was the true birth of the "atomic age." Yet Fermi's room-sized experimental reactor was far too small to produce usable quantities of Pu-239. A giant reactor had to be designed and built. This would require, first of all, the invention of an entirely new process for chemical extraction. To enable development of this process, a medium-sized reactor was built at Oak Ridge. Once the chemical engineering had been completed using this facility, industrial chemical engineers were able to draw up plans for the full-scale production reactors. These were built far from Oak Ridge, on a remote one thousand-square-mile tract along the Columbia River north of Pasco, Washington. Called the Hanford Engineer Works, it joined Oak Ridge as the two principal production plants of the Manhattan Project. The construction of the plant also meant that the Manhattan Project would develop not one, but two types of atomic bomb: one based on uranium and the other on plutonium.

REALITY CHECK
Plant Number 3

Even by 1944, there was no certainty that either the electromagnetic or the gaseous diffusion methods could be made to produce a sufficient quantity of U-235 for a bomb. Groves therefore ordered the implementation of a third method for separating the isotopes. Liquid thermal diffusion concentrated the lighter U-235 isotope near a heat source within a tall column. This required construction of a third Oak Ridge plant. Ultimately, all three methods were employed in order to produce enough "enriched uranium" (that is, U-235) to produce a bomb.

Even as one group of scientists, engineers, architects, and construction laborers worked on creating fissionable materials, J. Robert Oppenheimer, a brilliant and charismatic physicist, was chosen in 1943 to organize a central laboratory that would do the major work of translating atomic theory into a working bomb. While Groves directed the engineering and military aspects of the Manhattan Project, Oppenheimer was given responsibility for recruiting scientists and managing all aspects of the scientific research. Groves and Oppenheimer were obliged to work closely together. They were, in terms of personality, background, intellectual interests, political beliefs, and even physical presence (Groves was rotund and blustering, Oppenheimer nearly emaciated and soft-spoken), polar opposites, yet each recognized in the other consummate professionalism married to a passion for solving problems. Grudgingly at times, they developed an intense mutual respect and forged an unlikely but highly effective partnership.

Technicians at the giant Oak Ridge (Tennessee) nuclear weapons plant manipulate fissionable material to make the core of an atomic bomb.

Oppenheimer chose a remote mesa at Los Alamos, New Mexico, north of Santa Fe, as the site of the new laboratory. Isolated in the austere beauty of the high desert, Los Alamos drew the

REALITY CHECK

Staving off the Red Army

In addition to his conviction that the atomic bomb would save American lives, Truman had another compelling reason to use it. At Potsdam, both Truman and Churchill worked hard to persuade Stalin to fulfill the promise he had made FDR at Yalta by at long last declaring war on Japan. Truman understood that a Soviet presence in Japan might well result in that country—or at least the northern part of it—becoming a Soviet satellite after the war, but his immediate priority was defeating Japan and, to that end, he wanted a Red Army invasion. As soon as he received word that the atomic bomb had been successful, however, Truman wanted to use it to end the war before the Soviets began to invade. That way, he hoped to head off any postwar claim Stalin might make to that nation.

nation's most important physicists and chemists. If the team of Groves and Oppenheimer was a marriage of opposites, Los Alamos combined top-secret military discipline with the creative freedom and openness necessary for advanced scientific research. It was quite probably the most unusual scientific workplace ever established.

Los Alamos scientists had to invent methods of reducing the fissionable materials produced by the plants at Oak Ridge and Hanford to absolutely pure metal capable of being precisely machined into a shape that would both enable and enhance an explosive chain reaction. Mechanically, an atomic bomb had to bring together—very, very rapidly—enough fissionable material to create what physicists called a supercritical mass. This supercritical mass would produce a chain reaction—neutrons colliding with other neutrons, which, in turn collided with others, producing a spectacular release of energy in the form of a powerful explosion. If the fissionable material was brought together too slowly, supercritical mass would not be achieved, and there would be no explosion. If it were brought together in less than perfect alignment, the same result would occur—a failure to achieve supercritical mass. Thus, the bringing together of the fissionable material represented an exquisitely difficult problem of materials engineering. To make it far more complicated, this feat had to be accomplished within a bomb that could be carried in a bomber, released over a target, and detonated at precisely the optimum altitude above the target. Unlike most conventional bombs, which are designed to explode on impact, an atomic bomb had to be designed to detonate above ground zero so that none of its explosive force would be absorbed and dissipated by the Earth.

Trinity

By the summer of 1945, Hanford had turned out enough Pu-239 to produce a nuclear explosion. Thanks to the multitrack development system Groves had created, the Los Alamos scientists had, by this time, fabricated a prototype weapon ready to field test. At a desolate spot called Alamogordo, 120 miles south of Albuquerque, they built a tower from which the device—for reasons of security and, perhaps, dark humor, the scientists had taken to calling it the "gadget"—was suspended. At the site, the scientists had assembled observation and monitoring equipment to gather accurate data on performance—or failure. The test would be code-named "Trinity."

The scientists had been careful to choose a test site far from population centers, but the fact was that estimates of the "yield"—the explosive force—of the bomb varied wildly. It was one thing on which none of the scientists could agree. A few believed that there was a remote but theoretically possible chance that the detonation of the bomb would produce a chain reaction in the atoms of the very air. If that happened, a vast area would be destroyed. A more esoteric theory proposed that the detonation could ignite the entire atmosphere of the Earth, engulfing the planet. That was not the way anyone wanted to end the war.

At 5:30 A.M. on July 16, 1945, the Los Alamos scientists, together with Groves and a handful of VIP observers, hunkered down in hardened bunkers and in trenches positioned ten thousand yards from the test tower, their eyes protected by plates of thick, dark welder's glass.

A blinding flash was followed by a surging wave of intense heat and then—since sound travels so much more slowly than radiated energy—by a low roar and a visceral shock wave accompanied by a blast of wind. Long after the flash faded, an immense fireball hung above the Earth—the test tower had been vaporized—succeeded by a mushroom-shaped cloud that rose to a spectacular altitude of forty-thousand feet.

"Trinity" site, 33.6773° N 106.4757° W, near Alamogordo, New Mexico, July 16, 1945, 05:29:45 local time (Mountain War Time): The successful test of an implosion-design plutonium bomb, equivalent to the explosion of about twenty thousand tons of TNT. Los Alamos laboratory director J. Robert Oppenheimer said that, as he observed the test, a line from the Hindu Bhagavad Gita *came to mind: "I am become Death, the destroyer of worlds." Test director Kenneth Bainbridge reportedly replied to Oppenheimer: "Now we are all sons of bitches." According to Oppenheimer's brother, Frank, Robert actually uttered just two words: "It worked."*

The President Decides

President Harry S. Truman was in Potsdam, a suburb outside of war-ruined Berlin, meeting with Winston Churchill (who, voted out of office at the end of July, was replaced by the new British prime minister Clement Attlee midway through the conference) and Joseph Stalin to shape the fate of the postwar world. Secretary of War Stimson handed him a message from his Washington-based special assistant on atomic issues, George L. Harrison: "Operated on

NUMBERS

Explosive Yield

The Trinity test bomb produced an explosion equivalent in energy to what would be produced by fifteen thousand to twenty thousand tons of TNT.

REALITY CHECK

Theoretic Trials

The atomic scientists had to solve practical problems theoretically. Fissionable material was too valuable to expend on trials. It had to be conserved so that it could be used—as soon as possible—in finished, fully weaponized bombs.

this morning. Diagnosis not yet complete but results seem satisfactory and already exceed expectations. Local press release necessary as interest extends great distance. Dr. Groves pleased. He returns tomorrow. I will keep you posted." Truman now knew that he had an atomic bomb.

In later years, when asked about his decision to use the bomb, Truman consistently replied that it "was no 'great decision.'" The atomic bomb, he said, "was merely another powerful weapon in the arsenal of righteousness. The dropping of the bombs stopped the war, saved millions of lives. It was a purely military decision." George Elsey, a naval officer who served as one of Truman's wartime aides, observed that the president "made no decision because there was no decision to be made. He could no more have stopped it [the bomb] than a train moving down a track." Winston Churchill concurred. The "decision whether or not to use the atomic bomb to compel the surrender of Japan was never an issue. There was unanimous, automatic, unquestioned agreement around our table."

Major General Leslie Groves and Dr. J. Robert Oppenheimer were different in every conceivable respect: Groves was fat, Oppenheimer ascetically thin; Groves bellowed, Oppenheimer was soft spoken; Groves gave orders, Oppenheimer facilitated the work of genius; yet the two men worked brilliantly together to transform advanced theoretical physics into a war-winning weapon. Here, together, they examine what little remains of the tower from which the Alamogordo test bomb was detonated.

But even in high places, among those few who knew that a bomb was in the works, there was disagreement. Some argued that Japan was so close to surrender that there was no need to use the bomb. Informed of the existence of the atomic bomb, Dwight D. Eisenhower, fresh from victory in Europe, passionately argued against using a weapon he considered immoral, so terribly destructive that the world would never forgive the United States for using it. No less a figure than Leó Szilárd—the very man who had persuaded Einstein to prevail on Franklin Roosevelt to undertake atomic weapons research in the first place—secured hundreds of petition signatures from Manhattan Project scientists appealing to President Truman not to use the atomic bomb. Other scientists suggested that the Japanese officials be invited to a demonstration of the bomb at some remote site—that this might be sufficient to persuade Japan to surrender.

The arguments against using the bomb, now that the bomb had been created, were mostly moral. But some argued beyond morality, claiming that atomic weapons would bring into the world a force so powerful that civilization—quite possibly all life on Earth—would be menaced.

Truman understood the moral as well as the apocalyptic arguments against the bomb. As he noted in his diary on July 25, 1945: "We have discovered the most terrible bomb in the history of the world. It may be the fire destruction prophesied in the Euphrates Valley Era, after Noah and his fabulous Ark." But, for him, issues of morality and even the specter of apocalypse itself paled beside the reality of here and now, which consisted of an endless procession of murdered and maimed American young men. He wrote to his wife, Bess Wallace Truman, that the bomb would "end the war a year sooner . . . and think of the kids who won't be killed! That's the important thing."

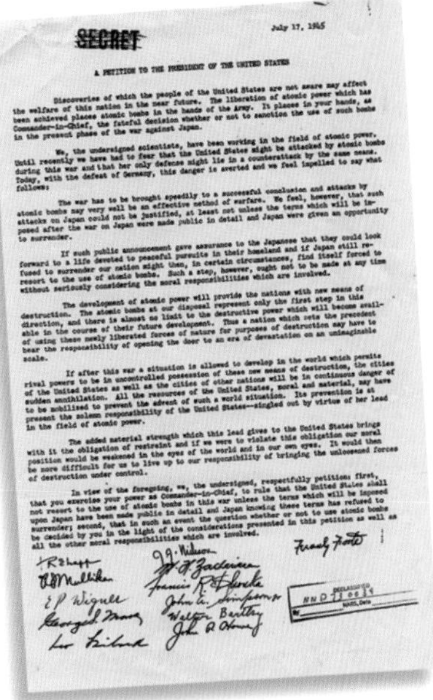

SECRET

July 17, 1945

A PETITION TO THE PRESIDENT OF THE UNITED STATES

Discoveries of which the people of the United States are not aware may affect the welfare of this nation in the near future. The liberation of atomic power which has been achieved places atomic bombs in the hands of the Army. It places in your hands, as Commander-in-Chief, the fateful decision whether or not to sanction the use of such bombs in the present phase of the war against Japan.

We, the undersigned scientists, have been working in the field of atomic power. Until recently we have had to fear that the United States might be attacked by atomic bombs during this war and that her only defense might lie in a counterattack by the same means. Today, with the defeat of Germany, this danger is averted and we feel impelled to say what follows:

The war has to be brought speedily to a successful conclusion and attacks by atomic bombs may very well be an effective method of warfare. We feel, however, that such attacks on Japan could not be justified, at least not unless the terms which will be imposed after the war on Japan were made public in detail and Japan were given an opportunity to surrender.

If such public announcement gave assurance to the Japanese that they could look forward to a life devoted to peaceful pursuits in their homeland and if Japan still refused to surrender our nation might then, in certain circumstances, find itself forced to resort to the use of atomic bombs. Such a step, however, ought not to be made at any time without seriously considering the moral responsibilities which are involved.

The development of atomic power will provide the nations with new means of destruction. The atomic bombs at our disposal represent only the first step in this direction, and there is almost no limit to the destructive power which will become available in the course of their future development. Thus a nation which sets the precedent of using these newly liberated forces of nature for purposes of destruction may have to bear the responsibility of opening the door to an era of devastation on an unimaginable scale.

If after this war a situation is allowed to develop in the world which permits rival powers to be in uncontrolled possession of these new means of destruction, the cities of the United States as well as the cities of other nations will be in continuous danger of sudden annihilation. All the resources of the United States, moral and material, may have to be mobilized to prevent the advent of such a world situation. Its prevention is at present the solemn responsibility of the United States—singled out by virtue of her lead in the field of atomic power.

The added material strength which this lead gives to the United States brings with it the obligation of restraint and if we were to violate this obligation our moral position would be weakened in the eyes of the world and in our own eyes. It would then be more difficult for us to live up to our responsibility of bringing the unloosened forces of destruction under control.

In view of the foregoing, we, the undersigned, respectfully petition: first, that you exercise your power as Commander-in-Chief, to rule that the United States shall not resort to the use of atomic bombs in this war unless the terms which will be imposed upon Japan have been made public in detail and Japan knowing these terms has refused to surrender; second, that in such an event the question whether or not to use atomic bombs be decided by you in the light of the considerations presented in this petition as well as all the other moral responsibilities which are involved.

Leó Szilárd, the Hungarian refugee physicist whose alarm over Nazi work on atomic weaponry had been the catalyst that launched the Manhattan Project, led sixty-nine fellow project scientists in signing a July 17, 1945, petition urging President Harry S. Truman to consider the moral consequences of using the atomic bomb.

Little Boy

As the Los Alamos scientists neared the end of their labors, a special unit of U.S. Army Air Forces B-29 air crews, commanded by Colonel Paul Tibbets, was training for a special mission. All they were told was that they would be dropping a single, very heavy bomb on a Japanese city. The phrase "atomic bomb" was never mentioned, but some guessed it.

Tibbets and the other members of the elite 509th Composite Group completed their training at Wendover Army Airfield in Utah, then were deployed to the Pacific island of Tinian, to which the first combat weapon to emerge from Los Alamos, a U-235 bomb dubbed "Little Boy," was delivered by the cruiser Indianapolis. The bomb was loaded aboard a B-29 that had been modified to accommodate the 9,700-pound, nine-foot-nine-inch device. Its explosive yield was predicted at 12.5 kilotons, the equivalent of 12.5 kilotons of conventional TNT. It would also generate tremendous heat and radioactivity, including radioactive contamination in the form of fallout. All of this made it far more deadly than 12,500 tons of any conventional explosive.

Hiroshima, a manufacturing center of some 350,000 people about five hundred miles from Tokyo, was selected by a U.S.-based "target committee" partly because it was a military production center but also because it had not yet been bombed. As a virgin target, it would allow military analysts to gauge the effect of the new

Little Boy, the uranium-core atomic bomb dropped on Hiroshima, rests on its cradle in a pit under the B-29 Enola Gay, *awaiting loading into the aircraft's bomb bay. The bomb bay door is visible in the upper- right-hand corner of the photograph.*

weapon more accurately. It would also demonstrate to the Japanese just how powerful the atomic bomb was. Seconds before the bomb detonated, there was a pristine city. Fractions of a second later, there would be ruin.

Colonel Tibbets flew the Hiroshima mission in the modified B-29 he had christened *Enola Gay*, after his mother. The aircraft reached its target at 8:15 (local time) on the morning of August 6, 1945. Little Boy was dropped by parachute and was detonated at precisely 1,885 feet above sea level.

Every wooden building within a 1.2-mile radius of the hypocenter (as the point of detonation was called) was completely destroyed by the blast. Structures made of reinforced concrete within 1,625 feet of the hypocenter were also totally destroyed by the blast. An area of five square miles was almost totally incinerated. Analysis of aerial photography revealed that 62.9 percent of the city's seventy-six thousand buildings were destroyed. No more than 8 percent survived without substantial damage. Most scientists believed the prediction of a 12.5 kiloton yield was close to the actual, if somewhat too conservative. Revised estimates ranged from 13 to 15 kilotons.

The detonation immediately killed half of those who had been within three-quarters of a mile of the hypocenter. Within one year, as of August 10, 1946, a total of 118,661 persons had died—from injuries, burns, and the effects of radiation. At the time of the detonation, 30,524 were severely injured, and 48,606 less severely injured.

Just before takeoff on August 6, 1945, bound for the skies over Hiroshima, Colonel Paul W. Tibbets Jr. waves from the cockpit of the B-29 he named after his mother.

Fat Man

When the bombing of Hiroshima did not elicit an immediate offer of surrender, Major Charles W. Sweeney flew another B-29, *Bockscar*, from Tinian on August 9. The primary target for this mission was the city of Kokura (now part of Kitakyushu), but thick cloud cover sent Sweeney to a secondary target, Nagasaki. At 11:02 in the morning (local time), Sweeney released "Fat Man," a bomb with a core of plutonium 239. Like the Hiroshima bomb, Fat Man was dropped by parachute and detonated at a preset altitude—in this case, 1,625 feet. It was a considerably more powerful bomb than Little Boy, weighing nearly ten thousand pounds and designed to yield a twenty-two-kiloton blast. However, the topographical situation of Nagasaki, which was located within narrow valleys bordered by mountains, tended to reduce the effect of the bigger bomb. About 2.6 square miles of the city were destroyed, compared with five square miles in Hiroshima. Approximately 23 percent of the city's fifty-one thousand buildings were destroyed or badly damaged, but just over 36 percent were almost entirely unscathed. Of the 270,000 people in the city that morning—this included 2,500 Korean slave laborers and 350 Allied prisoners-of-war—73,884 were killed instantly and 74,909 injured. As at Hiroshima, there were long-term ill effects from radiation exposure, but, as in the case of Hiroshima, the anticipated high rates of cancer did not occur.

On August 9, 1945, a second atomic bomb was dropped on a city in Japan. This photograph of central Nagasaki shows that only reinforced concrete buildings withstood the blast.

Hirohito Speaks

Although some militarists continued to resist surrender, the emperor himself, Hirohito, insisted that the time had come. On August 10, the official Japanese news agency, Domei, broadcasted a message declaring that the government of Japan was prepared to accept unconditional surrender, but with the understanding that the emperor would remain on the throne. Truman acknowledged that this was unconditional surrender with a condition, and some of his advisers counseled him to reject it. By this time, a third atomic bomb was ready.

But the president ordered that no more atomic bombs were to be used without his explicit directive. He told Secretary of Commerce Henry A. Wallace that he could not endure the thought of killing "all those kids," by which he meant Japanese kids. Instead, he decided that he could grant the single Japanese condition by adding a condition of his own. Japan could retain its emperor, who would, however, be wholly "subject to the Supreme Commander of the Allied Powers." This reply was transmitted on the very day the Japanese offer had been received, August 10. While awaiting the Japanese response, Truman ordered conventional air raids against Japan to recommence on August 13. Japan accepted the terms on August 14.

At noon on August 15, 1945, the people of Japan heard the voice of the emperor. On the fourteenth, Hirohito had recorded a message to be broadcast over the radio:

"The morning was still, the place was cool and pleasant. Then a tremendous flash of light cut across the sky. . . . It seemed a sheet of sun."

John Hersey, Hiroshima *(1946)*

DETAILS, DETAILS

Uranium Core

Little Boy was the only uranium-core atomic bomb produced during World War II. Both the Trinity device tested at Alamogordo and "Fat Man," dropped on Nagasaki three days after the Hiroshima bombing, were plutonium-based.

NUMBERS

Before and After the Bomb

About 350,000 persons were believed to have been in Hiroshima at the time of the bombing. Of this number, 118,613 were confirmed as living and uninjured as of August 10, 1946, one year after the attack. The majority of victims of the attack were civilian, but it is believed that about 20,000 military personnel also died as a direct result of the bombing. Radiation produced some long-term effects in those near the blast. These effects included elevated rates of genetic and chromosome damage, and birth defects, especially stunted growth and mental retardation, affecting some children born to parents who survived the blast. Physicians feared greatly increased rates of cancer, but, for the most part, these were not noted. Finally, about 4,000 citizens of Hiroshima went missing after the attack and have never been accounted for.

To Our good and loyal subjects: After pondering deeply the general trends of the world and the actual conditions obtaining to Our Empire today, We have decided to effect a settlement of the present situation by resorting to an extraordinary measure.

We have ordered Our Government to communicate to the Governments of the United States, Great Britain, China and the Soviet Union that Our Empire accepts the provisions of their Joint Declaration [the Potsdam Declaration, which demanded unconditional surrender].

To strive for the common prosperity and happiness of all nations as well as the security and well-being of Our Subjects is the solemn obligation which has been handed down by Our Imperial Ancestors, and which we lay close to heart. Indeed, We declared war on America and Britain out of Our sincere desire to ensure Japan's self-preservation and the stabilization of East Asia, it being far from Our thought either to infringe upon the sovereignty of other nations or to embark upon territorial aggrandisement. But now the war has lasted for nearly four years. Despite the best that has been done by everyone—the gallant fighting of the military and naval forces, the diligence and assiduity of Our servants of the State and the devoted service of Our one hundred million people, the war situation has developed not necessarily to Japan's advantage, while the general trends of the world have all turned against her interest. Moreover, the enemy has begun to employ a new and most cruel bomb, the power of which to damage is indeed incalculable, taking the toll of many innocent lives. Should We continue to fight, it would not only result in an ultimate collapse and obliteration of the Japanese nation, but also it would lead to the total extinction of human civilization. Such being the case, how are We to save the millions of Our subjects; or to atone Ourselves before the hallowed spirits of Our Imperial Ancestors? This is the reason why We have ordered the Acceptance of the provisions of the Joint Declaration of the Powers. . . .

A photographer aboard the USS Missouri, *riding at anchor in Tokyo Bay, recorded the signature that ended World War II. General Douglas MacArthur adds his signature to those of Japanese and Allied representatives to the document formally closing hostilities. Directly behind the seated MacArthur are Lieutenant General Jonathan Wainwright, who had been forced to surrender the Philippines in 1942, and British lieutenant general Arthur E. Percival, who had surrendered Malaya and Singapore. Both men had just been released from POW camps. Ill and emaciated after years in Japanese captivity, Wainwright quipped: "Last surrender I attended, the shoe was on the other foot."*

In Tokyo Bay

An armistice followed Japan's surrender, which was formalized on September 2, 1945, when representatives of the empire of Japan boarded the United States battleship *Missouri* anchored in Tokyo Bay to sign an Instrument of Surrender. Allied representatives included military men from Australia, Canada, China, France (Provisional Government of the French Republic), the Netherlands, New Zealand, the Union of Soviet Socialist Republics, Great Britain, and the United States. Presiding over the ceremony was General Douglas MacArthur, supreme allied commander, Pacific.

There was good reason for conducting the surrender aboard a great American ship of war. In part, of course, it was an act of powerful symbolism, but the Allies also feared that the people of Japan or military diehards might rise up against the Allied representatives, Hirohito's ministers, or both if the ceremony took place within Tokyo itself. As it turned out, no one need have feared this. The enemy that had fought so fiercely—to the death—greeted the emperor's command to complete surrender with absolute and uncomplaining obedience. World War II was at an end.

TAKEAWAY

Creation and Implementation

The Manhattan Project—the massive Allied effort to create an atomic bomb—was initially motivated by fears that Nazi Germany was working rapidly to produce atomic weapons. The war in Europe ended before German scientists were even close to creating a workable weapon, but it was decided to use the atomic bomb to force Japan into surrender.

CHAPTER 23

THE WORLD AFTER WORLD WAR

Picking Up the Pieces

V-E DAY—VICTORY IN EUROPE DAY—MAY 8, 1945, had been greeted in the United States and other Allied nations with spontaneous demonstration of joy and relief, tempered only by the knowledge that the defeat of Hitler did not mean the end of the fighting and the dying. Japan was still in the war.

Whereas V-E Day had come suddenly, V-J Day—Victory over Japan Day—approached more fitfully. On August 10, the day after the second atomic bomb was dropped on Nagasaki, the official Japanese news agency, Domei, broadcast a peace feeler to the Allies. This alone gave many Americans (and others) cause for celebration. On August 10, New York's Times Square filled with people, and office workers began to shower the streets with confetti improvised from torn-up paper.

Yet V-J Day had not yet arrived. The *New York Times* announced that official word of peace would be rolled across its building's famous news ticker just as soon as it was received. People kept watch. Over the next few days, knots of people gazed up at the sign. The United Press wire service sent out a flash announcing the peace—prematurely—on August 12 at 9:34 P.M., then immediately corrected itself, signaling editors to "Hold that flash." Too late. Celebrations began in Times Square and all over the nation and Canada.

That was Sunday. Monday, August 13, came and went, another day of war. Then, at ten minutes before two (New York time) on the morning of August 14, Domei broadcast the news that Japan had accepted the Allied terms. As word spread throughout the day, crowds

Celebrated Life *magazine photographer Alfred Eisenstaedt captured the very essence of V-J Day in New York's Times Square, August 14, 1945. "They were very elegant, like sculpture," the photographer recalled in a 1995 interview. "People tell me, 'Oh, you have taken pictures of [Sophia] Loren and [Marilyn] Monroe!' But* this *is what they know me for."*

gathered at Times Square and everywhere else people traditionally assembled to celebrate. The hours, however, continued to crawl by until, finally, at 7:03 P.M., the *New York Times* news ticker rolled: OFFICIAL—TRUMAN ANNOUNCES JAPANESE SURRENDER.

At 7:30, police estimated the Times Square crowd as ten times a Yankee Stadium sellout. By 10 P.M., there were two million. Eight thousand people per minute had been jamming themselves into the quadrangle bounded by 40th Street, Sixth Avenue, 52nd Street, and Eighth Avenue. New York, the nation, and the free world exploded in joy. In London, Winston Churchill quietly lit one of his trademark cigars, remarking, as he puffed it into ignition, "At last the job is finished." In Washington, crowds streamed to the gates of the White House, shouting, "We want Harry!" The president was at first reluctant to appear, but at last came out and proclaimed, "This is a great day for democracy." In Paris, a G.I.—an ordinary "dogface" private—was emboldened to say to the U.S. Navy nurse lieutenant standing next to him that the news made him want to kiss every American girl.

"Well, what are you waiting for, soldier?" she replied.

DISPLACED

ALL MAJOR WARS CREATE REFUGEES, but no war disrupted more lives than World War II. Officially, the homeless were called "displaced persons (DPs)", and no one knows how many there were, but the most widely accepted estimate is some 30 million—far more than in any other war in history.

"All the News That's Fit to Print"

The New York Times.

LATE CITY EDITION

JAPAN SURRENDERS, END OF WAR!
EMPEROR ACCEPTS ALLIED RULE;
M'ARTHUR SUPREME COMMANDER;
OUR MANPOWER CURBS VOIDED

HIRING MADE LOCAL

Communities, Labor and Management Will Unite Efforts

6,000,000 AFFECTED

Draft Quotas Cut, Services to Drop 5,500,000 in 18 Months

Third Fleet Fells 5 Planes Since End

SECRETS OF RADAR GIVEN TO WORLD

ALL CITY 'LETS GO'

Hundreds of Thousands Roar Joy After Victory Flash Is Received

TIMES SQ. IS JAMMED

Police Estimate Crowd in Area at 2,000,000—Din Overwhelming

PRESIDENT ANNOUNCING SURRENDER OF JAPAN

YIELDING UNQUALIFIED, TRUMAN SAYS

Japan Is Told to Order End of Hostilities, Notify Allied Supreme Commander and Send Emissaries to Him

MACARTHUR TO RECEIVE SURRENDER

Formal Proclamation of V-J Day Awaits Signing of Those Articles—Cease-Fire Order Given to the Allied Forces

Headline, New York Times, *August 15, 1945*

Most displaced persons were in the European theater of World War II. The crisis began even before the war started, as tens of thousands of Jews and other ethnic and political refugees fled Germany and, before escape was cut off early in the war,

THE FINAL COSTS

World War II was the deadliest conflict in history. The nations' militaries mobilized some 120,908,000 men, of whom at least 20,280,000 were killed and 47,980,000 wounded, a catastrophic casualty rate exceeding 50 percent.

Number of Troop Deaths and Wounded by Country

Nation	Maximum No. of Troops Mobilized	Dead (all causes)	Killed in Action Battle Deaths (KIA)	Wounded in Action (WIA)
Australia	680,000	37,467	23,365	39,803
Austria	800,000	280,000	n/a	350,117
Belgium	800,000	22,651	8,460	55,513
Brazil	200,000	n/a	943	4,222
Britain	4,683,000	403,195	264,443	369,267
British Colonies	n/a	n/a	6,877	6,972
Bulgaria	450,000	18,500	6,671	21,878
Canada	780,000	42,666	37,476	53,174
China	5,000,000*	2,220,000	n/a	1,761,335
Czechoslovakia	180,000	n/a	6,683	8,017
Denmark	15,000	6,400	1,800	2,000
Finland	250,000	82,000	79,047	50,000
France	5,000,000	245,000	213,324	390,000
Germany	9,200,000	3,250,000	2,850,000	7,250,000
Greece**	414,000	88,300	17,024	42,290
Hungary	350,000	200,000	147,435	89,313
India	2,150,000	48,674	36,092	64,354
Italy	4,000,000	380,000	110,823	225,000
Japan	6,095,000	2,565,878	1,555,308	326,000
Netherlands	500,000	7,900	6,344	2,860
New Zealand	157,000	13,081	10,033	19,314
Norway	25,000	3,000	1,598	364
Philippines	105,000	n/a	27,258	n/a
Poland	1,000,000†	597,320	123,178	766,606
Romania	600,000	300,000	169,882	n/a
South Africa	140,000	8,681	6,840	14,363
U.S.A.	16,353,659	407,318	292,131	671,801
USSR	12,500,000††	8,668,400	6,329,600	14,685,593
Yugoslavia	500,000†	305,000	n/a	425,000

* Recent historical research, still under way, suggests that these figures, staggering as they are, may have been grossly underreported.

** Includes casualties from 1937 to 1945.

† Troops mobilized include regulars and partisans, as does military dead of all causes; KIA and WIA include regulars only.

†† Troops mobilized include regulars only, but casualty figures include regulars *and* partisans.

The war was even deadlier for those who had worn no uniform. Civilian deaths due directly to the war—including victims of air raids, accidental crossfire, deliberate murder, and outright genocide, as well as war-related privation, starvation, and disease—have been estimated at from 30 million to 55 million. Beyond broad estimates, it is impossible to break down civilian deaths with any degree of accuracy. The Soviet Union lost more of its civilian population than any other country. Traditional estimates range from 7 million to 12 million, but recent scholarship suggests that the numbers may actually have been twice the higher estimate. In proportion to population—35 million at the outbreak of the war—no nation suffered more than Poland: 5,675,000 killed. Of this number, 3 million were Jews, victims of the Holocaust. About half of the 6 million Jews murdered in the Holocaust were Poles.

Civilian Deaths in World War II

Axis Countries

Austria: 170,000
Bulgaria: 10,000
Finland: 2,000
Germany—persons killed in air raids: 593,000 (includes 56,000 foreign workers and 40,000 Austrians)
Germany—victims of unintended crossfire in the west): 10,000
Germany—victims of unintended crossfire in the east and deliberate Soviet retribution: 619,000
Hungary: 290,000
Italy: 152,941
Japan: 658,595
Romania: 200,000

Allied Countries

Belgium: 76,000
Czechoslovakia: 215,000
France: 350,000
Greece: 325,000
Netherlands: 200,000
Norway: 7,000
Philippines: 91,000
Poland: 5,675,000 (including 3 million Jewish victims of genocide)
Soviet Union: 7,000,000 to 12,000,000 (possibly 25,000,000)
United Kingdom: 65,000
United States: 6,000 (of whom 5,638 were members of the U.S. Merchant Marine)
Yugoslavia: 1.2 million+

It is impossible to state in dollars the staggering cost of the war, especially in terms of property destruction and loss. It is estimated that, in Japan, 40 percent of dwellings were destroyed or severely damaged in the nation's sixty-six largest cities. In Germany's forty-nine largest cities, 39 percent of private dwellings were destroyed or severely damaged.

Civilian Property Loss in World War II

Belgium: 20 percent of dwellings destroyed or severely damaged
France: 20 percent of dwellings destroyed or severely damaged
Germany: 39 percent of dwellings destroyed or severely damaged in the 49 largest cities
Japan: 40 percent of dwellings destroyed or severely damaged in the 66 largest cities
Netherlands: 20 percent of dwellings destroyed or severely damaged
Poland: 30 percent of dwellings destroyed or severely damaged
United Kingdom.: 30 percent of dwellings destroyed or severely damaged
Yugoslavia: 20 percent of dwellings destroyed or severely damaged

Another measure of civilian loss is merchant shipping. Japan lost 80 percent of its merchant marine, France 70 percent, Belgium 60 percent, Norway 50 percent, and the Netherlands 40 percent.

Figures adapted from Micheal Clodfelter, *Warfare and Armed Conflicts: A Statistical Reference to Casualty and Other Figures, 1500–2000*, 2d ed. (Jefferson, N.C.: McFarland and Co., 2002), p. 582.

In the aftermath of the war, the initials "DP"—displaced person—were applied to millions of refugees. Here, German DPs, clutching what little has been left to them, wait in Berlin's Anhalter Station for trains that will carry them from the ruined capital to temporary shelter in a camp.

German-occupied countries. In the course of the war, invasion sent many into flight, while the strategic bombing of cities rendered hundreds of thousands homeless.

The world witnessed the first major flight of refugees during the disastrous Battle of France in the summer of 1940. The residents of Brussels, Lille, and Paris clogged the roads as they made their way southwest. The German occupation of Poland created a chronic refugee crisis when Adolf Hitler, in a program intended to "Germanize" much of the conquered nation, forced many Poles to move east. During the winter of 1944–45, the refugee tide turned against German civilians who had been resettled in "Germanized" Poland. As the Red Army approached, these people fled west, often deliberately into the arms of the Western allies.

The United Nations—chartered on June 26, 1945, even before the war was over—quickly created UNRRA, the United Nations Relief and Rehabilitation Administration, whose mission was to provide relief and resettlement for "displaced persons." UNRRA wasted no time in setting up "DP" camps throughout western and central Europe. The organization's most urgent priority was to shelter and feed refugees, but it also undertook a massive operation to reunite families torn apart by war.

"The people in the States do not know how lucky they are. They have come out of this war very easy. The country is all in one piece, and they have clean homes to go to. Over here the people have nothing."

James J. Fahey, diary entry, May 17, 1945, published in Pacific War Diary *(1963)*

AN ALLIANCE DISSOLVES

THE DIRE STRAITS OF WAR transformed the Soviet Union from implacable enemy of Western democratic capitalism into a gallant ally in the war against Nazism and Fascism. In the closing days of European combat, American and Soviet soldiers met at the frontiers that marked the extent of their respective eastward and westward advances. Together, they embraced, drank, sang, and even danced.

Then the leaders began to carve the burned-out remnants of eastern and central Europe. The Red Army occupied most of the territory between the Soviet frontier and Germany. Germany and Austria themselves were divided into four zones of occupation.

Eastern Germany was designated the Russian Zone. Northwestern Germany was occupied by the British. Southwestern Germany, bordering France, and western and southern Austria, bordering Switzerland and Italy, were designated the French Zone of occupation. The United States occupied much of central and southern Germany, south of the British Zone, east of the French Zone, and west of the Russian Zone and Czech border. The American Zone extended into the border area of Germany and Austria as far as the British Zone of Austria. Berlin, the ruined German capital, was in the heart of the Russian Zone, but was itself divided into four zones of occupation. All of these divisions were intended as temporary, strictly for the purposes of administering the land of a prostrate enemy. The Soviets, however, regarded the occupation as a foothold, from which they would claim political satellites that would remain in the Soviet orbit for some fifty years after the war had ended. These nations, in Winston Churchill's memorable phrase, fell behind an "Iron Curtain" and constituted the "Eastern Bloc" of the Cold War period, a "Communist World" inexorably opposed to the "Free World" of the West.

REALITY CHECK

An Icy Breeze

The incipient Cold War began freezing relations between the West and the Soviets—so recently allied—even before the war ended. Soviet authorities kept DPs who were in their territory beyond the reach of UNRRA. Stalin's policy was not to care for refugees, but to give them bare subsistence in exchange for forced labor in work camps.

In Asia an even more momentous division between Communist and non-Communist nations was beginning to crystallize. Liberated from Japanese occupation, Korea was divided into a northern Soviet zone of occupation and a southern American zone. Within a few years, this division would harden into the Democratic People's Republic of Korea—the Communist North Korea—and the Republic of Korea, democratic South Korea. The division would become the source of the Korean War of 1950–53.

Peace would be elusive in the postwar world. Soviet United Nation's representative Andrei Gromyko (in dark military cap) guides North Korea's premier Kim Hsong (hatless, at left of official party reviewing troops) during Kim's 1949 visit to Moscow less than a year before the outbreak of the Korean War.

Elsewhere in Asia, French Indochina had been occupied by Japan during the war, and when the French attempted to reassert their colonial domination of the country after the war, the Marxist leader Ho Chi Minh led an anticolonial war for independence, which developed into a civil war between North and South Vietnam even after the French had

DETAILS, DETAILS

Megabombs

As discussed in Chapter 22, the explosive energy of an atomic bomb is liberated by the splitting apart—the fission—of the atomic particles in the nuclei of the bomb's uranium or plutonium core. In a thermonuclear, or hydrogen, bomb, a fission reaction is used to create *fusion,* the joining together of subatomic particles of hydrogen atoms in the bomb's core. The fusion process yields even more energy than a fission reaction, and thus a hydrogen atom blast is far stronger. Whereas a fission explosion is measured as the equivalent of so may kilotons (kilo = 1,000) of TNT, a fusion explosion must be measured in megatons (mega = 1,000,000) of TNT.

relinquished their hold on the country in 1954. The Vietnam War became a twenty-year struggle in which the United States was deeply and tragically involved.

Most spectacularly, China had been torn by a long civil war between the Western-aligned Nationalists of Chiang Kai-shek and the Communist forces of Mao Zedong before the Japanese invasion of 1937 temporarily united the Nationalists and the Communists against the common enemy. With the defeat of Japan, the alliance between Chiang and Mao dissolved, the civil war resumed, and the People's Republic of China, the biggest Communist country in the world, emerged triumphant on October 1, 1949.

Slouching toward Armageddon

Within half a decade of V-E and V-J days, the world seemed once again to have divided itself into armed camps: the tenuously allied Soviets and Chinese Communists on one side and the U.S.-led West on the other. Just as World War I had failed to be what President Woodrow Wilson had hoped it would be—the "war to end all wars"—so World War II came to seem a possible prelude to World War III. And in what was now the atomic age, that was a terrifying prospect indeed. By the early 1950s, the United States had lost its monopoly on atomic weapons. Both the Soviet Union and America—soon to be joined by China as well—accumulated nuclear and even more powerful thermonuclear arsenals. Were a new world war to erupt, it would almost certainly be "the war to end all wars" by virtue of being the war that ended civilization itself.

Cold War

President Harry S. Truman presided over victory in World War II then found himself faced with the dilemma of defending the "Free World" against the aggressive expansion of Communism—without igniting a third world war that would almost surely bring Armageddon. Between the twin rocks of surrender and universal doom, Truman steered a course that U.S. State Department official George F. Kennan termed "containment." It was a policy of using diplomatic, political, economic, cultural, and very limited military means to meet and counter Communist aggression wherever and whenever it broke out in the world. It was a policy of limited war intended to curb Communist expansion without engulfing the world in a major conflict. In a speech of April 14, 1947, the eminent financier and presidential adviser Bernard Baruch called the condition that resulted from this policy a "Cold War." Truman and others had faith that this patient, tense, and often frustrating strategy of fighting limited conflicts, though rarely decisive in itself, would buy time during which the inherent superiority of democracy and capitalism would outlast and triumph over the innate weaknesses of Communism and a command economy.

"Our policy is directed not against any country or doctrine but against hunger, poverty, desperation and chaos. Its purpose should be the revival of a working economy in the world so as to permit the emergence of political and social conditions in which free institutions can exist."

George C. Marshall, announcing the Marshall Plan at a Harvard University address, June 5, 1947

THE MARSHALL PLAN

THE WARS IN KOREA AND VIETNAM, AS WELL AS OTHER, SMALLER WARS during the fifty years between the end of World War II and the collapse of Soviet Communism in the early 1990s, were armed battles of the Cold War. But arguably the most important "battle" of that war was waged not with guns and bombs, but with capacious humanity and a great deal of money.

The United States had been sending emergency economic aid to Europe even before the end of World War II, totaling some $9 billion by early 1947. The hope that Britain and France would recover quickly enough to care for their own populations and perhaps even extend aid to others soon faded. The problem was that the entire European economy had been shattered, for victors and vanquished alike. European farmers could still produce food, but urban populations, their infrastructures crippled or destroyed, had no way to pay for it. Even if industrial plants were rapidly rebuilt, neither city dwellers nor farmers could pay for the goods produced. The basic economic cycle had been disrupted.

U.S. secretary of state George C. Marshall (center) discusses with American and French officials the massive European relief plan unofficially named for him. Britain's Winston Churchill called the Marshall Plan the "most unsordid political act in history." U.S. undersecretary of state Dean Acheson stands at the left, with Maurice Petsche, French minister of finance, beside him. On the other side of Marshall are French minister of public works Jules Moch and U.S. secretary of the treasury John W. Snyder.

In this postwar crisis, American government officials proposed various plans to aid European recovery and jump-start the Continent's economy. That favored by George C. Marshall, who had been U.S. Army chief of staff throughout World War II and, in the

NUMBERS
Funds Distributed
Over four years, the Marshall Plan distributed $13 billion in economic aid, which helped the countries involved raise their gross national products from 15 to 25 percent over four years. Funds were offered to the Soviet Union and to the eastern European nations behind the Iron Curtain. The Soviet Union and its satellites rejected the offer.

Truman administration, had become secretary of state, was a plan for the United States to finance European recovery with the proviso that the European nations themselves jointly decide how the American-supplied funds were to be used. Marshall understood that much of Europe was in the grip of an acute humanitarian crisis, which required immediate relief. He was also keenly aware of how the harshly punitive Treaty of Versailles, which ended World War I, had created conditions conducive to the rise of Hitler. Germany, Marshall reasoned, had been the most powerful industrial force in Europe before World War II, and its economic prostration was now holding back the recovery of all Europe. Worse, the devastation throughout Europe made all the Western nations vulnerable to intimidation and domination by the Soviet Union. Truman and Marshall hoped that a massive infusion of capital would not only relieve the immediate humanitarian crisis, but also jump-start the entire European economy, restoring capitalism and blocking the inroads of Soviet influence.

Marshall introduced the proposed plan on June 5, 1947, in a commencement address he delivered at Harvard University. The details of what the press was quick to dub the "Marshall Plan" were filled in later. Marshall and Truman believed that the political, social, and economic future of Europe required the nations of that continent to overcome all motives of rivalry, vengeance, and nationalism. That meant that Europeans had to learn to act with a unity they had never known before. Marshall proposed that the nations of Europe meet to formulate a unified plan for the disbursement and use of funds. The United States would release no money until the plan had been made and agreed upon by every nation that wanted help.

The Marshall Plan was signed into law on April 3, 1948, and provided funding to Austria, Belgium, Denmark, France, Greece, Iceland, Ireland, Italy, Luxembourg, the Netherlands, Norway, Portugal, Sweden, Switzerland, Turkey, the United Kingdom, and western Germany.

JUSTICE

IN THE BROADEST SENSE, THE MARSHALL PLAN was an effort to restore social justice to a Europe that had been for so long deprived of it. The Allies were concerned to restore another kind of justice as well.

On August 8, 1945, representatives from the United States, Great Britain, the Soviet Union, and the provisional government of France signed the London Agreement, which included a charter calling for a military tribunal to try major Axis war criminals whose offenses had no particular or specific geographic location. The tribunal was authorized to convict any individual guilty of the commission of war crimes and also to find any group or organization to be criminal in character. The tribunal was made up of a member (plus an alternate) selected by each of the four principal signatories of the London Agreement.

The Soviet member, General I. T. Nikitchenko, convened the first session on October 18, 1945, in Berlin, and presided over the trial of twenty-four former Nazi leaders and members of various groups, including the German secret police known as the "Gestapo." After this initial session, all others, beginning on November 20, 1945, were held in the city of Nuremberg under the presidency of Lord Justice Geoffrey Lawrence, the British member.

In all cases, indictments consisted of four possible counts: crimes against peace (the planning, instigation, and waging of wars of aggression in violation of international treaties and agreements), crimes against humanity (exterminations, deportations, and genocide), war crimes (violations of the accepted laws and international conventions of war), and conspiracy to commit any or all of the criminal acts listed in those first three counts.

On October 1, 1946, after 216 sessions, the verdicts on twenty-two of the original twenty-four defendants were handed down. One defendant, Robert Ley, had committed suicide while in prison, and the aged Gustav Krupp von Bohlen und Halbach, the great German arms manufacturer, was judged mentally and physically unfit to stand trial.

Twenty-two were tried. Three—Hans Fritzsche (Goebbels's deputy in the Propaganda Ministry), Franz von Papen (briefly chancellor under Hitler and later ambassador to Austria, then Turkey), and Hjalmar Schacht (banker and economics minister just before the war)—were acquitted. Four were sentenced to prison terms between ten and twenty years. These included Karl Dönitz, mastermind of the German U-boat campaigns and the man Hitler, before committing suicide, named head of state; Albert Speer, Hitler's director of munitions, who was responsible

REALITY CHECK

Accountable Individuals

The tribunal established certain enduring principles of international law, including those embodied in the rejection of the chief defenses offered by the defendants. The tribunal rejected the contention that only a state, and not individuals, could be found guilty of war crimes. The court concluded that crimes of international law are committed by men and women and that only by holding individuals to account for committing such crimes could international law be enforced. The tribunal also rejected the defense that the trial as well as its adjudication were ex post facto. All acts of which the defendants were found guilty, the tribunal held, had been universally regarded as criminal prior to World War II.

Trial at Nuremberg: Nazi-era war criminals are called to account before an Allied tribunal during 1945–46.

for administering much of Germany's wartime slave labor program; Konstantin von Neurath, "Protector" of Bohemia and Moravia from 1939 until his resignation following a dispute with Hitler; and Baldur von Schirach, a Hitler Youth leader who expressed remorse at trial. Three were sentenced to life imprisonment. Foremost among these were Rudolf Hess, deputy leader of the Nazi Party; Walther Funk, Hitler's minister of economics; and Erich Raeder, commander in chief of the German navy until 1943; only Hess served out his term—the others were released early. The rest, twelve men, were sentenced to death by hanging. Among these individuals were Julius Streicher, chief articulator of Nazi anti-Semitism; Joachim von Ribbentrop, Nazi Germany's foreign minister; Alfred Jodl and Wilhelm Keitel, top German military officers; and Arthur Seyss-Inquart, who had served as Austria's puppet chancellor after that nation's annexation to Germany. Martin Bormann, Hitler's private secretary, was tried and condemned in absentia but was never brought to justice. Hermann Göring, the second most powerful man in the Third Reich and the head of the Luftwaffe, cheated the hangman by swallowing a cyanide capsule.

Less universally publicized than the Nuremburg Tribunal were the Tokyo War Crimes trials, conducted from May 3, 1946 to November 12, 1948, to try Japanese civilian and former military officers who had either killed prisoners of war or had been indicted for roles in instigating the war. Only twenty-eight men were tried by the Tokyo tribunal itself, but some twenty thousand defendants were tried in the countries of their victims. In all, nine hundred individuals were executed.

The Jewish Homeland

Many of the Nuremburg trials focused on the Holocaust, in which Germans at every level of the government and the military were responsible for the mass murder of six million Jews. At the time of

THE NAZI HUNTERS

Many important Nazis, including some associated with the Holocaust, managed to evade capture by the Allies at the end of the war. Agencies of the United States and other Allied nations tracked some—although it is also true that American officials sheltered a number of Nazis considered important in the areas of science and technology or in the fight against postwar Communism.

Although most of the Nazi perpetrators of the Holocaust who escaped capture immediately after the war were never brought to justice, there were notable exceptions. On May 11, 1960, three members of the Israeli Security Service (the Mosad) abducted Adolf Eichmann near Buenos Aires, Argentina, where he had been in hiding since 1950. The highest-profile surviving administrator of the "Final Solution," Eichmann was tried in Jerusalem and convicted of many charges, including "crimes against the Jewish people." His execution was the first—and, so far, the only—death sentence ever carried out by the state of Israel.

The most famous individual "Nazi hunter" was Simon Wiesenthal (1908–2005), a Holocaust survivor who, after the liberation, went to work for the War Crimes Section of the U.S. Army and in 1947 opened the Jewish Historical Documentation Center in Austria. Wiesenthal pressured governments into finding and prosecuting escaped Nazis and also uncovered and supplied leads as to their whereabouts. He was instrumental in tracking Eichmann, as well as such figures as Franz Stangl, commandant of the Sobibor and Treblinka death camps, and Karl Silberbauer, the Gestapo officer chiefly responsible for the arrest of Anne Frank and her family.

Another important Nazi hunter, Beate Klarsfeld, tracked down, in 1971, Klaus Barbie, infamous as the "Butcher of Lyon," who ruthlessly ran the Gestapo office in Lyon, France. For a time after the war, Barbie worked for American military intelligence. Not tried until 1987, he was convicted in France of crimes against humanity and sentenced to life in prison.

After surviving the Holocaust, Simon Wiesenthal (1908–2005) dedicated his life to bringing escaped Nazis to justice. In this 1978 photograph, he holds a poster urging Americans to write to the German government in support of abolishing the statute of limitations for prosecuting Nazi war criminals—the statute was abolished in July 1979.

REALITY CHECK

Small Steps

The impact of the war on race relations and the role of women in American life was important, but also limited. Racial inequality, including outright segregation, reemerged after the war, especially in the South, and most women, as soon as the men began to return, eagerly relinquished their jobs for what were perceived as the traditional roles of wife and mother. Still, there was no going back to the status quo. In the areas of racial and gender equality, wartime society had, at the very least, demonstrated a reality that *could* be.

World War II, Jews were a people without a homeland. During the nineteenth century, a Zionist movement had developed, aimed at securing Palestine as a Jewish state. The cataclysmic fate of the Jews in the war that had just ended persuaded not only the world Jewish community, but the governments of many nations, including the United States, of the necessity of establishing a Jewish state. In this way, World War II served as a catalyst for the founding of the state of Israel on May 14, 1948. Harry S. Truman declared America's recognition of the new nation barely fifteen minutes after it had been created. Other governments soon followed suit.

Occupation

THE WESTERN AND SOVIET POWERS OCCUPIED GERMANY from 1945 to 1949, allowing a gradual transition from Allied military administration to self-government—although, in the case of East Germany, the government was essentially a puppet of the Soviet Union. The occupation of Japan was a more dramatic story. From 1945 to 1952, the occupation government was headed solely by the Supreme Commander for Allied Powers (SCAP), who was, until 1951, General Douglas MacArthur, the very commander who had accepted the Japanese surrender. It would have been no surprise had the Japanese people resented being governed by their military conqueror, but, in fact, MacArthur proved to be not only a brilliant and enlightened administrator, who drew up the very constitution on which the modern Japanese democracy is based, but was extraordinarily popular. The U.S. occupation of Japan was without doubt the most successful, productive, and benevolent military occupation in history.

The American Home Front

THE SHARED EXPERIENCE OF WORLD WAR II profoundly affected American society. The manpower demands of the war, both in industry and the military, made important, if tenuous, inroads into the racial segregation that characterized most of American life, especially in the South. Those same demands brought millions of women into the workplace and into various aspects of the military.

One of the most remarkable social transformations was created by the federal government. On June 22, 1944, more than a year before

The National World War II Memorial on Washington's National Mall includes a Freedom Wall with four thousand sculpted gold stars representing the four hundred thousand American lives lost during the war.

the war ended, Congress passed and President Roosevelt signed the Servicemen's Readjustment Act, better known as the "G.I. Bill of Rights" or just the "G.I. Bill." This unprecedented legislation provided extensive and extraordinary benefits for returning veterans, including generous mortgage assistance and educational scholarships. Young men whose lives had been interrupted by war service were given the opportunity to get vocational education or a full college education—the latter hitherto available only to a relatively small fraction of young men. The G.I. Bill helped to produce the best-educated generation in American history, and its mortgage assistance provisions made more Americans than ever before owners of their own homes. The postwar generation was overwhelmingly middle class rather than working class, contributing to the perceived as well as the actual prosperity of America in the 1950s.

Last, Best Hope

The generation of Americans who had fought World War II not only anticipated—and to a remarkable degree realized—a future of solid prosperity at home, they had learned to see their country as a superpower. Whereas the American public rapidly retreated into isolationism after World War I, there was, after World War II, a far greater national will to engage with the world, to become a global power and, more importantly, a global force for good. America's role in World War II seemed abundant proof of the truth of the definition Abraham Lincoln had fixed to the United States during the darkest days of the Civil War in 1862. In his Second Annual Message to Congress, he had called it "the last, best hope of earth."

TAKEAWAY

Healing and Division

World War II was the most devastating human conflict in history. The United States took the lead in attempting to heal the wounds in Europe and Asia, but the war left the world divided, on either side of an "Iron Curtain," into two new armed camps, one Communist and totalitarian, the other both capitalist and democratic.

World War II Timeline

1938

March 13: Adolf Hitler proclaims Anschluss with Austria.

September 29: At the Munich Conference, British prime minister Neville Chamberlain attempts to "appease" Hitler by forcing Czechoslovakia to cede part of itself (the Sudetenland) to Germany.

November 3: Japan proclaims a "new order in Asia," effectively declaring its intention to dominate the region.

November 9–10: The Crystal Night (Kristallnacht) pogrom is the first officially sanctioned mass violence against Jews in the Third Reich.

1939

August 23: Hitler and Joseph Stalin conclude a nonaggression pact between Germany and the Soviet Union, also secretly agreeing to partition Poland and to allow the USSR to occupy Estonia, Latvia, and Lithuania.

September 1: The German invasion of Poland begins World War II.

September 3: Great Britain and France declare war on Germany.

September 5: U.S. president Franklin Roosevelt declares neutrality and national emergency.

September 17: The Soviet Union invades part of Poland and the Baltics.

September 27: Warsaw falls to the Germans.

November 4: The U.S. Neutrality Act of 1939 enables the sale of arms to the Allies on a cash-and-carry basis only.

November 30: The Soviet Union invades Finland.

1940

March 12: Finland surrenders to the Soviet Union, ending the Russo-Finnish War.

April 9: Germany invades Norway and Denmark.

May 10: Germany begins *Blitzkrieg* (lightning war), an attack on the Western Front, invading France, the Netherlands, Belgium, and Luxembourg. In Britain, Winston Churchill succeeds Chamberlain as prime minister.

May 24–June 10: In the evacuation of Dunkirk, 338,000 British Expeditionary Force (BEF) and French troops are saved, but most of the European continent is doomed to German occupation.

June 10: Benito Mussolini's Italy joins the conflict, declaring war on Great Britain and France.

June 22: France falls and concludes an armistice.

July 1: Marshal Henri Pétain organizes a puppet government at Vichy; Germany occupies northern and northwestern France.

July 10: The Battle of Britain commences in the skies above London and other British cities.

August 1: Japan formally announces the "Greater East Asia Co-Prosperity Sphere," a program by which they seek to dominate Southeast and East Asia.

September 3: The U.S. gives Britain surplus World War I–era destroyers in return for ninety-nine-year leases on British naval bases in the Western Hemisphere.

September 26: Seeking to curb Japanese aggression in China, President Roosevelt announces an embargo on strategic exports to Japan.

September 27: Germany, Italy, and Japan formally conclude the Tripartite (Axis) Pact military alliance.

October 28: Italy invades Greece.

December 9: British forces take the offensive against Italian forces in Egypt's Western Desert.

1941

January 22: The Libyan port of Tobruk falls to the British.

March 11: The U.S. Congress passes the Lend-Lease Act, permitting the supply of arms and other matériel, without a cash or other exchange, to any nations the president deems vital to U.S. defense.

April 6: Germany invades Yugoslavia and Greece to aid the ill-fated Italian campaigns in Albania and Greece.

April 13: Japan concludes a neutrality agreement with the Soviet Union.

May 20: Germans paratroops land and began to drive the British out of Crete.

May 24: HMS *Hood* is sunk by *Bismarck* and *Prinz Eugen*.

May 27: The British Royal Navy forces sink *Bismarck*, pride of the German surface fleet.

June 22: Abrogating the German-Soviet Non-Aggression Pact, Hitler invades the Soviet Union.

August 14: Roosevelt and Churchill publish the Atlantic Charter, formal basis of an Anglo-American alliance.

September 4: The U.S. destroyer *Greer* is attacked by a German submarine; the United States begins an undeclared naval war with Germany.

September 8: German troops commence the siege of Leningrad.

September 29–30: At Babi Yar, near Kiev, German soldiers massacre more than thirty-three thousand Jews.

October 18: General Hideki Tojo becomes Japan's prime minister; the nation is now a military dictatorship.

December 7: Japan attacks Pearl Harbor, Hawaii, home of the U.S. Pacific Fleet, inflicting extensive damage and many casualties. Simultaneously, Japanese forces attack the Philippines and Guam, both U.S. territories, and invade British-held Malaya. They also begin an attack on the British Crown colony of Hong Kong and Wake Island, held by a small detachment of U.S. Marines.

December 8: The United States and Great Britain declare war on Japan.

December 10: Guam surrenders, becoming the first U.S. possession to be occupied by the Japanese.

December 11: Germany and Italy declare war on the United States.

December 15: Japanese forces invade Borneo.

December 23: Wake Island falls to the Japanese.

December 25: The British Crown colony of Hong Kong falls to Japanese invaders.

December 30 (approximately): British- and Dutch-controlled areas of Borneo fall to Japan.

1942

February 15: Singapore falls to the Japanese.

February 19: Franklin Roosevelt signs Executive Order 9066, ordering the internment of Japanese-Americans living in coastal areas of the United States.

March 1: Japan defeats U.S. naval forces at the battle of the Java Sea.

March 11: Acting on orders from President Roosevelt, General Douglas MacArthur evacuates the Philippines via PT boat. After arriving in Australia, where he establishes a headquarters, MacArthur broadcasts on March 17 the famous promise: "I shall return."

April 10: The fall of Bataan signals the final fall of the Philippines. It is followed by the infamous Bataan Death March, to a Japanese prison camp.

April 18: Colonel Jimmy Doolittle leads a spectacular air raid on Tokyo and other Japanese cities.

May 1: Mandalay, Burma, falls to Japan. Japanese troops advance on India.

May 7–8: Battle of the Coral Sea ends in a tactical defeat for the U.S. Navy, but a strategic defeat for the Japanese, whose Pacific juggernaut is halted.

June 4: The Battle of Midway marks the turning point of the war in the Pacific, putting the Imperial Japanese Navy on the defensive through the end of the war.

JUNE 21: Under the "Desert Fox," Field Marshal Erwin Rommel, the German Afrika Korps retakes Tobruk, Libya, which the British had captured earlier.

JULY 1: At the first battle of El Alamein, British general Bernard Law Montgomery stops Rommel's advance near Alexandria, Egypt.

AUGUST 7: The Battle of Guadalcanal, in the Solomon Islands, begins; it is the first American ground offensive of the Pacific war.

AUGUST 19: British and Canadian forces raid Dieppe, France, and are disastrously repulsed.

NOVEMBER 4: Montgomery forces Rommel's vaunted Afrika Korps into retreat toward Tunisia.

NOVEMBER 8: Operation Torch commences. Under the leadership of U.S. general Dwight D. Eisenhower, American and British forces land in North Africa.

NOVEMBER 12: The naval phase of the Guadalcanal campaign commences.

NOVEMBER 23: At Stalingrad, forces of the Soviet Red Army cut off German-held Stalingrad in preparation for their major counteroffensive against the German Sixth Army.

NOVEMBER 30: The Battle of Buna marks the first high point of MacArthur's offensive against the Japanese in New Guinea—an effort to prevent an invasion of Australia.

1943

JANUARY 23: Tripoli, Libya, falls to Montgomery's British Eighth Army.

JANUARY 24: The Casablanca Conference between Churchill and Roosevelt concludes with an Allied agreement that nothing less than the unconditional surrender of the Axis will end the war.

JANUARY 27: U.S. Army Air Forces bombers raid Germany for the first time. The strategic bombing campaign begins and will continue until the end of the war in Europe.

FEBRUARY 1: Japanese forces begin to evacuate Guadalcanal.

FEBRUARY 2: The German Sixth Army surrenders at Stalingrad—the turning point of the war on the Eastern Front.

FEBRUARY 19–25: The U.S. II Corps suffers a humiliating defeat at Kasserine Pass, Tunisia.

MARCH 2–4: The U.S. Navy's victory at the battle of Bismarck Sea destroys Japanese troops and supply convoys of the so-called Tokyo Express.

APRIL 18: U.S. fighters shoot down an airplane carrying Isoroku Yamamoto, Japan's leading naval commander and the architect of the Pearl Harbor attack.

APRIL 19: The Jews of Poland's Warsaw ghetto rise against German occupiers in a heroic but doomed effort.

MAY 13: German forces surrender in North Africa.

JULY 5: The Battle of Kursk begins. Part of the Soviet counteroffensive, it is the largest tank battle in history.

JULY 10: The Allies commence Operation Husky, stepping off from North Africa to invade Sicily.

JULY 22: The Seventh U.S. Army, led by Patton, takes Palermo, Sicily.

JULY 25: In Italy, the Grand Council of Fascism ejects Mussolini (in office since 1922) and replaces him with Marshal Pietro Badoglio. Badoglio secretly negotiates a separate peace with the Allies.

AUGUST 17: With the fall of Messina to Patton, Sicily is occupied by the Allies.

SEPTEMBER 8: Italy unconditionally surrenders to the Allies. It is the first Axis power to fall.

SEPTEMBER 9: The Allies land on mainland Italy, at Salerno.

SEPTEMBER 12: German commandos rescue and evacuate Mussolini, who is set up as puppet ruler of German-occupied northern Italy.

SEPTEMBER 16: Lae, New Guinea, falls to the Allies.

OCTOBER 1: Under the command of U.S. general Mark W. Clark, the Fifth U.S. Army takes Naples, Italy.

November 6: Kiev, capital of Ukraine, is retaken by the Red Army.

November 18: British RAF bombers begin massive air raids against Berlin.

November 23: Tarawa (in the Gilbert Islands) falls to U.S. Marines, while neighboring Makin Island is taken by the U.S. Army.

1944

January 22: American troops land at Anzio, Italy, in an effort to flank German defenders.

June 4: Rome becomes the first Axis capital to fall to the Allies.

June 6: D-Day—Operation Overlord—the Allied invasion of Normandy, commences.

June 15: U.S. Marines and soldiers land on Saipan, Mariana Islands.

June 19–20: The U.S. Navy triumphs at the battle of the Philippine Sea.

July 9: Saipan falls to the Americans.

July 20: The Stauffenberg Plot to assassinate Hitler fails.

July 21: Marines assault Guam, Mariana Islands.

July 25: Operation Cobra begins—the great Allied breakout from Normandy.

August 1: Encouraged by the approach of the Red Army, partisans stage the abortive Warsaw Uprising against German occupiers.

August 3: U.S. and Chinese troops take Myitkyina, Burma.

August 15: In Operation Dragoon, Allied troops land in the south of France.

August 25: Paris is liberated by Free French and American troops.

September 17: Operation Market-Garden, Montgomery's attempt to break through to Germany via Holland, begins.

September 25: Market-Garden fails with heavy losses.

October 10: The Red Army breaks through to the Baltic Sea.

October 20: Fulfilling his pledge to return to the Philippines, General MacArthur wades ashore at Leyte.

October 21: Aachen is the first significant German city to fall to the Allies.

October 26: The naval battle of Leyte Gulf ends in the near destruction of the Japanese fleet.

November 24: American B-29s begin routine raids on Tokyo.

December 16: The Battle of the Bulge, a surprise German offensive, begins in the Ardennes region of Belgium and Luxembourg.

December 26: The Third U.S. Army of George S. Patton Jr. turns the tide at the Battle of the Bulge, delivering a decisive blow against the German army in the west.

1945

January 12: The Red Army advances across the Vistula River into Poland.

January 17: Warsaw falls to the Red Army.

January 27: Red Army troops liberate the Auschwitz death camp in Poland, beginning the international exposure of the Holocaust.

February 4: Roosevelt, Churchill, and Stalin meet at Yalta to plan the postwar world.

February 13: An Anglo-American bombing force stages an intensive incendiary raid on Dresden, Germany, igniting a firestorm that consumes the medieval city.

February 19: U.S. Marines land on Iwo Jima, beginning five weeks of intense combat to take the island.

March 3: Manila, Philippines, is liberated.

March 7: U.S. forces cross the Rhine at Remagen.

March 9: Army Air Forces general Curtis LeMay begins the firebombing of Tokyo.

MARCH 20: Mandalay falls to the Allies.

MARCH 29: Frankfurt falls to American forces.

APRIL 1: U.S. Marines and soldiers land on Okinawa, the last bastion defending the Japanese home islands.

APRIL 6: Japan uses kamikaze (suicide) aircraft attacks to defend Okinawa.

APRIL 12: President Roosevelt dies of a cerebral hemorrhage; Harry S. Truman assumes office.

APRIL 13: The Red Army takes Vienna.

APRIL 16: The Red Army begins the Battle of Berlin.

APRIL 18: Patton's Third Army enters Czechoslovakia.

APRIL 23: The long, frustrating, and bloody Italian campaign ends as American and British troops reach the Po River at Italy's northern frontier.

APRIL 25: U.S. and Red Army forces shake hands on the Elbe River at Torgau.

APRIL 28: Italian partisans execute Benito Mussolini and his mistress, Clara Petacci.

APRIL 30: Holed up in a bunker beneath the streets of a ruined Berlin, Adolf Hitler and his long-time mistress, now bride, Eva Braun, commit suicide. Admiral Karl Dönitz becomes head of state.

MAY 2: Berlin falls to the Red Army.

MAY 3: Hamburg falls to the British army. Anglo-Indian forces take Rangoon, Burma.

MAY 7–8: The German army surrenders at 2:41 A.M., May 7, at Reims, France, and, at Stalin's insistence, also at Berlin on May 8.

JUNE 22: Okinawa falls to the Tenth U.S. Army.

JULY 16: Near Alamogordo, New Mexico, U.S. scientists successfully test the first atomic bomb.

AUGUST 2: Meeting at the Potsdam Conference, Truman, Stalin, Churchill (then his successor, Clement Attlee), issued a declaration that nothing less than Japan's unconditional surrender will end the war against that empire.

AUGUST 6: The U.S. B-29 *Enola Gay* drops an atomic bomb on Hiroshima, Japan.

AUGUST 8: The Soviet Union finally declares war on Japan and initiates an invasion of Japanese-held Manchuria.

AUGUST 9: Another B-29, *Bockscar*, drops an atomic bomb on Nagasaki, Japan.

AUGUST 14: Japanese emperor Hirohito agrees to a surrender that allows him to retain the throne, his authority wholly subject to that of the Supreme Allied Commander, Douglas MacArthur.

SEPTEMBER 2: Japan formally surrenders in a ceremony aboard the U.S. battleship *Missouri* at anchor in Tokyo Bay. MacArthur presides. World War II is over.

Live and in Person

SELECTED WORLD WAR II MUSEUMS AND MEMORIALS

ALFRED M. GRAY RESEARCH CENTER
2040 Broadway Street
Quantico, VA 22134, USA
(703) 784-2240
www.mcu.usmc.mil/MCRCweb/index.htm
Comprehensive collection of the U.S.Marine Corps's role in World War II.

AMERICAN AIR POWER HERITAGE MUSEUM
Confederate Air Force Headquarters
Midland International Airport
P.O. Box 62000
9600 Wright Drive Midland, TX 79711, USA
(432) 563-1000
www.airpowermuseum.org
A collection of World War II aircraft.

AUSCHWITZ-BIRKENAU MEMORIAL AND MUSEUM
ul. Wiezniow Oswiecimia 20
32-603 Oswiecim, Poland
(48) 3 38 43 20 22
www.auschwitz-muzeum.oswiecim.pl
A memorial and museum on the site of the most infamous extermination camp of World War II.

AUSTRALIAN WAR MEMORIAL
GPO Box 345
Canberra ACT 2601, Australia
(61) 02 6243 4211
www.awm.gov.au
Museum dedicated to Australians at war.

BASTOGNE HISTORICAL CENTER
Colline du Mardasson
B-6600 Bastogne, Belgium
(32) 61 21 14 13
www.bastognehistoricalcenter.be
Museum dedicated to the Battle of the Bulge.

CANADIAN WAR MUSEUM
1 Vimy Place
Ottawa, Ontario K1R 1C2, Canada
819 776-8600
www.warmuseum.ca/cwm
Canada's major war museum, including extensive exhibits on World War II.

DIEKIRCH HISTORICAL MUSEUM
10, Bamertal
L-9209 Diekirch, Luxembourg
(352) 80 89 08 or (352) 80 47 19
www.nat-military-museum.lu
Museum dedicated to the Battle of the Bulge.

FLEET AIR ARM MUSEUM
Royal Naval Air Station
Box 06, RNAS Yeovilton
Somerset BA22 8HT, United Kingdom
(44) 19 35 84 05 65
www.fleetairarm.com
Museum covering aviation in the Royal Navy.

HIROSHIMA PEACE MEMORIAL MUSEUM
1-2 Nakajimama-cho
Naka-ku, Hiroshima City 730-0811, Japan
(81) 82-242-7798
www.pcf.city.hiroshima.jp
Memorializes the world's first nuclear weapons attack, August 6, 1945.

IMPERIAL WAR MUSEUM
Lambeth Road
London SE1 6HZ, United Kingdom
(44) 20 74 16 53 20
www.iwm.org.uk
Has a very extensive collection covering World War II.

LUFTVAFFENMUSEUM (GERMAN AIR FORCE MUSEUM)
Foerderverein des Luftwaffenmuseums der Bundeswehr e.V.
Bundesgeschaeftsstelle,Postfach 450 222
12172 Berlin,Germany
(49) 30 8 11 07 69
www.luftwaffenmuseum.de
Devoted to German aviation, including during World War II.

MUSÊE D'HISTOIRE CONTEMPORAINE
Hotel National des Invalides
75007 Paris, France
(33) 44 42 54 91
www.paris.org/Musees/Histoire.Contemp/info.html
Extensive World War II collection.

MUSEUM OF FLYING
www.museumofflying.com
A large aircraft collection scheduled to open in its new location at the Santa Monica Airport in 2008.

MUSEUM OF LONDON
150 London Wall
London EC2Y 5HN, United Kingdom
0870 444 3852
www.molg.org.uk
www.museumoflondon.org.uk/archive/exhibits/blitz/intro.html
Includes extensive coverage of the Blitz in London.

NATIONAL AIR AND SPACE MUSEUM
National Mall location
6th and Independence Avenue SW
Washington, DC 20560, USA
(202) 633-1000
www.nasm.si.edu/museum/flagship.cfm
Udvar-Hazy Center
14390 Air and Space Museum Parkway
Chantilly, VA 20151, USA
202-633-1000
www.nasm.si.edu/museum/udvarhazy/
America's premier collection of historical aircraft.

NATIONAL ATOMIC MUSEUM
1905 Mountain Road NW
Albuquerque, NM 87104, USA
(505) 245-2137
www.atomicmuseum.com
Includes extensive exhibits on the history of the Manhattan Project.

NATIONAL MARITIME MUSEUM
Greenwich, London
SE10 9NF, United Kingdom
(44) 20 88 58 44 22
www.nmm.ac.uk
One of the world's great naval museums, including extensive World War II exhibits.

NATIONAL MUSEUM OF NAVAL AVIATION
1750 Radford Boulevard
Naval Air Station
Pensacola, FL 32508, USA
(850) 453-2389 or (800) 327-5002
www.navalaviationmuseum.org
A magnificent collection of U.S. naval aircraft.

NATIONAL MUSEUM OF THE MARINE CORPS AND HERITAGE CENTER
18900 Jefferson Davis Highway
Triangle, VA 22172, USA
(877) 653-1775
www.usmcmuseum.org
Museum of Marine Corps history, including World War II exhibitions.

NATIONAL MUSEUM OF THE U.S. AIR FORCE
1100 Spaatz Street
Wright-Patterson Air Force Base, OH 45433, USA
(937) 255-3286
www.nationalmuseum.af.mil
Documents the history of the U.S. Air Force.

NATIONAL WORLD WAR II MUSEUM
945 Magazine Street
New Orleans, LA 70130, USA
(504) 527-6012
www.nationalww2museum.org
Formerly the National D-Day Museum; extensive collections on D-Day and the United States in World War II.

NAVY MUSEUM NAVAL HISTORICAL CENTER
Washington Navy Yard
805 Kidder Breese Street SE
Washington, DC 20374-5060, USA
(202) 433-4882
www.history.navy.mil
Extensive collection of U.S. navy's role in World War II.

ROYAL AIR FORCE MUSEUMS
Royal Air Force Museum London
Grahame Park Way
London, NW9 5LL, United Kingdom
(44) 20 8205 2266
www.rafmuseum.org.uk/london/index.cfm
Royal Air Force Museum Cosford Shifnal
Shropshire, TF11 8UP, United Kingdom
(44) 1902 376 200
www.rafmuseum.org.uk/cosford/index.cfm
Britain's major RAF museums.

ROYAL AUSTRALIAN AIR FORCE MUSEUM
RAAF Base Williams
Point Cook Road
Point Cook, Victoria 3027, Australia
(61) 3 92 56 1300
www.defence.gov.au/RAAF/raafmuseum
Documents the history of the Royal Australian Air Force.

U.S. ARMY AVIATION MUSEUM
P.O. Box 620610-0610
Fort Rucker, AL 36362, USA
(334) 598-2508
www.armyavnmuseum.org/
Documents the history of U.S. Army aviation.

U.S. ARMY CENTER OF MILITARY HISTORY
Collins Hall, 103 Third Avenue
Fort Lesley J. McNair, DC 20319-5058, USA
(202) 685-2733
www.army.mil/cmh-pg/
Comprehensive World War II collection.

U.S. ARMY TRANSPORTATION MUSEUM
300 Washington Boulevard, Bessen Hall
Fort Eustis, VA 23604-5260, USA
(757) 878-1115
www.transchool.eustis.army.mil
/museum/museum.html
A major collection of World War II U.S. Army vehicles.

U.S. HOLOCAUST MEMORIAL MUSEUM
100 Raoul Wallenberg Place SW
Washington, DC 20024-2126, USA
(202) 488-0400
www.ushmm.org
A living memorial to the Holocaust.

USS *ARIZONA* NATIONAL MEMORIAL (PEARL HARBOR)
1 Arizona Memorial Place
Honolulu, Hawaii 96818-3145, USA
(808) 422-0561
www.nps.gov/usar
For America, the place where World War II began.

YAD VASHEM
P.O. Box 3477
Jerusalem 91034, Israel
(972) 26 44 34 00
www.yadvashem.org/
A Holocaust memorial and archives.

Read More, See More

BOOKS

Adams, Michael C. C. *The Best War Ever: America and World War II*. Baltimore: Johns Hopkins University Press, 1994.

Ambrose, Stephen E. Citizen Soldiers: *The U.S. Army from the Normandy Beaches to the Bulge to the Surrender of Germany, June 7, 1944–May 7*, 1945. New York: Simon & Schuster, 1997.

Bartov, Omer. *Hitler's Army: Soldiers, Nazis, and War in the Third Reich*. New York: Oxford University Press, 1991.

Bergerund, Eric M. *Fire in the Sky: The Air War in the South Pacific*. Boulder, CO.: Westview Press, 1999.

———. *Touched with Fire: The Land War in the South Pacific*. New York: Viking, 1996.

Beschloss, Michael. *The Conquerors: Roosevelt, Truman and the Destruction of Hitler's Germany, 1941–1945*. New York: Simon & Schuster, 2002.

Bookman, John T., and Stephen T. Powers. *The March to Victory: A Guide to World War II Battles and Battlefields from London to the Rhine*. New York: Harper & Row, 1986.

Brinkley, Douglas, and Michael E. Haskew, eds. *The World War II Desk Reference*. New York: HarperCollins, 2004.

Buchanan, Albert Russell. *The United States and World War II*. New York: Harper & Row, 1964.

Bullock, Alan. *Hitler and Stalin: Parallel Lives*. New York: Knopf, 1992.

Burleigh, Michael. *The Third Reich: A New History*. New York: Hill and Wang, 2000.

Calvocoressi, Peter. *Total War: The Story of World War II*. New York: Pantheon Books, 1972.

Chambers, John W., and David Culbert, eds. *World War II, Film, and History*. New York: Oxford University Press, 1996.

Craven, Wesley Frank, and James Lea Cate, eds. *The Army Air Forces in World War II*, 7 volumes. Chicago: University of Chicago Press, 1948–58.

Dear, I. C. B., ed. *The Oxford Companion to World War II*. Oxford, U.K.: Oxford University Press, 2001.

Denfeld, Duane. *World War II Museums and Relics of Europe*. Manhattan, KS.: Military Affairs/Aerospace Historian Publications, 1980.

Flower, Desmond, and James Reeves, eds. *The War, 1939–1945*. London: Cassell, 1960.

Franks, Clifton R., ed. *The Second World War* (West Point Military History Series). Wayne, N.J.: Avery, 1984.

Gantenbein, James Watson, comp. and ed. *Documentary Background of World War II, 1931 to 1941*. New York: Columbia University Press, 1948.

Goldhagen, Daniel J. *Hitler's Willing Executioners: Ordinary Germans and the Holocaust*. New York: Alfred A. Knopf, 1996.

Goodwin, Doris Kearns. *No Ordinary Time: Franklin and Eleanor Roosevelt: The Home Front in World War II*. New York: Simon & Schuster, 1994.

Hart, Liddel, ed. *History of the Second World War*. New York: Exeter Books, 1980.

Hess, Gary R. *The United States at War, 1941–1945*. Arlington Heights, IL.: H. Davidson, 1986.

Jacobsen, Hans-Adolf, and Arthur L. Smith Jr., comps. and eds. *World War II, Policy and Strategy: Selected Documents with Commentary*. Santa Barbara, CA: Clio Books, 1979.

Keegan, John. *Encyclopedia of World War II*. London and New York: Hamlyn, 1977.

———. *The Second World War*. London: Hutchinson, 1989.

Keegan, John, ed. *The Times Atlas of the Second World War*. New York: Harper & Row, 1989.

———. *Who Was Who in World War II*. London: Arms and Armour Press, 1978.

Lamb, Richard. *War in Italy, 1943–1945: A Brutal Story*. New York: St. Martin's Press, 1993.

Langsam, Walter Consuelo, ed. *Historic Documents of World War II*. Princeton, NJ: Van Nostrand, 1958.

MacDonald, John. *Great Battles of World War II*. New York: Macmillan, 1986.

Michel, Henri. *The Second World War*. London: Deutsch, 1975.

Miller, Nathan. *War at Sea: A Naval History of World War II*. New York: Scribner, 1995.

Morison, Samuel Eliot. *History of United States Naval Operations in World War II*, 15 volumes. Boston: Little, Brown, 1947–62.

Murray, Williamson, and Allan R. Millett. *A War to Be Won: Fighting the Second World War, 1937–1945*. Cambridge, MA: Belknap Press of Harvard University Press, 2000.

Neillands, Robin. *The Bomber War: The Allied Air Offensive against Nazi Germany*. New York: The Overlook Press, 2001.

Noakes, J., and G. Pridham. *Nazism, 1919–1945*. Atlantic Highlands, N.J.: Humanities Press, 1983–88.

Overy, R. J. *Russia's War.* New York: Penguin Books, 1998.

Perret, Geoffrey. *There's a War to Be Won: The United States Army in World War II.* New York: Random House, 1991.

Shachtman, Tom. *Terrors and Marvels: How Science and Technology Changed the Character and Outcome of World War II.* New York: William Morrow, 2002.

Shirer, William L. *The Rise and Fall of the Third Reich; A History of Nazi Germany.* New York, Simon & Schuster, 1960.

Snyder, Louis Leo. *Louis L. Snyder's Historical Guide to World War II.* Westport, CT: Greenwood Press, 1982.

———. *Encyclopedia of the Third Reich.* New York: McGraw-Hill, 1976.

———. *The War: A Concise History, 1939–1945.* New York: Simon & Schuster, 1960.

Spector, Ronald H. *Eagle against the Sun: The American War with Japan.* New York: Free Press, 1985.

Stanton, Shelby L. *Order of Battle, U.S. Army, World War II.* Novato, CA: Presidio, 1984.

Taylor, A. J. P. *The Origins of the Second World War.* New York: Atheneum, 1961.

Terkel, Studs. *The Good War: An Oral History of World War Two.* New York: Pantheon Books, 1984.

Toland, John. *The Rising Sun; the Decline and Fall of the Japanese Empire, 1936–1945.* New York: Random House, 1970.

Van Creveld, Martin. *Fighting Power: German and U.S. Army Performance, 1939–1945.* Westport, CT: Greenwood Press, 1982.

Weinberg, Gerhard L. *A World at Arms: A Global History of World War II.* New York: Cambridge University Press, 1994.

Wheeler, Richard. *A Special Valor: The U.S. Marines and the Pacific War.* New York: Harper & Row, 1983.

Young, Peter, ed. *Atlas of the Second World War.* New York: G. P. Putnam's Sons, 1974.

WEB SITES

In addition to the Web sites included with many of the museums listed under "Live and in Person," the following are especially valuable:

Airborne assault
www.thedropzone.org/index_back.html

American Memory collection, Library of Congress
memory.loc.gov/ammem

Cyberlibrary of the Holocaust
www.remember.org/

General history
www.historychannel.com
www.thehistorynet.com
http://www.bbc.co.uk/history/worldwars/wwtwo/

Statistics
gi.grolier.com/wwii/wwii_mainpage.html
www.warmemorial.com

Weaponry
www.angelfire.com/ab/worldwar2weapons

TOP TWELVE WORLD WAR II MOVIES

12. *To Hell and Back* (1955)
    Directed by Jesse Hibbs and starring Audie Murphy
    America's most-decorated World War II soldier plays himself.

11. *Midway* (1976)
    Directed by Jack Smight and starring Charlton Heston, Henry Fonda, and Robert Mitchum
    A historically accurate portrayal of the great naval battle that turned the tide of the Pacific war

10. *A Bridge Too Far* (1977)
    Directed by Richard Attenborough and starring Sean Connery, Robert Redford, and Anthony Hopkins
    A gripping and meticulously researched depiction of Montgomery's failed Operation Market-Garden

9. *Memphis Belle* (1990)

Directed by Michael Caton-Jones and starring Matthew Modine and Eric Stoltz
Dramatization of the true story of the last mission of the Memphis Belle, *a B-17 whose crew was the first to survive twenty-five missions and earn the right to go home*

8. *Tora Tora Tora* (1970)

Directed by Richard Fleischer and Kinji Fukasaku and starring Martin Balsam, Sô Yamamura, Joseph Cotton, and E. G. Marshall
Pearl Harbor seen from both sides

7. *Das Boot* (1982)

Directed by Wolfgang Petersen and starring Jürgen Prochnow
A harrowing, intensely realistic drama of life and death on a German U-boat

6. *Saving Private Ryan* (1998)

Directed by Stephen Spielberg and starring Tom Hanks, Matt Damon, and many others
Great special effects and remarkable acting mark this portrayal of D-Day and a mission to rescue one soldier.

5. *The Longest Day* (1962)

Directed by Ken Annakin (British exterior episodes), Andrew Marton (American exterior episodes), and Bernhard Wicki (German episodes) and starring John Wayne, Henry Fonda, Robert Mitchum, Sean Connery, and many others
Beautifully shot in black and white, an ambitious and epic portrayal of D-Day from all sides

4. *Schindler's List* (1993)

Directed by Steven Spielberg and starring Liam Neeson, Ben Kingsley, and Ralph Fiennes
The chilling and inspiring story of the small-time German industrialist who decides to save his Jewish workers from the Holocaust

3. *Downfall* (2004)

Directed by Oliver Hirschbiegel and starring Bruno Ganz and Alexandra Maria Lara
Released in Germany as Der Untergang, *this masterpiece is a richly researched and intensely dramatic portrayal of Adolf Hitler's final days in his bunker under the streets of a ruined Berlin.*

2. *Flags of Our Fathers* and *Letters from Iwo Jima* (2006)

Directed by Clint Eastwood and starring (*Flags*) Ryan Phillippe, Adam Beach, and Jesse Bradford and (*Letters*) Ken Watanabe, Kazunari Ninomiya, and Tsuyoshi Ihara
Companion films present an extraordinary dual view of the Battle of Iwo Jima, from the American perspective (focusing on the men who raised the flag on Mount Suribachi) and from the Japanese defenders of the island.

1. *Patton* (1970)

Directed by Franklin Schaffner and starring George C. Scott and Karl Malden
This film biography of America's enigmatic and controversial warrior general, George S. Patton Jr., is driven by one of cinema's greatest screen performances: George C. Scott in the title role.

And for special consideration . . .

Directed by Fred Zinneman and starring Burt Lancaster, Montgomery Clift, Deborah Kerr, and Frank Sinatra, *From Here to Eternity* (1953) is a magnificent cinema realization of James Jones's novel about American soldiers on the eve of Pearl Harbor. It is a moving evocation of a country about to lose its innocence in a cataclysmic war. *The Best Years of Our Lives* (1946), directed by William Wyler and starring Frederic March, Myrna Loy, and Dana Andrews, focuses on the painful homecoming of men who had lived through war. Harold Russell, not an actor but a veteran who had lost both hands in the war, is featured as a wounded sailor coming home to the childhood sweetheart who knew him when he was whole.

Index

Picture Credits

Courtesy the Australian War Memorial, Negative Number 0180897: 236

Courtesy Archiv der Max-Planck-Gesellschaft, Berlin-Dahlem: 127

Courtesy Cacace Family: 146

Corbis: 272: © CORBIS; 293: © CORBIS; 349: © CORBIS

Maps courtesy of the Department of History, United States Military Academy: 107; 145; 192; 199; 226; 241; 253; 280; 286; 300; 313

Courtesy Department of the Navy—Naval Historical Center: 95; 98; 139; 218; 219 *t*; 219 *b*; 227; 235; 240 *t*; 240 *b*; 242; 243; 268; 271; 277; 281; 306

Getty Images: xvi–1; 25; 35; 39; 41; 74; 91: Time & Life Pictures/Getty Images; 177: Time & Life Pictures/Getty Images; 230: Time & Life Pictures/Getty Images; 238; 245: Time & Life Pictures/Getty Images; 255; 262: Time & Life Pictures/Getty Images; 267; 273; 272: Time & Life Pictures/Getty Images; 288; 313: Time & Life Pictures/Getty Images; 322: Time & Life Pictures/Getty Images; 324: Time & Life Pictures/Getty Images; 363; 365: Tim Graham/Getty Images

The Granger Collection, New York: 22; 28; 30 *b*; 32; 44; 47; 51; 54; 76 *b*; 114; 178; 259

Courtesy the Private Collection of Anthony Langley—www.greatwardifferent.com: 7; 11

Courtesy the U.S. National Archives and Records Administration, Washington, D.C.: 37; 40; 50; 68–69; 86; 88; 131; 134; 149; 161; 164; 183; 189; 246; 250; 258; 265; 266; 297; 302; 308; 311; 318; 319; 321; 342; 345; 347; 348 *t*; 348 *b*; 351; 353 *t*

Political Archive, German Federal Foreign Office: 126

Courtesy Library of Congress Prints & Photographs Division: 4: LC-USZ62-70672; 9: LC-USZ62-136086; 15: LC-USZ62-65032; 18: LC-DIG-ggbain-37518; 19: LC-USZC4-12051; 27: LC-USZ62-12667; 33: LC-USZ62-98333; 55: LC-USW33-019093-C; 79: LC-USZC4-4337; 81: LC-DIG-ppmsca-05354; 102–3: LC-USW33-018432-C; 119: LC-USZ62-36391; 120: LC-USZ62-132634; 137: LC-DIG-jpd-01794; 152: PR 13 CN 1999:154; 156: LC-USZC4-12821; 160: LC-USZ62-128769; 174: LC-DIG-ppmsca-13366; 176: LC-USZ62-99397; 182: LC-USZ62-99399; 186: LC-DIG-ppmsca-13336; 193: LC-USZ62-128337; 196: LC-USW33-026191-C; 197: LC-USZ62-67837; 200: LC-USZ62-25120; 202: LC-USZ62-98981; 206: LC-USZ62-67839; 207: LC-USZ62-106459; 209 *t* : LC-USZ62-121096; 210: LC-USZ62-98984; 212–13: LC-USZ62-78593; 220: LC-USZ62-99391; 223: LC-USW33-032360; 231: LC-DIG-ppmsca-13344; 256: LC-USW33-029494-KC; 276: LC-USZ62-92438; 278: LC-USZC4-3352; 291: LC-USZ62-106464; 294: LC-USZ62-121825; 296: LC-USZ62-121795; 303: LC-USZ62-94464; 304: LC-USZ62-104901; 307: LC-USZ62-103914; 310: LC-USZ62-93479; 312: LC-USZ62-25600; 316: LC-DIG-fsac-1a55001; 327: LC-USZ62-121815; 328: LC-USZ62-121804; 330–31: LC-USZ62-134192; 334: LC-USZ62-111426; 335: LC-USZ62-90918; 336: LC-USZ62-57665; 341: LC-USZ62-36967; 343: LC-USZ62-93234; 346: LC-USZ62-128768; 353: LC-USZ62-71629; 356: LC-USZ62-93707; 357: LC-USZ62-80619; 362: LC-USZ62-86919

American Memory Historical Collections: 13; 14

United States Department of the Army/U.S. Army Center for Military History: 155; 158; 159; 209 *b*; 234; 264; 282–83

United States Marine Corps: 248; 276

Courtesy Franklin D. Roosevelt Presidential Library and Museum: 94

Truman Presidential Library and Museum: 83

ullstein bild / The Granger Collection: 26; 30 *t;* 59; 64; 97; 109; 112; 116; 166–67; 287; 289; 298; 329

Courtesy of the United States Holocaust Memorial Museum (USHMM): 118: USHMM, courtesy of Library of Congress; 122: USHMM, courtesy of Unknown Provenance; 124: USHMM, courtesy of Moshe Zilbar; 130: USHMM, courtesy of Yad Vashem (Public Domain); 131: USHMM, courtesy of Archiwum Panstwowego Muzeum na Majdanku; 133: USHMM, courtesy of Moshe Kaganovich; 170: USHMM, courtesy of Gavra Mandil

Courtesy Wikimedia Commons: 43; 67; 76 *t*; 141; 185; 252; 260; 261